165

Asad Qureshi

Days

Prisoner of the Taliban

SCHIFFER
PUBLISHING

4880 Lower Valley Road • Atglen, PA 19310

For my parents, Farrukh, Sherry, and the enigmatic duo,
Khalid Khawaja and Sultan Amir Tarar (Colonel Imam)

Cover design by John Ferguson
Type set in Impact/Times New Roman

ISBN: 978-0-7643-6426-6
Printed in India

Published by Schiffer Publishing, Ltd.
4880 Lower Valley Road
Atglen, PA 19310
Phone: (610) 593-1777; Fax: (610) 593-2002
Email: Info@schifferbooks.com
Web: www.schifferbooks.com

For our complete selection of fine books on this and related subjects, please visit our website at
www.schifferbooks.com. You may also write for a free catalog.

Schiffer Publishing's titles are available at special discounts for bulk purchases for sales promotions
or premiums. Special editions, including personalized covers, corporate imprints, and excerpts, can
be created in large quantities for special needs. For more information, contact the publisher.

We are always looking for people to write books on new and related subjects. If you have an idea
for a book, please contact us at proposals@schifferbooks.com.

Contents

Foreword

This is a story of a most terrifying, grotesque, and barbaric experience, and it is *true*.

After getting numerous letters and telephone calls, I agreed to meet a man who wanted to work on a feature film. Never was somebody more ambitious and enthusiastic about film than this man.

So it was that, in the rainy summer of 1978, a young Asad Qureshi walked onto the platform at Keighley railway station, where I was standing with director John Schlesinger, filming location shots for the movie *Yanks*. This was the first time I'd laid eyes on him. I liked him from the outset.

When *Yanks* was finished, work began on assembling a production team for the Warren Beatty movie *Reds*, on which I was a production manager. I remembered Asad and mentioned him to production coordinator Vikki Manning. We asked Asad to come to London to work as a production runner on the film.

The film industry has a high dropout rate—starry-eyed youngsters desperate to be involved in something seen as glamorous often disappear after a few seventeen-hour days spent wading through mud—but I had a feeling this young man was in it for the long haul. I believed he'd go on to make his mark in the industry.

Since then, of course, his determination, his extraordinary work ethic, and his creative flair have seen him work as an assistant director on some of the major movies of the last thirty-five years, with some of the biggest names in the business.

And as a gifted maker of documentaries, he goes where most of us would fear to tread and he comes back with award-winning material. In 1992, I watched his film *The Bounty Hunter*. I was riveted. Proud to have had a hand in his career, I phoned him and said, "Now you're a director!" Since then, I've followed his progress with great interest.

I was horrified when he was taken hostage in 2010. When he's talked to me about his projects and where they'll take him, I've usually advised him not to go. But he's somebody who won't take no for an answer and will do what he has to do to make a good film.

Throughout the years I've known him, he's remained hardworking, tenacious, and, above all, engagingly modest. His tenacity served him well during the dreadful experience he recounts in the spellbinding book you're about to read.

It has to be read to be believed.

Nigel Wooll
Movie producer; London, May 2021

Preface

Whosoever killeth a human being for other than manslaughter or corruption in the earth, it shall be as if he had killed all mankind, and whosoever saveth the life of one, it shall be as if he had saved the life of all mankind.

—*The Holy Qur'an,* chapter 5 (part of verse 32)

This is a personal story. But it's a story that takes place in a political context, a multifaceted context that requires some comment.

We live in a tribal world. As humans, we like to feel we belong to a tribe of like-minded people. We look at people from other tribes and we see their differences. They're not like us.

Some of these tribes we like to draw lines round. We call them nations. Nations have friends and they have enemies. Just as in business, in love, and in the school playground, today's friend may well become tomorrow's enemy. Nowhere is this truer than in the region in which my story takes place.

While making films in Pakistan I've met people who have close connections with the Taliban. Some admire them, others revile them. The Taliban say that their fight is one of Jihad. We need a clear definition of what Jihad is.

There are two possible definitions—Jihad is a spiritual struggle against sin within ourselves; and, Jihad is a state-sanctioned war against unbelievers. I believe that all faithful Muslims pursue Jihad in the first sense. The Taliban has declared Jihad in the second sense, but, as I've explained, for a call to Jihad to be validated, it needs the official backing of the state. This is a step that the government of Pakistan has not yet taken.

The current situation in Pakistan is that members of the Taliban are not only opposed to the state but are deliberately working against the laws of the state. To my mind, therefore, they cannot be called Jihadists. They are renegades, criminals, and murderers, and those on the run from the law have congregated in the tribal areas of Pakistan. Kidnapping is one way in which they fund their activities.

I abhor everything about this movement and cannot forgive the countless killings of innocent men, women, and children at its behest.

Author's Note

The events described in this memoir involve the lives of real people. The names of several of those people have been changed to protect their identity.

Prologue

March 24, 2010

1:23 a.m. Ciragan Palace Kempinski, Istanbul

A young legal assistant from Pakistan falls into bed after another fourteen-hour day spent poring over court documents. The influential Pakistani lawyer she's apprenticed to is working her hard, but she's not complaining. This is a top job. Plus she gets to see a little of Istanbul.

"Heaven!" she says to herself, as she surrenders to the soft, generous mattress and cool sheets. It's good that she has no trouble drifting off to sleep—another seven o'clock alarm call awaits her, so she needs her sleep. But her sleep tonight will not be a restful one.

She's on the streets of an Afghan village. A bearded man engulfed by a mob. Beaten brutally. She asks why but no one answers her. A razor blade. Someone shaving the eyebrows of this man, then his hair, peeling the skin off. His face and bald head bleed.

She stirs into wakefulness but the dream pulls her back. A simple house. Mud walls. The mob again, now disemboweling the bearded man, still alive and conscious. He struggles. She sees his excruciating pain. An eye is gouged out with bare fingers. From the shadows, a man is watching this torment impassively. He rises but still she cannot see his face. He rushes toward her. . .

She screams. Her hotel room. The sounds of Istanbul under her window.

* * *

4:25 p.m. Tornol, outskirts of Rawalpindi, Pakistan

A heavy-set man in his forties stuffs a change of clothes into a plastic shopping bag. Around his right thumb, a long deep scar reminds him of the day, in the timber yard, when it almost parted company with the rest of his hand. His workplace is unregulated and dangerous. But he accepts danger. He has to. He has two wives and eleven children to support. He takes any work he can get.

Today's work is a little different. Instead of sawing wood and hauling logs around, he will be lugging cameras, lights, sound equipment. He's done it before, many times. His old friend, the crazy documentary filmmaker from England, has dragged him to some pretty dangerous spots over the years. But he accepts danger.

* * *

5:04 p.m. Islamabad, Pakistan

A retired Pakistan Air Force squadron leader pours two cups of tea. Tea helps him to relax and think clearly. He'll need to think clearly these next few days. He'll need to use all his intelligence contacts, his resources, and his street smarts to negotiate a way through the political minefield into which he has agreed to set foot.

He hands a cup to his distinguished guest. The ageing colonel accepts it with two hands, in the traditional way. He values tradition. He understands the importance of honor. He knows integrity will have an important part to play in the days ahead.

The retired squadron leader and the distinguished colonel drink their tea and wait for the others to arrive.

* * *

5:19 p.m. Islamabad, Pakistan

A documentary filmmaker emerges from the bathroom after his third shower of the day. His Texan wife has been quiet since breakfast. She hates it when he goes away. It's bad enough when she's left alone at home in the UK. Left alone here in Pakistan, with no car and no chance to walk the streets unchallenged, she'll simply stay indoors with her husband's elderly parents.

Her father-in-law is a pious man in his late eighties whose calm countenance she admires and covets. It's served them well on previous assignments. But this assignment is different. She feels it. The mother feels it, too, she sees. An unease in the body language. A pleading in the eyes as the filmmaker shoulders his bag with all the breezy insouciance he can muster.

When her husband hugs her, it's as if it were the last time.

"If I don't come back, please forgive me."

1
The Ambush

I'm woken from an uneasy sleep by voices intoning daybreak prayers. The unfamiliar room around me is strewn with baggage and with the boxes of cameras and lenses that travel the world with me. As I stretch myself and my senses return, I remember that we've slept in Kohat at the house of Jawaid Ibrahim Peracha, a friend of Khalid Khawaja. The night seems to have passed very quickly, and I know the day ahead will be long and tense.

The four of us—myself, Colonel Imam, Rustam, and Khalid Khawaja (known to us all as KK)—dress quickly. The breakfast served is not one I'm accustomed to—spicy curry, lambs' trotters, semolina pudding, fried naan bread. Being a veg-etarian, I settle for naan bread. This is washed down with the most revolting strong tea—a mixture of water, milk and sugar all boiled together in one pan. A far cry from my usual breakfast at home in the UK—lightly buttered toast and English breakfast tea.

The courtyard of Peracha's house reveals itself to us as the sun rises. Paint is peeling from the walls, and the heavy rain has taken its toll on the brickwork. The badly washed clothes of Peracha's bodyguards are strung across the yard on a rope.

We duck under the clothes, cross the courtyard, and emerge into the street. I dodge a cow tied to a wall. She eyes us with disinterest as her tail flicks away the flies that are already gathering. We climb into our battered white Toyota Corolla. The sky is clear and the sun already hot. With baggage and equipment packed into every corner of this modest vehicle, we edge away from the house and wind our way through the narrow streets.

It's the morning of Friday, March 26, 2010.

The events of this day will change our lives forever.

* * *

It's around 80 miles to Bannu, the town where KK's guide is to meet us, but the roads in this Khyber Pakhtunkhwa province of Pakistan (formerly the Northwest Frontier) are so poor that such a relatively short journey can take hours. Add to this the locals' rather cavalier attitude to road safety—huge trucks weaving in and out, overtaking buses flying past each other with only inches to spare, the constant blare of air horns—and any experience on the road is apt to prove a little unnerving.

I'm feeling decidedly nervous as we enter the walled town of Bannu. My watch shows 11:30 a.m. We've been on the road for four hours. It feels like eight. The town's narrow streets are littered with rubble and garbage. We pass the burnt-out wreck of a bus, its orange bumper wrenched off at a painful angle.

Bannu is not designed for traffic. Whichever way you turn, you find yourself in a long line of cars, trucks, and carts inching their way to their various destinations. The town has the forlorn air of being unwanted—it's a place you're transferred to as a soldier, or trapped in by accident of birth. It's not a town of choice.

But it has one saving grace—outside its walls, acres of luxuriant palm trees bear the succulent dates for which Bannu is justly famed.

This is the last major settlement before we reach the tribal area. Beyond this town, the laws of Pakistan do not apply. We'll be on our own in North Waziristan, the most dangerous place on earth. I wonder if I'm being brave or just plain irresponsible. I try to comfort myself with the thought that I'm in safe hands—KK and Colonel Imam are living legends in Pakistan.

KK is a difficult man to describe. Revered by some, a controversial figure to others, he is, to me, a man of integrity with a soft heart and eyes that are always smiling. He is trusting and generous to a fault. A former squadron leader in the Pakistan Air Force, he retired some years ago and joined Pakistan's premier intelligence agency, the Inter-Services Intelligence or ISI. He's party to many secrets of state, which makes him a man of influence in the shifting sands of Pakistani government. He feels passionately about the plight of Pakistan's legions of disappeared people, the dissidents spirited away by shadowy agencies, never to be heard of again. He visits their families. He sits with them and weeps with them. Perhaps his most remarkable quality is always to speak the truth, even in the face of death.

Sultan Amir Tarar is a retired Pakistan army officer and special warfare operations expert better known as Colonel Imam. A former member of the Special Services Group (SSG), he was for a time Pakistan's Consul General in Herat in Afghanistan. A veteran of the Soviet war, he is widely believed to have played a key role in the formation of the Taliban. After having helped train the Afghan Mujahedeen on behalf of the United States in the 1980s, he also trained Mullah Omar and other Taliban factions and remained active in Afghanistan until the 2001 US intervention. After the Soviet defeat and the collapse of communism, he was invited to the White House by US president George H. W. Bush, who presented him with a piece of the Berlin Wall carrying a brass plaque inscribed "To the one who dealt the first blow."

Today, Western intelligence agencies believe Imam to be among a group of renegade officers from Pakistan's ISI who continued to support the Taliban after Pakistan turned against them in the wake of the attacks of September 11, 2001. Once a tall, powerfully built man, the Colonel is now in his seventies and physically rather fragile but still a commanding presence with unshakeable convictions.

I am in safe hands.

I repeat this to myself as the chaos of Bannu swirls around me. The car has come to rest in the former marketplace that serves as the city's bus terminus. Multi-colored buses crowd the square, and the air is filled with the sound of honking horns. Smoke spills out from the clusters of stalls roasting peanuts, barbecuing seekh kebabs, and frying pakoras, their delicious aromas drowned by the stench of diesel and sewage.

My eyes zoom onto a man running a sharp knife over a chicken's neck. Blood gushes from her throat, then, after a few final convulsions, she succumbs. Soon she will be somebody's lunch.

The exotic pandemonium of this bus station is at once unnerving and oddly thrilling, and a strange mix of adventure and foreboding overtakes me while we are, albeit briefly, part of this chaotic world.

The legions of bus drivers are desperate to fill every seat. Each driver repeats his own frantic mantra—"Peshawar, Peshawar, Peshawar!," "Kohat, Kohat, Kohat!," "Miranshah, Miranshah, Miranshah!"

Miranshah. The next stop on our journey. KK's contact is to meet us here, at the bus terminus, and conduct us safely to Miranshah. But he's not here, and KK can't reach him. He's been trying the man's mobile for hours, without success. He paces up and down outside the car.

"Why doesn't he answer? Where is he?" KK is becoming frustrated.

I am in safe hands.

Rustam steps out of the car and walks over to a stall where a bearded Pushtun is selling green halwa, its uncovered sweetness providing plentiful nourishment for the flies. It turns my stomach to see Rustam consume a slice of this insect-fodder with relish as he chats casually with the man, but at the same time I recognize the ridiculousness of my British sensibilities in this corner of the world.

As my assistant on many projects, Rustam has always been a dedicated worker whose impressive physical strength makes him a first-rate porter and bodyguard and more than compensates for his lack of education and skills. He has eleven children and two wives, so I pay him well. When he's not hauling equipment around for me, he works in a timber yard, chopping wood and moving logs around. It's hard work in an environment where health and safety regulations play no part. On one occasion, he nearly severed his right thumb. I see the scar as he lifts his hand to finish the halwa and, with some trepidation, I catch the stallholder's question.

"What are you doing with those two?" He's referring to KK and Colonel Imam.

"Work. Why?"

"They are dubious."

"I don't know anything about them. I've come to assist my friend."

I signal Rustam to come back to the car. I don't want him discussing our plans with anyone. There are so many shadowy agencies in Pakistan and our project (and, indeed, our personal safety) could easily be jeopardized if details fall into the wrong hands. Besides, we have a car full of expensive film equipment, and we're carrying cash. Rustam makes his excuses to the man and returns. My nervousness makes me irritable with him.

"Why are you talking to strangers?" I demand. He shakes his head and climbs into the car.

KK announces that a different guide is on his way, and we are to travel onward by minibus. After a quarter of an hour, an unshaven young man introduces himself as Saddam. I nod but refrain from shaking the grubby hand he extends. Saddam says that, in order to cover our tracks, we should change vehicles a few times. He suggests taking a minibus as far as Thal, then finishing the journey to Miranshah in a hire car. This seems oddly excessive to me, but, with reluctance, I agree. Without Saddam's help, I have no idea how we can get there.

We try to secure a minibus for our exclusive use by offering the driver extra money, but he refuses. He seems suspicious, so we switch to another bus and accept that we'll have to squash in beside other passengers—here, a twelve-seater carries eighteen people. KK pays for the four of us. I try to give him money but he refuses. A typical Pakistani gesture of hospitality. Any insistence on my part will be considered offensive, so I decide not to push it.

As the packed minibus pulls out of the terminus, I'm very conscious that we're leaving the relative safety of the jurisdiction of Pakistan and heading into no man's land.

We drive through tiny villages, along winding unpaved roads. The farther we drive, the more uneasy I become. I try to interpret my unease as the feeling that I'm missing my family, and I comfort myself with the knowledge I'll soon be returning home. I don't normally need to use this tactic. Normally, I go out on a shoot full of enthusiasm. But this time the unease is running deep.

After some time, we stop by a patchwork of puddles that will be a river in the rainy season. Passengers climb off the bus and go over to the river to wash for prayers. Colonel Imam comments on the beauty of this area, and he's right. Waziristan has amazing rock formations everywhere, symmetrical patterns of rock reminiscent of those paint patterns you make as a child by dabbing paint on a sheet of paper then folding it in half. One outrageous rock formation looks like a Roman amphitheatre. In the face of such beauty, it's easy to forget that we're standing in the most dangerous territory in the world, ruled by tribesmen whose skill in combat has been legendary since they were a thorn in the British side over a century ago.

After prayers, the minibus continues its journey along dusty winding roads. Through an open window, a fragrant breeze announces the imminent arrival of spring.

We make an unannounced stop at a small village. The driver gets out and goes into a house made entirely of mud. As the minibus sits, children of seven or eight approach and try to sell us little packets of heroin. I am immeasurably saddened to see that children at this tender age have contact with heroin and are not afraid to handle it. It strikes me that these same children are doubtlessly also familiar with guns. Among them are future suicide bombers and Taliban warriors. There is simply nothing else for them to do in this God-forsaken land.

My mind returns to a visit I made to South Waziristan in October 2009, during which I discovered a house used for the brainwashing of young children. Alongside colorful murals of lakes and mountains depicting paradise were slogans on the wall, painted in blood, announcing "Death to Musharraf." Nearby was an altar made of bricks, with a drainage area around it. The altar was covered in dried blood. The place was used for beheading captured soldiers and hostages. I imagined the horrific initiation ceremonies these young souls had taken part in.

Rustam is becoming agitated at this unexplained stop. He wonders if the driver is phoning through to someone and alerting them to our presence in the area. I can't imagine that any telephone network extends to such a remote rural area.

"Why would he do that?" I whisper. Rustam just shrugs.

I look around at my fellow passengers. We're different from these people. We dress differently and speak differently. Maybe they see us as fair game. I remind myself I am with KK and Colonel Imam.

I am in safe hands.

The driver returns with no explanation and we continue our journey.

After about thirty minutes, the minibus comes to a halt and the five of us alight. This is where we part company with the bus.

We stand by a roadside tire repair shop while Saddam walks a few hundred yards down the road to hire a car for the rest of our journey. Across the road, a group of people sit under the shade of a large tree. I walk over into the shade. A man dressed in a traditional *shalwar kamiz* and a dark turban looks up at me.

"What are you doing here?" he asks.

"Work."

There is an edge of hostility in his tone. I decide to rejoin the others, who are watching an old man and his young assistant fix a tire.

I see a white Toyota hatchback emerge from behind the bushes and park next to the man with the turban. Its windows are blacked out. I feel the occupants are watching us. Fear engulfs me. The others haven't noticed the car, so I keep my worries to myself while continuing to watch the Toyota as it inches up the road about a hundred yards then disappears into the bushes again.

Saddam drives up with a similar Toyota. These are the workhorses of this region, smuggled over the border from Afghanistan, sold very cheaply and kept inside the tribal areas to avoid customs duty.

"I could only persuade one man to go to Miranshah. The others are all afraid of army checkpoints."

It proves to be a tight squeeze indeed. As the tallest, Colonel Imam takes the front seat alongside Saddam, leaving KK, Rustam, and me to squash into the back seat. The car's owner spreads himself on top of our bags and equipment in the back. We make off in the direction taken by the other car.

We're now off the main road, driving through scrubland and over deep gravel that makes progress very slow.

"This man knows the back way to Miranshah," KK says. "No army checkpoints."

I'm conscious that we're in a very remote area indeed. If something happens to us here, no one will know. What if the car breaks down? We have no food or water. I console myself with the knowledge that I've survived many a tricky situation while filming.

And I am in safe hands.

"Why don't we film an interview with you while we're driving?" I ask KK.

"Okay."

We stop the car and assemble the equipment. The Colonel looks around. He seems uneasy.

"We should have some cover story. In case someone stops us. I should have brought my revolver."

KK tries to reassure him. "Not to worry. We are here now."

"We need a cover story," the Colonel insists. "We say we are doing missionary work, and these two are making a film about it."

I'm unnerved and puzzled by the uncertainty of this exchange at such a late stage in the game. I climb into the front seat with my camera and twist round to frame up on KK in the back. I signal to Saddam, and he pulls away slowly, but even at this slow speed, progress is bumpy and it's difficult to keep KK in frame.

I give "Action" to KK and he starts to talk.

"I am here in North Waziristan, possibly the most dangerous place on earth. War is being waged between the Taliban and the Pakistan army and, just a few miles across the border, NATO troops are trying to contain the Taliban insurgents along a border so porous that people come and go between Pakistan and Afghanistan completely undetected. The government of Hamid Karzai has very little control of Afghanistan. As Madeleine Albright once said, Karzai is no more than a mayor of Kabul. All the other provinces are controlled by warlords. We desperately need to bring peace between all the different factions and put an end to the violence and the suicide bombings in this region."

There's a crack of gunfire. Saddam slams on the brakes and the tires skid to a halt, biting into the gravel. A man in a black hood is suddenly standing at my window, his eyes and mouth covered in black gauze. He points a machine gun at me. I keep my head very still but, from the corner of my eye, I see another gunman a few yards away. He too points his gun at me. I spot the white Toyota hatchback by the roadside, its bonnet open, the driver feigning a repair.

The gunman issues an order in Urdu. "*Bahar niklo.*" Get out.

My world seems to have gone into slow motion, and I am unable to react to the gunman's order at first. I see again my mum's anguished face. It's clear she doesn't want me to leave. I replay my farewell to my wife, Sherry, and my last words to her: "If I don't come back, please forgive me."

After what seems forever, I recover my senses, but the door lock is jammed and will not open from the inside. I point to the lock. The gunman pulls the door open and drags me from the car by my arm. My camera is left on the seat. My heart is pounding. Who are these people? Are they going to rob us, kill us, or what?

Rustam stands a few paces behind me. The gunman fires at his feet, and I see gravel fly up inches from his toes. Instinctively, I do what people do in the movies. I put my hands up.

I see KK kneeling on the ground. His cap is missing and his hair is ruffled—he's been struck on the head.

The owner of the hired car makes a run for it. There is a crack of gunfire. I dare not move my head. No further sound. The man has been shot dead.

Colonel Imam tries to reason with the gunman. "I am your friend. Why are you doing this?"

The masked man punches the Colonel in the face and pushes him to the ground. Rustam and I are pushed from behind to lie face down on the ground.

"Hands behind your backs," someone shouts.

I feel handcuffs go around my wrists and tighten unbearably. I'm hauled from the ground by the scruff of my neck and pushed into their car. Colonel Imam is frogmarched to the back of the car, but he resists. Another gunman runs up and kicks the Colonel in the face and forces him into the boot, where he's tied up with rope before the door is slammed shut.

I have entered a world that is totally alien to me. *I will see violence. I will feel pain. I may never see my family again.*

Rustam and I are flanked by a gunman on one side and Saddam on the other.

"Heads down! Heads down!" the gunman barks. He does not wear a mask but has his face covered with his turban. We obey. A sheet is thrown over our heads.

One of our captors talks into a radio. "*Mitha Khan. Mitha Khan.*"

No response.

"*Mitha Khan. Mitha Khan.*"

Still no answer. Another gunman grabs the radio.

"*Mitha Khan. Mitha Khan, Singri Singri Singri.*"

"Yes," comes the reply.

There is more dialogue between our car and the car that KK is in. I wonder why seven of us are crammed into one car and KK is held alone in the other.

We drive for what seems like hours. I move my hands inside the handcuffs in an attempt to make them less uncomfortable, but this only makes them tighter. The sheet over our heads makes me feel very hot and claustrophobic. Everyone is sweating.

There's a sniffing sound to my left and I realize Saddam is crying. But it sounds like fake crying. He stops for a while and then starts again. Every now and again, one of the gunmen shouts at him.

"*Oye, chotay. Sur neachay.*" Oi, shorty. Keep your head down.

I wonder why Saddam would pretend to cry.

Rustam begins to cry as well. His handcuffs are too tight to bear. I expected him to be stronger.

I think of an email from my dear friend, Nigel Wooll. It was Nigel who gave me my first job in the industry, on the film *Reds*. I directed *The Battle of Swat Valley* for the BBC's Panorama in 2009, and, after it aired, Nigel emailed me—"Congratulations on a very impressive piece of filmmaking. It looks exceedingly dangerous. I hope you'll make that your last foray into Taliban strongholds. Life is too precious."

What would he say if he could see me now? He was so right. Life is too precious. I've come here to get the scoop of my life, an interview with the top Taliban commander. But is it worth my life to get it?

I recite the prayers my parents taught me. I pray to God to save us and bring this ordeal to an end.

I'm sweating profusely, and I'm unbearably thirsty. The man in front takes a swig from a bottle of lemonade.

"Please give me some—I'm very thirsty," Rustam pleads.

The man leans over and offers the bottle to Rustam but keeps hold of it.

"Give me some too," I say.

"Later. And we will also give you food."

This refusal is a blow. I'm dehydrating rapidly. From the boot comes the sound of Colonel Imam reciting prayers, which, for me, underlines the seriousness of our situation. I'm very concerned about KK. Why have they kept him away from us? I have to admit I'm also concerned about the expensive equipment I've left behind in the other car. I'm sure these men will have no respect for it.

We've been driving for so long the sun is beginning to set. The Colonel asks if he can offer evening prayers. He's told that he can, but we're not stopping. The Colonel has to pray in contorted confinement.

I hear the gunmen discuss crossing the border into Afghanistan at a place called Khost. I hear a horse galloping. "This is the type of horse that the Taliban use for training," says one of the men.

More hours on the road. A stop at a petrol station to attend to a flat tire. An interminable delay while a replacement is found. More driving. I'm exhausted and dehydrated and my clothes are wet with perspiration. I'm in a hostile foreign country. I have no papers other than a photocopy of my ID card.

Suddenly the car stops. The sheet is removed. I catch a brief glimpse of the darkness around me before a hood is pulled over my head. Inexplicably, the car pulls away again and, for a while, I feel that we're driving in narrow streets.

The car stops again. We're bundled out and led into a room. We're told to sit. A wooden seat. A musty smell in the room. Much cooler than outside. Someone is pacing up and down. I hear a rifle being pressed to my temple. I recite the first Kalima:* "There is no God but Allah and Muhammad is his prophet." I wait for the bullet to enter my skull. I see the faces of my mother and father. How will they take the news of my death?

A sudden surprising peace comes over me. I have had the presence of mind to think of God and to ask for forgiveness before my death.

I remember hearing that, just before his execution, former Iraqi president Saddam Hussein recited similar words. At the time, I was mystified by his calmness. Now I understand it. Faced with death, it seems we want to confer the last rites upon ourselves before we enter a state from which no one has returned.

A voice near my ear.

"I am going to remove your handcuffs. Any sudden moves and they go right back on."

"I won't move."

He unlocks the handcuffs. After hours of excruciating tightness, what a relief to have my hands free!

Still hooded, I ask, "Can I lie down? My back is hurting."

Someone acquiesces and I grope around and stretch out on the floor. The same voice again.

"You people get money from Manmohan Singh and come into Pakistan to cause terrorism."

KK's response. "We are not terrorists. We are here to make a film about the peace process."

"Be quiet. Be quiet. Don't lie. What are your names?"

The roll call starts with KK.

---

* The first pillar of Islam.

"Khalid Khawaja."

"Sultan Amir."

"Rustam Khan."

"Asad Qureshi."

"You have very pretty names but you are terrorists."

KK again. "Asad here is an award-winning filmmaker and he is making a film."

"Be quiet."

"What are you going to do with us?" KK asks.

"We are going to send you somewhere else."

"Are you going to sell us on to someone else?"

"Be quiet."

"Can I have some water?" I ask.

I'm offered a metal container. The water tastes of diesel but I'm so thirsty I don't care.

The man who removed our handcuffs returns. He removes my Fossil watch from my wrist, a treasured gift from my wife, Sherry. He puts his hands in my pockets and takes my money—80,000 rupees (around $750) and the photocopy of my identity card.

"Keep these safe," he says to someone.

"Can I keep my Chapstick?" I ask.

"Yes." Relief.

KK is asked how much money he has.

"100,000 rupees."

Our hoods are removed. KK's black briefcase is taken off him. I look around and see we're in a mud hut. The ceiling is decorated with paper flags and bunting, and the walls are covered with large sheets of card bearing the logo of Colgate toothpaste, presumably taken from a factory where they were to be cut into individual packets.

Some food is brought, but I don't like the look of it at all. I decide not to eat it. After a while, I ask if there's any other food. A carton of milk and some cookies are produced, which KK shares with me.

As soon as we've finished eating, Colonel Imam is handcuffed, shackled, and led away, as are KK and Rustam, leaving me on my own.

After a few minutes, I hear frantic banging on a wooden door, and Rustam's voice.

"There's a snake down here! Open the door!"

Down here? He must be in some sort of pit.

"Be quiet."

"Open the door!"

The sound of a key. A latch. A chain.

"Yes?"

"There's a snake in here. There!"

A crack of semiautomatic gunfire. My blood freezes. The thud of a door. Footsteps retreating. With relief, I hear Rustam vomiting in his hole. I can hear nothing of KK or the Colonel.

One of the gunmen returns and once again I'm hooded and handcuffed. Then my hands are chained to a wooden bed. My door is locked and I'm alone in the darkness, wondering what will happen next.

The night is long, uncomfortable, and sleepless. I have plenty of time to think. I speculate on the details of my situation. It occurs to me that the gunmen are likely to be from Inter-Services Intelligence (ISI), patrolling the tribal areas for foreign Jihadists. We've been apprehended by mistake. All will become clear. They'll let us go in the morning.

I think about filming interviews with the Taliban hierarchy, about what a difference it would make to the peace process once the interviews were broadcast. If we could show the world that the Taliban are willing to enter into peace talks and end the bloodshed, the world would be a better place. The streets of Pakistan would be much safer and life could get back to normal. Instead, the Pakistan army is leveling houses it identifies as Taliban hiding places. There are drone strikes. Endless fighting. It pains me to see this region at war, to know that there has not been peace for over a hundred years, to think of the countless lives lost.

I'm already awake when the door to my room opens. My hood is removed, and I now see the man who first removed my handcuffs. He gives me water to wash so I can offer my prayers. I'm comforted somewhat by the knowledge I'm with the right people.

Rustam is led into my room by an unmasked man who makes him sit on the floor next to me. The men sit and stare at us. I feel a tension in the room. To break it, I speak.

"Can you let my family know I am all right? My mother worries a lot. I want her to know that I am alive." I begin to cry.

He nods his head. Rustam comforts me. The man leaves. His place is taken by the man who yesterday kicked Colonel Imam in the face. I see now he's quite young, probably in his late teens. He speaks to us in Pushto. Rustam translates.

"I am not like the others. Don't worry. No one will hurt you."

Given his violent behavior yesterday, I find it hard to see him in the role of good guy.

Another man comes in. Armed but without a hood, he has a distinctive long nose and a short beard. After surveying us for a few minutes, he leaves the room, then returns wearing dark glasses. I can't see the point of the glasses, now that we've all seen his face without them.

A man we haven't seen before comes in carrying a breakfast of tea and cookies. He too wears no hood. His complexion is dark. He doesn't look like a local man.

"What is going on?" I ask him in Urdu.

"I am a translator from the Indian embassy, working for NATO. We catch a lot of terrorists here. We question them. Afterward, we hand them over to their country of origin."

I'm reassured. *Once they establish who we are, we'll be on our way.*

After breakfast, Rustam is led away again, and I'm chained to the bed once more, no blindfold this time. I stare at the ceiling and wonder what's in store for me.

I watch a fat gecko on the ceiling. I don't relish the idea of him falling into my lap, but I'm unable to move. Time drags on. I keep thinking we'll be on our way home before long. Nothing happens. From time to time, someone looks in on me. I'm occasionally untied so I can relieve myself outside, although a blindfold is always applied, making this function difficult to perform.

Time drags on.

Another night is about to fall. I'm no wiser as to where I am or what's going to happen. I'm becoming irritated at my situation. *Why has my liberty been taken away for no reason? I've done nothing wrong. Why am I in this place?*

Morning comes. The translator enters the room. He helps me up, then blindfolds and handcuffs me. He leads me out of the room.

We walk a few paces. The translator helps me up through what must be a small elevated doorway. I crawl into what seems to be the house next door.

I'm led into a room and made to sit on the floor by a wall. I feel the cold mud wall against my back. Still hooded, I can nevertheless sense the presence of others in the room. I decide to greet them.

"*Asalaam alaikum.*"

"*Walaikum as Salaam.*"

There is a collective response from several people. Then the questions begin.

"What is your name?"

"Asad Qureshi."

"Are you Sunni Muslim or a Shia?"

"Sunni, but I don't have a problem with other sects."

"What are you doing in Waziristan?"

"I'm filming a news report about the peace process between the Taliban, the Pakistan government, and the army. When we've finished, we want to do a similar report on the Kashmir issue. We want to bring it to the world's attention. A British reporter is helping us."

A different person speaks.

"Who are you working for?"

"A channel in England has commissioned the report. My producer, Asif Jameel, has fallen ill. He couldn't come. I decided to proceed without him."

Another voice.

"Why do you think you are qualified to make this news report?"

"I may not be qualified. But I am in a position to make this report. To bring it to the world's attention."

"Don't you think that your report will embarrass everyone?"

"Well, it could prove to be a double-edged sword. But we have to show the reality on the ground."

A sound like a booklet being thrown onto a table. A different voice.

"According to our investigation, you are an MI6 agent."

"I'm not an agent. Like I said, I'm a filmmaker."

A pause.

"You can check my website. You will see who I am."

"Anyone can make a website." An aggressive voice.

"Okay, then check me out with the ISPR.* I know everyone there. Talk to Colonel Faisal, Colonel Farooq, Colonel Jawad. They'll all vouch for me. I've worked with them all on several projects."

I begin to feel more at ease. These are my own people, checking that I'm not a terrorist. I give them more information, about my films, the people I know at the ISPR. More questions.

"Have you been to Waziristan before?"

"Yes. I've been to both North and South Waziristan. In the south, I went to Wana, Shakai, Ladha, Razmak, Jandola, and Makeen."

I tell them of my visit to the Taliban brainwashing center. That I was the first person to film that place. That I even filmed outside the demolished house of Baitullah Mehsud, the former leader of the Pakistani Taliban. "And I've been to Miranshah as well. I'm making a film about the army's work in North Waziristan. How they're trying to win the hearts and minds of people in this area. They took me to Datta Khel and Barmand for a reconnaissance trip. I stayed at the Tochi officers' mess."

"Which one? There is one in Mir Ali."

They're trying to catch me out.

---

* Inter-Services Public Relations, a branch of the Pakistani armed forces liaising with the media on military affairs.

"The Tochi officers' mess in Miranshah. You can check me out with the ISPR. I've been there before through them. I've even worked with the Ministry of Information and Broadcasting to promote the image of Pakistan. I am no terrorist. I am a good Pakistani. I made *The Battle of Swat Valley* for the BBC. It's on my website. Look on my website."

"We will check your website."

Thank God. Once they look at my website, I'm in the clear.

"And how do you know Khalid Khawaja?"

"Journalists from all over the world know him. They contact him for stories. He's a great source of information. Robert Fisk, the famous journalist from the *Independent* newspaper in England, interviewed him not long ago."

Another question is fired at me.

"How long have you known Khalid Khawaja?"

"I first met him in 1997, and then again in 2005 when I was working on the film *The Journalist and the Jihadi: The Murder of Daniel Pearl*. We were in Karachi when I first introduced him to my producer, Asif Jameel."

"Who is Colonel Imam?"

"I don't really know Colonel Imam. The first time I met him was at Khalid Khawaja's house on the day we set out from Islamabad. Khalid decided to bring him along. I didn't question him."

"And who is Rustam?"

"I've known him for thirty years. You can check him out from the shop below our Rawalpindi house."

"Where?"

"It's on Murree Road."

"Do you have any friends in England?"

"Yes, I do."

"Who?"

"There's an old friend of mine, Vajih Khan."

"How can we contact him?"

I give them a phone number.

"What about the person you are working with. How do we contact him?"

"Asif Jameel." I give his number. "His wife, Warda, may answer. Asif may still be in Pakistan."

"And what do you know about this young boy, Saddam?"

"I've never seen him before. I've no idea who he is. I thought he was our guide."

"He's a good-looking boy. He does not answer questions. We have beaten him, severely, but he will not answer questions."

"I don't know anything about him."

Suddenly, my interrogation is over. I'm led back to my room. I've answered many questions but my own questions remains unanswered: Who are these people? Am I in trouble? When will they let me go?

It's the morning of Sunday, March 28, 2010. I have witnessed violence. I have been manhandled, hooded, and handcuffed. I have felt the muzzle of a rifle against my temple. But I am alive. Thank God.

2
Five Years Earlier

I'd started out in the film industry as a runner. After many years of working in various positions, I became an assistant director. But my heart was set on directing a film in my own right. When a documentary idea came my way, I collaborated with my friend, Asif Jameel (known to everyone as "Alu"), and made the controversial film *The Bounty Hunter.*

Since our first meeting in 1984, Alu and I had worked together on many films. We were something of a double act: embracing one minute, then at each other's throats the next. But this love-hate relationship had stood the test of time.

When I moved to Pakistan in 2005, I worked as consultant to the Ministry of Information and Broadcasting and I also made numerous films for the army. I'd made many contacts in Pakistan and found it easy to get permissions to film throughout Pakistan.

The world was a very different place after 9/11, and Pakistan was a country in which this transformation was very apparent. The country had become a Mecca for journalists, all of them looking for a scoop. In January 2002, just a few months after the events that shook the world, Daniel Pearl, a journalist from *the Wall Street Journal*, made the pilgrimage to Pakistan to interview Sheik Mubarak Ali Gilani in connection with 9/11. In Pakistan, Daniel Pearl was betrayed, abducted, and consequently beheaded.

In April 2005, I took a call from Alu. He wanted to make a film about Daniel Pearl, with the title *The Journalist and the Jihadi: The Murder of Daniel Pearl.* The film would investigate the circumstances of Daniel Pearl's abduction and death by retracing his movements. I had just relocated to Islamabad from the United States so I was conveniently placed to shoot the film for Alu.

But crucially for him, I could bring something extra to the project: my connection to Khalid Khawaja.

It was in 1997 that I first met KK, while preparing to film the first all-Pakistani mountaineering ascent of Mount Everest, to commemorate Pakistan's Golden Jubilee. As soon as I arrived in Islamabad with two cameramen from London, we hit a snag.

Since the expedition was going to climb from the north side of the mountain, which is in Tibet, we needed the Chinese embassy to issue visas to my cameramen. Around this time, the Chinese authorities were particularly suspicious of westerners entering the province because of the unauthorized filming that had been done for the movie *Seven Years in Tibet*. We could not afford to be delayed as the mountaineers were waiting for us in Kathmandu.

In my frustration, I asked my brother Farrukh if he could help me get the visas. He suggested I talk to Khalid Khawaja, a well-connected friend of his who would know which strings to pull.

I spoke to KK and, just a few days later, got a call from him saying that the visas had been arranged. I was amazed at his influence.

Around this time, KK asked me to do some filming in connection with a human rights case he was involved in. Two men from Karachi had been missing for nine months, and KK, a prominent human rights activist, was a very outspoken critic of the Pakistani government's lack of interest in missing people.

Through my work for him on this project, I had firsthand experience of his widespread influence within the country. He had access to everyone, and he seemed to be aware of every item of news before it broke. He carried several mobile phones, the combined contacts lists of which read like a *Who's Who* of Pakistani life.

Daniel Pearl had met with KK in 2002. He believed that KK could get him access to Sheik Mubarak Ali Gilani, an author and cleric with a very large following in the United States. Daniel Pearl wanted to interview him in Pakistan in connection with his investigations into the case of Richard Reid, the shoe bomber, and into unrecorded transfers of Al Qaeda money, money which it was suspected helped to fund the 9/11 attacks.

When Daniel had met KK and asked him for access to Gilani, KK had assured him that Gilani would not agree to an interview. Daniel was told to forget it. But Daniel Pearl knew that persistence is the journalist's most valuable tool and he'd refused to take no for an answer. Sadly, it was this persistence that had led to his death.

Because of KK's involvement in Daniel Pearl's story (he was one of the first to know of Daniel's arrival in Pakistan, and of his subsequent disappearance and death), I knew it would be desirable to interview him for Alu's film. Fortunately for me, I'd already met KK on a number of occasions in the past, as my older brother Farrukh had known him for over twenty years, and, although our meetings had not always been cordial (indeed, we'd fallen out quite badly a few times), he'd agreed to see me and be interviewed.

It wasn't going to be easy to shoot this film. Daniel Pearl's was not a name *anyone* could go round dropping inside Pakistan, let alone a filmmaker. The whole enterprise would have to be cloaked in secrecy.

I scouted a few locations in Islamabad and selected a tall building with a backdrop of the Margalla Hills, to give a typical depiction of the city. The interview with KK went very well—he was a natural in front of the camera—and it was clear that it could be used to string the various episodes of the film together nicely.

In tracing Daniel Pearl's movements, two other locations for the film would have to be visited: the Akbar Hotel in Rawalpindi and the Village Restaurant in Karachi.

I drove the 12 kilometers from Islamabad to Rawalpindi in the company of a local cameraman. We parked by Liaquat Bagh, a park opposite the Akbar Hotel, a cheap and nasty establishment on the busy Murree Road, the main thoroughfare between Rawalpindi and Islamabad.

We filmed some exteriors of the hotel and its surroundings, the traffic bumper to bumper and the air filled with heat, noise, and exhaust fumes. Then we went inside for interior shots of the hotel's restaurant, the place where Daniel Pearl had met Omar Sheikh, the man to whom Daniel had subsequently turned for access to Sheik Mubarak Ali Gilani.

We walked into the hotel with the camera running and simply panned around, capturing whatever we could. I was disappointed to see the place pretty much deserted. This seedy joint was known to be a nexus for all kinds of underworld activities and, had the place been busy, it would have given us just the atmosphere the film needed. As it was, a glance at my watch showed we'd arrived after lunch. People were having their siesta. This was an unfortunate miscalculation, but we needed to make the best of the situation. To return later, with a camera, would attract too much attention.

Initially, we placed the camera on a table and let it roll, but because so little was happening, I decided to walk across the restaurant and sit at a table by the window, so that I was on camera. I scribbled some notes to give an impression of activity. I knew that in postproduction my image could be blurred sufficiently for me to pass as a stand-in for the American journalist. Job done.

The following morning, I stepped off a plane in Karachi, made my way to the Sheraton Hotel, and again engaged the services of a local cameraman.

The Village Restaurant, the site of Daniel Pearl's kidnapping, is next to the Metropole Hotel, on a large island in the city center. I'd identified the hotel itself, a faded remnant of the British Raj in the throes of being demolished, as a good spot from which to capture shots of Karachi and of the nearby American embassy, as well as of the restaurant itself. Luckily for us, security around the hotel site was nonexistent and, via dusty and crumbling staircases stained red with expectorated betel nuts, we managed to gain access to the roof without difficulty.

We got a few good shots of the embassy. Then my cameraman spotted the embassy's surveillance cameras inching round to stare right at us. You don't mess with American security—we needed to clear out. With bags of equipment swinging from neck and shoulders, we vaulted down the steps four at a time, jumped into the rental car, and sped away. A lucky escape.

The following day, I'd arranged to meet Alu at the Sheraton. He arrived with Massoud Ansari, the production coordinator, and a local Karachi man who was to act as a guide. Karachi is Pakistan's largest city, with a population of over twenty-one million. If we were to blend in and travel around the city efficiently, this man would be a useful member of the team.

Before going back to the Metropole to retrace Daniel Pearl's movements, we filmed more general shots of Karachi, for context and local color, starting in a *madrassah*, a religious school where poor families send their children to board and learn the Qur'an by rote. We filmed the children rocking their heads back and forth as they memorized passages from scripture.

Cruising the streets for more local color, we passed an open, unrefrigerated truck loaded with freshly slaughtered cows. I caught on camera the swarm of flies shadowing the truck in the subtropical heat, a stomach-churning sight that endorsed my vegetarian lifestyle whilst not exactly whetting my appetite for lunch.

Then we drove to the Village Restaurant by the Metropole Hotel. Here we were to recreate the circumstances of Daniel Pearl's kidnapping. We hired a cab that would act as the taxi Daniel had arrived in, and I asked Massoud to play the role of Daniel, filmed only from the waist down.

A comically frustrating hour ensued in which the taxi driver repeatedly missed his mark, then had to negotiate the one-way system to repeat the shot, then, with typical Pakistani chutzpah, began bombarding me with directorial advice. Your only choices in this situation are good humor or a fist fight. In the circumstances, the former seemed the best policy.

We moved to the next setup, recreating the scene in which Daniel Pearl is bundled into a car and driven away with a motorcycle escort. We recruited some locals and their vehicles as stand-ins and set up the equipment near an underground car park, a good place to make the abduction believable.

The stand-in motorcyclists didn't take direction well, and we had to retake various shots several times. I was frustratedly aware that the light was beginning to fail.

Several men suddenly appeared out of nowhere. Some of them surrounded the motorcyclists and Massoud. Others approached me.

"What are you doing?" one of them demanded.

These people were not casual bystanders. They spoke with an easy authority that suggested official status and belied their civilian clothes. But whether they represented the Intelligence Bureau, the American embassy, or the police, I knew from past experience that such tense situations can often end in beatings, confiscation of equipment, even arrest. If these men saw the slightest trace of panic, we were done for. Alu seemed nonplussed, so I spoke up.

"It's my student film. I'm studying at the NCA [National College of Art]. This film is for my graduation," I answered.

The men just looked at me. Mustering as much nonchalance as I could, I shouted over to Massoud and the motorcyclists.

"Come on, lads. We need to move on to the next scene right away."

Thankfully, they quickly followed my lead, and within a few seconds we were speeding away to a different part of Karachi, Alu and I in convulsions of laughter at my flimsy excuse. A film student at my age? It was the first thing that had come into my mind. But this middle-aged man with graying hair had pulled it off. Another lucky escape.

I wanted to continue the abduction scene with a few action shots of the car and the motorcycle escort, to convey the pace and drama of the situation in which Daniel Pearl had found himself. The cameraman was not at all keen on the idea, so the only option was for me to operate the camera personally from the pillion seat of one of the bikes. I found myself enjoying the thrill of these action shots, my left hand gripping the seat and and my right hand clutching the camera as we weaved at speed through the traffic of downtown Karachi.

The Journalist and the Jihadi went on to be a very successful documentary film and is widely regarded as the definitive account of the events surrounding Daniel Pearl's death, events later dramatized in the Hollywood movie *A Mighty Heart*, starring Angelina Jolie, with, somewhat bizarrely, Alu himself taking on the role of KK.

But there would be more chances for me to work with KK and others in this troubled region.

I made many friends in the ISPR, the publicity wing of the Pakistani army, as a result of making a documentary film about the army rescue operation that followed the earthquake of October 2005.

These connections came in very useful when, in 2009, Alu and I collaborated on a further documentary film, *The Battle for Swat Valley*, for the BBC's *Panorama* program. The Taliban had moved into this picturesque area with the intention of implementing Sharia law and, to that end, had carried on a bloody campaign of intimidation and murder. The Pakistani army had engaged with them and had eventually driven them out, and our film documented the struggle between these two forces.

It was by no means an easy film to make (we came under fire numerous times), but it was such a resounding success that, in spite of the very real risks involved, we felt emboldened to do more.

The army had moved its operation to South Waziristan and was continuing the struggle against the militants. Alu contacted me from London, looking to film a news report that would require army support. My relations with the ISPR were by now very good and permissions were readily granted. Soon, Alu and I were flying into South Waziristan by helicopter under the protection of the army. Again the report was well received. We seemed to be making a reputation for ourselves as the documentary team of choice for reports in the badlands.

Our work continued with a project that followed up events in the Swat Valley. During their operations, the Pakistani army had apprehended many child soldiers, whose presence in their hands was problematic: they were too young to be imprisoned but too old to be allowed to go scot free.

A school was set up in Malakand as a means of rehabilitating these boys. It was given the moving and poetic name *sabaoon*, meaning "first ray of light from the morning sun."

Journalists came from all over the world to report on the progress of the school, but I was privileged to be the only person allowed to make a documentary film about it. The film, titled *Defusing Human Bombs*, was screened in Pakistan in 2011 to great acclaim.

After working with Alu on a number of projects, I didn't see much of him for quite some time: I was living in Islamabad and he'd returned to London. But a number of incidents in the ensuing years brought me into contact with KK again.

He knew a lady in Karachi whose husband ran a film company. The husband had become embroiled in an affair that resulted in his being arrested and packed off to Guantánamo Bay, leaving behind a lot of expensive video equipment. KK asked me to manage the rental of this equipment as a way of providing an income for the man's wife, which I was glad to do. But there was a falling-out when, some months later, he insisted, out of the blue and in the middle of a rental, on the immediate return of the equipment.

Then, in the summer of 2009, KK's mother died. When I heard the news, I went straight to his house to offer my condolences. He seemed stricken. We hugged and were friends again.

Alu got in touch with another idea for a news report, about rumors of a behind-the-scenes peace initiative between the Taliban and the Pakistan government.

My connections with the ISPR gave me access to the Pakistani army and, indeed, in my various forays into sensitive areas, I'd relied on practical support from the army several times in the past. But I suspected that, for this report, it would be difficult, if not impossible, for them to provide any practical support at all, given the sensitivities involved. It seemed to me that KK was the only man who could get us the access and the information we needed.

I met him at my niece's wedding in September 2009 and spoke to him of our hopes for the project. He was enthusiastic and declared himself ready to help.

For his age, KK had an incredible amount of energy. He wasted no time in traveling to North Waziristan. A few days later, I received an excited phone call from him. A senior figure in the Taliban leadership had agreed to be interviewed for our film. KK had got us our "ace in the hole."

Alu and I were entering uncharted territory in documentary filmmaking. But we'd taken risks before and had emerged relatively unscathed and with valuable footage. And this time we were poised to produce a genuinely groundbreaking piece of work. There was every reason to be positive.

3
The Beginning

Prior to filming, I met with a few of my contacts at the ISPR and told them about the planned interview with a Taliban commander. I suspected we couldn't rely on them for practical support in making the report, but I felt it was important to keep my ISPR contacts in the loop.

One colonel took me aside and advised me not to tell anyone of my plans. The fewer people who knew about our project and our whereabouts, he argued, the less danger we'd be in.

Nevertheless, I was secretly hoping for a little support from the army and, to that end, I met with Brigadier Iftikhar at ISI headquarters and tried to persuade him to meet KK—I felt that such a meeting might secure army help. But the brigadier was not interested. It was simply not possible, given the height of the armed conflict at that time, for the army to release troops from frontline duty in order to escort a bunch of civilians into Taliban territory. The brigadier knew that, without the army to airlift us into the territory, we'd be forced to travel by road, and this he urged us not to do, for our own safety.

I reiterated my wish to set up a meeting between him and KK, but he refused point blank to entertain such a meeting. Nevertheless, later that day I emailed him the questions I was planning to ask the Taliban leadership in the interview. I wanted the ISI to know what I was up to.

Our report was to be filmed in two parts—the first part in Balochistan province, in the towns of Quetta and Chaman, and the second part in North Waziristan. For all previous reports in Pakistan, I'd had the support of the Pakistani army. The lack of support this time round was beginning to hit home. I was apprehensive.

At Islamabad Airport, Asif and I checked in for our flight to Quetta. Sitting in the departure lounge, I was thinking about KK. Normally a bundle of energy, he'd seemed pensive the last few times we'd spoken. I thought of all the ups and downs we'd been through as friends in recent years. I thought of what an infuriatingly stubborn man he could be at times, but also what a remarkable man, so full of integrity and with a deep desire to make the world a better place.

I had witnessed his tireless work for the families of missing persons, people whose disappearance the Pakistan military government had, for nefarious reasons, arranged. KK worked night and day on such cases, filing petition after petition with the Supreme Court of Pakistan, forcing Chief Justice Iftikhar Chaudhary to ask some uncomfortable questions of the government and securing widespread media coverage of the growing divide between the judiciary and the military rulers. When the government demanded that the chief justice resign, his refusal had led to civil unrest that in turn resulted, in 2008, in the toppling of the military regime of Pervez Musharraf. A caretaker civilian government had held elections and, three months later, the Pakistan People's Party came to power. The people had spoken—no more dictatorship.

Another thing that KK felt strongly about was the Taliban. The Pakistan government had created the Taliban but, in pursuit of American money and support, it was now persecuting them and supporting US-led drone strikes that were killing civilians. KK was working to bring this story to the forefront. And our report was to be instrumental in presenting a balanced view of the situation to the Western world.

His integrity and honor, combined with an incredible work ethic, had helped him make friends in high and strange places—he had a bewilderingly diverse and extensive network of acquaintances, giving him access to people and places that a journalist like me could only dream of.

Asif and I were beginning to feel that the film was centering more and more around KK, and we'd come to the decision to give it the title *Travels with Khalid*.

As the wheels went up, I reflected that, in a few short days, KK and I would be companions once again, embarking on perhaps the most difficult journey of our lives.

I tried to think of this is as the beginning of something exciting, valuable, good. But the truth was it felt more like an end.

It was 9:30 a.m., on February 23, 2010.

We settled into our seats. Unlike me, Asif seemed fairly relaxed. I was feeling distinctly like a fish out of water, thanks, largely, to the traditional *shalwar kamiz* and turban, traditional Pakistani dress that we'd been instructed by KK to wear so we'd blend in with the local population in Quetta. Asif had bought some readymade suits, while I took my father's *shalwar*, as we're about the same size. I'd managed to tie the turban correctly on my fourth attempt.

When the snacks were served, I was given a chicken spread sandwich. I asked Asif to ask the flight attendant if she had any vegetarian snacks. She was clearly bewildered by the request. No, nothing vegetarian was available. I might have been dressed like a Pathan, but I wasn't fooling anyone.

I looked out over the beautifully rugged mountains of Balochistan lying below us. Pakistan's largest province, it's also its least populated and is the hub of illegal activity across the Pakistan-Afghanistan border. A beautiful but dangerous place.

A few hours later, we were collecting our luggage, which, owing to a decision to travel light, was a considerably less extensive array of film equipment than usually travels with me on assignments like this. The matte box and filters had been left behind—I'd be using a polarizing filter only. Nothing fancy. Just juicy interviews.

Thanks to a newspaper cartoon, our passage through Quetta airport security did not go smoothly. The furore surrounding an image of the Holy Prophet hiding a bomb under his turban, printed in the Danish paper *Jyllands-Posten*, had made the whole world wary of turbans, even in regions where the turban was a standard item of dress.

An airport security guard asked me to remove my turban. I told him I couldn't (I knew the whole thing would unravel in my unpracticed hands). He asked why. I fumbled for a convincing explanation.

"It's new," I offered, feebly. "I'm not used to tying it yet."

It was as clear as day to the guard that the turban was not my usual attire. He knew it, and he knew I knew he knew it. A tense few seconds followed. A glance to his colleague. An impassive stare returned. To my relief, he settled for running the metal detector over my head. I was cleared through security but I was now the object of public attention.

As I passed through the airport concourse, I noted with irony the array of beautifully starched and tied turbans of the local men around. When KK stepped forward to greet us, it was clear he wasn't overly impressed at my attempt to blend in. He bundled us out of the airport and took us directly to the army mess where we'd be lodging while he set about making arrangements for filming.

While KK was away, Asif and I decided to explore Quetta. It was muddy after the heavy rains and we had to negotiate puddles every step of the way.

I remembered the last time I'd been in Quetta, in 1995, when I was shooting a film for the Pakistan Tourism Corporation. It was the coldest winter for fifteen years and I'd walked through the town wearing the same turban I had on today, only then it had been tied for me by my driver, Abdul Sattar, in Chaman style. In those peaceful days, I was wearing my Barbour raincoat with the turban, a curious combination that attracted lots of smiles and thumbs-up gestures.

In this post 9/11 climate, it was a different scenario altogether. Even though I was dressed in a traditional *shalwar*, I stood out like a sore thumb in my inexpertly tied turban.

I stopped a local man and asked him, with as much humility and dignity as I could muster, to help me tie my turban. He was a handsome, warrior-like Afghan from Kabul and I didn't understand his language, nor he mine. All I could make out was his instruction to face Mecca. Then he retied my turban with astonishing flair and handed it to me. I thanked him warmly.

As Asif and I walked through the bazaars, we saw color everywhere—beautifully embroidered shawls, fabulous hand-knotted rugs, finely crafted sandals.

Night was falling and with it the temperature. I decided to buy a shawl and haggled the vendor's vastly inflated starting price down to the price I'm sure he'd wanted in the first place.

We made our way back to the barracks, with me feeling a little more in character in my shawl (although marveling at how women handle a huge shawl and a handbag at the same time).

KK returned from his negotiations with the news that the situation had changed. Originally, the plan had been to leave for Chaman at 5:00 a.m. and cross into Afghanistan at a point nearby. Now it seemed we were to go to some undisclosed destination instead, still inside Afghanistan, to meet a different person for an interview. KK did not reveal the person's identity, or the location, and we knew better than to press him.

The senior producer from the UK television channel called Asif and asked him for an update—where were we going and what were we going to film? Asif was lost for words.

"Just tell him *West*," I said, hoping that the person at the other end of the phone would understand that we meant Afghanistan but, even if we'd known ourselves at that stage, we couldn't safely be more precise over the phone.

Asif had given KK £5,000 up front to organize the logistics. This had initially seemed ample, but KK hadn't banked on a visit to Quetta by Asif Ali Zardari, the Pakistani president. Asif remarked that KK was spending money on security "like a sailor on shore leave." It was clear he thought that Asif and I had lots of money. He was in for a shock.

This cloak-and-dagger stuff had reinvigorated my enthusiasm for the project. I said to Asif that this would be an experience money couldn't buy. We'd be dining out on the story of our exploits for years to come. KK, too, was convinced that we were onto a good story.

But the mood changed suddenly.

KK got a call. The man we were supposed to meet wanted to see him alone. With the recent arrest of Mullah Barader and other Taliban commanders, our potential interviewee was being cautious. KK warned us that, if we were to be allowed access to this figure, whoever he was, he would probably insist on our being blindfolded. In addition, we'd be required to forgo our own clothes and wear only items provided by him, in case we had microchips sewn into our clothes that could reveal our location to the US units organizing drone strikes in the region.

KK emphasized the importance of not asking him or the people accompanying us any questions. He said it was for our own safety that we knew very little about the arrangements.

Both Asif and I were unnerved by his instructions. Besides, for my own part, I wasn't relishing the prospect of being forced to wear someone else's smelly, sweaty clothes. We were told to wait for further instructions.

The waiting continued.

My partnership with Asif had, over our many years together, seemed to consist more and more of days spent waiting around. It seemed the more valuable the footage was likely to be, the longer we were kept waiting to get it. We were experienced enough not to despair, but it was nevertheless frustrating when, days later, still nothing had happened. On top of the frustration, every day we're out in the field, we're spending production money. There are awkward phone calls from the commissioning channel. Convincing excuses have to be found. Assurances given. Egos massaged. The wait is draining.

In 1992, Asif and I were filming *The Bounty Hunter*, a *Cutting Edge* documentary about the work of Taher Mahmood, a private detective of sorts engaged by Asian fathers and husbands to track down daughters and wives fleeing the life that their patriarchal society arranges for them. A controversial figure.

During our research, we'd spoken with Mahmood and he'd given us assurances that he'd arranged access to numerous families who were willing to speak openly about their circumstances.

Alas, this was not to be. After six weeks of filming, we'd gathered nothing of any use. As this was my debut as director, I was feeling under particular pressure. To make matters worse, I'd fallen sick on day three of filming, with acute pancreatitis. But, in order to salvage something from the project, I had to treat the hospital like a hotel—days spent on location filming, nights spent recovering and being treated in the hospital.

My persistence paid off in the end, and we emerged with a successful film. To this day, Asif and I say that *The Bounty Hunter* was essentially made in just one day, when everything finally fell into place.

We've been in situations like this many times together, and things always work out. Asif often flatters me by saying, "Asad, you always deliver!"

At 4:30 p.m., KK called and told us to be ready to move. There'd been a drone attack earlier that day and two people had been killed. Perhaps our interviewee thought it unlikely there would be a second attack on the same day and it was therefore safe to move.

At around 5:10 p.m., KK arrived in a white Toyota Hilux pickup, with four other men. These men were carrying guns, and they looked hostile and formidable. KK asked us to move off right away. I loaded the equipment into the pickup and asked if I could sit in the front passenger seat, with KK positioned behind the driver, so that I could film him. The man in the front passenger seat seemed to be the leader and was not at all happy about moving. KK eventually managed to convince him, he moved to the back, and we got under way.

We made it clear to the leader that we wouldn't attempt to roll the camera until he gave us permission to start filming. We weren't there to trick anyone.

I waited and waited, but no word came from him. The sun was setting and I was concerned that we were losing light fast. How was I going to film?

After a few more miles, the leader suddenly said, "Bypass." The pickup turned and drove for a few hundred feet before he said, "Stop."

The driver obeyed instantly. Two of the men got out and asked me to sit in the back. I was puzzled. We'd agreed I'd film from the front seat, but I hadn't done any filming yet and now I was being moved into the back.

The second man came over with what looked like three rolled-up black bags. As he unfurled them, it became clear they were, in fact, hoods. I watched the man put a hood over KK's head, which gave him the look of a condemned man. A video image flashed into my mind—Saddam Hussein refusing a hood, then, seconds later, a trapdoor opening and his body dropping.

My turn next. I made a feeble protest about being claustrophobic, but to no avail. On went the hood, pulled so tight that I was rendered completely blind. To make matters worse, the hood had an indescribably unpleasant smell. I wondered what atrocities it had been party to. I felt panicky and sick. I felt helpless and completely at the mercy of these men. Unlike me, KK seemed very matter of fact about the situation.

Into my mind came an image of the murdered US journalist, Daniel Pearl, kidnapped on the pretense that he was being taken to his interviewee.

And, five years on, here we were—KK, Asif, and I—hooded and in the back of a truck. On our way to meet a Taliban commander? We hoped so. Perhaps we were stupid even to hope for that, but it was still my hope.

I thought of my parents and my wife. As a son and a husband, perhaps I was being grossly irresponsible in exposing myself to such great danger—I knew my whole family strongly disapproved of the choices I often made as a documentary filmmaker—but I felt a strong sense of duty to shine a light in dark corners. Plus, if I'm honest, I found the sense of adventure you experience in these situations quite intoxicating and addictive.

I tried to regain that sense of adventure during our long blindfold drive, a drive so long I almost dozed off a number of times. Almost. The acrid odor of the hood would, like smelling salts, always jerk me back to wakefulness.

The truck came to a halt. The doors opened, the men jumped out, and our hoods were pulled off.

The men seemed less hostile than before. More nervous and circumspect. Perhaps they were regretting the access they'd agreed to allow us. Their unease immediately eased my fears of being kidnapped, and I became a filmmaker again. I glanced around at the darkness. How was I going to film anything in this light?

Asif asked them if I could film his and KK's hoods being taken off. They muttered objections, but Asif persisted and the men eventually agreed. The hoods went back on and I got a quick shot of them being removed. I got a wide shot of the area, and a shot of Asif and KK walking into a mud hut.

Inside, four men were seated. The leader said I was not to film or even look behind me. I could feel that there were more people in the room, watching the proceedings. I was too nervous to do anything other than oblige him.

This leader introduced himself as Aminullah, a Taliban leader from the Oruzgan province of Afghanistan. He sat in the middle of the room, with a gunman on each side of him. A fourth man seated nearby was covered from head to toe in a white sheet. A translator, we were told. Aminullah was wearing dark glasses, but the rest of his face was uncovered.

As there was practically no light in the hut, I got a circular LED light and mounted it onto the camera microphone. This would be the only light to illuminate these men. Men with a message of global significance.

There was a clear mood of urgency in the room. The Taliban group wanted us out of the way quickly, perhaps out of fear that our presence might bring a further drone strike, or that their dealings with westerners might put them at risk with the wider Taliban leadership. For our part, we would be glad to be on our way soon too.

In this hurried atmosphere, I completely forgot about the second camera I'd brought along, still in the truck. I had hoped that Asif would be able to use it for cutaway shots. Now there was no chance of that.

KK asked the questions we'd prepared. The translator relayed them in Pushto to Aminullah, who replied without delay or equivocation. I couldn't see much of his face in the low light, but from his manner it was clear he had a strong sense of himself as a leader.

We learned that he'd fought the Soviets during their invasion of Afghanistan and had lost his father in that war. Like his father, he too was willing to die in this war. His conviction was impressively strong.

As the interview continued, I was struck by a number of things Aminullah said. He was at pains to emphasize that, contrary to the widespread perception in the West, there is *no* connection between the Taliban and Al Qaeda.

"We want to convey our message that we are fighting the foreigners because they have invaded our lands and they call us terrorists but they themselves are the terrorists. They are perpetrating crimes against us and have invaded Afghanistan. We are not terrorists; we do not have any connection with terrorists or Al Qaeda."

And he balked at my reference to the United States as a superpower.

"America is not a superpower. Allah is the superpower. It is Allah who has created the whole world. If He is with you, then America, Russia, Britain cannot defeat you."

With the interview over, the mood relaxed somewhat, and when the men made their *maghrib*,* I was allowed to film them.

---

* Prayers said at sunset.

After prayers, the men who'd transported us were keen for us to be on our way quickly. Aminullah reiterated that it was very dangerous for us to be out here this late.

Before leaving, I offered Aminullah the almonds and sweets that Sherry had packed for me. He accepted graciously.

"You are very kind. I wish we could eat together, but it is not safe for you."

As we stepped out of the hut, I saw one of the gunmen grab the bag of almonds and sweets.

"In case there's a tracking chip in the bag," KK whispered.

So much suspicion, on all sides.

Outside the hut, it was completely dark. A total blackout. I had to use the small LED camera light so I could see to load my equipment back into the truck. One of the Taliban gunmen asked me to turn the light off. In this darkness, any light could be seen for miles, he said, making us an easy target. He didn't have to ask me again.

Once in the truck, we were made to wear the hoods again, even though it was pitch dark. Through the thick blackness of the hood, I could see a faint light shining into my face. The leader was checking with his torch that the hoods were doing a good job.

I wondered where they'd taken us. I suspected we'd crossed the border into Afghanistan. It would have been too risky for any Taliban commander to set foot in Pakistan.

The man sitting in the front issued a caution—if the van was to stop on the way and we heard someone talking outside the van, we must remain silent. He repeated himself. A clear warning.

KK and Asif said nothing, but I was keen to let him know that I understood.

"Yes, sir."

We were on our way back to Quetta, but we were clearly not out of danger yet.

After some time, I began to be aware that the road was not bumpy any more. We were back on tarmac. We went over a few speed bumps, and I could even make out an odd street light through my hood.

In the middle of a conversation between KK and Asif, the truck suddenly stopped. I heard someone outside and immediately shushed the other two. The man in front also told them to be quiet.

We were silent for a good couple of minutes. Then the man announced that we could remove our hoods. What a relief! We were alive, back in civilization.

Asif and I asked if we could keep the hoods as souvenirs, and the man agreed. The truck pulled away.

Asif was on a high and the sense of adventure returned. We'd pulled through. KK was relieved that the interview was behind us. Aminullah was a major figure in the Taliban leadership, he told us, with sixty commanders reporting to him and perhaps thousands of ordinary soldiers.

We'd been blindfolded and driven deep into Taliban territory, had been held at gunpoint, and had been at risk of a drone attack, all for the love of filmmaking. It had been some day!

Back at the officers' mess, KK asked me for the two tapes I'd shot. He said he had to show them to someone, to get everything we'd filmed cleared for broadcasting. I was reluctant to hand over this precious material, but he'd given his word to the Taliban that we would play with a straight bat, and I knew Asif and I had to do as he wished. Besides, I didn't want us to jeopardize any future interviews.

KK told us that the next plan was to go to Chaman the following morning and, from there, into Afghanistan. After KK had left us, Asif was pensive. I asked him what was wrong. He told me he had a confession to make.

"I couldn't stand being hooded again. I can't do it."

"But we survived, didn't we? Look, we've been through scrapes before. We always survive. Like you always say, 'We deliver.'"

"*You* deliver, Asad."

"With your help."

"I can't do it. I can't go. You'll have to go alone."

"Come on, Asif. We're in this together. Look at what we've achieved already."

Asif said nothing. He didn't seem convinced, but we left it at that.

KK had told us that the plan was to leave for Chaman at around 10:00 a.m. At 7 o'clock, we got a text from him telling us we'd be leaving instead at 8:00. Never a dull moment with KK. It was February 25, 2010, our third day in Quetta.

We were picked up at the army mess in the same vehicle as the previous day, with, incredibly, the same driver and same two armed escorts, but in place of the previous day's leader was a guide who introduced himself as Shahid.

It all seemed very strange to me. Here we were, staying at any army mess on an apparently secure and fortified military base, yet these men, whom we knew nothing about, could roll up at will and spirit us across the border into Afghanistan to meet with a senior Taliban leader, then bring us back again. I couldn't make sense of it. For our own safety, it was perhaps best not to try.

We set off for Chaman, on the border with Afghanistan. In the morning sun, the hills around us were a stunning bright red that took my breath away.

On the way, Asif interviewed KK and I filmed it as best I could, given the bumpy roads and my cramped position on the front seat of the pickup. After thirty minutes or so, suddenly there was a thud. The driver stopped to investigate, and we all stepped out of the truck. One of the rear wheels had lost all its nuts and the wheel itself had worked loose. A few seconds later and the wheel would have fallen off, damaging the truck and, with it, our plans for the day.

One of the escorts ran back down the road, to see if he could find the nuts. Although he only managed to find two of the six, they would hold the wheel on long enough to get us to the next town and a garage.

While our escorts were busy dealing with the wheelnuts, KK took Asif and me to one side. He was at pains to stress the importance of last night's interview. He seemed to think we underestimated Aminullah's position in the Taliban hierarchy. Perhaps he thought we were being too casual, too blasé. For my part, I think I understood our position perfectly, and was fully aware of the danger we were placing ourselves in. But, as a filmmaker, I couldn't allow myself to dwell on the danger. If we were to emerge from this adventure with a broadcastable piece of work, it was important to be professional and cover as much ground as we could.

On the road again, we continued to gain altitude, the soft red hills of early morning giving way to jagged brown peaks. The road was so dusty that every time we were overtaken, I hurriedly rolled up the window to keep our equipment clean.

We made a number of stops so I could film some location shots and, for context, some establishing shots of the truck on the road.

The road to Chaman was full of trucks, all of them heavily laden with supplies and equipment for the NATO troops stationed in Afghanistan, all of them painted in regulation mushroom camouflage, all of them armed to the teeth (I saw a rocket launcher on the back of one truck). All good context material for our film.

After a few more miles, we stopped at a prearranged spot, a police checkpoint a few hundred yards from Chaman, in order to change cars. While we were waiting, I filmed more shots of trucks driving by.

A policeman walked over. I must stop filming, he said. This was a government area and all photography and filming was prohibited. He ordered me to hand over my film. Shahid intervened and tried to placate the officer. While they were talking, our transport arrived. Knowing we couldn't afford to hang around, we drove off, still in possession of the film, leaving Shahid to sort things out with the police.

We were still a couple of miles from the Afghan border, but already we could see the long line of trucks awaiting customs clearance, and the line was getting longer and longer ahead of us.

In the distance, we could make out the Friendship Gate, the structure that marks the border between Pakistan and Afghanistan. Our plan for the film was to emphasize KK's influence in the region by showing him driving into Afghanistan unchallenged. Our new guide, Bilal, suggested we avoid the Friendship Gate and cross the border at some other point. Nevertheless, I wanted some shots of this prominent border crossing, so we approached.

On the Pakistan side, there are regular checkpoints. Security is very tight—papers are checked, questions are asked, eyes meet eyes. Checkpoints are thin on the ground on the Afghan side, and standards are relaxed. I filmed people going across the border. On the Afghan side, they got a quick pat down and that was it. Some people even walked through unchecked, especially young children.

From the Friendship Gate, I could see far into Afghanistan and I took a few shots of Afghan streets busy with traffic and hundreds of people milling around. The line of the border is marked by a ditch about 4 feet wide and the same deep. We decided to drive alongside it, to get some shots of the wider border area.

Bilal reassured us that he would handle any difficulties with the Pakistani police. Within a mile or so, we came to a checkpoint. When two officers stepped toward the car, Bilal jumped out and walked up to them. We watched the exchange from the car. The officers clearly wanted to know what we were doing there. Bilal gave some explanation that seemed to satisfy them. The mood was cordial. One of the officers came over and invited us for tea, but we excused ourselves, Bilal jumped back in, and we carried on.

As we drove farther along the border, the ditch petered out, leaving no visible border separating the two countries. We could see houses and children on the Afghan side. There was nothing stopping people crossing unhindered from one side to the other, even though there were Pakistani checkpoints at intervals.

We crossed onto the Afghan side. Then I filmed some shots of KK and Asif standing in Afghanistan, with me operating the camera from the Pakistan side.

After we'd driven farther on, I suggested stopping so I could get some shots of the car driving on the Afghan side. While Bilal and I were standing at the side of the road, an Afghan soldier approached us and asked what we were doing. Bilal told him we were surveyors, working on the road. Although we had absolutely no equipment of that nature, this feeble explanation seemed to satisfy the soldier, and he left us in peace.

We'd got some good footage of border, and had been able to show how incredibly porous it is, but I was still waiting for the big interview that we'd set off for and that KK had assured us would happen.

I asked KK about it. He seemed to think it was too dangerous to press on now. We should be satisfied, for this trip, with the Aminullah interview and leave it at that.

I was disappointed. But I was also relieved at not having to spend a few more hours in a smelly hood and someone else's dirty clothes. I knew that Asif, too, would be glad we were giving that a miss.

We headed back, on the Pakistani side again, toward the Friendship Gate. Another soldier flagged us down. He asked what we were doing. Bilal gave a breezy reply. The soldier was not impressed. He wanted us to meet his superior officer. He would accompany us. Rather peremptorily, he moved toward the back of our car and opened the door to get in. Bilal leaned over and said that our arrangements were all in place, and that we had no wish to meet anyone. The soldier insisted and went to climb in. At this, Bilal jumped out of the car, flashed a card, and, to my surprise, pushed the soldier bodily away. On seeing the card, the soldier's mood changed instantly. He backed off and let us go on our way.

The influences at work in Pakistan never fail to surprise me. With the right connections, one can do almost anything. On this trip, numerous people we hardly knew were ready to accompany us and were opening doors for us effortlessly. I reckoned Bilal was probably a member of the ISI. It was wisest not to ask any questions.

Back at the Friendship Gate, I was feeling a little peckish. A boy was pushing a cart of peanuts along the street. I asked him how much for a bag? He put his hand up.

"Free."

He could see I was not a local and he was treating me as a guest. What incredible hospitality these tribal people show! This generosity underpins the code of *Pukhtunwali* that they live by, its principles being honor, justice, bravery, loyalty, righteousness, the giving of asylum, trust in God, courage, and the protection of women.

But their sense of honor is so ingrained that a tribal feud can last for decades. Revenge is a major way of life for them.

Our work in Quetta was done. Asif managed to get a flight out to Karachi, but it was not clear at this stage that there was a seat for me on the plane back to Islamabad.

There was only one flight a day leaving Quetta. I didn't relish the prospect of spending another night here. The standards of hygiene at the army mess left a lot to be desired. Besides, I was impatient to return to Islamabad to reassure my parents that all was well—I knew the last few days would have been an anxious time for them.

KK kept assuring me that he'd get me on that plane. After a tense few hours, KK received a call confirming my seat. He'd come through for me again.

After seeing me off at Quetta airport, KK headed to North Waziristan. Terrorists were carrying out suicide bombings in Rawalpindi and Lahore, and he wanted to use his influence to get them stopped. At the same time, he would secure permission for us to interview another senior Taliban commander.

I was also hoping that KK might arrange an interview with commanders from the Haqqani network, who we'd heard were actively involved in the peace deal. Jalaluddin Haqqani commanded the Mujahedeen army from 1980 to 1992, and he's credited with recruiting foreign fighters, Osama bin Laden among them.

The Haqqanis and Al Qaeda evolved together and they've remained intertwined throughout their history. The significant difference between the two organizations is that Al Qaeda's goals are global and they operate on the world stage, whereas the Haqqani group is solely interested in Afghanistan and the Pushtun Tribal regions. Jalaluddin Haqqani is more interested in the influence of Islamic law over Afghanistan than in the global Jihad.

KK visited me in Islamabad a few days later, with important news. He'd made contact in North Waziristan with Hakimullah Mehsud, the leader of Tehrik-e-Taliban Pakistan,[*] and with his deputy Wali-ur-Rehman, and he'd got their agreement to be interviewed for our film.

This was a scoop indeed. It had been reported around the world that Hakimullah Mehsud had been killed in a drone attack. But KK had known all along that this top Taliban commander had simply gone underground. And what's more, he knew how and where to find him, and was able to get access to him. Again I was stunned by KK's network of contacts.

During his meeting with Hakimullah, KK told me that, at one point, the group had heard the sound of something landing on the roof of their hideout. They suspected it was a package containing a microchip marking them as a target for a drone strike, and, fearing an imminent attack, they'd fled the building, continuing their meeting in an open field.

In this part of the world, everyone is suspicious of everyone else. A common way of earning money is by planting a microchip wherever there is the suspicion of a gathering of Taliban hierarchy, but it's a risky way to make money. If Taliban supporters, who are legion, discover someone in possession of a microchip, their fate is sealed. They are shot and their body is laid out on the street with a note pinned to the chest—*This man was a spy.*

KK stressed that we'd need to shell out a lot of money on security, but it would be worth it for access to such a senior figure in the Taliban regime. The opportunity to talk to someone like Hakimullah was thrilling. We would be the journalists who revealed to the world that he was still alive.

[*] The Pakistan Taliban, often referred to as the TTP.

4
The Journey

For the people in the street below my bedroom window, this was just another day. For me, it was the day I would set off for the lawless wilderness of North Waziristan to get the scoop of my life.

Asif had withdrawn from the trip owing to ill health. My brother, Farrukh, had jokingly accused him of cowardice, of feigning illness in order to avoid dangers that he had no stomach for. He was abandoning his friend and colleague at a time when I would need him most, Farrukh jested.

A rather sheepish Asif didn't seem capable of jocularity. "I'm not well enough to travel."

The adventure of a lifetime. That's certainly how it felt to me as I spent the day preparing my equipment and my belongings for the journey. As with any adventure worth its salt, there was an awareness of the potential dangers. I had jumped from enough helicopters in enough trouble spots to understand the risks of consorting with armed groups like the Taliban.

Evening came and with it the time for me to leave. I didn't relish the prospect of saying goodbye to my wife, Sherry.

We were like magnets—when the alignment was good, we were drawn together by a powerful attraction; when it wasn't, we were forced apart.

In the early years of our marriage, one major cause of misalignment was Sherry's mother, Ann. As someone much more famous than me once said, there were three of us in the marriage.

Ann hadn't liked me from the first moment she'd laid eyes on me. While there can be love at first sight, there can also be hatred at first sight, and this characterizes Ann's response to me. She was deeply suspicious of my ethnicity. She told Sherry outright that I bore a personal responsibility for the events of 9/11.

But, in spite of Ann's antipathy, Sherry and I were very happy in those early years. We bought a rundown house and set about the monumental task of remodeling it. One evening not long after we'd bought the house, we were driving past Home Depot with Sherry's brother, John. John pointed to the store. "That place is going to be your best friend."

He wasn't wrong. My skills in the DIY department were pretty limited. At first, I never measured things properly. I sometimes sawed skin off my fingers. I was always hitting my thumb with a hammer. And I'd often get fed up and walk off the job.

But I became more proficient, although I never got to the point where I actually enjoyed the work. Sherry was endlessly patient with me. She'd tell me how great I was. She'd look at my handiwork and tell me it was wonderful. She'd offer to hire someone to finish the work (although we both knew we didn't have the money for that).

And she was blissfully unselfconscious. If someone paid her a compliment, she'd bat it back to them, or find a way to downplay it. She had a passion for cotton print dresses. Once, when were walking along Sundance Square in Forth Worth, a woman driving by slowed her car and shouted across to Sherry.

"I LOVE your dress!"

"Thanks. And I lost 10 pounds!"

And she was quite a homemaker, with a voracious appetite for collecting. The little house was full of vases she'd picked up from all over the world, which she'd fill with flowers. And every inch of wall was covered with watercolours she'd bought in Djibouti or Cape Town or Kuala Lumpur.

It didn't take much to make Sherry happy. An hour on a park bench in the sunshine with a tub of hummus and some French bread and she felt like the Queen of England. She'd pick berries by the side of the road and eat them there and then. When I objected that they hadn't been washed, she'd look at me like I was crazy and then laugh. I loved her laugh. Like her, it was so carefree.

But life in Pakistan had changed the dynamic. And it had changed her.

Growing up in Texas, Sherry had been used to migrating freely around her environment. Here in Pakistan, life was, even with me around, very different for her—a total culture shock.

And I was often away on assignments. And with an absent husband, no Pakistani driver's license, and, as an American and a woman, no prospect of venturing out safely alone, she was effectively housebound, confined to quarters with my elderly parents.

This reality was taking its toll on our relationship. I knew things were not good between us. We'd had a few separations in our long history together. I wasn't sure we could survive another.

I would be leaving her with a heavy heart indeed.

As to my parents, I was always uneasy about leaving them behind. I knew my profession gave my naturally anxious mother tremendous cause for worry, and she'd always worried more about me than about any of my siblings. She prayed for me constantly whenever I was gone.

When I was directing my first film and came down with pancreatitis, I'd urged Asif not to tell my family about my hospitalization, but, dutiful family friend that he was, he'd called them first thing the following morning, and they'd learned of my illness over breakfast.

When they arrived at the hospital a few hours later, they found me on a drip with a tube up my nose, sedated and incoherent. The very shock of seeing me in this state had caused my mother to collapse. The doctors had moved her in two floors below me, where she'd stayed for two of the ten weeks I was there.

They say that opposites attract. Mercifully for domestic harmony, my father's personality was the antithesis of my mother's.

A deeply pious bibliophile in his late eighties, my father was a retired English teacher. He'd taken early retirement in England and, following their move to Pakistan, had for a while lectured in the Islamic University in Islamabad. A man with incredible reserves of patience, he had a close relationship with God that gave him a deep sense of contentment which all who met him admired and envied.

My mother herself was not without patience. In the 1970s, she'd worked in an electronics factory, assembling parts for television sets. Then the company shut down and she'd never worked again, instead devoting all her energies to raising her family and fretting about their welfare.

They were the ideal inseparable couple who loved each other as much today as they did when they were first married. I had to hope that my father's calm countenance would be enough to assuage my mother's worries. Her anxiety was palpable as she followed me outside to the car, something she never normally did. I hugged her and felt her hold me tight.

I shook hands with my father, and he gave me his customary warm smile, tinged, I felt, with something akin to resignation.

I shook hands with Jawaid, our housekeeper, who, unusually, had also come outside to wave me off.

I looked at Sherry. We embraced, then I stood back and looked her in the eyes.

"If I don't come back, please forgive me."

Tears rolled down her cheeks. I knew that nothing I could say would comfort her. I'd always joked with friends that my work was my first wife, and Sherry had always known how committed I was to it and accepted that commitment. But this parting felt like an incredible wrench.

I climbed into the car with Rustam, and as we pulled away, I didn't look back.

Rustam's baggage consisted of a plastic shopping bag containing a single change of clothes. When I looked at it quizzically, he responded, "We're only away for a few days."

Something of my mother's natural anxiety has rubbed off on me, at least where preparedness for travel is concerned. When I go away for a day, I pack for a week. Expecting to be away for several days this time, I had packed for a month. Add to this personal baggage all the bags of cameras, lenses, and tripods, and my assignments are apt to resemble polar expeditions.

At the root of this overzealousness in matters of packing is a deep-seated regard for general cleanliness and personal hygiene also instilled in me by my mother. More than any misgivings I might ever have about my personal safety, this is the one thing that makes working on location tough for me. Putting up with dirty accommodations and food prepared in less-than-hygienic conditions is something I dread. It's fair to call me a clean freak or germaphobe.

When we were young, in summer my mother would make us all take a cold bath before breakfast. Even though it was a refreshing experience, one day I refused. I wasn't asking to take a hot bath instead; I just refused to bathe at all. As a result, I was sent to school without breakfast. I never refused to take a bath again. The habit of bathing daily has stayed with me ever since, and I take a shower every day, no matter where I find myself.

Rustam and I arrived at KK's house at about 6:00 p.m., as planned. KK himself crackled with the enthusiasm of a man on a mission. But he was not alone. I was introduced to a tall elderly man with a long gray beard.

Sultan Amir Tarar was known to almost everyone as Colonel Imam. I had not met the retired ISI officer before, but his national reputation as a special operations commander preceeded him. Thought to have played a key role in the formation of the Taliban in the Soviet days, he was a man whose presence on this assignment confirmed its seriousness.

We shook hands. I engaged him rather cheekily.

"I hope you speak English. I plan to conduct our interviews in English." He looked at me with a smirk on his face.

"A little bit."

KK welcomed me with an embrace, but eyed Rustam with apprehension. He hadn't known I'd be bringing Rustam along, he said, and didn't think it was a good idea. I explained that Rustam would assist me in recording the sound, and would carry the equipment I needed. KK suggested a local man in Waziristan could be hired to do that work. I insisted I wanted a trusted and dedicated person for this important job and was unwilling to risk someone new and untried. Rustam was going and that was that. KK was annoyed, but I was adamant. Old tensions bubbled under the surface.

Also present was KK's friend, Shah Abdul Aziz, a former member of parliament with a lot of influence in the town of Karak and the tribal areas into which we were venturing. A handsome man with a beard and a fair complexion, Aziz chatted urbanely with us about what we expected this encounter with the Taliban hierarchy to achieve.

It was clear from the conversation that, while for me this was a major international news assignment, for KK and Colonel Imam their motive was to be of service to the Taliban, to make it clear to the wider world that the Taliban felt betrayed by the Pakistani government.

This quagmire developed with the Russian invasion of Afghanistan in 1979, when billions of dollars were pumped into Pakistan by the USA and the UK for the purpose of training the Mujahedeen as the bulwark against the Russians. For their part, the Mujahedeen saw themselves as the defenders of Islam. After the Russians withdrew from the region, Mujahedeen groups spread to various countries, including India, Chechnya, Bosnia and Herzegovina, Kosovo and Macedonia, Iran, Iraq, and Somalia. Their influence in Afghanistan waned.

This void was filled by the Taliban, the self-styled Students of Islamic Knowledge. They have an antimodern ideology, perhaps best characterized as an interpretation of Sharia that also incorporates elements of Pushtun tribal code.

They ruled an Afghanistan that had regressed to near-medieval standards in terms of infrastructure and social order and still served, from a Western point of view, as a protection against post-Soviet influence.

Then, following the events of 9/11, because the Taliban had given sanctuary to Osama Bin Laden, as is decreed by ancient Pushtun codes of hospitality, they were ousted from power by the US military. Pakistan became America's ally in the war on terror and the marginalized Taliban became the new enemy, with Sharia law presented by the Western media as proof of their barbarism. Islamophobia whipped up by the media branded the Taliban the new global boogeyman.

So our film was to peek behind the media curtain and present an in-depth view of the situation on the ground. Yet, to my mind, my colleagues' faith in the Taliban was unreasoning—they were like a mother who can see no wrong in her children.

I asked Shah Abdul Aziz to join us on our trip. "My dear brother, I must be in court the day after tomorrow and cannot go with you."

I knew the case he was referring to. He'd been implicated in the killing of a Polish engineer, Peter Stanczak, kidnapped by the Taliban in September 2008—a serious charge. I understood his reluctance to miss this day in court. The wheels of the Pakistani legal system grind very slowly, and his next chance to clear his name might not come for months or even years.

It was a shame for us. He would have been an ideal man to accompany us, with his close links to the Taliban hierarchy.

The time came for us to leave, and KK said his goodbyes to his wife and his son, Usama. KK's wife had packed a weekend bag for him, but he declined to take it.

"I won't need much. The clothes I'm wearing are enough."

She accepted his statement without protest. He picked up a black briefcase and his three phones. KK was the type of individual whose phones are constantly monitored by the security agencies. I was concerned that multiple phones meant multiple opportunities to trace and monitor us.

"Why don't you leave your phones here?" I suggested.

"Good idea. Well, I'll just take one. Usama can answer the others."

We took our seats in the hired car, Colonel Imam (as the tallest) in the front passenger seat, next to the driver, and Rustam, KK, and I in the back. As we drove off into the darkness, Usama stood waving, with, I thought, a rather forlorn look on his face.

We drove several hours, with KK on his phone constantly, fretting about being unable to contact our guide. When we stopped for prayers at a mosque by a roadside petrol station, I think we were all relieved to stretch our legs and cool off. As we were too late for congregational prayers, the Colonel was asked by KK to lead prayers.

It was very late when we arrived in Karak. We were met by a stout man, a nephew of Shah Abdul Aziz, who took us to a restaurant. The best in town, he said.

The place turned out to be little more than a roadside café, and a rather grubby one at that. Taking in its dusty floors and sticky tabletops, I wondered what the worst restaurant in town was like. At home in London, I deployed my ever-present bottle of hand sanitizer whenever I was out in public. My concern for hygiene was so great I even refrained from touching the handrails on escalators. There was no way I was accepting food prepared here, so, although ravenous after the long drive, I politely refused everything while the others ate.

After dinner, we made our way to Shah Abdul Aziz's *madrassah*. Rustam and I elected to sleep outside in the courtyard, staring up at a night sky full of stars. Our driver Abbasi, a rather portly gentleman, slept in a nearby room and kept us awake and entertained with his regular, rumbling snore. We managed to catch a few hours' sleep before sunrise brought swarms of flies buzzing round our heads. Sheltering under the covers was useless—far too hot—so I accepted defeat and decided to get up and face the day.

Having arrived in the dark, we hadn't seen much of the *madrassah* the night before. In daylight, and with a chance to explore, we realized how huge this place was. A 10-foot-high perimeter wall surrounded a vast courtyard the size of five football pitches. There were innumerable classrooms and even a mosque. Land must be cheap in Karak, I thought.

Whereas the previous night the complex had been deserted, now the whole place was alive with students, or *tulba*, the local Urdu word from which the word *Taliban* is ultimately derived.

I continued my tour with a visit to the kitchen. A huge clay oven or *tandoor* was presided over by two men making hundreds of chapattis. A kidney bean curry was being served in huge dishes from which eight people were eating communally. The air was thick with flies. My chances of a healthy meal were not improving.

When Rustam and I met up with KK, he was on his phone again. This set the pattern for the day, with KK sometimes climbing up to the roof in search of a better signal. When he wasn't making calls, we all sat together discussing world affairs, in the company of Shah Abdul Aziz's younger brother, Hussain, who was glad to have company from outside. Mindful of my role as a journalist, I made notes of all my observations.

KK's numerous phone conversations had yet to translate into activity—he still hadn't managed to make contact with our guide.

Although it was now early afternoon, like the others, I hadn't bathed. Eager to stay clean, and conscious of the fact I'd slept in someone else's bed, I decided to take a bath.

While I performed my ablutions as best I could in the very cramped and untidy bathroom, I heard a text ping. Preoccupied by my attempts to make myself clean in these rather dingy surroundings, I forgot about it. When I emerged from the bathroom, KK and the Colonel announced they were ready to leave.

"I think we should push on. We're just wasting time here," said KK.

"What about the guide?" I asked.

"He's probably got a problem with his signal. We'll make contact once we're closer."

I looked at KK. He was asking me to trust him.

"Well," I said, "we're here now, so we might as well carry on."

We loaded our things into the car, said farewell to our hosts, and drove off, a trail of dust flying behind the car. Half a mile along the road, we passed a mosque where people were gathering for *asr*.* Colonel Imam asked the driver to stop so we could join the congregation.

After prayers, coming out of the mosque, I reached into my jacket for something, touched my phone, and remembered the text. It was from KK's son, Usama. It read:

"They know you are coming. Permission for journalist not cleared. Please return home."

The message was sent to KK's cell phone that he had left at home, and Usama had forwarded it to me.

I showed the message to KK. He looked at it intently, his lips moving slowly as he read. Then he looked at me and said, "Okay, I think we should go back."

My reaction was, strangely for me, pure relief. This was the first time I'd ever been apprehensive about a shoot. I was glad to be going home to Islamabad, home to my parents, and home to Sherry, who really needed me now. I phoned Sherry and told her to expect me home around 10:00 p.m. that night.

Then I called Asif and told him we'd decided to abort the trip, and explained about not being given clearance. He seemed happy to hear the news. Now that he was sure I'd be safe, he'd leave for Karachi in the morning to spend time with his family.

Night was beginning to fall. Driving anywhere in Pakistan is never easy. Most roads are poorly made and surfaced. People drive recklessly, which is hardly surprising given the test—driving around a police compound for ten minutes, with no other traffic. With connections, you can get a license with no test at all. Driving at night is worse still. Street lighting is virtually nonexistent and all oncoming vehicles have their headlights on full beam. You can barely see the road.

* Late afternoon prayers.

We reached a junction. Into the darkness ahead, our lights illuminated a road sign. Islamabad right, Kohat left. KK told the driver to stop. He punched numbers on his phone.

"*Asalaam alaikum*, Peracha *sahib*. I hope you are well. Where are you?"

"I am on my way home to Kohat."

"That is good. I am very near Kohat."

"Good. You come over and we will have dinner."

"Thank you. See you soon."

KK hung up. "That was Jawaid Ibrahim Peracha, who lives in Kohat. Maybe we can stay the night with him and go to Waziristan tomorrow."

I was dumbfounded.

"But the text. I don't have clearance. The Taliban don't want me there."

Colonel Imam weighed in.

"We must return to our homes. We have been exposed. Going on now would be a mistake."

My heart was no longer in this assignment at all. It was back with my wife and my family.

"I really think we should go home. Please. Let's go back."

KK was adamant.

"Look. It is either now or never." Then in a more conciliatory tone: "I will make some phone calls. It will be all right."

I didn't like this development. We seemed to be making policy on the hoof. I didn't know Peracha from Adam. And I certainly didn't like the idea of waltzing into a Taliban stronghold against their express wishes.

On the other hand, I'd known KK long enough to know that, with his vast network of contacts, he could pull a rabbit out of any hat. I also suspected he'd already placed himself at considerable personal risk to get us this far, and I appreciated he wanted to salvage our mission. Defying KK now would likely result in friction between him and my brother, Farrukh, which I was keen to avoid.

I looked at Colonel Imam. He looked back at me with a steady gaze. We appeared to have no choice.

KK nodded to the driver and the car veered left, toward Kohat.

I felt uncomfortable, no longer in control. I tried to focus on KK's skill as a tactician, rather than his belligerence—the latter was making me irritable and afraid. I also tried to take comfort from the fact KK had a court appearance in Sarghoda on March 30, in five days' time, in connection with the case of five American boys detained on terrorism charges (KK, in his capacity as a human rights activist, was working with the defense).

I knew my parents would be unnerved, especially so soon after hearing news I was coming home. And I dreaded calling Sherry to update her, but this I did first. She took the news badly and the conversation was brief, her responses curt. It broke my heart to dash her hopes of my coming home. I felt a heavy burden; the last thing I wanted was for her to be unhappy and lonely. Knowing she was so far away from her family in Texas, I used to keep her as busy as possible, but I had to work and assured her I'd be home soon. I called Asif and told him we'd be spending the night in Kohat, then traveling on to Miranshah in the morning. With his journalist's hat on, he wished us well.

The car proceeded slowly along the Kohat road, the dots of light from the lanterns of roadside stalls that stretched into the distance giving the road the appearance of a dimly lit runway. Despite frequent and widespread power cuts, life went on as usual. People adapted. Business continued. By the light of a lantern.

On the outskirts of Kohat, KK instructed the driver to take a left turn. The car edged into a dark and very narrow street. In the distance was a small corner shop lit by a single lamp. When we reached it, KK told the driver to stop. The car could go no farther, KK said. The track was too narrow. We'd have to walk the last few yards to Peracha's house.

The Colonel, KK, and I set off down the narrow alleyway, leaving Rustam and the driver to unload the car. The proprietor of the shop eyed us with suspicion as we walked past.

It was a still night, and the putrid smell from the drainage canals that flanked the street hung heavy in the darkness. For the residents, foul air must be a fact of life, I thought.

As a member of parliament, Peracha had police guards posted outside his house. The guards must have been forewarned, as they let us into the house straightaway.

Peracha greeted us warmly. He was a rotund figure in an ill-fitting suit that bore all the hallmarks of fine tailoring but which, over the years, he had simply eaten himself out of. Despite the ethnic disparity, his bulbous nose gave him a resemblance to the veteran Hollywood actor Karl Malden. After the initial pleasantries, we were invited to take a seat. Peracha and KK talked extensively as if the Colonel and I were not there.

Rustam and the driver had been hanging around near the shop, waiting to be invited in. I went outside to beckon them. Rustam told me the shopkeeper had accosted him and demanded to know why he was with "those two" (KK and the Colonel). They were dangerous people, he'd said.

"What did you tell him?" I asked.

"I told him you are my boss, and I go where you go."

Peracha's servants came into the room and laid a cotton sheet on the floor. Two more men began to bring in large trays laden with food. There was fish, rice, meat curry, chapattis, roast chicken, and lots of fruit. I wondered how on earth they'd prepared all this food so quickly.

We sat down on the floor and began to eat the delicious meal. Having seen conditions in the surrounding streets, I was glad we were not eating out. It occurred to me this would probably be my last good meal for several days, as there was no telling what we would be served once we were in Waziristan.

After dinner, KK suggested we film an interview with Peracha. I couldn't really see the point—the focus of our report was interviews with Taliban commanders. Still, he had offered us his hospitality, and it would do no harm to indulge him, even if the resulting footage would never be used.

I unpacked the camera and set it up. I framed up on Peracha. Through the lens, the resemblance to Karl Malden was even more striking and brought a smile to my lips.

KK started the interview. It was clear from Peracha's body language that he was enjoying being filmed.

After we wrapped up, I took a call from Asif. He'd been to the ISPR in Rawalpindi to see Colonel Faisal, to let him know that we were pressing on to Waziristan. Asif told me the Colonel had also been keen for him to see Brigadier Azmat, to update him as well.

So, my contacts with the ISPR were up to speed. That was good. A small safety net. There were people behind us who knew (broadly) of our intentions and our whereabouts. We had support.

As I lay in bed that night, though, I reflected on a universal truth—on the most important journeys of your life, you are ultimately alone.

It was the night of March 25, 2010.

5
The Torture Begins

My third day in captivity. I knew this to be true because I'd been repeating it to myself. At intervals, I tapped my foot against the frame of the bed—one, two, three. The third day. I knew it but didn't feel it. What I felt was a suspension of time. The world stopped.

The dark-skinned unhooded man came into my room. The self-styled translator from the Indian embassy. He released the chains from the bed. Silently, he hooded me and led me out of the room. Once again, I had to climb back through a window-like opening in the wall. Back to the interrogation room, then.

The translator spoke.

"I told the officers you didn't like the lizards in the other room, so they moved you here."

"Thank you." I felt a wave of emotion—relief at experiencing kindness—wash over me.

"What's your name?" I ventured. They'd insisted on knowing our names; it seemed reasonable we should know theirs.

"Krishan Lal," he replied.

I heard a door open and he led me inside, holding me gently by the elbow. An unpleasant dankness, a mixture of damp mud and urine, assaulted my nostrils and made me gag.

My hood was removed and I surveyed my surroundings. I seemed to be in the neighboring house. Thick walls, at least 2 feet thick, I guessed. A tiny, dingy room. A bed like a child's cot, with a mosquito net slung over it. In the corner, a bathroom of the most basic kind—no sink or toilet, just two brick slabs to squat on. No running water. A tiny drainage hole about the diameter of an old British penny. I'd only be urinating, clearly.

I was beginning to feel claustrophobic. How would I cope in such filthy confines, and for how long?

I tried to latch ont o a consolation. The mosquito net was fairly sound. A barrier between me and the creepy crawlies, at least.

A closer inspection of the bed shattered this notion. The bedding was grimy, the two pillows practically black with dirt and emitting a putrid smell. I wondered how many people had used the bed before me, and what had happened to them. I stared at the bed and tried to picture myself on it. How on earth could I sleep in such filth?

I scanned the room. A flashlight on the floor. On the ceiling, a fan—good. And a light. They would not always work—long and frequent power cuts are a fact of life in this region—but at least they would work some of the time. At least I had a flashlight. If it worked.

Krishan Lal shackled my feet, handcuffed me, and told me to lie on the bed. Without a word, he left the room. After he'd closed the door, there was almost total darkness. I heard the door lock.

I realized with alarm there were gaps around the edge of the mosquito net, and I couldn't move my hands freely to close them. I looked around for creepy crawlies but in the darkness could see nothing. I closed my eyes and tried not to picture the array of large insects that were likely marauding around the floor and up the walls.

The single window in the room was bricked up with a curtain on the outside. Occasionally, the curtain flapped in the light breeze, which allowed a little light in through the gaps not filled in with cement. A curtain also hung outside of the door, masking any gaps between the doorframe and floor. It was impossible for me to catch any glimpse of the outside, and the curtains also restricted the flow of air.

A cramped filthy hovel, and now an airless one. Was this to be my grave? I thought of Captain Scott's description of the Antarctic wasteland: "Great God! This is an awful place."

To take my mind away from thoughts of death, I tried to focus on my physical surroundings. I stared at the ceiling. Two thick wooden beams ran across the room's width. There were narrower logs running lengthways, thatched with twigs above.

Eager for a mindless task to occupy me, I started to count the logs that ran the length of the room. Seventeen. Then I counted the places where nails had been hammered into the wall. Twenty-seven. That was it. Two beams, seventeen logs, twenty-seven nails, one window, one door. The count had taken me around two minutes. It couldn't have taken the builders much longer to throw the place together.

I became acutely aware of my body. My back ached, which was hardly surprising as I'd done little else but lie down for three days. When I adjusted my position to ease the pain in my back, the chain and shackles jangled and the wound on my right wrist from the handcuffs shot sharp pain up my arm to my shoulder.

For the first time, I felt genuinely hungry. Three days without food. Perhaps knowledge that the food I'd been offered and ignored had been prepared in deeply unhygienic conditions had forced me to put hunger out of my mind.

Well, it was on my mind now. I thought of all the wonderful dishes my mother cooked for me. I remembered how, when I'd suffered from kidney stones, my mother had painstakingly removed all the seeds from the tomatoes she used in her dishes so they wouldn't give me any pain. I thought of the many, little things she did to make my life better and which I'd always taken for granted. I missed her love and her affection.

The warmth of these thoughts relaxed me, and I dozed off.

Sometime later, I don't know how long, I was roused by the sound of the door opening. Krishan Lal handed me two vanilla and strawberry cream cookies and a small carton of milk. Then he left. I was happy to consume prepackaged food like this—I knew it was clean. Or at least I made myself believe it was.

As soon as the cookies and milk hit my system, my stomach started to rumble. I needed to use the bathroom. I managed to get myself upright, shuffle across to the door and knock on it with my cuffed hands.

"What do you want?" Krishan Lal.

"Toilet."

"Wait."

After a few minutes, the door opened. A younger, slimmer, hooded man came into the room.

"Face the wall."

I turned around. He put a blindfold on me. I felt his face close to mine. He was inspecting the cloth around my eyes to make sure they were completely covered. Once satisfied, he led me out of the room slowly. He warned me to step over the threshold and keep my head down—there were wires overhead, he said.

I had stepped into a more open space, some sort of courtyard. I heard voices around me. I remembered an old film, black and white, in which the protagonist is kidnapped and, later, having escaped, retraces the route of the kidnapping by the sounds he'd heard—traffic noise, a clock striking the hour, children laughing and shouting in a school playground. These memories had helped track down the criminals. Would I have the ability to do the same? To use the sounds I could hear to retrace my where-abouts? I doubted it. This was real life. There was no telling where I was.

"Be gentle with him, Mukhtar. He's a guest." I heard Krishan Lal from a few feet away.

A guest. Yes, they were just holding us while they established our identities. Another day or two and we'd be back with our families. Safety. Clean beds. Edible food.

We came to a halt. Mukhtar's shrill voice.

"There is a big step. Lift your leg."

I had to strain to lift my leg high enough. The step must have been almost 2 feet high. We took a few steps then stopped. Mukhtar explained it was a latrine type of toilet and I had to squat over it. I didn't like these toilets at the best of times; I could never keep my balance. But refusing to use this toilet was not an option, and my stomach was being very insistent.

"I will get you some water."

I heard a thud and a splash. He'd placed a container of water at my feet.

"Okay."

"What about the blindfold?"

"Blindfold stays."

"Then I don't want to go. I can't balance."

I stood there, anxious but determined not to lose my dignity.

"Look down! Look down!" he shouted, as he roughly untied the knots in the cloth covering my eyes. I saw the floor and a disgusting hole in the ground. Scores of flies flitted around the hole. The stench was so awful I wanted to vomit. For a clean freak like me, this was hell.

"Let me know when you've finished. And make sure you don't look anywhere. And hurry up."

No door. Just a curtain of grubby, tattered blue cloth. I looked around for soap. Nothing.

When I'd completed the operation as best I could, I called out, and Mukhtar came and angrily blindfolded me and returned me to my room.

A few minutes later, Krishan Lal came with a plastic bucket full of water. He walked at an angle across the sloping floor in order not to spill the water (a precious commodity for them, too). A plastic jug floated on top of the water. He placed the bucket in the corner of the room designed to be used as a bathroom.

"Now you can wash yourself. This water is for *whudu** and has to last you four days. Don't be having a bath."

"I can't use this place as a toilet. The whole room will smell."

"Well, I can drill a hole in the wall for you, if you like."

A joke, surely? No, he was serious.

"No, no. I don't want a hole in the wall. Thank you."

My distress at these very basic conditions was amusing him. He approached me slowly.

"If you use too much water, you see this?" He clenched his fist. "You will get this in your face."

I couldn't work this man out. One minute he was friendly, the next hostile and threatening.

He left the room, bolting the door and leaving me in darkness again.

A little later, Mukhtar came in carrying a black plastic container and a roll of pink toilet paper. The plastic can was the type that usually contained car engine oil. It had a hole cut on one side, near the top, and its original cap was still screwed on.

* Ablutions for prayers.

"You can use this to urinate in."

I looked at the black gallon container and wondered how long it would be before they emptied it. More indignity. But I needed to make the best of it. I looked at the roll of toilet paper and prayed they'd release me before it ran out.

I searched through my bag and took out my toiletries. I placed them in the so-called bathroom. Sherry had packed me a soap dish, which would at least keep the soap out of contact with the filthy surfaces around me. There was a tiny alcove cut into the wall. The perfect place to store my toilet bag.

I'd been wearing the same clothes for several days and they were beginning to smell. I normally go through two changes of clothes a day, so this was unbearable.

I heard the call for prayers from a mosque nearby. Krishan Lal walked in to unlock my handcuffs and shackles. I washed myself and offered prayers. I prayed with deep conviction. I asked God to free me and my colleagues from this hell.

After prayers, I took the opportunity of being unshackled to exercise before Krishan Lal came in to handcuff and shackle me again. I walked across the width of the room. Seven paces. The floor sloped down to one wall. I noticed that in the middle of the floor there was a slight depression, about the size of my heel. I arranged my paces so my right foot would land in the depression. It's amazing what boredom leads to.

Just as I was getting into a rhythm, Krishan Lal entered the room. I froze instantly, terrified in case he suspected me of peeking outside.

"I was just exercising," I said, as he closed the door behind him.

"Okay." He threw the handcuffs and chain on the floor. "You can put these on later." He left.

I continued my pacing, and with each pace I prayed I'd be released and out of this cramped and filthy hellhole.

Back and forth, back and forth, back and forth. Always making sure I kept the same stride, a neat seven paces to the other wall. Pacing. Like Steve McQueen in the film *Papillon*. Except I wasn't watching the film on my couch. I was living it.

I managed to offer night prayers before Krishan Lal came back to handcuff me. After that, I lay on the bed.

I heard a plane fly overhead and thought of freedom. Of people in a warm clean aircraft cabin, an upholstered seat, a newspaper. I wondered if news of our kidnapping had reached the media. I wondered how my parents were coping. My father would deploy the vast reserves of spiritual comfort at his disposal. But my mother would be going through hell.

Too many negative thoughts. I had to make my mind busy and healthy. Trivia. I was good at that.

I began to list all the states of America. I counted those beginning with "A" on my fingertips—Alabama, Alaska, Arizona, Arkansas. Then I moved on through the alphabet. I managed to count forty states. Not bad. What next? Pick a continent and list as many countries as I could. I did Europe and Africa. More than twenty countries in each. I finally fell asleep somewhere in Asia.

I was woken by Krishan Lal. He came into my room to top up the drinking water. He was barefoot and had his *shalwar* rolled up to his knees. He walked over to the window ledge, unscrewed the water cooler's lid, and poured more water in. He then walked over to me and unlocked the handcuffs and shackles. What a relief to have my hands and feet free!

"What happened to my equipment?" I asked.

"We have it in a safe place."

"Can I have it? I can look after it here."

"No, we cannot do that."

"Well, can you please let me have my diary? And a pen. You'll find them in my equipment bag."

I'd been writing a diary of this production from the outset. It was a habit I'd started when making the documentary on the expedition to Mount Everest in 1997. I'd made a meticulous record of the events of the expedition. The expedition leader, Nazir Sabir, had often turned to me for clarification of facts. It was valuable exercise, inspired by watching *Robinson Crusoe* on TV when I was younger. He'd kept a diary by carving on tree trunks. He knew the importance, for your own mental well-being, of recording events as they happened.

When I'd returned from Everest, I'd given my diary to my friend, Mohsan, to type up. He'd stayed up all night reading it, riveted, he'd told me. I wondered what he would say about this diary.

Krishan Lal produced a pen from his pocket. It was mine. I'd bought a dozen like it before we'd set off.

"You mean like this?"

"That's mine."

"I wanted something to remember you by, so I took this."

It's not like we were friends. He was just a liar and a thief.

He gathered the chain and cuffs. "From now on we only use these at night. What do you think?"

"I would like a pen and some paper. Do you think you can do that for me?"

"Let me see."

"Thank you."

I was relieved. I thought this hint of goodwill might be a little progress toward my release.

He took the chain and handcuffs and left the room. I could hear him hanging the chain on the wall outside as he bolted the door.

I thought about my expensive film equipment. There was no telling what condition it would be in now. I knew these people would have no respect for it.

Still, the equipment was not really the issue here. I was concerned for our welfare. I'd dragged Rustam away from his large family and exposed him to danger. I felt particularly bad about that.

KK I felt less responsible for. He'd been more gung ho than any of us in plowing ahead with this assignment. He was still something of an enigma to me. I was perplexed by his apparent pride in his son's involvement with Al Qaeda and Jihad, and by his commitment to social justice. He was a shadowy figure in some ways—he seemed to have access to anyone and everyone—but he loved the camera and relished giving interviews. Indeed, from the beginning of this project, he'd been very vocal about his aspirations to become a journalist. Asif and I had encouraged him, but, to be honest, I wasn't sure he would make a good journalist. He was too opinionated. Too polemic. A good analyst, perhaps.

As far as Colonel Imam was concerned, I had no idea why he'd joined us on this assignment. It seemed to me KK was responsible for his involvement.

But here we all were, our destinies intertwined. I couldn't believe that, with all KK's connections, we'd ended up here.

A short while later, the door to my room opened again. Krishan Lal hurled a booklet and ballpoint pen toward me. It was not the diary I'd been writing in. It was just a school exercise book. But it was better than nothing and I was pleased to have it. At least now I had, as it were, someone to talk to.

I backtracked to the morning of March 26, three days ago, and filled in the gaps up to the present day. It felt good to have my mind occupied.

After several pages of writing, I switched the flashlight off and lay back on the bed. I put my hand as close to my eyes as possible. It was so dark I couldn't see it. You could have uncovered a 1,000-foot roll of motion picture film stock in the room and, in that darkness, it wouldn't have been the least bit exposed.

The door burst open and the room was flooded with light. In the doorway were two backlit figures that stood and stared at me.

I got up as the figures approached. Both men wore hoods. They sat on the floor (there was nowhere else to sit) and leaned back on their elbows, relaxed. Through his hood, I could see that one of them had a long thin face. The long-faced man had a pen in his right hand. He played with it while his colleague just looked at me.

"*Asalaam alaikum*," I ventured.

"*Walaikum asalaam*," came the reply.

There was a long pause. I waited nervously to hear what they were going to say.

"So, Asad *sahib*, how are you finding it here?"

In spite of the hoods, they seemed friendly. I felt a sense of relief. The long-faced man did not have a Pushtun accent. I'd have said he was from the Punjab province.

"Why are you holding me and when will I be allowed to go home?"

"We are in the process of making some inquiries at the moment."

"What kind of inquiries?"

"We want to know if you are who you say you are, and what you are doing here."

"I told you. You've seen my identity card."

"Yes, we have seen your card but that is not original. It is a copy. We have no way of verifying it."

He was right. Most people in Pakistan don't carry their original identity card for fear of losing it. Once lost, it is a major hassle to replace. So people just carry a copy.

"Yes, but you can see it's my photograph. Everyone in Pakistan makes a copy of their identity card. I'm no exception."

"Yes, they are also masters of fraud. A copy is not acceptable."

"So, what's going to happen now?"

"Don't worry. You will be home soon. In fact, this will be an adventure for you."

This made me angry. "What, being locked up?"

The men laughed. I wondered what was so funny.

"Tell us about your Murree Road property."

"It's our ancestral home. It belonged to my grandfather. It's been in our family ever since."

The men were listening intently. Long Face spoke.

"I see. We will have to make our inquiries, you understand?"

"How long will all this take?"

"We have many things to do. You are not the only case. Be patient. As I said, think of it as an adventure."

The men got up and left the room. Once again, I was left in darkness.

The thought of staying here much longer was difficult to accept. I lay back on the pillow, trying to get comfortable. I wondered what I'd done to deserve this. A ridiculously naïve thought, when you looked at it. After all, we'd come to North Waziristan. Without any papers. With no visible protection. Based on KK's reconnaissance. And connections that had disappeared. What did I expect?

We'd wound up in a situation that was totally alien to us. I wondered about the others. How were they coping? Why had we been separated?

Several hours passed. Then I heard a shrill voice. Mukhtar. He was shouting at someone. I could hear a mumble in Colonel Imam's voice. Mukhtar was baiting him relentlessly.

"You smell. Why don't you take a bath?"

I heard the Colonel's feet shuffling. Sounds of pushing and kicking. It didn't sound like the Colonel was resisting. I didn't blame him—it was better to be pushed and kicked by one person than to antagonize him and have all of them weigh in.

I heard him push the Colonel into his room and lock the door.

As I'd stopped eating, thinking I'd have a good meal when I got home, I imagined the Colonel would be thinking the same about washing. Why wash in this grubby hellhole? Better to wait and have a good bath in a few days' time.

But were we all in a state of denial? Were we here for the long haul? Look at me, desperate to stay clean and healthy, and all the while urinating into a plastic can in the corner of the room. The smell of stale urine was a constant reminder of my situation. I felt hopeless. Like I was living in a sewer.

I must have dozed off.

Sometime later, the door to my room burst open. Two hooded men rushed toward me. Behind the gauze of his eyehole, I could tell that one of them was Krishan Lal.

Both men pulled me off the bed violently and blindfolded me roughly. I was terrified. A sense of dread engulfed me.

"What's the matter? What are you doing?"

"Just shut up!" Krishan Lal shouted in my ear, almost deafening me.

The other man held my hands behind my back, and Krishan Lal handcuffed me so tightly that the pain from the wound in my right wrist almost made me vomit. My heart was racing. I was more scared now than when we'd been ambushed.

He put another set of handcuffs around my ankles and made me bend over. I was shaking with fear. I thought I was about to be raped. I knew that the Pathans had a penchant for boys. I knew that prisoners around the world were subjected to rape as a form of torture. I was trembling uncontrollably.

"What are you doing?" I shouted.

"I told you to be quiet," Krishan Lal yelled in my face.

I felt a sickening stinging sensation in my hands. While Krishan Lal was holding me, the other man started beating my hands with a stick. With each blow, pain flashed through my body like a lightning bolt. Before I could recover, another blow. Again. Then again.

I was pushed to the floor. The man started beating me on my feet. Blow after blow. No respite. A different pain. A dull ache that never stopped.

After what seemed like forever, and when I was no longer aware of any sensation in my feet, the man switched targets, now focusing on my back. Each blow sent shivers down my spine. Each blow was delivered with greater force than the last.

I could hear the swish of the stick as it traveled through the air. I tried to block the pain out of my mind by diverting my thoughts to God. I prayed hard. *Oh God, please help me. Take me out of this dreadful situation.*

"Are you going to tell the truth now?" the man screamed. "Tell the truth. Tell the truth."

The man was merciless and using all his strength and energy. I could hear his heavy breathing.

"What do you mean? I've hidden nothing!"

The stick was breaking into fragments. It sounded different each time it struck my back.

"I said tell the truth!"

"I have told the truth! Would you rather I lied to you?"

"How dare you answer me back!"

He kicked me in the face. I fell on my side. He took a step back.

"No food or drink for him."

The two men walked out of the room. I heard the door slam. I heard the bolts. I lay on the floor. Still blindfolded, with my hands and feet tied. Every part of my body ached—hands, feet, back, face—and I was beginning to feel cold. In spite of all this physical discomfort, I was relieved that my only punishment had been a beating. I had feared rape. My body had been severely abused—I felt a level of pain and exhaustion that brought me close to death—but I still had a sense of dignity and self-respect. I had not been completely degraded by these people.

The rag they had used to blindfold me smelt strongly of sweat and faintly of cologne. They must have torn a shirt into strips.

Several hours passed. Still I lay in the middle of the floor, unable to move. I felt as if I'd been trampled by a team of horses.

My body got colder and colder. The pain from my injuries intensified. I could smell the earthen floor's dampness.

My mental strength started to return. Lying on the floor, I started to worry about being bitten by insects.

I remembered the last time I'd been beaten with a stick. Secondary school. A couple of boys had misbehaved and the teacher had decided to cane all of us. That same stinging sensation on the palms of my hand. I remembered a kicking. A fight I'd lost around the same age.

Then I heard violence erupt in a neighboring room. Colonel Imam. A different noise from the stick. A whipping noise. No screams. No protests. Just a muted grunt each time a blow struck.

He told me later he'd been made to lie on his stomach. His hands and feet had been tied to each corner of the bed. Krishan Lal had a stick with a truck's transmission belt nailed to it. These belts are made of reinforced steel fibers and Kevlar, the material used in bulletproof jackets.

Each time the belt had struck his back, it had dug into his flesh. Each blow produced a line of blood on his cotton shirt, so that, by the end of the beating, his shirt was a dense network of red lines.

I heard voices taunting him.

"*Apney betay ko Shia larkey key saath shaadi kernay though gey!*" So you let your son marry a Shia girl!

These people regarded Shias as non-Muslims.

The beating was relentless. Blow after blow after whipping blow. But, although he was approaching seventy years of age, the Colonel proved very strong and composed. Just a grunt through gritted teeth. I would have been squirming and screaming with pain. His Special Services training had made him a very tough individual.

KK was given the same treatment. His slightly built frame took the beating badly. The swishing blows of the belt and KK's shrill screams echoed round the damp walls of my dark prison for twenty minutes.

Then I heard a scuffling of several pairs of feet, Rustam's baritone grunting something, then, a minute later, more distant blows with a stick. I'd learn later that Rustam had been blindfolded, lifted out of his hole, tied to a tree in the yard, and subjected to the same beating I'd received.

We'd been the lucky ones. The transmission belt was a particularly wicked taskmistress.

Sometime after Rustam's ordeal, I must have dozed off. I was woken by the call for evening prayers. I'd been lying on the floor for several hours.

I heard the door unbolt and a chain being dropped next to me.

"So, how are you?" Krishan Lal asked, in a rather breezy manner, like an old pal popping in for a coffee.

He took my blindfold off. I blinked a few times, adjusting my eyes to the light. I looked around and saw the remnants of the broken stick strewn all over the floor. Krishan Lal looked at me and smiled.

"This was just an introduction to what these men can do. You must tell the truth."

He unlocked the handcuffs and rehandcuffed my hands to the front. My right wrist was extremely painful and I flinched as the clasp went round my wrist. He then proceeded to put the shackles on my feet, and attached the chain from the handcuffs to the shackles.

"Can you loosen it by a few notches?" I looked at him appealingly.

Krishan Lal stared at me for a few seconds, then loosened the handcuffs by two notches. Click, click. Now I could keep the wound on my wrist from coming into contact with the cold metal. I felt he'd softened a little, and this emboldened me.

"Why did you wear a mask? Why did you treat me so badly? I've been honest with you and I've cooperated with you all along."

"When I come to see you on my own, I don't wear a mask. But I have to in front of my superiors."

The Nuremberg defense. Just following orders.

I tried to get comfortable. It was still too painful for me to lie on my back, so I positioned myself on my side.

He left the room, turning the light off and leaving me in pitch darkness. I replayed the beating in my mind.

One thing I remembered was that I had stayed still. Remarkably still, when I thought of the pain, which should have had me writhing and squirming a lot more. I guess, since I'd been blindfolded throughout, I just hadn't seen the stick coming toward me. I'd only reacted when it had struck me.

I tried to visualize the man who'd beaten me, to imagine what he looked like without his mask. I pictured him having a long ugly face. He'd have very low self-esteem. He probably took pleasure in beating people, as it was the only time it gave him power. No doubt he was illiterate and poor, and he'd been brainwashed into thinking he was a righteous man. As he considered me an infidel, by beating me he probably thought he'd been doing God's work.

What a fool.

6
Concern at Home

My brother, Farrukh, had to return to Istanbul in connection with a legal case. He called his assistant, Nudrat, to brief her on the progress of his meetings. And for the first time he voiced his concerns about me. He knew it wasn't like me not to call home.

"He was supposed to be back on the twenty-eighth. That was two days ago."

Nudrat tried to console him by telling him what he wanted to hear—that I was in a remote area, probably with no phone signal; that my mobile may have got lost or stolen; that we had more work than we realized. But Farrukh wasn't convinced. "There are public call offices. He knows how much our parents worry. It's just not like him."

He was agitated. Nudrat had never known him to be like this. She couldn't find any words to console him.

And she was struggling to console herself. She remembered a recurring nightmare. She's on the street of an Afghan village. A bearded man is engulfed by a mob and beaten brutally. She asks why but no one answers her. A razor blade. Someone shaving the man's eyebrows off, then his hair, peeling the skin off. His face and bald head bleed.

She sees a simple house. Mud walls. The mob again, now disemboweling the bearded man, still alive and conscious. He struggles. She sees his excruciating pain. An eye is gouged out with bare fingers. From the shadows, a man is watching this torment impassively. He rises but still she cannot see his face. He rushes toward her …

She wakes, screaming.

* * *

Meanwhile, in Islamabad, a man by the name of Khalid Khattak, a business associate of KK's, called on my mum and dad to say we were well and that our delay was due to the fact I'd been able to get more access to Taliban commanders than expected, and that, although this was good for the overall project, it meant we were overrunning by several days.

KK's wife, Shamama, confirmed this when she too visited my parents' house. As the language of these visits was Urdu, Sherry didn't understand much about what was going on. And my father, in his wisdom, tried to protect her as much as he could by reassuring her. Still, Sherry sensed from my mother's demeanor that the situation was unnerving.

As the proposed date for our return receded further into the past, my parents became increasingly worried. KK's wife visited again, with her eldest son, Usama, and told my parents they'd been communicating with KK through an intermediary, Usman Punjabi, who'd given assurances about our welfare and told them we hadn't traveled to Miranshah until March 26.

This relief was short lived.

* * *

In the business class lounge at Istanbul's Ataturk Airport, Farrukh answered his phone. A bomb was about to drop.

"Hello. This is Rodney Henson from the channel in London. As you may know, Asad has gone to North Waziristan to make a news report. I'm sorry to tell you that we've received reports, now confirmed, from local sources in Waziristan that Asad and his group have been abducted, probably by a faction of the Taliban. So far, the abductors have not demanded a ransom."

Farrukh listened intently, lost for words. Rodney continued.

"I want to assure you that the channel will be there to support your family in every way we can. A member of the channel's risk management team will be flying out to Islamabad as soon as possible."

Farrukh was speechless. His worst fears had been confirmed. Listening to Rodney, Farrukh just nodded in cold silence, imagining the headlines in tomorrow's Islamabad papers. He said goodbye and hung up.

Farrukh had always thought of himself as good at dealing with stress, but this bombshell would test his mental strength to the full. How on earth would our parents take this news? What was the best way of breaking it to them? Should he do it before the newspapers came out the following morning? Should he do it over the phone, or wait and do it in person? He wondered if I was still alive. So many questions!

After sitting in silent thought for perhaps fifteen minutes, Farrukh called his friend, Asghar, and told him to ensure that no newspapers made it into our parents' house for the time being.

Asghar was Farrukh's most trusted friend. They'd been best friends since their days together at Carlton Grammar School in Bradford. Like all other people around Farrukh, Asghar revered his friend and was selfless in his friendship. Asghar knew Farrukh better than anyone else. He'd witnessed all the ups and downs of Farrukh's life. When Farrukh had moved to Islamabad, Asghar himself had upped sticks and settled there, just to be close to him. Farrukh knew that, until he arrived himself, Asghar was the best person to protect our parents' interests.

Farrukh then called Nudrat and told her the news.

On the plane, he couldn't sleep at all. The thought of facing our parents and dealing with their anxieties was making him deeply unsettled. If only he could sleep, then wake up to find this was all a dream. If only he had some magic way of sheltering our parents from this horrifying reality.

* * *

Rodney wanted Asif to go to Islamabad immediately and talk to KK's son, Usama, who had given an interview to the Pakistani media about the abduction. Rodney knew that publicity would only harm future negotiations.

Rodney told Asif to make sure the channel's name was kept out of the picture. Rodney's stringers were telling him that KK and his team had boasted about their British media credentials. Asif said that was nonsense. The mood had always been cautious, secretive. KK would never have risked our safety, or our cash and equipment for that matter, by being so indiscreet. Rodney's stringers were badmouthing the team out of envy—they weren't making the report. Asif was angry with Rodney for involving these local journalists, for giving credence to their rumors and for his high-handed attitude to Asif.

"I'm not some foot soldier you can order about! I've been producing news reports for over twenty years! You can't tell me what to do!"

"I want you out there!"

"To do what? To meet whom?"

"I've never lost a journalist, and I won't let it happen now."

"And you think I will? Asad is not a journalist. He's my friend."

The slugging match continued. Asif repeated his intention to go to Islamabad only when he'd made some enquiries. He still suspected government or ISI involvement in our abduction. Rodney persisted in his request that Asif should accept his responsibilities as producer and fly out now. Asif wanted Rodney to provide some form of security—he had serious concerns about his own safety. Rodney offered to send security but stressed that, in such a lawless region, there could be no cast-iron guarantees in relation to Asif's personal safety. Asif retorted that, on the Security Assessment Forms for the assignment, it had been made clear that Farrukh was to be the first port of call in the event of danger. He would go to Islamabad, as Rodney wanted. But he would deal with the situation through Farrukh. Rodney wasn't impressed. He wanted a producer on the ground dealing with the situation directly. He would send someone from London. The two men parted on very bad terms.

Asif reflected on the situation and on his tussle with Rodney. He didn't like the idea of a producer from London, someone completely unconnected with the project, wandering around Waziristan putting his foot in it. He decided to register his objections in an email:

Islamabad, April 5th

Rodney,

I completely disagree with you sending people here from London who will jeopardize the safety of Asad and the others and probably up the ante. You think your actions will help but they'll only make a dangerous situation worse.

Calm and informed action is what's needed. I know the politics and the mindset in this part of the world, and we need to proceed slowly, carefully, and very much behind the scenes.

If you do send someone, whoever comes must coordinate with me. They must keep a very low profile. Don't make bookings for them anywhere in the channel's name. They must appear to be independent.

We must proceed with extreme caution.

Asif

* * *

Once on the ground in Islamabad, Farrukh made straight for a newsstand. The first front page he saw carried this report:

ISLAMABAD: Two former officials of the premier intelligence agency, Inter-Services Intelligence (ISI), and a freelance journalist, have gone missing from Kohat in suspicious circumstances.

Family sources of the missing ISI officials Colonel (retired) Imam and Squadron Leader (retired) Khalid Khawaja revealed that these officers were assisting freelance journalist, Asad Qureshi, in the making of a documentary on the Taliban and Al Qaeda.

They were on their way back home after having a meeting with the Taliban leadership, in tribal areas, when they were allegedly picked up by unknown people. It is not yet clear who has kidnapped them. However, it is pertinent to mention that both former ISI officers are thought to have access to the leadership of both the Taliban and Al Qaeda.

Farrukh did not relish having to impart the news to our parents. An inseparable couple married for fifty-eight years, our parents had witnessed the deaths of many friends and relatives. But now death was stalking their own child.

At our parents' house, Farrukh found Mum sitting in the drawing room. Dad told him she'd been on sentry duty in that seat since the day I'd left. Staring at the gate. Feeling things were not right. Hoping to see me walk in. She'd rearranged the furniture, he told her, to get an unobstructed view of the gate. Then Dad told Farrukh about Sunny, my beautiful white Persian cat.

"The cat?"

"Your mother has been watching the gate. The cat had been watching it also. For days."

Farrukh looked out of the window. Sunny wasn't there.

"She sat by the gate, with her chin resting on her paws." Then Dad explained what Shahgufta, our domestic help, had seen.

"Shahgufta went to pick her up and saw that the fur on her face was wet. As she looked, she saw tears flow from her eyes. For her it was a bad omen. I told her to take the cat and give her a bath."

Washing Sunny wasn't an easy task. She hated water and always struggled. Shahgufta had needed help from her husband, Jawaid, to keep Sunny under control. But they'd eventually washed and dried and brushed her lovingly. Once released, she'd immediately taken up her post by the gate again. Then a strange thing had happened.

"Jawaid set her food out but she didn't come. When he went to the gate to fetch her, she wasn't there. He went out into the street to look for her, but she was nowhere to be found. He looked for hours, with several of the neighbors. He took the jar of biscuits and shook it—you know she normally comes running when she hears that—but nothing. She's gone."

Farrukh knew this incident would confirm all our mother's fears. She was a born worrier.

He remembered how anxious she'd always been when, as teenagers, he and I had dared to arrive home even a few minutes after the expected time. She was never angry, but, sometimes, she'd shiver with stress and worry. That was Mum. Whenever I was traveling, I had to call her when I arrived at the airport. Then call her again when I checked in. One more call from the departure lounge. She needed a final call once I was onboard the aircraft. All the time assuring her that everything was okay. When I got to the other end, my first job was always to call Mum. It was difficult to relax.

Now in her late seventies, Mum had a weak heart, so her worry was a real cause for concern. We were often at pains to hide things from her. If there was ever any bad news to break, my two brothers and two sisters would always talk to Dad first and then see how best to tell Mum. A worrier.

I wouldn't change her for the world.

Now that I was several days overdue, lost in a country where I'd be viewed as a foreigner, Mum's face was the one Farrukh feared the most as he broke the news of our abduction.

He played it down. We'd been apprehended, probably by the Taliban. They would ask for money. And he would pay the money and then the group would be released. There was no need for concern. He explained that since I was accompanied by KK and Colonel Imam, who were both familiar with Waziristan, it was only a matter of time before this misunderstanding was sorted out. We would soon be on our way home.

He wasn't sure how much he believed this, nor how much Mum believed it as she sat silent, tears rolling down her cheeks. Farrukh could not imagine the pain Mum was in, but he knew that, in her condition, bad news could have serious consequences. If feelings could take a physical form, Mum's fears would be a monstrous beast, the sight of which few people could bear. Farrukh was a strong man, but not strong enough to confront his mother's tears. She'd had a bad feeling all along about this trip.

"I saw it. I saw it on his face. He was worried when he left. He never turned round to wave goodbye to me. I knew then that something was wrong."

Dad never panicked; never let his emotions rule him. But now he looked stricken and exhausted, and he collapsed silently into a chair, as if his legs couldn't support him anymore.

Farrukh tried to calm them both. He suggested that they go to England as planned, for the marriage of their granddaughter, Aisha. They were booked to leave on April 1 (ironically, I was supposed to be taking them to the airport). They weren't sure. They didn't want to leave me behind. Farrukh tried to reassure them.

Knowing that Pakistani journalists are worse than most, Farrukh knew our parents would be hounded relentlessly if they stayed in Islamabad, now that the news had broken. He'd make the arrangements for them to leave. They should go soon. But Mum wasn't having any of it. She couldn't leave knowing that I was missing. Farrukh tried to reassure her.

"All is well. There is no proof that Asad is among enemies. Chances are he's with ISI personnel. I have contacts. I'll bring him home, I promise you. There's no need to worry."

He'd pulled on a mask—eyes shining with hope and confidence—that he was desperate not to let slip. In his head, he repeated a sentence over and over—*I cannot let them see through me. I cannot let them see through me.*

With our mother, it seemed to work. Mum was a woman easily persuaded and influenced, particularly by Farrukh. He could see the belief he had communicated to her.

But Dad, eighty-nine years old and with the wisdom of ten men, knew that there could be no easy escape from this situation. He was not reassured. But he was tactful enough to keep his reservations to himself, as much for Farrukh's sake as for Mum's. He could see the falseness of Farrukh's assurances but felt an incredible tenderness toward his elder son.

When Farrukh explained the situation to Sherry, my last words to her ran through her mind: *If I don't come back, please forgive me.* She burst into tears.

Farrukh and my father looked on helplessly—Muslim men don't touch other women to comfort them. Sherry hugged my mother and wept uncontrollably.

Having done all he could at home, Farrukh knew he had to face the tasks ahead. His office was the best place for that. Looking back at the house, he saw a wife with her head buried in her hands and two frail and elderly parents sitting in forlorn silence.

This would be the biggest challenge of his life.

He called in at his office to begin the task of putting together a plan of action. His staff informed him that the phones had been ringing off the wall all day—endless calls from relatives, friends, and TV channels.

He met Nudrat and asked her to rearrange a flight to England for Mum and Dad. Even though Mum was refusing to go, he knew he could persuade her.

"My parents need to go. I'll never feel safe with them around. Seeing my mother's fragile face every day would break me. And I cannot allow myself to break. I need to stay strong for my parents. For Asad's sake."

"But having them around might give you strength."

"It would never work. I need to be alone to deal with this."

Nudrat could see how this would play out. She'd seen Farrukh muster his strength and self-control many times in court. He could not be advised against what he'd already decided. He would isolate himself in order to concentrate his resources. Become an island. Withstand the waves that came battering at the shore. And he was strong. But his eyes betrayed the anxiety he was desperate to contain and conceal. Red eyes. Moist eyes.

A heartbreaking sight for her.

7
Our Last Steps Are Retraced

Asif arrived at the office in a state of shock. He was also anxious about meeting Farrukh, who he imagined blamed him, at least in part, for all that had happened.

Farrukh had been in the dark about the exact purpose of our trip—he was a busy man, and we didn't get to see each other that often. Had he known the details, he would almost certainly have dissuaded us from going.

Now he wanted to know everything. He knew that Asif could give him the information he needed.

"Lives might be at stake now. I need you to be absolutely truthful with me, no matter what level of confidentiality had been agreed within the group."

Asif understood the need for frankness.

"The plan was to cover the story about the peace negotiations between the government and the Taliban. KK arranged everything. Interviews were going to be filmed and a documentary made for the channel in London."

Now things were falling into place for Farrukh. The call from Rodney. No wonder he was in the loop and offering support. The channel had commissioned the report. But he wondered why they had sent us into the line of fire without any protection.

All Asif could tell him was that it was a legitimate channel commission. This was the first comforting thought Farrukh had had since the call at Istanbul airport. Small comfort, though.

Asif went on to tell him that we'd filled out all the necessary security and hostile environment forms; also that I'd informed the ISPR of my mission (about which Farrukh was very glad) and had been advised by them against undertaking it (about which he was not so glad). Asif also told Farrukh that arrangements were in place for a channel reporter to come to Pakistan to do follow-up interviews with KK.

Farrukh asked Asif to leave for London immediately. If his presence, as a representative of the channel, were to become known, he too would be at risk, since his links to me were well documented. Another problem for Farrukh to deal with.

Farrukh and Asif still had some suspicions (hopes, really) of ISI involvement in our disappearance. They determined to pursue this hope.

During the course of the day, they managed to gain access to the ISI colonel with responsibility for North Waziristan. To the dismay of all parties, the colonel categorically denied all ISI involvement in our abduction.

A worried and frustrated Asif went to see his friend, Hamid Haroon, the owner of *Dawn* newspaper. He told him of my kidnapping. To Asif's further dismay, Hamid hinted that people seized in Waziristan generally didn't get out alive.

The need for Asif to leave Pakistan was agreed by all, including Rodney, and Asif flew out the very next day.

Farrukh went to see Usama, to find out how much he knew about the circumstances of our abduction and captivity. Usama told him about the phone call from Khalid Khattak, who'd apparently spoken to KK in Bannu on March 26 and had urged the family to remain in contact with a man called Usman Punjabi, who they believed to be an intermediary.

Usama also mentioned a man he called "the Doctor" (the same "Doctor" whom KK had been unable to raise by phone on the way to Karak—Farrukh would later learn that his name was Abdul Qayyum). The Doctor had been in touch with KK's family to say that clearance had not been obtained from the Taliban leadership for us to enter Waziristan and that we should return. The Doctor had said that clearance had specifically not been granted for me but that he would continue to make contact with the Taliban to arrange for us to go some other time. My life would be in danger if we tried to proceed without the necessary permissions, he'd said.

But Usama had also spoken to his father directly by phone, around 5:00 p.m. on March 25. KK himself had said we were turning back, and Usama remembered how disappointed he'd sounded. He'd been looking forward to making this documentary—for him, bringing the story of the Taliban to the fore was a public service. But the message that we were turning back was clear. Usama remembered his father's exact words:

"As there is no clearance for Asad, we are returning."

Yet Usama went on to say that KK had later phoned, on the morning of March 26, and spoken to his wife, Shamama. She'd told Usama that his father had said he was getting the necessary permissions from "the other side." Usama told Farrukh he didn't understand what "the other side" meant. What had happened that had made them change their mind? Usama had no answer for that.

But Shamama had been upbeat, Usama said. His father had been very excited about the project, which he was sure would be a great success, and he felt himself to be a proper journalist. They'd been able to get some very good interviews, he'd said.

Shamama had taken all this to mean that our group was pressing on into Waziristan. If this had been true, Farrukh wondered why I hadn't called to share this information with Mum and Dad. What had stopped me? Maybe KK had asked me to keep my phone switched off. After all, Farrukh had no reason to doubt that KK really had spoken to his wife and given her this information.

So, to everyone on the outside, it seemed our intention had been to go on into North Waziristan and conduct interviews with senior Taliban leaders. Farrukh trusted that KK would not have put me in any danger, and so concluded that there must have been a very good reason for us to press on in spite of the earlier instruction to turn back owing to lack of clearance for me. It was baffling. It occurred to Farrukh that, by March 25, KK had no longer been in charge of things. Maybe the phone call of the twenty-sixth had been made under duress.

What was clear was that, after March 26, there had been no direct contact between our group and the families.

Usama went on to tell Farrukh that he'd received a phone call, on March 29, from a man who'd identified himself as Usman Punjabi. This man had told Usama that we'd met with a senior Taliban leader and were safe. At the time, Usama had had no reason to doubt what this Usman Punjabi had told him.

But several days later, on April 4, the whole picture changed. Usama was contacted by General Aslam Beg, the former chief of the Pakistani army staff, a man who was well known to KK and who had known connections to the Afghan Taliban. Usama knew General Beg's sources to be impeccable. General Beg told Usama categorically that we had not reached the Taliban leadership and that all previous information regarding our movements and our safety should be regarded as unreliable.

Farrukh further discovered from Usama that the news carried by the newspapers on April 5 had been given to the press by Usama himself, in a panicked response to the revelation from General Beg, in order to prompt someone to come forward with information. Usama had wanted to use the media to learn as much as he could about our disappearance and, in fact, had learned from journalists that the intelligence agencies had records of several telephone conversations in which KK and Colonel Imam talked to two Punjabi Taliban commanders in Miranshah, namely Usman Punjabi and "the Doctor," during the last day of our disappearance.

Again, Farrukh could not understand why, after having aborted the mission for very good reasons, we had decided to go ahead.

* * *

In Bradford, my sister, Rakhshindah, was visiting friends and delivering invitations to the wedding of her daughter, Aisha. Standing on the doorstep of Mubeena's house, she took a call from our younger brother, Fayyaz, as she was ringing her friend's doorbell.

"Where are you?"

"I'm at Mubeena's."

"Come home."

"What is it?"

"I just spoke to Farrukh. Asad's been kidnapped."

The door opened and Mubeena came out smiling. Her expression changed when she saw my sister clinging to the wall, her knees buckling.

"Rakhshindah! What on earth's wrong?"

My sister was too numb to speak. She handed Mubeena the invitation, turned, and rushed home.

* * *

The same day, Farrukh received a call from a woman called Nancy, sent by the UK news channel, who wanted to meet with him. He was eager to meet her and hear what information, if any, she'd picked up from their local stringers.

Dressed in his best Canali suit, he went to Nancy's hotel, where he was also introduced to a man called Robin, from the channel's risk management team.

Nancy and Robin gave him assorted fragments of information which amounted to no more than he already knew from the newspapers. But the pair assured him of their support and promised not to interfere with the decisions he took. Farrukh was in charge, they stressed, and, in fact, he would have to be seen to be the person at the forefront of the operation to secure our release—the risk management team was only there to give advice. They also warned him that, while a situation like this would be easy to tackle at the beginning, as time went on it would become increasingly difficult and stressful.

Inside, Farrukh was terrified, but he knew this was not the time to show it. He looked at Robin with courage and defiance. "Come what may," he said.

The following day, Farrukh was contacted at his office by another figure from the channel, Brian, who sent him a questionnaire. Brian said that Farrukh's answers would help to establish who knew what. Farrukh and Nudrat sat down together and tackled each question one by one, given all the information they knew about our trip and what had happened to them since we'd left the UK.

After returning these questions to Brian at the channel, Farrukh set about searching for more clues.

He managed to find the car rental company that KK had used for our journey to Bannu. He phoned the manager and asked to speak to the driver who'd taken us. Farrukh was told that the driver was away with a client and wouldn't be back for another two days. When Farrukh called again two days later, he was told that the driver was in fact away for fifteen days. Farrukh became angry at what he saw as the company's evasiveness. He warned the manager against being obstructive and threatened to involve the police—they'd waste no time in picking up the driver for questioning. The manager told Farrukh to do his worst.

In a fit of rage, Farrukh called an associate of his law firm and instructed him to begin filing a First Information Report* against the driver. As the complaint was being drafted, the rental company manager rang again, apologized for his attitude, and said the driver, Abbasi, was on his way over to Farrukh's office.

Farrukh called his close friend, Atique Tahir, and explained the situation to him. He felt he needed the help of a trusted friend. Atique came over and Farrukh asked him to go to Bannu with Abbasi and KK's son, Usama, to see where we'd been dropped off. Atique was to get clear information about what had happened, and where. Farrukh told Atique to be very careful—he didn't want any more people to go missing.

Atique was perplexed that, as a close friend who often confided in him, I hadn't told him the full truth about our trip to Waziristan. He'd assumed I was going with members of ISPR. Had he known I was going in the company of KK, he would have dissuaded me. He didn't approve of KK's activities.

In order to retrace our footsteps, Atique, Usama, and Abbasi went to Kohat first and met Jawaid Ibrahim Peracha. Peracha told Atique he'd advised us not to go to Waziristan, something I do not recollect him saying at all.

The next day, Atique and Usama drove to Karak and there met Shah Abdul Aziz at his *madrassah*, where they were shown the beds we'd slept in—not particularly useful information.

The following day, Shah Abdul Aziz accompanied Atique and Usama to the Bannu bus station. There they asked around about us and about the red minibus we'd boarded. They were told that nothing out of the ordinary had happened—people get on and off buses of all shapes, sizes, and colors, and it's not remarked on. Taliban were often seen in the area and no one thinks anything of it.

But they did learn that there were four checkpoints along the main road out of Bannu, and they were told it would not have been possible for four people to get through these checkpoints undetected, certainly not with film equipment. Had we been detained by the army, news of that detention would have reached them by now. The conclusion was that we must have bypassed the checkpoints and gone off the beaten track.

After this fairly fruitless trip, the trio headed back to Islamabad. Abbasi told Atique and Usama about our discussion in the car on the night of April 25, as we'd approached the Kohat fork. He told them that most of the group had wanted to return home but that KK had opposed the idea and insisted we turn back and go to Waziristan. That's why we'd ended up spending the night at Jawaid Ibrahim Peracha's house.

Usama was saddened by the news that, as it seemed, his father was largely responsible for our predicament. He phoned his mother and told her.

---

* Which prompts a police investigation.

When they got back to Islamabad, Atique told Farrukh the bits and pieces of information they'd gleaned from the trip. Farrukh was unnerved by the suggestion that we'd taken the back roads out of Bannu. He knew that, if that were the case, all the statistics were against us. According to the International Press Institute's Death Watch, in the last two years alone, fourteen journalists had been killed in Pakistan. Seven of the deaths had occurred in the Khyber Pakhtunkwha Province.

In August 2009, an Aaj TV correspondent, Sadiq Bacha Khan, had been gunned down in broad daylight on his way to work in Mardan, a town in the province.

In January 2009, Muhammad Imran, age twenty, a trainee cameraman with Express TV, and Saleem Tahir Awan, age forty-five, a freelance reporter with the local dailies, *Eitedal* and *Apna Akhbar*, had been killed when a suicide bomber blew himself up in front of the Government Polytechnic College in Dera Ismail Khan, also in the Khyber Pakhtunkwha Province.

And in February 2009, Musa Khankhel, a reporter for Geo TV and the English-language newspaper *The News*, had been shot dead by unidentified gunmen while on assignment covering a peace march led by Muslim cleric, Sufi Muhammad, in the Swat Valley.

David Rohde, a *New York Times* reporter on leave to research a book, and his local colleague, Tahir Ludin, had been held in North Waziristan for several months after being kidnapped in Afghanistan's Logar Province, before escaping from their captors in June 2009.

Farrukh tried not to think about these disturbing realities. Something else was bugging him. From reports he'd read on the internet and elsewhere, it seemed the channel had a policy of equipping journalists venturing into danger zones with ultradiscreet tracking technology. Why had this technology not been made available on this occasion, in this most lawless region? It was an uncomfortable question he'd not yet asked the people from the channel. It would be difficult to ask the question *and* maintain a friendly relationship with them.

As for Mum and Dad, Farrukh had very little to tell them, but what news he did have he was careful to release to them gradually, bit by bit, so as not to raise their hopes, but also not to leave dispiriting gaps with no news at all.

A few days later, Shah Abdul Aziz volunteered to go to North Waziristan to plead with the Taliban leadership to release us. He told Farrukh he would appeal to their sense of honor—we were their guests and they were responsible for our welfare. He would be away for a week to ten days, he said, and was confident he'd be bringing us back.

His assessment gave some comfort to Farrukh, whose strength had been badly dented by reports in the newspapers.

The Pakistani media was very much in its infancy at this time. Gaining independence only during the Musharraf era, its reporting was still often wildly inaccurate. The variety of accounts of our movements had Farrukh's head reeling—we had spent time in Wana, the capital of South Waziristan, one report said, where we'd interviewed Taliban commanders; another report had us vanishing on our way to Tank district; yet another that we were in the protective custody of the security agencies.

Usman Punjabi, the supposed intermediary, was bombarding Usama with phone calls, portraying himself as a friend with inside information about our abduction. Usama had gradually come to suspect that Usman Punjabi was himself the kidnapper. Punjabi's information was becoming more inconsistent and, on one occasion, Usama saw through him. He told Usama that he didn't know which group had taken us, but he suspected that Hakimullah Mehsud, a senior Taliban commander, might have been responsible, as revenge for KK's supposed involvement in a US drone strike— KK was suspected by the Taliban of having planted the microchip that had guided the drone, Punjabi had said. Usama knew this was a lie and had told Punjabi so. Shah Abdul Aziz had accompanied KK on that trip and, had Mehsud's men suspected KK, they would have had no trouble in arresting him, yet both men had moved freely in the area.

Usama spoke to Shah Abdul Aziz, now in North Waziristan, about his suspicions. He confirmed that Punjabi was involved in our abduction.

Usama decided to file a First Information Report with the Islamabad police, in relation to the disappearance of his father. This was Usama's second cry for help.

Farrukh knew that filing an FIR was pointless. In these circumstances, the system would not come to Usama's aid. After all, details of our abduction had, by this time, been in the public domain for several days. Not a single state agency had contacted Farrukh to offer help.

On top of all this, Farrukh had the differing accounts of KK's son, Usama, and of Jawaid Ibrahim Peracha to contend with.

And the fact that no one had yet claimed responsibility for the kidnapping only added to the tension Farrukh was feeling.

He derived some comfort from the fact that Colonel Imam was known for his pro-Taliban views and had been Pakistan's counsel general in Herat, in Afghanistan, during the Taliban years. If we were indeed being held by the Taliban, well, Farrukh was confident they wouldn't harm the Colonel. And if the security agencies were holding us, the Colonel would be influential enough to get us out. Hopefully.

But it was a waiting game. It was becoming clear to Farrukh that patience was going to be his most powerful weapon. And his biggest challenge.

8
The Call

My door was flung open. A sudden flood of light into my darkness. A hooded figure in sharp silhouette. A movie shot. Except this was for real.

Squinting through shaded eyes, I could make out a plate of food, which was then clattered onto the floor in front of me before the figure retreated and the door was closed once again, returning me to darkness.

I looked at the food, a plate of rice. I pushed it to one side. Not hungry.

What was happening? Why couldn't an organization as professional as the Pakistan army or the Intelligence Service just run some checks on me, establish my credentials, and let me go? What was taking the time?

I thought about my parents, leaving for England for their granddaughter's wedding. I'd promised to run them to the airport, saying I'd just be away for a couple of days. Already we were several days overdue. They'd be worried sick.

And here was I, isolated from my colleagues and prevented from performing my duties as a son. Why? WHY?

I turned over on my little bed, the handcuffs cutting into my wrists. Never in my life had I imagined myself handcuffed and shackled. It was ridiculous.

A few hours later, my door was flung open again. Krishan Lal came in. He stared at me with hatred, as if I'd insulted his wife.

"You are not to sleep. I will be knocking on your door and you had better answer. If you fall asleep, you will get another beating. Understand."

About five minutes later, I heard a sharp knock on the door. Krishan Lal shouted in.

"Are you awake?"

I raised my head, expecting him to come in. But the door stayed closed. I shouted out.

"Yes, I'm awake."

I could hear him knocking on other doors as well. As with the other day, this was a collective punishment.

Some minutes passed, and I was beginning to doze off when he knocked at my door again. This time, I didn't wait for the question.

"Yes, I'm awake."

This went on. And on. My head began to feel like a huge weight. A medicine ball on my shoulders. I couldn't keep it upright, couldn't keep my eyelids open, but Krishan Lal was relentless in knocking on our doors. He continued all night. Five-minute intervals. For hours. The noise of the knocking was almost as bad as the discomfort I felt at not being able to close my eyes and succumb to sleep.

I knew that sleep deprivation was used as a form of torture, but I'd never imagined I'd find being deprived of sleep so challenging. I knew I had to fight hard to keep my eyes open. I couldn't take another of their beatings.

Normally, when I can't sleep, I think about things—I review my day and make plans for the days ahead—and this busy mental state that I induce sends me to sleep. In this situation, I had to do the opposite. Keep my mind blank. Banish the slightest stray thought. But it wasn't a welcome, Zen-like, yogic emptiness that resulted. The emptiness I strove to achieve was the result of an extreme athletic effort that was utterly draining. I had no energy to fight the thoughts that were my enemy.

I felt as if my brain was loose in my head. I shook my head. I seemed to be aware of my brain moving around inside my skull. It was surreal.

I heard the call for the morning prayers. I was aware of a faint light through the little gap left in the window. Dawn.

While my captors relished inflicting the torture of sleep deprivation, one of them always came in the morning to unlock my handcuffs for prayers. On this particular morning, the hooded figure was someone I'd never seen before. A small masked figure, perhaps a boy, wearing all black. He brought with him the pungent aroma of cheap cologne.

I was completely exhausted, and it was almost impossible for me to offer prayers. My body swayed from side to side and my eyelids were so heavy that even my strongest effort couldn't keep them from falling. But, no matter how tired I was, in my present situation I had no one but God to look to up to for help. Missing prayers was not an option.

The boy returned sometime later, tightened the handcuffs and shackles, then left. Moments later, I heard the familiar knocking sound again. Then Krishan Lal's voice.

"Are you awake?"

"Yes, I am."

Here we go again, I thought. How much longer are they going to do this? I had a thumping migraine. The sound of the knocking was becoming intolerable. I felt like a zombie, neither alive nor dead. My senses were numb from lack of sleep. I no longer felt any physical pain from my injuries, and, although I'd not eaten for over twenty-four hours, I felt no hunger whatsoever. The body can go much longer without food than it can without sleep—this much I knew from reading about experiences of torture—and that's what makes sleep deprivation so effective. A week without sleep can kill a person. My desire to succumb to sleep and be left alone was completely overwhelming. I craved sleep. No knocking, no voices, no interruptions. Just peace. And sleep.

Some minutes passed. Another knock, but a different voice.

"Are you awake?"

"Yes, I am."

The voice of one of the original captors. The man with the machine gun, who had pulled me from the car. So Krishan Lal was resting. The hours of knocking had taken its toll on him too. The knowledge that he was no tougher than us, in spite of his bravado and his threats, made me despise him. It made me smile and gave me strength.

But his replacement seemed to be enjoying his role. There was a relish in his voice when he asked the question. My strength began to falter. I wondered how much more of this treatment I could take.

Time dragged, on and on. Each interval between knocks felt like hours, although I'm sure it could have been no longer than a few minutes. Some physical sensations returned. An overwhelming feeling of cold. A deep desire to let my body shut down. Rest. I must have rest.

When I heard the call for evening prayers, the knocking came to a halt. Such a sweet relief!

No one came into my room to untie me for prayers. They must have been just as exhausted as we were.

I reveled in the silence. So good to hear nothing. No knocking, no voices, no interruptions. Peace.

But I found myself unable to sleep. How could this be? It had been the one thing I'd been wanting desperately to do for hours and hours and hours, and now, released from the oppression of denying myself sleep and given the freedom to do what had been my one desire, I simply couldn't. I was physically and mentally incapable of sleep. But I was also incapable of thought. It felt like my brain was dead, literally.

* * *

Mum and Dad were bidding a tearful farewell to Sherry. It was April 7, and Sherry was sobbing uncontrollably.

Mum too was feeling the pain. In her eyes, in leaving Pakistan she was abandoning me. She wanted to be home when I returned.

But Farrukh couldn't bear to see her suffering, day in and day out. So he was sending them away. But it had been the most difficult decision of his life. So far.

In the car on the way to the airport, Dad was silent. Thoughtful. From Mum, the tears flowed steadily, punctuated by emotional outbursts.

"I want to be here when he phones."

"He can call you in England. Please don't worry. Everything is going to be all right."

Farrukh tried to believe it, but the burden he'd assumed, for my sake and for the sake of our parents, was already weighing very heavy on his shoulders.

He'd said goodbye to Mum and Dad many times before, at this very airport, but this was the most difficult parting he'd had to endure. He only hoped that, in England, they'd be busy with Aisha's wedding, which would offer some distraction. But it was a forlorn hope and he knew it. As I've said, our mother's anxiety was compulsive.

Sending Mum and Dad away was one less worry for Farrukh. But that still left Sherry. The American wife of a Pakistani documentary filmmaker currently held in a region where American drones were missing their targets and killing innocent people. Keeping Sherry out of the picture was now Farrukh's biggest concern.

Nudrat was deputed to keep her busy. It was decided they'd go shopping, have lunch, then, at Sherry's request, pay a visit to the hairdresser's—she fancied having highlights in her hair. The shopping and the lunch went fine, but the visit to the hairdresser's did not go well.

Sherry wasn't happy with the highlights. She became tetchy and insisted that the treatment be repeated. Nudrat and the staff couldn't see what it was that Sherry was unhappy with. After the second treatment, she still wasn't happy and again asked for it to be repeated. When Nudrat became embarrassed and quietly asked Sherry what the problem was, her mask slipped, her self-control crumbled, and she simply broke down.

The newspapers of April 8 brought disturbing news. They reported Taliban suspicions about Khalid Khawaja. A Taliban leader, Mufti Wali-ur-Rehman, was linking KK to a US drone attack on his secret location near Miranshah, a site that KK had visited when he'd interviewed Hakimullah Mehsud two months earlier. KK was being accused of planting a homing device at the site.

I'd interviewed KK on his return from this interview in Waziristan, and he'd told me that, before he'd met with Hakimullah, his men had very respectfully asked him to change into clothes they'd provided. They trusted him, they'd said, but, unbeknown to KK, someone else could have placed a drone homing device into his clothes or his baggage. KK had told me he'd been as sure as he could be that no such device had been planted on him.

But this was news. And now Farrukh feared that we'd been picked up because the Taliban thought KK had betrayed them. He knew how jumpy people were about American connections. He knew that the punishment for traitors was death by be-heading or shooting. He remembered the story of a man from Waziristan who'd been found in possession of an American man's business card. The Pakistani man had been taken for a spy. Hours later, he'd been executed.

Farrukh noted wryly that the newspapers were also reporting that the British High Commission was investigating our kidnapping. Farrukh had had only a brief meeting with one of their representatives, Jacqueline, in the course of his discussions with the risk management team. The High Commission had shown only a perfunctory interest in the matter. Later that day, our sister in England had received a call from the Foreign and Commonwealth Office telling her everything was fine, and I'd be home soon. It seemed to Farrukh that they were uninterested and they were getting their information from very unreliable sources. So much for Her Majesty's Government.

But the following day's newspapers brought better news. Reports stated we were safe and staying with Commander Wali-ur-Rehman in North Waziristan. We were still working on the project, reports said. Wali-ur-Rehman was known to belong to the Mehsud militant group. We'd reportedly spent a night with Jawaid Ibrahim Peracha and had interviewed him, then we'd left the next day for South Waziristan under Taliban escort. Wali-ur-Rehman had dispelled rumors we'd been kidnapped. He was quoted as saying he trusted us, and his people had taken us to their strongholds in South Waziristan, where we were staying with them "as guests."

He went on to say our visit to Waziristan had been planned, and Taliban commanders were waiting for our arrival in Mir Ali. He knew Colonel Imam and his colleagues were making a documentary for a foreign news channel, and they'd happily consented to help, as the Pakistani media had stopped covering their activities. He said we were currently in Shaktoi, an area of South Waziristan still under Taliban control.

It was in this area where US drones had carried out a number of missile attacks back in January, including a strike on a suspected militant hideout in the course of which, it was believed by US and Pakistani intelligence agencies, Hakimullah Mehsud had been killed. The Pakistani papers were claiming Hakimullah was still alive in an underground location.

Wali-ur-Rehman said there were no landlines and no mobile signal in the area, which is why we'd not made contact with our families.

Farrukh wanted to believe what he was reading. It was certainly the case that he and Asghar had called my mobile many times, at different times of the day, in the past week, with no luck. This tallied with the point about the lack of signal. As to the rest, that we were safe and being treated as guests … Well, Farrukh was unconvinced but hopeful as he went to bed that night.

By the morning, though, the newspapers' assurances were starting to wear thin. The risk management team, unconvinced by what they'd heard from local journalists, had become suspicious about our safety.

Farrukh was so consumed by our situation that his practice was suffering. Nudrat was managing the office and was having to pester Farrukh to deal with clients' issues in order not to embarrass the firm. All the while trying her best keep her eye on Sherry, who was persistent in the belief that we'd be released soon and determined that I wouldn't be coming home to an empty house.

*　*　*

However, a few days earlier, Warda, Asif's wife, had been just getting home from work when the telephone rang. She answered it.

"Hello?"

"Is Asif Jameel there?" An assertive voice.

"No, I'm sorry, he's not at home."

"Make sure that he is at home this time tomorrow."

The caller hung up. Warda didn't know what to make of this call. She told Asif about it and, the following day, Asif stayed at home and waited for the phone call. But nothing happened. He waited in the next day, but again no one called. Then, on Saturday, April 10, the phone did ring.

"Asif Jameel?" A man's voice.

"*Gee Asif Jameel hoon*," Asif replied.

"*Asad Qureshi hamari harasat mey hey*. Asad Qureshi is in our captivity. I will call you again in forty-eight hours with our demands."

The man hung up. Asif froze. This was the call. The one he'd been briefed about. The one he'd been dreading.

Without hesitation he called Rodney, who contacted Simon, the channel's security advisor. Within minutes, Simon called Asif and arranged to visit the following day.

Simon arrived early. He told Asif they were working behind the scenes to get me released. They'd been waiting to be contacted. Now negotiations could begin in earnest. This was progress.

Asif fired a barrage of questions at Simon. Who could be holding us? What did they want? When would we be released?

Typical Asif. Always asking questions that people can't answer. He was like that whenever we worked together. It always drove me mad.

Simon said that this contact was a good sign, that the next call would be a ransom demand, and that meant that I wouldn't be harmed.

He gave Asif an earpiece microphone and recorder, and said he would stay with him in order to be there when the next call came. He said Asif should tell the kidnappers clearly that he had no authority to talk to them, and they should call Farrukh. Asif was to establish that the caller had a pen and paper then give him Farrukh's number, a new number specifically obtained for this purpose.

A few hours later, Farrukh received a call from the risk management team, inviting him to a meeting. Another briefing, Farrukh thought. More advice on how to stay calm if kidnappers called. When he turned up, Robin broke the news to him.

"Farrukh, the first contact has been made. Asif was called earlier today by a stranger who has admitted to having Asad in his custody."

Farrukh felt his spine turn to ice. This was it. His worst fear. In spite of everything the papers had said. Reality was now staring him in the face.

"They called Asif?"

"Yes, but they won't call him again. I've told our security colleague to advise Asif to change his number. So they call you instead."

"How will they know to call me?"

"They'll know."

Farrukh swallowed hard.

"Farrukh, the storm is now going to center on you. Do you think you can handle the pressure?"

"I'm Asad's only hope. I will do whatever needs to be done."

Farrukh knew if he couldn't handle it, no one else in the family could. But he was scared. Not about losing money, or losing his business and with it his (considerable) reputation. But about facing our parents if he failed. Bringing me back alive was the goal, for my sake and for the sake of Mum and Dad.

So he put on a brave face. But the more Robin talked about how the situation might develop, the more Farrukh realized what a testing challenge this would be. The kidnappers' language would be uncompromising. They'd mention violence. They'd likely send videos containing disturbing images. Images of physical torture.

The mention of torture made Farrukh's stomach turn.

But Robin seemed to know what he was talking about, and, through his growing unease, Farrukh drew some small comfort from this fact.

Robin presented Farrukh with a detailed script for how to proceed when the kidnappers called. He was to identify himself and who he was speaking to, get proof that he was talking to the right person, arrange a call back for the following day, and agree to nothing at this stage. It was important to build in delays. And if a financial demand was made, to make it clear that it was well beyond anything he could afford, true or not.

It was decided that, for security reasons, the channel and the risk management team would, from now on, be collectively referred to in all communications between them as "the A Team."

Farrukh left Nancy and Robin with very mixed feelings—it was good he was not alone, but he felt deeply uneasy about what lay ahead.

He went back to his office and told Nudrat and Asghar the grim news. His head was spinning. When he thought about what lay ahead, then looked at the work that had piled up, there simply weren't enough hours in the day. He knew he was going to find it impossible to have other people around him. He felt he needed to be alone. When he said this to Nudrat and Asghar, they both understood. They left him to himself.

It was about 7:00 p.m. when Farrukh's phone rang.

"Hello."

"Farrukh Qureshi?"

"Yes."

"*Asad Qureshi hamari harasat mey hey*. I will call you again in forty-eight hours with our demands."

The man spoke Urdu like an Indian. From the number that appeared on his phone, Farrukh realized the call had been made from a satellite phone. So it could have been made from anywhere. The call he'd been dreading. The call that had finally unleashed the full force of the nightmare. The nightmare that had been simmering away at the back of his mind for days. Except he wasn't asleep.

But, as we know from childhood, a nightmare loses much of its power if we share it with someone. Farrukh called his friend, Shoaib Suddle, a former police chief and now a tax ombudsman. Farrukh didn't need or want advice, just an ear. Shoaib said that, in any case, in matters like this the police couldn't do much.

Farrukh decided there and then not to involve the police, or any of the other agencies. He'd need to get through this on his own. Although Colonel Imam and KK were big names in Pakistan, still nobody had come forward to offer any assistance. How could Farrukh expect help in respect of me, an unknown filmmaker in what was essentially a foreign land?

The time to tell Mum and Dad would come soon, but not tonight. But he had a duty to tell Sherry, so he called Nudrat and asked her to bring Sherry over so he could break the news to her personally.

By the time Sherry arrived, in the company of Nudrat and Asghar, Farrukh had clothed himself in his lawyer's persona. Calm. In control.

"How was your day?"

Sherry nodded, holding back her tears. Asghar looked down at the floor. He was bracing himself for Sherry's reaction.

"Earlier today I got a call from the people who are holding Asad. I'm afraid he has indeed been kidnapped."

Sherry began to sob. Nudrat stepped forward to comfort her.

"I know this is not easy for you. It's a difficult situation that might continue for a long time. I think it would be better, for you and for Asad, if you went back to America."

"But I don't want to leave Pakistan. Not with Asad here, suffering who knows what."

She lowered her head and sobbed into her lap.

"You do understand that I need to concentrate on Asad. I cannot spare the energy and attention to worry about how other people are reacting."

"I'm not leaving."

"Very well. In that case, I suggest you stay here, at my house. So that you are not alone."

"I'll come over tomorrow."

On the way home in Nudrat's car, Sherry didn't say a word. She was alone, to all intents and purposes. Alone in a foreign country, with a foreign culture—an American-hating culture—with no one to turn to.

When Nudrat dropped her off, it was at a dark and lonely home. The home I'd left her in, two weeks ago. Then she'd at least had the familiar faces of my parents for company. Now she was all alone. Alone and frightened.

That night Farrukh lay in bed thinking about God and destiny. He remembered the time he'd first introduced me to KK, and how we'd fallen out soon after, so massively he'd been sure we'd never talk to one another again.

But we'd met again at the wedding of Farrukh's daughter, and the friendship had clicked back on and the idea of the documentary had been born. Destiny. Farrukh felt he was responsible for reuniting us.

The words "what if" filled his head. KK and I had met again. We'd resolved our differences. We'd formed an idea that Asif had instantly taken a fancy to. Colonel Imam had made a last-minute decision to go along with us.

How different the situation might have been now if only one of these things *hadn't* happened. How meticulously circumstances had conspired to bring us all to this point.

But that was in the past. The only question now was what fate had in store for us. What if he failed me now? Then he'd also be failing Mum and Dad. What if he made a wrong decision? He'd made some very difficult decisions over the course of his professional career, but not ones that had involved the lives of others. Was he strong enough to make the right decisions now, when the time came?

These were the questions that kept him up through the long night.

9
The A Team

Several days in a darkened room had thrown my body clock into disarray. I'd effectively become nocturnal and was staying awake well into the night. The electricity level had clearly dropped—the light was very dim and the ceiling fan was groaning and struggling to turn.

To pass the time, I was reading a book that Krishan Lal had given me, about the giving of alms. It was full of accounts of the lives of people who'd given away money in the name of God and had been subsequently rewarded many times over. I was finding it fascinating.

Suddenly, I heard heavy breathing outside my room, and sounds of a struggle. I sat up. Someone was being punched. Heavy punches in quick succession. Like a boxer trying to finish the fight by using all his reserves to knock out his opponent. Not the crisp punching sounds we hear in films. Those are made by men in boxing gloves punching an animal carcass. That sound is sharp and clean. The sound outside my room was dull and ugly. I could tell the person was being punched really hard.

Then the punching sounds stopped, and I heard two gunshots in quick succession. Seconds later, someone unlocked my door. My heart started racing. My time had come.

Krishan Lal marched into the room and stood over me, his terrifying face twisted with rage.

"Do you want to see some human blood?" he bellowed.

"No, no. No, I don't."

He stared at me, his heavy breath hot on my face, his bulging eyes drilling into mine as if they were about to pop out of their sockets. I was so scared by the sight of his face that I dropped the book I'd been reading. But I didn't want to antagonize him by staring back, so I lowered my gaze, in the hope he'd go away. But still I could feel his eyes burning into my face. I was sweating now, a cold sweat on my face, under my arms and down my back. And my heart was pounding so hard I could hear it. *This is it.*

Then, from the corner of my eye, I saw him turn around and walk out. I let out an audible sigh and felt nauseous with relief. I lay back on my bed. A life had just been taken only a few feet away from me.

I'd been convinced I was next. I imagined the scene outside my room—imagined being beaten up then shot at point-blank range.

The only other time I'd been physically close to anything like this was on an assignment in Saudi Arabia. There'd been a commotion in the street—a crowd had gathered quickly, their voices raised in a frenzy of anger. I'd asked a colleague what was happening. A man was being beheaded, he'd told me. I'd felt sick for the rest of the day.

Sleep eluded me. I spent the night tossing and turning. In the morning, one of the men came in to untie me so I could offer morning prayers (they were meticulous about affording me this freedom). On this particular morning, another man came into my room, shortly after prayers. He wasn't wearing a hood but he had part of his turban wrapped around his face so it was well hidden. He sat down and stared at me. It was a little unsettling, but not the terrifying experience I'd had with Krishan Lal.

I could hear a lot of helicopter activity overhead and felt brave enough to ask a question.

"Where are all these helicopters going?"

"Islamabad."

Islamabad? How strange. I wondered why helicopters would be flying to Islamabad from Afghanistan. As far as I knew, the Pakistani army had no presence in Afghanistan—they had enough to deal with in their own country. And if they were in Afghanistan secretly, I was sure my contacts in the ISPR would have told me. But the whole situation was so complex, I supposed no one really understood it.

"We should be flying back as well. But we have been held up because of you."

"What do you mean, you've been held up?"

"It is time for our vacations, and we should have been going back. But we have been asked to stay behind and look after you people."

"Well, I've done nothing wrong. I shouldn't be here. So why don't they let me go?"

"Soon, they will let you go. And we will most likely fly back to Islamabad together."

This relatively normal exchange had both calmed and emboldened me. I asked another question.

"Tell me—have you ever killed a person?"

"I can't tell you that."

The stock response. Of course he must have. Anyone with a gun who lives in this region cannot avoid killing people.

A bang on the door, and Krishan Lal's voice.

"Come on out, Nauman." The man I now knew as Nauman got up straight away and left the room.

After that, Nauman's visits became a regular feature. Every morning he would come and sit with me. Every morning I would tell him I was innocent of any crime and should be allowed to leave. Every morning he would nod his head and not say much.

I was no further forward in my quest to be released, but it felt good to have someone who was at least listening to me. I thought I might eventually get through to him, and he'd go back to his superiors and persuade them of the truth—I was merely shooting a news report and was no terrorist.

I had the idea to put my case in writing. Write a letter to the kidnappers that might persuade them to release me. Since my handwriting was terrible, I decided to write in capitals. It was a long and laborious task, but I now felt an urgent need to explain my situation.

The next time Krishan Lal came to see me, I gave him the letter and asked him to give it to the necessary people. I hoped they'd understand.

"When the officer pays a visit, I will pass it on."

I was encouraged by his use of the word *officer*. Someone with a bit of sanity. Someone with clout. I allowed myself to hope.

A few days later, on his morning visit, Nauman brought me an orange. It was a welcome variation on the standard theme of biscuits and milk. A little consideration at last. I thanked him. Since he seemed to be showing me some kindness, I ventured to ask him for more.

"Is it possible you could remove the curtain draped on the outside of the door? I'm suffocating in here."

"No."

"Then can you just raise it a little? So fresh air can come in from underneath?"

A slight nod of the head. I took that as a maybe. A loud banging on the door and Krishan Lal's voice.

"Come on out. You know I don't like you going in there."

Nauman left and bolted the door behind him. A few seconds later, a chink of light appeared at the bottom of the door. Then a waft of fresh air. He'd raised the curtain. It was only a couple of inches—they obviously didn't want me peeking outside and seeing them with their hoods off—but it was enough to make life for me a little less oppressive. I was grateful.

* * *

For Farrukh, there had been three days of excruciating waiting and no news. He was still unable to turn his attention to the work he knew he was neglecting, and Nudrat was here again, trying to nudge him in that direction.

Then the phone rang. The new phone. Farrukh dashed across the room to turn on the recording device given to him by the A Team, his heart racing with every ring. The machine started and he picked up the phone.

"Hello."

"Hello. Am I speaking to the brother of Asad Qureshi?"

"Yes, this is Asad Qureshi's brother."

"I am Ali Raza. Your brother is in our custody. We are the Asian Tigers. Listen very carefully to me. You should talk to the British and Pakistani governments and arrange for the sum of ten million US dollars to be found. If you want to see your brother alive. Do you understand me?"

"Yes, I do."

Farrukh had resolved to be very submissive, although it was not his true nature. But before he could say anything else, Ali Raza hung up.

A pin dropped.

Although Farrukh knew the mask of calm had not slipped from his face, when he looked at the hand holding the phone, it was trembling.

He sat down to compose himself. What to do now? He played the recording of their brief conversation. Nudrat listened too. Farrukh asked her if she would make a transcript for the A Team.

The Asian Tigers. From the name, apparently *not* an Islamic group. Nudrat did several internet searches and found no reference to them. A mystery.

Farrukh called the A Team and requested a meeting with them. He took his friend, Asghar, with him. He met with Robin, Nancy, and Brian. They'd now been joined by Simon, the member of the risk management team who'd previously visited Asif in London. A very composed Robin took the lead and introduced Simon to Farrukh.

"This is a good sign. Contact has been established and the kidnappers have accepted you as the first point of contact. No question now of the kidnappers calling multiple people."

Farrukh was heartened by Robin's optimism.

"Everything is on track. We're here to help you and guide you every step of the way. Tell us what happens and exactly how it happens. Wait for the next call. When it comes, make it clear that neither the channel nor the UK government will negotiate with them. For them, *you* are the only hope and *you* are the one they must contact."

Robin repeated these instructions several times, so he could be sure Farrukh had absorbed the information. He knew Farrukh would not be in a fit state of mind to concentrate normally.

"Farrukh, you need to establish who you're talking to. You need to assert very forcefully that you are just the brother and absolutely *not* a representative of anyone."

Farrukh nodded.

"If the kidnapper becomes angry, it doesn't matter. You need to drive this point home. And we need you to arrange four more phones. Small ones, since we're all carrying at least three each. Nancy and I can't buy them and register them in our names."

Farrukh started to think of people he could ask to do that.

"Phones can only be monitored by outsiders if they have the numbers. For these four new phones, only the five of us must know the numbers and only we five are to call each other from them. No one—and I mean *no one*—outside the five of us must use them. The person registering the phones cannot be linked to any of us. So choose someone with a tenuous connection to you. A friend of a friend. We'll monitor the designated phone you'll be using for the kidnappers."

Arranging the phones would be relatively straightforward—Farrukh had an enormous network of contacts—but he didn't relish the task of pressing home a point that would antagonize someone in control of his brother's life.

Robin continued to set out his instructions.

"You must tell the kidnappers you have spoken to the British government and they have a strict policy *not* to pay ransoms. They will not budge on this. You are the *only* one who can solve this problem. No one else. It is paramount you convince the kidnappers that you alone can solve this problem. Tell them the channel will not be involved and stress also that the Pakistani government will not pay a ransom for Asad."

Farrukh agreed to follow this line of argument. Nancy told him not to go to the media. As negotiators, they needed to stay under the radar of the press, for the sake of the captives. Farrukh was naturally a media-shy person anyway and was happy to toe the line on this point. Then Robin asked the question that Farrukh had been waiting for.

"How much would you personally be able to pay as a ransom?"

"Not more than one million rupees. All my tangible assets are in my wife's name."

"Can you get a bank loan?"

"Not to pay a ransom. That's not possible in this country."

"Okay."

Farrukh was uneasy about the direction the conversation was taking.

"Tell me, what rights do Asad and his colleagues have? Aren't they insured against an event like this? What happens if they don't come out of this alive? What then?"

Robin paused. He appeared deep in thought for several seconds. Then he replied. His words were striking in their coldness.

"Unfortunately, they have no rights or insurances. All the channel would be able to pay would be actual expenses incurred."

"What about Asad?"

"The same, with an additional sum for loss of earnings."

But Robin had misunderstood Farrukh's question. It wasn't about money—it was about the protection the channel had in place for me and my team. Robin was clearly absolving the channel of any responsibility. Farrukh was shocked and angered by Robin's response, but he knew a confrontation with Robin at this stage would not be helpful, so he resolved to let the matter drop. For now.

Robin gave Farrukh additional questions he should put to the kidnappers when they called again: "How is my brother?" "Can I speak to him?" "Is he with the others?" "How are they?" He was also instructed to say, "What you have demanded is impossible. I need a figure that is more realistic. It all takes time. I am trying to get the family together."

Farrukh was convinced that, when the kidnappers did call again, they wouldn't give him time to pose all these questions. But he read them and reread them, so they'd be clear in his mind when the call did come.

Robin told him KK's son, Usama, and Colonel Imam's son, Major Nauman, had both received a similar initial call.

Farrukh left the meeting with the A Team in much lower spirits. When he told his friend, Asghar, what had been said, and told him about the channel's desire to keep their name out of the media, Asghar became angry and suspicious. But Farrukh explained that media exposure, and the revelation of a link to a UK TV channel, would only inflate the kidnappers' demands and make it less likely I'd be released. He knew it was time to be pragmatic, in spite of his inner rage at Robin's detachment.

In the wake of this initial tumult, Farrukh reflected on his own personal situation. Life could hardly have been heavier with duties and responsibilities: he was concerned about our elderly parents' fragile health and the devastating results any shock might have; one of his own daughters was expecting a baby; he had Sherry to worry about and keep away from the media; and his business had come to a virtual standstill.

It's hardly a wonder he wasn't sleeping.

To his usual, dark, nighttime thoughts was added the realization he also had a duty to the family of my assistant, Rustam, caught up in this deadly business as a direct result of his willingness to help me. Farrukh knew Rustam was a desperately poor man with many children. With their father unaccountably and indefinitely detained, they'd be going through a very tough time financially. Farrukh would have to provide for them.

The following morning, Farrukh asked his colleague, Atique, and another colleague, Sadiq Dar, to pay a visit to Rustam's family.

They lived on the outskirts of Islamabad, in a small house which still lacked basic utilities, such as a gas supply. They found the small courtyard full of Rustam's children, playing.

The two men met Rustam's eldest son, Jawaid, and Rustam's wife, Bas Bibi. Like Rustam, she was illiterate. She didn't read, so no newspapers ever made it into the house, and the family didn't have a television, so she was completely unaware her husband had been kidnapped.

Atique gave Rustam's wife some money, which she accepted gratefully, and Sadiq explained the situation to her and gave her assurances her husband would be home as soon as Farrukh could arrange it. Her reaction stunned both men. Bas Bibi said Rustam could stay away as long as he wanted—she only wished to be kept informed of his whereabouts just once a year.

In the conversation that followed, she explained to Atique and Sadiq what I already knew, that Rustam had married a second woman, Shahmim Ara, much to the displeasure of Bas Bibi. He'd had a son with this new wife and provided for her fairly well, while neglecting Bas Bibi and her children. Rustam's absence was welcome, she said. And the money the men had given her more welcome still.

Back at his office, Farrukh was coming to the conclusion that it was best for him, and for the family as a whole, if his wife, Rhuksana, and his children went away to England. With everything that was going on, he was hardly with them in body anyway, and certainly never with them in mind. And he worried about the safety of his wife and children almost as much as he was worried about me. No one knew as yet who the kidnappers were. Perhaps they were part of some terrorist network with long arms that reached right into the heart of Islamabad.

He knew sending his family away was the right thing to do, although he also realized that living alone was not going to be easy for him. He knew how pampered he was. I'd always joked with him that he had the life of a senior Buddhist monk (in Buddhism, the more senior the monk, the less he has to do)—his clothes were always pressed and ready when he came out of the shower; his food was always waiting on the table whenever he sat down; his house was kept immaculate. Farrukh never had to bother himself with domestic matters of any kind—everything was taken care of.

On the morning of April 7, he told Rhuksana she and the children had to go to England. She wasn't expecting him to say this. It was one thing to send Mum and Dad away, but, to her mind, splitting up his own family was quite another. She wanted to be near him and be able to give him real support, tending to his needs. She told him she wouldn't go.

Farrukh explained her staying would only add to his problems. She should leave, and she should also take Tahira, their middle daughter, who was expecting a baby. She was not in a great position to travel, but Farrukh insisted it was, on balance, the safest option. Their eldest daughter, Sarah, who lived in her own house, could stay behind provided she didn't visit the family home, as she might be followed.

It was with a very heavy heart that Rhuksana started packing for the trip. She also set about packing up the house for the indefinite period of her absence. By the time she'd finished, with belongings packed away into cupboards and furniture draped in white sheets, her home looked empty, as if its owner had died.

Tahira's husband, Haroon, wanted to accompany his pregnant wife to England, but he didn't have a visa. Farrukh wanted to get them all out of the country as quickly as possible, so he paid a visit to Jacqueline at the British High Commission. Jacqueline promised to process the application within hours.

She looked at Farrukh's exhausted face and asked how he was coping. He said he was fine. She admired his resignation, she said. Then she lowered her voice.

"Off the record, you shouldn't worry so much. You're in good hands. The channel always takes care of its people."

"I feel like I'm on my own. That has been made very clear."

"Well, it's true the government won't pay any ransom. But the channel will. They've paid ransoms in the past."

Farrukh was astounded. In all their discussions, Robin had been at pains to point out the channel had no financial safety net in place. There'd be no material support. If what Jacqueline was saying was true, they'd misled him grossly. He was livid.

He still held the channel responsible for our predicament. He felt it only right they should pay the ransom, or at least make a significant contribution to it. And, deep down, he thought it scandalous they were trying to keep their name out of everything, leaving the whole burden on him, emotionally and financially.

On April 10, Farrukh took his family to the airport. It was a flight into uncertainty. None of them knew when they would be reunited. Nor under what circumstances.

10
The Realization

Krishan Lal entered my room, carrying handcuffs and a chain. He asked me to get out of bed. I got out and stood up. Out of habit, I offered him my hands for cuffing.

"Some people are coming to ask you a few questions. You need to be honest and tell the whole truth."

"I understand," I agreed, feebly.

He put the chain around my ankles. Then he blindfolded me and led me to the corner of the room. He asked me to sit on the floor. I heard a rustling noise—he was rummaging through his pockets for something. Then a click. A flashlight. He was shining a flashlight all around the blindfold, to make sure no light was getting to my eyes. Since I didn't flinch, he knew the blindfold was secure.

I was nervous. I had nothing new to tell whoever was coming to interview me. No privileged information. No secret truths to reveal. Nothing. But these people clearly thought otherwise. Where could we go from here?

The wall felt cold on my back and, even with its straw mat, the floor didn't feel any warmer.

Krishan Lal then left the room. Robbed of one of my senses, and unable to see facial expressions, catch an exchange of glances, read their eyes, I'd be even less well equipped to work out what was going on. But whoever was coming didn't want to be encumbered by a hood, perhaps felt he was above covering his face, and had ordered my face to be covered instead. Was it another way of subjugating me?

I heard the door open and several feet walked past me, one after the other. Perhaps three or four people. I thought one of them was bound to be Krishan Lal.

Something metallic was laid on the floor in front of me. A gun?

I thought it would be both polite and prudent to offer a greeting.

"*Asalaam alaikum.*"

'*Walaikum asalaam*,' came the reply in unison. I was right—three or four at least.

"Asad *sahib*, do you have family?"

"Yes. I live with my parents in Islamabad."

"Children?"

"No. No children."

"Are you married?"

"Yes."

"Which city is your wife from?"

"She's not from Pakistan. She's from America."

"Pakistani American?"

"No. American American."

"Muslim?"

"Why do you need to know about her? Is this necessary?"

"We want to know everything about you."

"Is she Muslim?" A different voice.

"Half and half, I would say."

"Half and half?"

"What about your parents?" First voice again.

"They're retired."

"Brothers and sisters?"

"Yes, I have an elder sister and brother and a younger sister and brother."

"What do they do?"

"My elder sister is a teacher in England. My elder brother is a lawyer in Islamabad. My younger sister doesn't work. My younger brother is a trained lawyer as well."

"Tell us about your connections with the ISI."

"I'm not connected with the ISI. I'm a filmmaker. I've had meetings with the ISI, in connection with my film, but that's it."

"Do you know General Pasha?"

"No, I don't. I've never met him."

"Where are the ISI headquarters in Islamabad?"

I was perplexed. Why would they ask such a question? Surely they knew the answer? Was it a test? I shook my head in irritation.

"Where are these questions going? I don't understand."

"Please look straight ahead."

I could hear something being adjusted in front of me. Metal on metal. Ah—a camera on a tripod. They're recording my interview, so they can verify my story. They'll establish my credentials, they'll find everything is in order, and they'll let me go home. I felt suddenly relieved and relaxed. Not long now.

"Tell us about the ISPR. How many barriers do you have to go through to get inside the ISPR headquarters?"

"Just one check-post. And after that, a gate."

"What about the ISI offices?" Second voice again.

"ISI offices? Well, I can visualize where they are, but I don't know the address."

"Shall we give you access to the internet?"

A third voice. A strange voice, with an accent totally alien to me. I couldn't place it at all. But, hang on, there were people from all over the place in the armed forces. Odd accents from far-flung places were entirely to be expected. *Calm down.*

But then again, why these silly questions? It didn't make sense. They knew who I was. Why were they trying to trip me up? Why the games?

"No, no. It's okay. I'm just trying to think."

I tried to see the ISI complex in my mind and visualize the roads around it. I could see the complex clearly but couldn't remember the name of the road. Then I remembered Gerry's Travel Agents nearby. That gave me a fix in the city.

"Where Seventh Avenue meets Aabpara. That's where the ISI complex is."

"Did you tell anyone at the ISI you were coming here?"

"Yes. I had a meeting with Brigadier Iftikhar and told him what I was doing."

"What else have you done with the ISI?"

"I haven't done anything. I've never worked *for* the ISI. I just consult with them. That's all."

"What about the ISPR?"

"Yes. I made a film on the earthquake for them. They've allowed me access to the Sabaoon school in Swat, to film boys who are being rehabilitated. After being trained as suicide bombers."

"Why are you making this film?"

"Well, it's a good thing the army is doing. It's good they're training them to be electricians, carpenters, mechanics. Rather than put them in prison. Some of them will even go to university."

"But what about these boys? What if they relapse? What if they tie bombs to themselves again? Blow themselves up? Just like the Pakistani soldiers did in 1971?"

1971? A slip of the tongue, I thought. He was referring to events in the war between India and Pakistan. Indian tanks had been advancing on Lahore. Pakistani soldiers had tied bombs to their bodies and rolled under the tanks and blown them up, effectively repelling the Indian army. But that was the war of 1965.

1971 was the war that led to East Pakistan separating from West Pakistan and becoming Bangladesh. These were important dates in Pakistani history.

A slip of the tongue. Surely.

"What if these boys want to be martyrs? What if that is all they want to be? They have heard the stories of their brave compatriots from 1971 and they want to prove their bravery. They want that honor. What then?"

No. Not a slip of the tongue. Not a second time. 1965 is a date stamped on every Pakistani soldier's brain. Major Aziz Bhatti was killed in that war. He was posthumously awarded the *Nishan-e-Haider*, Pakistan's highest military honor. In 1965. Even I know that. And I'm not a soldier.

And neither are these men. Not Pakistani soldiers, anyway.

My God! How stupid I've been! How naïve! Whoever these men are, sitting in front of me, they're not ISI. Definitely not.

All this time, I'd taken it for granted I was being held by the ISI. It all had the ring of officialdom. Investigations. Interrogations. Carrying out inquiries. I'd assumed an official structure and official processes. And Krishan Lal had given me no cause to think otherwise.

I'd suspected something was wrong when they'd asked me about the Tochi army officers' mess, and said there was one in Mir Ali as well as one in Miranshah. At the time, I'd thought they'd been trying to trip me up.

I'd thought all along I was just biding my time here until they'd concluded their inquiries. But these people had never told me who they were. I'd assumed everything. Assumed they were ISI. And assumed they were on my side.

But now I knew I was in serious trouble.

I tried to stay calm and maintain a composed posture but, somehow, being blindfolded only intensified my fear. My heart started to race. I'd told them everything about me. Things I shouldn't have revealed. Details about my family. My wife. My *American* wife. That had been particularly unwise. That revelation had surely scuppered any chance I had of being released soon. Of being released at all.

I tried to think beyond my feelings of panic and terror. I realized I must not display my fear or let them see a change in my mood. I needed to play ignorant. If only to save me from another beating.

"Okay. We are finished." First voice.

I heard them gather their things together. Scrapes and clicks as the tripod and camera were dismantled. The opening of the door and the sound of footsteps retreating.

I sat there motionless for several minutes, contemplating my fate.

The door opened again. My blindfold was untied. Then Krishan Lal removed my handcuffs and shackles.

"Your questioning is over now. You did well. Now you will be moved to the American compound. You will get good food and satellite television before we let you go home. You will be our guest."

"I don't want to go there. I just want to go home now."

"We can't do that. Enjoy yourself first."

None of that made sense. If they were the dangerous people I was now assuming them to be, why was there talk of release? Were they trying to confuse me?

Krishan Lal gathered the chain and handcuffs.

"They said you are to move your bed over there," he said, pointing to the area directly in front of the door. I'd be right there, in front of them, as soon as the door was opened. Well, for one thing, I'd be farther away from the stench of the bathroom.

Krishan Lal pointed to the handcuffs and the chain.

"From now on, we only use these at night. What do you think?"

"Thank you." I was relieved. "How are the others?"

Instantly, his mood changed.

"Just because he wears a long beard, it does not mean he is a saint. Even the devil wears a beard." Vitriol in his voice.

"What do you mean?"

"Your Colonel Imam! His son is married to a Shia woman. How does he offer his prayers?"

"I don't know."

"*We* know! Sometimes with arms folded and sometimes with arms by the side!"*

Krishan Lal brought his face close to mine.

"What do you think to that?" He spat the words out.

"I don't know what to say."

"And you! What do you mean, your wife is half half?"

"She ... Well, she's not sure."

"And Khawaja. He's no good. He's been saved from hanging. But he's no good."

With these words he flew out of the room and bolted the door behind him, leaving me to my thoughts.

None of it made sense. I was now convinced I wasn't being held by the ISI or any Pakistani agency. But if these people were Taliban, well, KK had close connections with them. Why would Krishan Lal speak about KK in that way? And speak about hanging? Surely they wouldn't harm KK?

It was a complete conundrum.

I thought about the day they'd captured us. I remembered hearing them talk about a horse that had galloped past us, and how the Taliban used such horses for training. And they'd talked about Khost, the border crossing into Afghanistan. Were these people then Afghan Taliban? But the Afghan Taliban were fighting the Americans. They wouldn't have any business with us.

---

* Sunni Muslims offer prayers with their arms folded, while Shia Muslims pray with their arms by their side.

Then I thought about Krishan Lal. A Hindu name. What was he doing here, among Muslims? He was the odd one out here. He'd told me he'd worked as a translator for the Indian embassy. Perhaps he also had a connection to RAW, India's Research and Analysis Wing, the equivalent of Pakistan's ISI. They had a major presence in Afghanistan. Perhaps they had taken us.

Yes, that made sense. Some sort of prisoner exchange. Us in exchange for Indian prisoners held by the Pakistani secret service. Part of some big game well above our heads.

Late in the evening, Krishan Lal came into my room. I was lying on my bed, reading.

"I need your email address and passport."

I looked up at him and thought "passport?" I wasn't carrying my passport with me. They knew that. The only ID I did have—a copy of my Pakistani identity card—had been taken from me at the outset. And I wasn't comfortable with them having access to my email.

"I don't have my passport here."

"I want your email address and its passport."

Ah. He meant *password*. Well, I wasn't at all keen to give them access to my email, but, if I didn't offer it up voluntarily, they'd only beat it out of me in the end.

Then he asked me for Sherry's email address and password, which I also gave him, albeit very reluctantly. He scribbled the details on a small piece of paper, using the ballpoint pen he'd taken from my kit.

They'd taken my belongings and my freedom. Now they were slowly chipping away at my personal life.

I consoled myself with the thought that going through my emails would only give them further proof that I was who I said I was. Perhaps that would expedite my release.

But the following morning, Krishan Lal burst into my room in a foul temper. He shook his fist under my nose and I recoiled.

"Your wife's password! Give me the right one! I want the right one!"

Sherry's password was her phone number, which I'd rattled off automatically when he'd asked me. Maybe I'd transposed some of the numbers by mistake, or perhaps he'd copied the numbers down wrong, but either way the numbers had become muddled and now here I was facing this pathetic man's wrath.

I apologized and went through the numbers again, hoping this time they were in the right order.

I felt as if I'd betrayed Sherry. It was awful they'd be monitoring her as well. A terrible intrusion. But there was nothing I could do about it. I closed my eyes and willed Sherry not to send any emails.

Krishan Lal was a liar. I wasn't going to any American compound. If that had been their intention, they wouldn't have been snooping into my email, and into my wife's email. This nightmare was going to continue for some time yet.

Overhead I heard a plane, full of people enjoying the simple freedom to travel from one place to another. Freedom. I looked at my handcuffs and my shackles. I felt it would be a while before I tasted freedom again. Perhaps I never would.

That dismal thought kept me awake for hours. Counting sheep had never worked for me, but my variants on the traditional method sometimes did. I started to list all the film directors I could think of. When that didn't do the trick, I moved on to actors. Eventually, several hours later, sleep came.

* * *

Usman Punjabi continued to call Usama, pestering him to make the arrangements to meet the demands that would secure our release.

But Usama had neither the contacts nor the resources to make that happen. He had no option but to stall him by saying he was trying his best. The truth was he was helpless and his helplessness was playing right into the hands of the kidnappers.

When Usama asked Punjabi what *he* could do to move things along, Punjabi insisted he was only a media man—he didn't know how to get Usama's father back.

Usama had had his differences with his father over the years. KK's passion for social justice had often taken him away from his children, and there was some resentment about that on Usama's part. Usama often said that his father had neglected them, that he'd pursued his various projects regardless of their impact on the family. That, in fact, he'd given his family only poverty.

In spite of all that, though, Usama had himself been involved in several of KK's missions and had worked with him in helping to protect human rights, notably in KK's intervention to stop the massacre at the Lal Masjid (the Red Mosque), over the course of which hundreds of young innocent lives had been lost.

So, although he didn't always agree with the path his father had chosen, he often helped him, out of duty and out of love.

And now he desperately wanted to bring his father back. But he didn't know which way to turn.

He spoke to Major Nauman, Colonel Imam's son, and together they decided they wanted to go to the press. They visited Farrukh at his office and told him about the calls they'd received and about their plans to get the media involved.

Farrukh argued that was exactly what the kidnappers wanted, and he repeated what he'd told Asghar—media exposure would be damaging. But, despite Farrukh's objections, they were adamant about giving a press statement. Farrukh knew he was in no position to stop them, so he asked Nudrat to help draft the press release and told her to keep the channel out of it at least.

In the evening, the A Team invited Farrukh to another meeting, also attended by Jacqueline from the British High Commission in Islamabad. She emphasized to Farrukh that the British government did not negotiate with or pay ransoms to terrorists. In order to make this clear to the terrorists, she suggested Farrukh tell them to visit the British High Commission's website, where, at bullet point number five, this policy is clearly stated. Jacqueline said she would get the IT department to move this item to bullet point number one, clearly expecting Farrukh to be impressed by this intervention.

Ever the diplomat and pragmatist, Farrukh managed to conceal his disgust at the lightweight level of involvement on the part of Her Majesty's Government, which made news reports of British High Commission "investigations" into the kidnapping pretty hard to swallow.

Farrukh's sense of outrage deepened later that evening when our elder sister, Rakhshindah, called him from England to say she'd received a call from the British Foreign Office. They'd assured her everything was fine, and I'd be home soon.

The following morning, the families of KK and Colonel Imam gave a hastily arranged press conference. It was Usama's third cry for help and he did all the talking:

On April 4, 2010, my father, Khalid Khawaja, son of Muhammad Ishaq Khawaja, along with Mr Asad Qureshi, son of Abdul Karim Qureshi, and Colonel (Retired) Sultan Amir (aka Colonel Imam), son of Ghulam Ali Tarar, left Islamabad at the precise invitation of the High Command of the Tehrik-e-Taliban of North and South Waziristan, and as their respected guests, for the purpose of making a documentary film highlighting the present situation in the area and its impact on the indigenous population. The invitation contained assurances of safe passage throughout the journey.

On their way, my father and his companions conducted some interviews and on March 26, 2010, they reached Bannu, from where they made their last contact with me. At about 12:30 p.m., when they contacted me, they were about to leave Bannu for Mir Ali and points beyond. After that, they disappeared into thin air. Until yesterday.

Last night, the evening of April 14, 2010, we were contacted by a faction calling themselves the "Asian Tigers." They demanded ten million US dollars for the release of the group. A threat to eliminate those kidnapped was also voiced by the Asian Tigers' spokesperson.

I hereby humbly beg the Taliban authorities who are in control of the Tribal Area where this unfortunate incident has taken place, and on whose invitation my father and his companions were visiting their land as respected guests, to please help recover my father and his companions from the hands of this faction and ensure their safe return home. I also beg the government of Pakistan to assert all its powers to do the same.

And with that, the press conference was over.

It hadn't been well attended, but making the situation public had given Usama and Major Nauman some comfort and some hope that action might be taken on their behalf.

11
The Price

I looked at the few words I'd written. My mind was almost completely blank. The words weren't registering at all. I was mentally exhausted and I had drifted into a sort of trance.

I don't know how long I was in this state, but I was suddenly snapped out of it when Krishan Lal entered the room. Behind him were three other men, all of them hooded. The sight of the hoods made my blood freeze. My time had come.

Krishan Lal signaled to me to stand up with a slow lift of his index finger. Nobody spoke. The silence was unbearably tense.

"What is it?" I asked.

"Keep quiet. Nothing is wrong," Krishan Lal replied.

One of the men stepped forward with a cloth in his hand and proceeded to blindfold me, while another handcuffed my hands behind my back.

"Something is happening. Please tell me what you are going to do!"

I was terrified of another beating. I knew these people were absolutely merciless. There was no limit to the physical pain and humiliation they were prepared to inflict on me.

I heard the door open and close. Then footsteps. A thud behind me, then I was pushed back and stumbled onto a chair placed behind me. I kept quiet. I marshaled the meager remnants of my mental strength to prepare for whatever was coming my way.

I could hear someone fumbling through my bag.

"Where is your shaving kit?" A voice I'd not heard before.

"The black bag," I said. I wondered what they needed my shaving kit for.

"Sit up straight," said Krishan Lal.

I sat up so my head was facing forward. Someone adjusted my blindfold so it was just above my sideburns. I felt lukewarm water being applied to my beard, with my faithful Kent shaving brush, bought from Harrods over twenty years ago. An image of a Knightsbridge Street flashed across my mind. Then another of the gleaming glass counter of the gentlemen's grooming department. Right now that was a different planet. I couldn't be farther away from the civilization I was used to.

My shaving foam wasn't used. Instead, a bar of soap was plied to my beard, then lathered up with the shaving brush. Then the razor was dragged sharply down my cheek.

Prior to this, I'd only once in my entire life been shaved by someone else. I'd gone to a traditional barber's, just to see how close they shaved. The finished shave hadn't been that impressive, but the whole process, with hot towels, a preshave, then slow, careful strokes with the razor, had been relaxing to the point of being almost hypnotic.

This was anything but relaxing. This felt like a punishment. A violation. It often is, literally, in this part of the world. Half of a man's moustache or beard is forcibly shaved off to punish and humiliate him. A walking insult.

I tried to stay as still as possible, out of fear of being cut. The person shaving me made quick strokes with the razor, occasionally cleaning it in a plastic mug of water.

A whispered exchange. I was too afraid to concentrate on what was being said. Then someone spoke to me.

"Do you want a mustache?"

"No. No, it's okay."

The full shave was completed. Roughly. Then I heard footsteps retreat. I was pulled up by my collar and made to stand, with Krishan Lal holding me. More scuffled activity in my room, but I couldn't work out what was going on. I stood patiently awaiting my next ordeal.

Then my blindfold was loosened and my eyes were uncovered. I saw a sheet hanging on the wall in front of me. It had a scene painted on it, of a lake surrounded by palm trees and a jetty with a white boat tied to it, rendered in a very kitsch, unsophisticated style. The kind of picture you'd see in a cheap restaurant.

Krishan Lal unlocked the handcuffs and pushed me toward the wall where the cloth was hanging.

"Sit."

I sat down with the scenery behind me. The earthen wall felt cold against my back. If they'd just wanted me shaved, why hadn't they asked me to do it myself, instead of subjecting me to this rough treatment? Krishan Lal left the room. I sat there waiting, wondering what was going to happen next.

The door to my room opened and a hooded man walked in. He was new—I'd definitely not seen him before. He was fairly tall and very well built. Not the kind of man you'd want to tangle with. He both frightened and repelled me. I would later learn he was Sabir Mehsud, the group's leader.

I sat up as he walked closer. Krishan Lal appeared behind him, then another very big man, dressed in what seemed to be hessian cloth. His face was covered. He stood in the doorway, keeping watch. A very intimidating presence.

Sabir Mehsud looked around the room. His eyes caught the pile of empty milk cartons on the window ledge.

"I see that you like milk."

I nodded.

"How are you?"

Well, I've been locked up, severely beaten, mentally tortured, and starved. I live in the shadow of death. And you want to know how I am!

"I'm fine."

"We are the Asian Tigers. Our elders have found you guilty of spying and colluding with the enemy. We are holding you as our hostage. We want ten million US dollars for your release. If we do not get it, we will kill you. Do you understand?"

My mouth became instantly dry. A film of cold sweat formed over my whole body. I began to tremble.

No one would pay ten million dollars for me. Nobody I knew had anything like that amount of money. My death warrant had just been signed. I was going to die in this God-forsaken place.

He stared at me, seeing the impact of his words. He signaled to Krishan Lal, who went out of the room and brought me a cup of water. A dirty blue plastic cup. But this was not a time to reflect on hygiene. On the hygiene of the people who had drunk from it before me. On their rancid breath. Their rotten teeth. Not a time to reflect on any of that, but, stupidly and inexplicably, I did.

The cold water ran over my tongue and down my throat but did nothing to quench my thirst. I took a deep breath and struggled to compose myself.

"Can I have some more water?"

Krishan Lal took the plastic cup from my hand and went out to get some more.

This situation was frustrating and terrifying. I had done nothing wrong. Why couldn't they accept that? Accept that I wasn't a threat? Who did they think I was, that they had any hope of securing such an outrageous ransom? They might as well shoot me there and then.

Krishan Lal appeared with the water. He was also carrying a small video camera and my tripod. He tried to set the equipment up, but the quick-release plate was missing from the tripod (it was still screwed to the bottom of my video camera), so he had to settle for resting his camera on the tripod's head. *Be careful with my tripod.* Another stupid thought.

"We want you to make a statement in front of this camera."

"What do you want me to say?"

Sabir Mehsud gave me a sheet of paper and a pen.

"Here. Write on this."

I took the pen and paper and, for a second, made eye contact with him. But I quickly turned away. He had cold, piercing eyes. I had no desire to look at them.

"Write what you need to say to the outside world and tell them what we want."

I thought I'd better address my brother. He was officially my next of kin. And, with his connections, he was the one who'd be negotiating my release, as remote a possibility as release seemed. I scribbled some notes with an unsteady hand. Then I looked up at the camera.

"Cry when you speak," Sabir Mehsud ordered.

I was in such a state of numb shock that tears were impossible. Ten million dollars was an impossible amount. How could they think someone would pay that sum for me? I knew Osama Bin Laden had a bounty of twenty-five million dollars on his head, but how could they think of me as remotely in that league? It made no sense.

I took a few deep breaths and composed myself. I wanted more water but was too bewildered and scared to ask:

Dear Farrukh, I hope you're well. I'm fine and I'm being well looked after. At the moment, I'm not sure of my location but I'm being detained by the Asian Tigers. They are a very strong force. They're demanding a sum of ten million dollars for my release. Please talk to Asif and tell him to speak to his people at the channel about my predicament. I'm very sorry to have put everyone to so much trouble. Do assure everyone not to worry about me. If there's anything you can do, I'd be very grateful. They have given you a deadline of ten days to pay. The government of Pakistan is not doing anything to get me released.

Once I'd finished, Sabir Mehsud asked me to record another message, for Human Rights Watch:

This is a message for Human Rights Watch. I, Asad Qureshi, am being held by the Asian Tigers. I am a journalist and filmmaker. They are demanding ten million US dollars for my release. My family has no means to raise such an amount. I appeal to you to help me. The deadline for settlement is ten days. Please help me. I have no means of raising such an amount.

As soon as I'd finished reading this second statement, Krishan Lal put the handcuffs back on, and the shackles, and I lay back down on my bed.

Things were as bad for me as they could possibly get. The more I thought about it, the less I could understand and accept the situation. It seemed frighteningly surreal. Given KK's extensive network of connections, at the highest level, how on earth had we ended up here? It was a ridiculously impenetrable conundrum.

By now, I was an emotional wreck. Of the four of us, I was the weakest in every way. Of the four of us, as a British national, I was the most valuable. But I knew the British government had a policy of not negotiating with terrorists. And, as no one known to me was in a position to pay such a huge sum of money, my fate was sealed. I wasn't going to come out of this alive.

The shock of this reality had affected my concentration. I was finding it almost impossible to read, or write in my diary. At times, I felt as if my brain was completely empty. I had nothing to do, nothing to look forward to. I was often in a trance for several minutes, with no thoughts in my mind at all. A state of utter emptiness.

I supposed my time was up. Death had placed me in the care of these terrible people, and now they were going to kill me.

I thought about prisoners on death row. With repeated appeals, they can hold death at bay for twenty years or more before they're finally executed. At best, I had ten days.

I thought about Major Mumtaz from the ISPR, and my friends Haroon Toor and Fawad Naeem. I'd asked them all to come with me on this assignment. Thank God they hadn't.

I shook myself up. I needed to accept the situation. Make it easy on myself. No point worrying about the inevitable. The reality was no one would pay ten million dollars for me. My family would know I'd understand they were completely unable to raise that kind of money. Nobody should feel guilty. I'd decided to come here of my own free will and I now had to accept the consequences.

And there had been signs.

My words to Sherry—"If I don't come back, please forgive me." Had I known, unconsciously, I wouldn't be returning home? It had been an odd way to say good-bye, but those were the only words that had come to me.

And at the roadside, waiting for Saddam to bring the hire car. I'd spotted the white Toyota, lurking. I'd had a bad feeling. It had been justified.

It all seemed like a master plan. Fate.

For me it was the end, but for my family there would be months of pain, perhaps years. They would never completely recover. I prayed they would find peace.

My reverie was broken by the sound of KK's voice. He was shouting, perhaps one or two rooms away.

"Kill me if you like, but please let the others go. They only came here because of me."

He sounded weak and tired, but still brave. In my view, we were a team. I wouldn't want him to sacrifice himself for me. But I was deeply touched by his concern for me. My eyes filled with tears.

More voices shouting in his room. Then the voices softening. Several voices, though. Doubtless it was his turn to make a statement.

I thought about what lay in store for KK, and for Colonel Imam and Rustam.

I thought again about my parents and what they must be going through. They were such wonderful people. They didn't deserve all this.

I thought about Sherry. She'd wanted a lifetime contract with me. Instead, I'd be making her a young widow. I wondered how she'd take the news.

I felt deeply guilty. I should not have embarked on this job. I'd been incredibly selfish, naïve, and stupid. I'd wanted adventure. Well, this was adventure all right! Asif had insisted all along we send some other person to go out and shoot this film, but somehow I hadn't been able to bring myself to listen to him.

Besides, I'd reasoned, if there was danger, why should we allow someone else to face it? After all, that person would have a family who'd worry about him. I couldn't put someone else in the line of fire and sit back and make money from his efforts—that wasn't my way. I was a hands-on person. This was our project. If we wanted a film, we should be the ones on the front line, not some poor unsuspecting cameraman. I'd been right (I still think that). But I hadn't anticipated the dangers involved.

As a cameraman, I often feel detached from the action in front of me. I guess that detachment is what gives me the courage to carry on filming. I know if my mother found out the risks I often take she'd never let me out of the house.

I've interviewed many people and I've always tried to put my subject at ease before the interview has begun. And on the few occasions I myself have been interviewed, my interviewers have extended me the same courtesy and I've felt comfortable.

Today's experience in front of the camera had been horrific. I'd been forced to beg for my life and have the world watch me do it. I wouldn't wish that on my worst enemy.

I lay in my little bed, staring at the ceiling. I felt as if I had been hypnotized. I guess there was just too much to think about and, as a result, my brain had shut down.

* * *

Farrukh hadn't been in his office long when his phone rang.

"Hello. This is Ali Raza. We have sent you a video of your brother. If you want to see him again, tell the British government to give us ten million dollars. You now have ten days to come up with the money."

Before Farrukh could say anything, Ali Raza hung up.

A similar call was received by KK's family, and the Colonel's, but no ransom demand. Instead, the kidnappers were demanding the release of senior Taliban leaders. People like Mullah Baradar, Mullah Maulavi Kabir, and Mullah Mansoor Dadullah. People who'd committed truly heinous crimes.

Much as he wanted to see his brother's colleagues set free, Farrukh was certain the government would never release these men.

Mullah Baradar, believed to be number two in the hierarchy of Afghan Taliban, had been arrested the previous February in Karachi, in a joint raid conducted by US and Pakistani intelligence services. He was one of the people we'd been due to interview.

Mullah Kabir had been captured in the northwestern town of Nowshera, by Pakistani intelligence, in February 2010. Having been governor of Afghanistan's Nangarhar province while the Taliban had been in power, he'd been high on the wanted list.

Mullah Dadullah had replaced his brother Maulvi Dadullah as the top commander in southern Afghanistan during the summer of 2007. He'd been arrested by Pakistani security forces in January 2008.

Farrukh rushed to the A Team's hotel. They had warned him that this would happen. That things would get worse. That there would be videos. Disturbing things. He remembered what his old friend, Dawood, had told him about the Taliban. That they show their kidnapping victims clips of captured soldiers being slaughtered by twelve-year-old boys.

He took the lift up to the sixth floor. Nancy, Brian, and Robin greeted him. Nancy held a CD in her hand.

"The kidnappers have sent this video to the BBC and other news agencies. Since we have a pact not to publicize hostage situations involving journalists, we've prevented this video from being broadcast."

Brian explained that the main aim of the kidnappers was to gain as much publicity as possible. If the film was suppressed, their goal would be frustrated. This would make the kidnappers realize their demands would not be met with ease and it would force them to negotiate.

Nancy put the disk into her laptop and turned it in Farrukh's direction.

Farrukh looked calm and pensive but, inside, his heart was beating fast and a feeling of helplessness washed over him.

As the film played, Nancy allowed herself an occasional glance in Farrukh's direction. Apart from my voice coming from the laptop, the room was silent.

The voice stopped.

"There's more."

My voice again. The appeal to human rights watch:

This is a message for Human Rights Watch. I, Asad Qureshi, am being held by the Asian Tigers. I am a journalist and filmmaker. They are demanding ten million US dollars for my release. My family has no means to raise such an amount. I appeal to you to help me. They gave ten days for settlement. I appealed for an extension of fifteen days. Please help me. I have no means of raising such an amount.

The message ended.

There was a long pause, each person waiting for the other to say something. Robin looked at Farrukh and broke the silence.

"He's in good health. There are no signs of physical abuse. He's very composed. I think we have to be thankful for all that."

Farrukh nodded but he was lost for words. He hadn't known what to expect, but he'd known that, no matter what it was, it would be upsetting for him.

From childhood, I'd always been the one behind the camera. I'd always been the one who took the family photographs and videos. To see me front of the camera, and in these conditions, was a terrible shock for him.

With an enormous effort, he mastered himself.

"What now?"

"Well, the crux of the matter is the money. What can you arrange? Have you given any more thought to the ransom?"

Farrukh's anger boiled over.

"How do you expect me to raise ten million dollars in ten days?"

Robin looked away. To break the tension, Nancy ejected the CD and gave it to Farrukh and tried to calm him.

"Let's not lose focus now. This is going to be a long-drawn-out affair. We all need to put our thinking caps on."

But Farrukh couldn't think. He got up and left.

He knew he'd never be able to come up with such an enormous sum, even if he sold his soul. For the rest of the day, he couldn't think of anything else but the money. How on earth was this situation to be resolved?

Jacqueline's words kept running through his mind, over and over again. *The channel had paid a ransom in the past.*

So what was different now? Why was the channel putting the entire burden of this affair on him? The more he thought about the channel, the more agitated he became. He felt he was being used. Duped.

After all, it was they who'd sent me into this lawless region, with no security and apparently with no insurance. Farrukh was formally listed as the next of kin, so they were dumping the whole responsibility for the ransom on him and washing their hands.

Farrukh was a maelstrom of anger and frustration. In the evening, he spoke to Nudrat and Asghar about the A Team's behavior and how disgusted he was with them. He was beside himself with rage. Nudrat had never seen him so angry. He was going to raise hell and cut all ties with them, he said. If the channel wasn't going to help, there was no point taking instructions from them.

He spent the long night staring at the ceiling. He had just ten days to negotiate the most important deal of his life.

12
Sherry

Sherry collaborated with me on this chapter and hers is the narrative voice.

In January 1998, I was working as a flight attendant for the charter airline Tower Air. We were operating the Hajj flights—carrying planes full of faithful Muslims to Mecca for their pilgrimage.

It was our first flight into Islamabad and the first layover for all of us. We were all pretty excited, eager to explore the sights, sounds, smells, and flavors this exotic country had to offer.

First on my list was a pair of pointed shoes. After checking in at the hotel, I grabbed John, my fellow flight attendant, and hailed a cab.

"Where are we going, Sherry?"

"Shopping."

"For what?"

"Genie shoes."

John looked puzzled.

"Those little pointy slippers. How can I visit Pakistan and not leave with a pair of genie shoes!"

The streets were packed solid with traffic and people and lined with shops selling gold jewelry and stalls selling food. We passed a cow sitting on the pavement in front of a three-story shopping mall, all glass and chrome. At an intersection, a small motorcycle stopped alongside, carrying an entire family—dad, mother in front holding a two-year-old girl, and, at the back, a ten-year-old boy holding a ladder. I smiled and the boy smiled back.

Then we hit a whole street of shoe stores. Nothing else, just shoes. Heaven. Across the street, one store window had racks of colorful shoes on a display that rotated slowly. Maybe the long flight had done something to my head, but I found this simple display enchanting and simply *had* to be in that store.

I pointed across the street and told the driver to stop. But he refused to let us out on the wrong side of the road. Too dangerous, he said.

Now, this was a busy street—no doubt about it—but I'm from New York City. Which means I'm a professional jaywalker. But this driver had his own professional pride and a deep sense of responsibility for the safety of us gentle foreigners, so I didn't push it.

When we finally got turned around and onto the other side—involving maneuvers that seemed to wilfully invite collision—John and I paid the driver handsomely and headed straight for the spinning shoe racks.

Within minutes, I'd selected several pairs and was bargaining with the clerk, a young boy. But the young boy was an old hand, practiced at extracting the maximum profit from rich tourists.

I was about to settle at a price a couple of notches down from his opener when a very distinguished man sitting quietly in the corner started speaking to the young boy, in a language I took to be Urdu. At first, we assumed it was a private conversation but, as it continued, it became apparent the man was negotiating on our behalf.

When I realized this, I spoke to the man.

"Excuse me. What did you just say?"

"I told him he should give you a better price."

"That's okay. I can speak for myself."

"Well, you're not from here and he'll take advantage of you."

"I'm happy with the price I'm getting, but thanks. Who are you anyway?"

"My name is Asad Qureshi. My parents own this shop."

I thought *yeah right*. This man didn't look like a shoe salesman. Too cool. Too stylish. A bomber jacket and well-cut trousers. Everything black, apart from a pair of wonderful lime-green socks. But his shoes were a very peculiar shape, and actually rather ugly.

But they would grow on me. Just like Asad would grow on me.

John and I asked Asad to direct us to the old Rawalpindi. We were looking for scarves. Asad said we'd never be able to negotiate the labyrinth of narrow streets in the old town, and he offered to show us round, so we walked together.

It was pleasant talking to him but I wondered what the catch was. What did he want from us?

We passed a poster advertisement for cigarettes.

"That's my work."

"What do you mean?"

"I'm a filmmaker, but I also do advertising work."

Hmm. I wasn't sure about this guy at all. I knew John was thinking the same, waiting for the sell—a trip to a fancy scarf shop that happened to be run by his brother, a lunch recommendation and an inflated check in a restaurant owned by his friend, and, at the end of it, a cab driven by his uncle who'd whip out a photo album and shove it under John's nose—*My seven daughters. Which one do you want to marry?*

The streets were narrow and it was dark. There was raw sewage running down the sidewalk, so there wasn't space to walk three abreast, which meant John and I took turns walking next to Asad.

We both found him immensely interesting to talk to and would each quietly tag the other and whisper "my turn now," so each of us got to speak with this fascinating character as he led us round the bazaars of Rawalpindi.

In January in Pakistan, the days are warm but the evenings are very cold. At dusk, the air was filled with the smell of gas and charcoal and woodsmoke. Round one corner, we'd come across stalls with huge vats of milk cooking over open fires and the clamor of crowds of people, then we'd dive down a narrow passage again, then find the next corner absolutely deserted.

It was all so different and exciting. We both felt safe, although, looking back, we were completely vulnerable.

John and I joked with each other about how attractive Asad was and about which of us we thought he was interested in. "It's you," I said. And John said, "No, it's definitely you."

Asad was utterly charming. He offered to carry my bag.

"No, thanks. I have it."

"There are not many gentlemen left, so take advantage while you can."

By the time we'd finished our shopping, it was approaching midnight and Asad had spent nearly six hours showing us around. We tried to give him some money for his time, but he smiled and politely refused. We offered to take him to dinner, but he declined, explaining he was visiting from England and his mother's cooking was always the best part of the trip—no restaurant chef could match her. He spoke about his family, particularly his mother, with a warmth that was deeply affecting. I was smitten.

Over time, I would come to feel that warmth myself, and to learn some of the secrets of preparing the dishes she lovingly crafted for her precious vegetarian son.

Since Asad was refusing all our offers of recompense for his time, John came up with the idea to get a gift for his mom instead. We didn't know much about this culture, but we'd already figured it was an insult to refuse a gift.

We spotted a gorgeous embroidered shawl, and John and I bought it between us and presented Asad with a fait accompli.

I needed the bathroom, but Western-style facilities are very hard to come by in Asian cities as old as Rawalpindi. Asad said we should wait, come back to his parents' house, and use their bathroom. That way, we could also present the gift to his mother personally.

When we arrived, his parents were both still up, although it was well past midnight. His mother and father met us at the door, looking distinctly unhappy, perhaps because of how late it was or because Asad was bringing home strangers.

Asad introduced us and also explained we needed the bathroom. John went first. While he was away, there was a very heated exchange between Asad and his mother which, although conducted in a language I didn't remotely understand, left me in no doubt that his mother was very upset indeed.

Feeling responsible, and wanting to defuse the tension, I dashed off to get the shawl we'd bought for Asad's mother. I presented it with a smile and with my head bowed. Whatever the problem was, maybe the shawl would make it go away. She accepted it graciously but I could see it hadn't completely done the trick. Her face was veiled with emotion. Not just anger. Something else. Fear?

At that moment, John returned from bathroom.

"Let's give her the shawl."

"I just gave it to her."

"Without me?"

"You don't understand how upset she is."

In his parents' eyes, Asad is a foreigner in Pakistan. He was born there, but he was raised in England. As a foreigner staying in Pakistan, they see him as vulnerable. They weren't angry about the lateness of the hour. They weren't offended he'd brought strangers to the house.

They thought he'd been abducted.

Most of my aircrew colleagues were not getting layovers, especially not regularly in the same place. But just a week after my first trip to Islamabad, and an afternoon and evening in Asad's delightful company, John and I again found ourselves exhausted from a long and busy flight, standing in the same hotel lobby waiting for the keys to our rooms.

We had the afternoon to ourselves, and John went off to see if the hotel had a pool. He came back with news. There was a very nice restaurant and there was a pool. A pool with a big party going on around it, thrown by the famous mountaineer and environmental campaigner Nazir Sabir. There were journalists, cameras.

"And guess who's also there?"

"Who?"

"Asad."

Yeah right. Asad had left for England last week. The day we'd met him was the last day of his stay in Pakistan. He'd caught a flight home the following day. John was messing with me.

But the fresh air would do me good after ten hours of pressurized cabin, so I decided to humor him. John was right—there was a pool.

When I came back in, John looked excited.

"Did you see him?"

"Nice try. I saw the pool, though. Looks good."

"He's here! Come. Come on. I'll show you."

We stood on the terrace and I scanned the crowd. John pulled me down the steps and along a side wall. He stopped at the corner and beckoned me with a flick of his head.

I stepped round the corner and came face to face with Nazir Sabir. The famous climber was laughing and joking with a friend. A distinguished man in snappy clothes.

"I thought you were leaving for England."

"I was supposed to. Work. I had to change my flight."

He smiled.

"And you said you wouldn't have any more layovers here."

"Well, we shouldn't have. They changed it two days ago. A fluke."

We'd spent a pleasant afternoon and evening the previous week, but that had been it. No numbers exchanged. No plans. No future.

But here we were.

After his meeting with Nazir Sabir was over, Asad joined John and me in a Chinese restaurant nearby. The food was pretty good but it was the conversation that sparkled. Asad was interesting and funny—he often had us both in stitches—and again I found him charming.

And his manners were impeccable, stemming from what I saw as an impressive sense of decency and thoughtfulness. He seemed constantly to be seeking to do things that would make us—me, in particular—most comfortable. It was beguiling.

I asked him if he'd have time to help me do some shopping the following day—I just wanted more time in his company.

He took me to handicraft shops. Again he negotiated prices on my behalf. This made me a little uncomfortable. I felt he was being too hard on the locals—they had to make money too. But he was adamant he didn't want me to be taken advantage of.

He took me to one shop that sold wonderful glassware from Herat, in Afghanistan. We had a lot of fun looking at vases, fabulous turquoises and deep, deep blues. My friends back home were going to love them.

It was a few months before we met again. Another chance layover. He was back in Pakistan in connection with a film he was editing, and again he was meeting with his friend Nazir Sabir. Both men were sitting in the lobby coffee bar when I walked into the hotel with my case. You couldn't miss Asad—always stylishly dressed in clothes that really stood out, this time a lavender shirt with a red cravat tucked inside it. Rakish and refined at the same time. He looked impossibly handsome.

Both men stood up as I approached and both greeted me warmly, Asad with sparkling eyes.

"I hope I'm not breaking up the meeting?"

"No, not at all," said Nazir. "We've just finished, haven't we?"

I looked at Asad.

"Do you have time for tea?"

"Sure."

"I'll check in and dump my bags."

I rushed to my room, dropped the bags and freshened up with as much speed as I could muster. I dashed back down, then slowed to a saunter when I hit the lobby.

Nazir had left. Asad ordered some tea.

We talked for two hours. About our families, our jobs, what we wanted for ourselves. I admitted to tiring of the transcontinental life.

He smiled, mischievously.

"You should find yourself a nice man and get married."

My heart was in my mouth. His words had brought tears to my eyes. I knew what I wanted.

"Can that nice man be you?" My heart was pounding.

Asad did a double take—my words had floored him—but he smiled. That smile!

He was leaving the country the following day. I couldn't keep leaving this to chance. I might never have seen him again. For me, it was now or never.

The following morning, he called me from the airport.

"I've thought about nothing else."

"Me either."

"We're of different faiths, of course."

"I don't see that as a problem."

One phone call and my life had changed. I was in shock.

Those lime-green socks. They'd been the first thing to catch my eye, but I'd fallen for the man himself on first sight.

I returned to Jeddah, the city in Saudi Arabia where we operated out of and where, already, I was studying Islam with some Muslims I knew.

So many practical questions now! Where would we be married? Where would we live? How would I tell my mother and, most importantly, my grandfather? I was really close to him. We had a great relationship. He was always kidding me. I thought of something he'd said the last time we'd been together.

"So, you gonna be an old maid?"

"What are you talking about?"

"That's what we used to say. If a woman got to thirty and is still single."

"Well, you're the one who told me not to get married till I ran out of things to do."

"That's right."

"I haven't run out of things to do."

"Hmm. Maybe we should redefine that."

Well, now I had. I couldn't wait to tell him. I knew the news would be bitter-sweet for him. As a devout Christian, he'd worry for my soul. As with all religions, the Christians think they're the only ones going to heaven. For that reason, I wanted to tell him face to face.

I phoned my mom from Jeddah and told her the news. She asked about Asad and I told her what a charming, intelligent, and fascinating gentleman he was. I told her about his parents and their lovely big house in Islamabad.

She said she was thrilled, and she certainly sounded it, but there was a note of reserve too. I knew what would be going through her mind. She'd seen a lot of movies about conflicts in interracial marriages. She'd be sceptical. And not just about race and faith.

We were southern people. My family's accomplishments were from blood, sweat, and tears. Nobody we knew had servants. Nobody in our family had ever been to college. I wanted to say, *Don't worry, Mom,* but that would have been admitting I knew what she was thinking.

At least now she could start getting used to the idea and start working on strangling her worries and complexes. But my grandfather would have to wait.

Except my five-year-old cousin, Owen, had other plans. She'd overheard my mother talking about my news quietly with a friend. A couple of days later, she was helping my grandfather clear under the house. It's a pier-and-beam type, with a space about 4 feet high under it, dark and full of cobwebs and spiders and perhaps a snake or two. My grandfather was bent double, pulling up weeds, when Owen spoke.

"So what you going to wear to Sherry's wedding, Papa?"

My grandfather was so shocked, he stood bolt upright and hit his head on the bottom of the house.

When we moved to Texas a few years later, Asad spent a lot of time with my grandfather. I enjoyed sitting back and watching the two of them interact, these two men I loved.

Asad was remodeling our little house in Texas and, gentleman that he was, would ask my grandfather for advice. The older man would sometimes look over Asad's shoulder at me and smile. He was very fond of my young man and genuinely happy for me.

Sometimes the two of them would surprise me at work (I was now in sales and marketing) and I would take my break with them. Asad had the bona fide Texan hat just like my grandfather's, which my Papa had selected for him *so you don't look like a drugstore cowboy.*

But some Texan ways can't be taught. One summer's night, the three of us were driving along a dusty track near the house, the windows down. Asad wrinkled his nose.

"Do you smell petrol?"

We two Texans in the car erupted into laughter. One thing you don't get in London—skunks.

Life together in Pakistan wasn't easy.

We lived in Islamabad, in Asad's parents' gorgeous house, with its ample grounds, its fine furniture, and its servants.

But I was never completely at home there. I was a grown woman. I'd always been independent and in charge of my life. Surrounded by servants and security staff, I felt stifled.

I frequently talked to Asad about us getting our own place. I didn't care what. A three-room house, rented. Just something we could call our own. A house I could put together myself and fill with all the things we'd picked up from our travels around the world. We'd be surrounded by our stories, a constant reminder of our life together, the two of us.

But Asad enjoyed talking to his parents and would stay up late into the night, never coming to bed until he'd massage his mom's legs to relieve her constant pain and, having dismissed the servants, heated some milk for her to take to bed.

He was a very devoted son. It was one of the reasons I'd fallen in love with him. But his devotion was beginning to drive me away.

While I loved and respected his parents, and enjoyed talking to them in the evenings, I spoke the language hardly at all, so there was a limit to how involved I could be. Besides, sometimes I just wanted us to snuggle up together and watch a movie.

But whenever I mentioned a house of our own, he was evasive and came up with reasons for us to stay where we were. I knew he'd never leave, and I felt like I couldn't stay.

And the film trips, which he couldn't take me on, became longer and more frequent. I became resentful.

Two days before he was due to leave to meet Khalid and the Colonel, I made the decision to pack up and move back to Texas. If I left while he was away, I reasoned to myself, it wouldn't cause him as much pain. In my heart, I knew I just didn't want to be around to see it.

I posted a message on Facebook—*I'm wondering how the job market is in Texas now? My strong point is marketing and sales. Does anyone have a room for rent, or a garage apartment?*

When he was leaving, I tried to hide the emotional turmoil I was in. He, too, seemed unusually disturbed.

"If I don't come back, please forgive me."

"Well, I'll have another kiss please."

"Sherry, I really must go. People are waiting for me. We've delayed long enough."

With that, he left. That only strengthened my resolve to escape from Pakistan now, without having to face him. Besides, his parents were preparing to leave for England, for his niece Aisha's wedding. I'd have the house to myself to pack and go.

Then Farrukh came and told us the bad news. I couldn't believe he'd been taken. Then, a few days later, Khalid's family came and told us they were delayed because there was more work to be done. Khalid's wife kept visiting to speak with Asad's parents. I felt sidelined and frustrated. Not having direct contact with him was driving me crazy.

I tried to convince myself he was simply under house arrest. Three meals a day, with tea at 4:00 p.m. sharp. An armed man at the door. I imagined him sitting around in a comfortable house, playing cards, watching old movies, and talking about politics. Talking about how this movie they were making was going to be even bigger, now that they'd been captured.

It would be just like him to put a positive spin on the situation. He'd even be trying to film interviews with his captors.

And he's such a demanding person on issues like cleanliness and diet. It was not unusual for him to take three or four showers a day and change into fresh clothes, freshly pressed by the servants.

He was obsessive. Everything had to be just right. Only food prepared by his mother, by his sisters, or (at a pinch) by me was ever good enough.

I imagined his fussiness driving his captors mad. They'd probably release him soon just to get rid of him. He always wanted to be in control of the situation.

I remembered one day on our honeymoon, when he drove my mother and grandfather up to the Murree hills. The road was very narrow. We came face to face with a police vehicle. Machine guns hanging out of the back and sides.

An officer stepped out and Asad went up to greet him. They spoke in Urdu. I looked at the guns and shouted to him to get back in the car. Asad ignored me. The officer pointed. He appeared to be ordering Asad to back up and let them pass.

I pleaded with him again, and again he ignored me.

A minute later, after much discussion, Asad climbed back into the car.

"What's happening?"

"It will be just a moment. They're going to back up so we can pass."

He was fearless. Except in the face of frogs.

We'd been married just three days. Asad went to brush his teeth. I heard a shriek from the bathroom.

"What's wrong?"

"You must do something."

"What is it?"

"A frog. Here. In the bathroom."

"Well, get it out."

"I can't. I'm sorry. I'm afraid. Can you do it for me?"

A tiny baby frog. The kind my brother and I used to catch by the bucketful. I threw my shawl on it, gathered it up, and laid it on the ground outside. I watched it hop away.

Farrukh advised me to move out of the house. The kidnappers might have extracted information from Asad, including the fact his wife was an American. The last thing Farrukh needed was to have me kidnapped as well.

Well, I'd already made the difficult decision to leave, so of course I was happy to comply with Farrukh's wishes.

But, when I packed up, I was careful to leave some things behind. I didn't want to strip the place of all my things. I wanted to minimize the impact of my absence on Asad. I was leaving him, but he was still the love of my life.

I thought again of the conditions he might be experiencing, and I tried my best to picture him under comfortable house arrest.

After all, Pakistanis are renowned for their hospitality. If you go to someone's house, they always offer you refreshments of some sort. Usually the best they have to offer, even if they're a desperately poor family and this is the last morsel they have, they offer it to you. Even if they don't know where the next meal is coming from. Kindness is cultural.

Then I remembered Asad's parting words. Had that just been one of his melodramatic moods? Or had he had some sort of premonition?

I spent the following couple of days scurrying around, packing, preparing for the trip, and visiting favorite places one last time. There were no friends to say goodbye to—I didn't have any. I was completely alone. Asad was all I had to live for in Pakistan. And now he was gone.

Two suitcases were all I took. I left behind so much of my life. Things I'd collected from my travels around the world. And family heirlooms it broke my heart not to take, particularly a tea set that was my Italian grandmother's, that she'd bought in Japan. I remembered, as a young girl, holding the cups up to the light to make the delicate painting of a geisha come to life, like a hologram. It was the only thing I had from that grandmother, who had passed away many years ago.

And a smaller version of the set that my best friend, Karrie, got for me, knowing how much I'd love it. Karrie, too, now passed away.

No room for either of them.

But some mementos I did have room for. One of Asad's passport photos, a recent one. Another photo of him with his trademark pink scarf. The scarf itself, which I liberally sprayed with his Bronnley English Fern cologne and put in a plastic ziplock bag.

I remembered, the week we were married, standing on a restaurant balcony, a big family event going on inside. The scent of his cologne wandered out to meet me and, without looking, I put out my hand and pulled his seven-year-old nephew close to me. He'd been messing around in Asad's things.

Cologne to comfort me. To go with the memories. To make me smile. Whenever I'd have a dream, I'd smile and remember how he'd ask me about a dream, then put on an analyst's face and decipher it. He'd work so hard to keep a straight face and convince me his interpretations were valid, and not the hokum I knew them to be, that I'd burst out laughing at his solemnity.

He made me laugh a lot. I was going to miss that.

I went to stay at Farrukh's house. It was like living in a very swish hotel—immaculate decoration, luxurious furnishings, cordon bleu cooking—but with a lovely intimate and fun atmosphere that his wife and daughters effortlessly created.

They took it upon themselves to entertain me, to keep my mind off the horrible reality of my husband's absence. They played games with me. They took me to the movies. They took me to dinner at fancy restaurants.

And Farrukh was patience and serenity itself. I was not to worry. He'd talk to the kidnappers. He'd keep me posted. There was no real cause for concern.

But each day we waited. Each day we heard nothing. Farrukh was working tirelessly to find Asad and figure out who the kidnappers were. But he also had a busy law practice, one that frequently involved international travel. He'd had to put all that on hold. He'd had to disappoint a lot of people. Influential people. But for him the choice was clear.

I decided I should be completely honest with him, and I told him I'd already been planning to leave Asad, before the kidnapping. He was very troubled by this revelation but he respected my choices and my reasons. Understood them, even. Again, he told me not to worry. He would take care of everything once Asad came back.

"How long will that take, do you think? How long do these things usually take?"

"Months, not weeks."

It was hard to throw everything on his shoulders but I knew I needed to leave, and I knew if I didn't go right away, I'd probably never go. And nothing would change. And I couldn't accept that.

Farrukh was a man of immense mental strength. When he said he would take care of something, you just knew he would.

He'll never know how much I appreciated his strength at that time. And his support for my decision, even though he knew it would likely break his brother's heart.

In the departure lounge, we watched TV. Me, Farrukh, and his trusted friend, Asghar. A news report came on, about the kidnapping. Asad was not mentioned by name, but they mentioned Khalid and the Colonel.

I began to shake. I had to work hard not to cry. My husband was being held against his will, doubtless in horrendous conditions, possibly by a bunch of amoral fanatics. And I was leaving him. Abandoning him. It was too much to bear.

Farrukh told me not to worry. If I was not happy, my decision was sound, and I should stick to it. He would deal with everything.

Asghar produced an envelope thick with money. At least $10,000. He pressed it on me. I said no.

"You'll need it. There'll be a ransom. Whatever I need, I'll get from my family. But thank you. It means a lot."

My flight changed in Dubai. In the bathroom in Dubai airport, I got to talking with a fellow passenger. She talked about her husband—she was looking forward to seeing him again. Then she asked me if I was married. I fell apart and told her everything. I just needed to let it out. And this total stranger just happened to be there.

My heart was in turmoil. I felt Asad had chosen his family over me. And I appeared to have chosen mine. But I still felt terrible. I prayed. Asked for guidance. I loved my husband—I *still* love him—but I knew I could never go back to Pakistan. Yet should I be holding on to our marriage? Holding on to some future together?

13
Thoughts of Suicide

Captain's log, star date … unknown.

That's what I scribbled in my diary. I'd lost track of time since my last entry and had settled into a routine of boredom and inactivity. I tried to work out how many entries I'd missed—how many days—but my thoughts and memories were a muddle.

Looking back over previous entries, I saw my diary was a pretty grim read. Doom and gloom. Time for humor.

It's strange how certain events haunt us. I remember vividly seeing the television images of John F. Kennedy's assassination. I was six years of age at the time. I've seen the same images, and others from that awful day, countless times since. Each time I see them I am once again a six-year-old boy standing in my parents' drawing room in Islamabad.

Two other world events I remember very clearly. The Iran hostage crisis, which started in November 1979 and lasted for 444 days, and the Soviet invasion of Afghanistan, which began in December 1979 and lasted for ten years.

I was working as a production runner on the film *Reds* when these events hit the news. As a young man looking to make his way in the film business, I devoured news reports on these incidents from the safety of my cocoon in England.

Then a friend working in documentaries asked me to go with him to Afghanistan to film the Mujahedeen fighting the Soviets. Excitement at last.

But it was short lived. My mother put her foot down. No way was her precious son walking into the valley of the shadow of death. So the BBC was the closest I ever got to the Soviet-Afghan war. Its images, though, still haunt me to this day.

Just like the number 444. How had those poor American hostages survived 444 days in captivity?

How many days had it been for me? No idea. Who'd have thought I'd end up in a hole like this? Well, lots of people, actually. I'd been operating in danger zones for years. Was it inevitable? Was there some sense in which I'd not only expected it but actively willed it? To validate me in some strange way? Or was that superstition?

I remembered an incident on a fishing boat. I'd been filming a report. I'd begun to whistle. Immediately, the fishermen asked me to stop. The wind is the fisherman's enemy, I was told. Whistling in the wind encourages the wind and brings trouble for the fisherman. Fishermen are superstitious people.

Was I being the same? Just prey to ridiculous superstition?

These uneasy thoughts had taken me into the outside world. An outside world I suddenly realized I might never see again.

I was a prisoner. That's all I was. That was my identity. A prisoner of men who had no respect for humanity. They reveled in inflicting physical pain and mental torment, and I was powerless to fight back.

I knew that, had I been a free man looking at this situation, I would have said, "I'd rather die than go through that humiliation." But I'd already suffered that humiliation. And now here I was with a ten-million-dollar ransom on my head. I'd never heard of anyone paying such a sum for a person's release, let alone a person like me. I wasn't important or famous. I wasn't worth ten million dollars. And nobody would pay such a sum for me.

I couldn't possibly see a way out. I was going to die here.

I thought about my parents and how worried they'd be. My mum especially. She'd be wondering what they were feeding me, whether the place was clean, how they were treating me. She'd be worried. She was a twenty-four-hour worrier at the best of times. But these weren't the best of times, and I had no idea how long these times would last. 444 days?

My elderly parents were already carrying the usual health problems that come with age. This extra burden of worry I was piling onto them would only be making their health worse. My father was a pragmatic man and would be suffering in silence, but my mother would be praying and weeping and damaging her health.

I think sometimes it's better to bring finality to a problem rather than prolong it. I'd become a source of great pain for my family, and they didn't deserve to suffer. And I didn't want to suffer anymore either.

That thought made my situation immediately unbearable. Confinement. Dirt. The putrid smell from the container I had to urinate in. I wished they'd just burst in and shoot me now and get it over with.

I looked up and saw a wooden beam running right across the ceiling. The ceiling was low.

Years ago, I worked on the television series *Traffik*. I learned how to tie a hangman's knot from the special-effects man. I looked at the drawstring on my *shalwar*. At the water bucket.

It would be quick. I would escape their threats and their beatings. I would escape this misery. This uncertainty. I smiled at the thought of them finding my lifeless body. No collateral. Nothing to bargain with. No ten million dollars for them.

They were laughing now, but the last laugh would be on me. It was a tantalizing thought.

I fixated on the beam. It seemed to be beckoning me. I could prepare everything during the hours when I was not handcuffed or shackled. I'd stand on the bucket, tie the knot around the beam, then hide it by laying it along the beam's top side. I'd wash with the water from the bucket. I'd wear clean clothes from my black bag, still in the corner of the room.

I'd do it in the night. To stop the chain from jangling, I'd wrap it tight around my legs. That would work. I'd do it in the middle of the night. When they were all asleep. That beam would be my passport to freedom from this hell. To a world from which no one has ever returned.

I started to prepare myself to die. I thought of my family. Time to say goodbye.

I thought of my father and what a wise, supportive, and wonderful dad he'd been to me. Of my mother, who had the knack of making all her children feel special—to me that made her the most beautiful woman in the world. I loved them both and felt so privileged to have been part of their lives. To have been their son. I'd always caused them the greatest concern. I'd always done unwise and dangerous things. But they'd always accepted and supported and forgiven me. I loved them so much.

One by one, I thought of my siblings. My older sister and older brother. My younger sister and younger brother. And me in the middle. Wednesday's child. So full of woe.

I thought of my wife, Sherry. I remembered the time we lived together in Texas. What a rough time we'd had. All the ups and downs. The rows. I remembered the day she'd brought a fleet of trucks to the house and emptied it of all our furniture. Then she'd emptied our bank account. Such a low time for me. In an alien place, my relationship in ruins, and me thousands of miles away from my family.

Looking for consolation, I'd phoned my elder sister, Rakhshindah. During our conversation, I'd begun to cry. She'd comforted me with kind, uplifting words.

"Asad, you are the strongest man I know."

I remembered an assignment to film a mountaineering expedition to Mount Everest in 1997. On the way to Advance Base Camp, I'd become exhausted in the rarefied atmosphere. I'd told my colleagues to carry on while I rested for a while.

I'd lain down on a rock and had made the very dangerous mistake of falling asleep. In such extreme conditions, it takes only a few minutes for hypothermia to set in. You never wake up.

I'd had a dream. My mother was shaking me with great force, and shouting at me to open my eyes. I'd sat up immediately.

My mother had connected with me in a dream and had saved my life.

Looking up at the beam again, I shook my head. How could I let my sister down by killing myself? To her, I was the strongest man she knew. And my mother had always watched over me. Every day, she came out into the driveway to see me off to work. She'd mumble a prayer then blow on me, so the prayer would protect me.

How could I take my own life now? Destroy what they'd worked so hard to preserve and nourish?

It was such a cowardly response to my situation. And so selfish. They would blame me, and rightly so, for giving up. For turning my back on the possibility of escape. If my captors murdered me, well, my family would remember a cherished loved one who had died if not with dignity then at least with honor.

I sighed with relief. I had talked myself out of it.

Then it occurred to me that, as a Muslim, I am forbidden from taking my own life. I thought about my faith, and I began to draw strength from it. I was not at the mercy of these crazy people, monsters who groom children into becoming suicide bombers. Islam prohibits suicide and it prohibits murder. The notion of a suicide bomber's actions opening the door to heaven is a gross misinterpretation of Islam. The innocent victims of suicide bombers will go to heaven but the bombers will not.

I was not at the mercy of these people. I was at the mercy of God alone.

In order to survive, I knew I had to put up a fight. I resolved to make some changes. I would eat the food they gave me (I was growing tired of biscuits and milk anyway) and I would embrace the lack of hygiene around me.

I remembered my mum telling me about her uncle. He'd been a prisoner of war, held in the jungle for weeks by the Japanese. He and his fellow prisoners had only ever eaten at night. That way, they hadn't had to see the insects crawling over their food.

That uncle survived. He'd been strong. He'd come home, got married, and had several children and a good life. I would be strong, too (although perhaps not strong enough to eat bug-infested food).

Your life isn't your own. It belongs to your family and friends. To the people who love you.

I settled back on my little bed and looked up at the beam that had almost enticed me to end my life. My situation wasn't good, but I had the strength to survive as long as I could. I'd always told myself my motto was: *No is not an answer and defeat is not an option*. Now it was time to live according to that principle.

If they decided to kill me, there was nothing I could do about that. But I knew I wasn't going to kill myself.

I thought about a future life outside. If I ever got out, I'd make some real changes.

I'd begin with Sherry. I made a list in my diary of the places I'd like to take her. Number one on my list was Lahore and the old city. She'd adore it. She'd be bowled over by the Mogul architecture and, as a foodie, she'd delight in the fragrant and spicy Punjabi cuisine. I'd enjoy showing her the sights, enjoy the feel of her hand in mine as we walked around the city, enjoy the light in her eyes as she gazed up at the enormous white marble domes of the Badshahi Mosque.

Next on the list were the northern areas. Spectacular mountains and lakes. The legendary Khyber Pass. But in more peaceful times, perhaps.

Sherry and I had always had a tumultuous relationship—we were two very different people, from completely dissimilar backgrounds. And life in Pakistan was hard for her, even without the strains that my job imposed. Sometimes she could accompany me when I was on location somewhere, but there were times when it just wasn't practical or safe. That meant periods apart that were hard for both of us, but perhaps especially for Sherry, stranded in a foreign place and a foreign culture with hardly any friends and no independence. *Driving test. Must deal with that when I'm out.* At least then she'd be able to get out and about while I was away. Knowing she had some freedom to enjoy herself would make me miss her less when I was away. I always missed her then.

I missed her now.

The low hum of activity outside my room stilled. Meal time. But, as always, one voice made itself heard—that of Krishan Lal. Such a loudmouth. I could even hear him eating—chewing loudly, licking his fingers, and burping. Perhaps table manners were too much to expect from such an animal.

As always, it was only when they'd finished eating that they'd deliver food to my room.

Mukhtar brought in a plate of rice and placed it on the floor. As always, he stood for a second, waiting for my instruction to take it away.

"Can I have a spoon, please?"

"You are going to eat this?"

"Yes."

In this part of the world, people eat rice with their hands, but that was not my custom. A spoon might not be easy to find. But Mukhtar dashed off and, a few seconds later, returned with a spoon. I examined the spoon to make sure it was clean, which it was, relatively.

I took a mouthful of the rice. There was too much salt and oil in it, which gave it a rather gooey texture. But this was prison food and I was a prisoner, so I took a few more spoonfuls. Then the salt content became too much. I wondered how my friends were coping with this food. I slipped the spoon into my pocket in case, the next time, Mukhtar wasn't so obliging.

When he came back to collect the plate, I thanked him. I thought it only right to show some appreciation.

"You are very lucky. You are being treated like a VIP. We have had people here for over ten years. They live in holes in the ground. They have long hair and long fingernails."

"Really?"

"Yes. We have about twenty places like this. Where we keep people. And our people are everywhere. In the army. In the government. All over the world."

I looked at him quizzically.

"We are not a small organization."

"I believe you. And I appreciate the kindness shown to me, by you in particular. You seem not like the others. You seem … better."

Mukhtar just stared at me.

"As if you deserve better than this."

Mukhtar continued to stare. He picked up the plate and left. He hadn't noticed there was no spoon.

I washed the spoon with my bar of soap and packed it in a little plastic bag I had in my clothes bag, to keep dust and insects off it. Then I hid it under my bed, ready for the next mealtime.

My switch into survival mode was already making my situation more bearable, and the small triumph of the spoon lifted my spirits further. Then I looked around my shabby and stinking cell and thought about what Mukhtar had said. If this was what they called VIP treatment, these people must have had a very basic and animalistic upbringing indeed. I thought about what he'd said about holes in the ground. No way could I have coped with that.

But maybe these were all scare stories. After all, if the Asian Tigers were as big as Mukhtar said, how come I'd never heard of them before? And why would they have Krishan Lal, an Indian, in their number? It didn't make sense. Even if Krishan Lal was a Muslim, he was still from India and an enemy of Pakistan and therefore of the other men. And what about the man from the last interrogation, whose accent I couldn't place?

The whole sinister affair was beyond my comprehension. There must be some greater force at play here. If what Mukhtar had said was right, and their people had infiltrated the government and the armed forces, and had not just sympathizers but agents in high places, how was that going to affect any negotiations for my release? Would it help or hinder? I didn't know.

Late into the night I was jerked awake by a deafening noise. Automatic gunfire. Rocket-propelled grenades screaming through the air, then exploding thunderously. It sounded like the apocalypse was happening just outside my room, with firing from either side and me in the middle.

The walls of my mud hut were about 2 feet thick, but the roof was thatched and flimsy. If a grenade landed on the roof, the whole structure would be blown away, and I'd be buried under the rubble. Handcuffed and shackled. No escape.

The ground shook with the force of a huge explosion just feet away from my hut. What was going on? A few hours earlier, I'd seriously contemplated suicide. Now I found myself in the middle of a battle. Death was stalking me.

Well, if this was my time, I had no option but to wait for death to tap me on the shoulder.

Had the army tracked us down? Was this a rescue attempt? Or perhaps a rival terrorist outfit was storming the place, looking to grab us for themselves.

Still the noise came. The cracking of rifles. The whir and scream of grenades. The ground-shaking thunder of their impact.

After about an hour, the noise stopped, as if someone had flicked a switch. I looked around. Miraculously, my room remained totally intact, and I was completely unharmed. I thought of my colleagues and hoped they were all right.

The next morning Mukhtar came in to unlock my handcuffs for morning prayers, looking casual, as if nothing had happened the night before.

"What was all the firing about?"

"It was nothing."

I thought better of pushing the point. Mukhtar was a temperamental man. No point in provoking another beating.

I asked him for another roll of toilet paper and for fresh batteries for my flashlight. I allowed myself a moment of half hoping this would be my last roll and my last set of batteries, but of course it wouldn't be.

There was no end in sight. And I was running out of things to keep my mind occupied. I'd counted all the countries in the world, and all their capitals. I'd counted actors and directors, vegetables and flowers, all the states in America. I'd gone round and round these lists several times. My mind was stale.

My body was suffering too. My muscles and joints were stiff from lack of use. People in solitary confinement can usually expect an hour's exercise a day—I wasn't getting any, apart from the walk to the outside toilet.

I longed to see the world again. To stretch my limbs under a blue sky and fill my lungs with fresh, clean air.

I longed for freedom.

Impatience and irritation crowded in on me again. Why was I here? What had I done wrong? What gave these men the right to deprive me of my freedom?

I thought again of the American hostages held in Tehran for 444 days. 1979, then all through 1980 and into 1981.

Thirty years later, here I was. A hostage in a foreign land. Who knew for how much longer?

14
Farrukh Meets Mr. Z

April 18, 2010, was Farrukh's first day alone in Islamabad. With the exception of his eldest daughter, Sarah, his family was now in England. Safety for them. Freedom for him to focus on getting me out.

But it was hard to focus. He'd been neglecting his many influential clients and some of them were making impatient noises. On top of that, he wasn't sleeping. He knew he'd need to fix both of these things in order to be as efficient a negotiator as possible.

The A Team called. The kidnappers had sent another video to the news agencies. They were emailing him a copy.

He watched the video with Nudrat. He saw me with a long grey beard. He knew I was scrupulous about shaving daily and deduced the beard was a demonstration of control by the kidnappers. He was upset at how much weight I'd lost.

I was holding on my chest a copy of *Dawn*, Pakistan's respected English-language daily newspaper, to prove I was alive on the day it was issued. A dirty sheet on the wall provided the backdrop to the dimly lit scene.

"Looks like some sort of cave," Nudrat said.

They listened to me read the words Sabir Mehsud had written out for me to speak. They heard Mehsud's grammatical mistake, which I'd deliberately not corrected in the hope people would see these were not my own words.

"My name is Asad Qureshi. I am an England citizen. Please have them set me free. I am being detained by the Asian Tigers."

Farrukh and Nudrat watched the video a second time—Farrukh wanted to see if my hands were tied. Then, because he'd been unsettled by the A Team's mention of torture, he watched the video a third time to look for any sign I'd been mistreated. But the image was dark. He couldn't be sure.

Videos of KK and Colonel Imam were sent through by the A Team. The format was the same, with the same location, but with, in each case, an Urdu daily newspaper as proof of life.

"My name is Khalid Khawaja. I have been in the air force for eighteen years and I was in the ISI for two years. I came here on the request of General Hamid Gul, General Mirza Aslam Beg, and the ISI's Colonel Sajjad."

Colonel Imam's statement was similar to KK's.

"My name is Sultan Amir. I am better known as Colonel Imam. I was in the army for eighteen years and eleven years in the ISI. When I came to Waziristan I discussed it with General Mirza Aslam Beg."

These short statements were bombshells for Farrukh. Up to that point, he'd harbored the belief that the presence of KK and Colonel Imam was a trump card—their influence over the Taliban would get us all out of any situation. But the videos made it clear we were being held on charges of spying.

Farrukh knew that no person charged with being a spy had ever walked out of Waziristan alive.

To be linked so closely and publicly to former and serving members of the ISI was, however untrue, catastrophic for our cause and for Farrukh's chances of negotiating a successful outcome.

The email that accompanied the videos was even more disturbing.

Khalid Khawaja and Col. Imam in Taliban custody. Both ISI persons are enemy of Islam and Muslims. We demand release of Mullah Baradar, Mullah Mansoor Dadullah, and Maulavi Kabir. We will send list of other mujahedeen within a few days. Ten days time, if government not released mujahedeen, then we will kill ISI officers or other decision.

Or other decision.

Was that a sign that there was some flexibility? Or did it mean that they were planning to kill those not accused of being ISI members?

Would they start by killing the least important person in the group? Who would that be, in their eyes? He thought of Rustam. A humble man. But a man who had colluded with people the kidnappers regarded as the enemy. In their eyes, he was disposable. It seemed a distinct possibility they would kill Rustam first.

Once again the news agencies kept their word and observed a blackout on reporting about me, but the videos of KK and Colonel Imam had started to play on the television channels.

The newspapers carried statements from the generals refuting claims in the videos that they had directed KK and Colonel Imam to go to Waziristan. General Hamid Gul admitted having met KK the night before he left, but emphasized he'd advised KK to be careful, as foreign agencies were working in the area.

Usama was constantly being contacted by Usman Punjabi, urging him to arrange the ransom so his father and his companions could be released. The hapless Usama did not, of course, have the contacts or the resources to procure what Punjabi was demanding and had no option but to tell him that he was trying his best. Whenever he pressed Punjabi for help and guidance, Punjabi always responded by saying he was only a media spokesperson and had no influence over what the kidnappers did and he could offer Usama no practical advice in getting his father back, which left Usama feeling desperate and miserable.

The following morning, he and Major Nauman went to see Farrukh and told him they were both now receiving calls from Usman Punjabi. Punjabi had given them a list of prisoners the kidnappers wanted released. In spite of his insistences that he was just a middle man, it seemed to them Punjabi was involving himself in the negotiations. Major Nauman remarked that Ali Raza, the kidnapper who had made the original calls, had warned him to beware of a third party who may call with demands. Had Ali Raza been talking about Usman Punjabi?

It was not at all clear to Farrukh what the status of Punjabi was. Was he one of the kidnappers? If so, why was he making calls when Ali Raza seemed to be the guy in charge? Was that evidence of a split in the kidnappers' camp? If not, what game was he playing? Why were they putting up with his nonsense? Nothing was making sense.

Farrukh tried to stay calm, and he reassured Usama they would unravel this tangled mess, all the while thinking ten million dollars was an impossible sum to raise. Even if the British government wanted to pay the ransom, which seemed unlikely, he thought they would probably come under pressure from foreign governments not to negotiate.

Farrukh went to see the A Team. He was advised by Brian that, given the size of the ransom being demanded, there was no quick fix. The key, he said, was to avoid appearing desperate and, in talking to the kidnappers, to incorporate as many delaying tactics as possible. The longer the process took, the easier it would become to negotiate and the stronger the team's position would be.

Farrukh told Brian he was uneasy about playing a long game. I was his younger brother. An uptight clean freak who wouldn't last long in an environment of squalor.

Brian dismissed Farrukh's concerns. The long game was the only game to play, he insisted. The only way that might get me back at all.

Brian suggested he should ham it up.

Farrukh, a sober and serious individual, regarded this piece of advice with disdain. If the game was to be cool and avoid appearing desperate, he would play that game with a straight bat, not indulge in histrionics.

He was also told my website needed to come down as soon as possible. The kidnappers could use it to learn more about my background and my associations with UK TV channels, all of which would be harmful to our cause. And it was once again stressed that both the government and the name of the channel should be kept out of the conversation.

Farrukh left the A Team feeling despondent and none the wiser as to how the situation was likely to resolve.

And his worries were not confined solely to my welfare. He had our mum and dad to shield from this torment as well. Now that my niece's wedding was over, they'd have more time to dwell on my situation. In England, they had access to Pakistani television channels and Dad, in particular, was an inveterate flicker between channels (just when you were getting into a program, Dad would switch over to something else—it was irritating). Farrukh called our sisters, Rakhshindah and Farhat, and told them to keep Mum and Dad away from the television news and to make sure Dad never got his hands on the remote control.

Farrukh made sure he appeased Mum's chronic worrying by feeding her with information piecemeal. There's a four-hour time difference between England and Pakistan, and Farrukh always stayed up until 2:00 a.m. local time to ensure his call to England was the last one Mum and Dad received before they went to bed in England at 10:00 p.m.

All of which messed up his sleep patterns even more.

For as long as I can remember, Farrukh has played a pivotal role in our family.

From an early age, he assumed family responsibilities and, in doing so, took many burdens off our parents' shoulders. Even to this day, there's not much that goes on in our family without his knowledge or his say-so. He's incredibly generous and kind-hearted and has never, to my knowledge, refused help, financial or other-wise, to anyone who has asked him.

I remember my mother once proudly telling me that, at a function attended by many people, one influential man was so impressed with Farrukh he asked to meet her and Dad. He wanted to see the parents who'd raised such a remarkable individual.

Of course, Farrukh's generosity has endeared him to many people, although some of them have, in my eyes, been little more than mercenary hangers-on. But Farrukh seems content to let it be that way, and I'm sure it's for this reason that God has blessed him with a busy law practice and a good income.

He takes an interest in a number of charities. His friend Dawood (introduced to him, as it happens, by KK) runs a hospital and a school, and Farrukh helps to keep them running. Both men have great respect for each other and meet each other at Friday prayers. Most of Dawood's friends know Farrukh, or know of him, and his generosity is legendary among them.

A while back, Farrukh received a visit at his office from a man in his thirties. He was dressed in the traditional *shalwar kamiz*, and he had a long black beard. He had a laid-back manner. He introduced himself as Salim, a friend of Dawood's.

"Farrukh *sahib*, I have an emergency and am in need of some money. Can you help me?"

Farrukh has a number of bank accounts. He picked up a check book and looked at the balance.

"Well, Salim *sahib*, in this account I have 202,000 rupees. Why don't I give you 200,000 rupees. I'll keep the 2,000 rupees so the account stays active."

Salim nodded his head in agreement. Farrukh signed the check with his trusty Mont Blanc ballpoint pen and handed the check over. With a hint of embarrassment, Salim accepted it, said goodbye and left.

Now, a year or so later, Dawood mentioned to Salim that Farrukh was in difficulty. He explained about the kidnapping. Salim presented himself at Farrukh's office.

"*Asalaam alaikum.*"

"*Walaikum asalaam,*" Farrukh replied.

"I've just heard the terrible news about your brother. I am sorry that you, of all people, have run into difficulty. I have always prayed to God to take special care of you, and of those you care about."

"Thank you for your kind prayers. I believe God will find a way for us."

"Farrukh *sahib*, ever since you helped me, I have wished somehow I could do something in return for you."

"I appreciate that very much. Thank you. Pray for us, especially for my parents. They are fragile and old."

"Yes, I will. But perhaps I can help in some other way."

Farrukh was a little embarrassed. He's a proud man who, although he gives help freely, finds it very difficult to accept aid from others. He never likes to admit he needs help.

And he was puzzled. Was Salim about to offer him money? As kind as that would be, Farrukh knew that any amount Salim was in a position to offer could not possibly pay the ransom.

"I might be able to talk to some people."

"I see." Farrukh was intrigued but a little incredulous.

"Sometimes I teach children at a *madrassah*. I know a man there who might be able to help."

"A man. Who is he?"

"His name is Fazlur Rehman Khalil."

This got Farrukh's attention. He'd heard the name before. It had been mentioned by Shah Abdul Aziz, the friend who'd gone to Waziristan to get information about our movements. Dawood had mentioned this name too, a few days ago, at Friday prayers. A coincidence? Could this man be helpful? Or was he somehow connected to the kidnapping? *Wait a minute*, thought Farrukh. *What is happening to me? Where is my positive outlook? Here is a man trying to help me.*

He looked at Salim. His eyes were sincere. Honest. A man whose judgment he could trust. Whose help he should not be too proud to accept.

Perhaps God wants me to meet this man, he told himself. Perhaps that is why his name keeps cropping up. Think positively.

"You believe he can help us?"

"Yes. I have been telling him about you ever since Dawood *sahib* told me about your brother. I will talk to him again."

Farrukh spent another long and largely sleepless night thinking that here, at last, there might be a chink of light in the darkness. Early the following morning, Salim called. There was a mixture of pride and excitement in his voice.

"Brother Fazlur Rehman Khalil will meet you."

"When can we go?"

"He has asked for us to be there in two hours."

"Very good. My friend Asghar and I will pick you up."

Desperately trying to keep a tight rein on the impatience, excitement, and optimism that was overtaking him, Farrukh called Asghar.

"I want to come across as an ordinary middle-class man. Western dress might offend him. He might take me to be a non-Muslim. Should I wear a *shalwar kamiz*? I can't risk offending him. I can't afford to lose this lead."

"Yes. I'll put on a *shalwar* as well. We'll go in my car—yours is too expensive."

Asghar's blue Toyota Corolla drove for forty minutes into the outskirts of Islamabad. The three men came to a dirt track that looked like a road to nowhere.

"This is it," said Salim.

They took the track, pursued by a cloud of dust. The dust settled ten minutes later as the car came to a halt in front of a pair of large iron gates, incongruous in the middle of this sparsely populated area.

A guard they hadn't noticed stepped out from under the shadow of a tree and walked over to the car. He bent down to look in through the window and, seeing Salim, walked silently back to the gates and opened one of them, allowing ample room for Asghar's small car to slip through.

Once inside, they were instructed to park the car. The guard gestured for them to get out and follow him.

After a walk of several hundred yards, they came upon a collection of buildings, among which were an imposing mosque and a substantial *madrassah*. The guard led them through a narrow gate. Asghar caught a glimpse of a cluster of small houses, built for the teachers, no doubt. They turned down an alleyway. Off to the left, another residential development, with larger and more luxurious abodes. Asghar wondered what kind of person lived there.

They arrived at a door. Fazlur Rehman Khalil's office. They entered. The room was large but spartan. A few bookshelves held several copies of the Qur'an and some other volumes. The only concession to comfort was a cheap-looking carpet of garish design.

Resting with his back against the far wall, Fazlur Rehman Khalil sat on the floor, a set of rosary beads in his right hand. He slowly flicked through one bead after the other with his thumb. He looked like an ordinary man. Farrukh knew he was not.

The former leader of the HuM,[*] Fazlur Rehman Khalil now led *Ansar ul Umma*, a group with a similar agenda. He had fought against the Soviets during the Afghan war and had killed his first Soviet soldier at the age of eighteen. In order to save bullets, he'd used a knife. It was said he'd lost count of how many Soviet soldiers he'd killed with his Kalashnikov. On operations in the Afghan wilderness, he'd survived by eating leaves.[**]

On the wall behind this outwardly unassuming man hung a flag. Black, white, and green horizontal stripes, with a globe in the middle that carried the words *Ansar ul Umma*.

Farrukh noted that Fazlur Rehman Khalil was a man of good build. He wore spectacles and had a long brown beard. He was wearing a clean *shalwar kamiz* and an immaculate white turban. He struck Farrukh as an altogether pleasant individual. The three men shook hands and Fazlur Rehman Khalil gestured for his guests to sit.

Salim was the first to speak.

"Farrukh *sahib* is the elder brother of Asad Qureshi, the filmmaker I have been telling you about. Asad Qureshi is a very good man and Farrukh sahib has a problem a man like him cannot resolve on his own. He needs someone powerful and influential like you. He is a very decent fellow and would not even kill a fly. His family is harmless and not rich. They are going through a very difficult time. His parents are old and fragile and cannot handle the stress of their son being in captivity. You have contacts and can help him. If you turn him away, there is no other place for him to go. He is a good friend of mine and of Dawood *sahib*."

Salim spoke like a preacher. You gave him a topic, and he could speak endlessly on it. After he'd finished this impassioned speech, he took a breath.

Fazlur Rehman Khalil nodded his head. This was the cue for Farrukh to tell him the story.

---

[*] The Harkat-ul-Mujahedeen, a militant group operating mainly in Kashmir.
[**] At the time of writing, FRK is listed by the US State Department as a "specially designated terrorist."

"My brother is a very simple man. He has an obsession with film-making. That is what he has chosen as a career. He is a harmless man. He has no hidden agendas and no connections to the Taliban or to the government. He simply wants to film a report. He is a good man."

Fazlur Rehman Khalil nodded again. Did he want more information? Farrukh looked at Asghar, whose face was expressionless. Farrukh decided to press on.

"He went to North Waziristan because Khalid Khawaja told him he could get him some good interviews. My brother met Khalid Khawaja through me. I am a lawyer. Khalid came to me in connection with a missing person's case my office was dealing with. Asad met him in my office. I am not aware Khalid Khawaja has any hidden agenda in traveling to Waziristan but, if he does, kindly take my word for it that my brother would not have known that. All he wanted was to make a film."

Fazlur Rehman Khalil nodded again.

"Sir, my parents are old and frail. They are unable to take this stress."

Farrukh had followed closely the guidelines given to him by Salim and, like the good lawyer he was, had driven home those points Salim had told him would be most persuasive. If ever there was a time for pragmatism, it was now.

As Farrukh talked, Fazlur Rehman Khalil held his gaze, all the time working through prayers on his rosary. He had listened patiently and had not said a word.

He now turned his attention to Salim.

"What is your connection to this?"

"Farrukh *sahib* and I are close. Like brothers." Pragmatism.

"Very well. Come and see me again tomorrow. I will see what I can do."

And with that, the three men seemed to be dismissed.

It all seemed very anticlimactic to Farrukh. He'd expected a more immediate response to his plea. He felt crestfallen. But he was tactful enough not to press matters. He stood and thanked the esteemed cleric for his kind attention. They all shook hands, and the three visitors respectfully withdrew.

Salim could see the disappointment on Farrukh's face.

"Don't worry. I am sure he will come up with something."

"I hope you are right."

As Asghar's car pulled out of the compound, followed by another cloud of dust, Salim once again sought to reassure Farrukh.

"You know, Fazlur Rehman Khalil is a serious man and very well connected. I am sure he can help you."

"Thank you. I trust you are right. He is my last hope."

"Have other people failed?"

"Well, other people are in the wings, offering a little support. I don't have much faith in them."

"Will you tell them about Fazlur Rehman Khalil?"

"No. At least, not yet. And I don't think we should speak about him by name, not even among ourselves. He is my only chance to get Asad back. I don't want to blow it by bandying his name around."

"We need a code name."

"Mr. Z. Let's just call him Mr. Z."

That night, Farrukh slept for five hours. The best sleep he'd had in days.

The following day, Farrukh and Asghar returned to the compound. Salim was waiting for them there. Also waiting to see Mr. Z were KK's son, Usama, and Colonel Imam's son, Major Nauman.

Farrukh had been keeping his distance from them. He didn't agree with their policy of speaking to the press—he thought that was playing into the hands of the kidnappers.

He'd only stumbled upon Mr. Z by chance, through his connection to Salim. Usama and Major Nauman clearly knew of Mr. Z independently of Salim. And they hadn't shared that information with Farrukh.

Asghar waited outside while Salim and Farrukh were led in to Mr. Z's office. He gestured for them to sit.

"I have made some enquiries. The first thing to tell you is your brother and his friends are alive."

This was the first piece of good news Farrukh had heard for days.

"But I must also tell you that I can do nothing for Khalid Khawaja and Colonel Imam. You should forget about them and focus on your brother."

Farrukh was shocked at this blitheness.

"And, regarding your brother, his chance of coming home alive is remote. Less than 1 percent."

Farrukh felt the room close in around him. He felt sick.

"Your brother is in serious trouble. I don't know what I can do for him, given the company he is keeping."

Mr. Z leaned forward and looked Farrukh in the eye.

"Why did he go to Waziristan with Khalid Khawaja?"

"Sir, please believe me. My brother is just a filmmaker. I don't know how he was persuaded to go with Khalid Khawaja and Colonel Imam. I don't know what they said to him."

"Your brother is from England. He is associated with a news channel that is seen here as anti-Islamic. It is difficult to see how I can get him out of there."

Farrukh hung his head. What was he going to say to Mum and Dad? How could he sweeten this pill?

"Mr Farrukh, do you realize once someone has been accused of being a spy in that region, his death is sealed? Your brother's group has been accused of spying."

"But, sir, my brother is innocent."

"To these people, that does not matter. A wealthy man was once kidnapped by them. They held him for ransom. They discovered he was a doctor. One of the kidnappers told him his mother had been seriously ill and her doctor had failed to save her. Not this man. Another doctor. Completely separate. But the kidnapper shot the man anyway. Just for being a doctor. You have to understand the kind of people we are dealing with. The only language they understand is violence. Violence is all they know."

Farrukh felt numb. No hope for KK and Colonel Imam. Virtually no hope for me because of my connection to a UK broadcasting company. And he didn't even know about my American wife.

"What will become of Khalid Khawaja?"

"Forget about him. We need to concentrate on your brother."

"But what will happen?"

"I don't know. His son is here again. He came to me yesterday also. I have told him I can't do anything for him."

"Nothing?"

"You must give all your energy to your brother. If you want my help, you have to trust me. I am not going to guarantee you anything. But if I am to help you, you must do exactly as I say."

"I understand. Whatever you say."

"We need to separate your brother from Khalid Khawaja. We will deal only with your brother. The others will have to take their chances."

This was a hard reality for Farrukh to accept. He had played down my association with KK in order to get Mr. Z's support. But KK was an old friend. To abandon him in this way felt like a betrayal. But now was not the time to argue with Mr. Z.

Farrukh tried to convince himself that, given KK's near-mythical status in the region, there would be many people negotiating on his behalf. He tried to convince himself.

The atmosphere in the room changed. Mr Z was looking hard at Farrukh. He seemed to sense his unease over KK. Farrukh needed to get him back on his side.

"Please, sir. Please help us. Our parents are very old and very worried for their son. If we never see Asad again, they will never recover. For the sake of our parents, please help us."

There was a long silence. Mr. Z counted the beads on his rosary and his lips moved noiselessly. Occasionally, he paused, seeming to weigh options in his head, like a chess grand master with his hand hovering over the queen.

"Can you assure me your brother has no other agenda?"

"I assure you."

Another pause.

"Well, with God's help, we may succeed."

Farrukh smiled. It felt good to smile. It was something he hadn't done for quite some time. It seemed to loosen his body.

"I will begin the work. The first task is to persuade the kidnappers to remove the death sentence on your brother. Then I will seek to separate him from Khalid Khawaja and Colonel Imam."

"Yes. I understand."

"This second task is the hardest. Your brother has camera equipment with him. It is clear he was in the region to make a film. That he was collaborating with Khalid Khawaja and Colonel Imam."

"Yes, I see that."

"What I am saying is … do not have high hopes."

A rock in Farrukh's stomach again.

"Given the company he is keeping, you need to accept what I have said. That the chances of your brother coming home alive are very slim."

Farrukh stared into space. He thought of Mum and Dad.

"I need to know how much ransom you will be able to pay."

A difficult question. What was the right answer? What figure can you put on your brother's life?

"I am a reasonably wealthy man. I'll pay whatever I can afford. But the kidnappers want more than I can afford."

"Very well. If the kidnappers contact you again, do not discuss money with them."

"I understand."

On the drive home, Farrukh tried to stay hopeful. But the more he rehearsed the conversation in his head, the more hope eluded him. Then he thought of Dad. He turned to Asghar.

"My father is a very pious man. You know that."

"Of course I know it. I am privileged to call your father my spiritual guide."

"My father has never hurt anyone. In his entire life, he has never caused anyone harm. Would you agree?"

"Yes. That's right. And?"

"Well, I know Asad is in a great deal of danger."

"Yes. He is."

"But … I don't believe God would do that to my father. God would not put my father through the pain of witnessing his own child's death."

Farrukh was smiling again.

"I just know He wouldn't."

15
KK's Confessions

As the deadline for the ransom was approaching, Usman Punjabi made a telephone call. The man who took the call was allegedly none other than Pakistan's venerable television anchor, Hamid Mir. No one involved in efforts to secure our release, nor indeed the Pakistani public at large, would have imagined that such a prominent broadcaster could have links to this terrorist group. The full extent of his connection to them was soon to become clear, with dire consequences for us.

The two men talked as if they were well acquainted. From the outset, Hamid Mir appeared to know Khalid Khawaja was in Punjabi's custody. He asked Punjabi what progress had been made with KK. He suggested to Punjabi that he beat information out of KK. He told Punjabi KK was the man behind the Lal Masjid (Red Mosque) massacre in 2007 and it was he who had compelled Maulana Abdul Aziz to leave the mosque in a burqa, a flight which had brought shame on him. Hamid Mir also implied KK was a *Qadiani** and, on top of that, a CIA agent, owing to his links to the American political analyst and Democratic Party fundraiser Ejaz Mansoor, himself a *Qadiani*.

The Taliban are vehemently opposed to *Qadianis*. Hamid Mir would fully understand such an accusation could have nothing but grave consequences for KK.

I should point out that it has yet to be conclusively established that it was indeed Hamid Mir whose conversation with Usman Punjabi had been made public.

Some days later, on the night of April 22, the A Team contacted Farrukh to say they'd received video footage of confessional statements made by KK, confirming he was working for the CIA and the ISI. In the video, KK wore a red cap, like the students of Lal Masjid (the brutality of the Lal Masjid massacre was still fresh in people's minds). His confessions were lengthy and detailed:

> The people and the media think they know me. I look like a modest, re-ligious, and sympathetic person, but in fact I have been working for the ISI and CIA. I am shameful of my deeds and am paying the price for my sins; I remember burnt bodies of the young girls and boys who studied at Lal Masjid

---

* A member of a branch of Islam dismissed by its many critics as non-Islamic.

because I forced Maulana Abdul Aziz Ghazi, the imam of Lal Masjid, to escape. Maulana Abdul Aziz is a very simple person and sincere in the implementation of true Islam in the country. We trapped him and consequently he was arrested.

KK went on to criticize the Pakistani army and to claim his mission had been to defame Taliban commanders and create infighting between Mujahedeen. He named various Islamic organizations which were being supported by the government. He claimed these organizations did nothing without the permission of the government and various Pakistani agencies used these organizations for their own purposes.

Then he named some international organizations working in Pakistan which, though they purported to have a welfare agenda, were in reality agents of the CIA who paid bribes to the Pakistani army. These organizations should get out of Pakistan, he said. He denounced as un-Islamic other organizations set up for the benefit of women and children. He called for them to be bombed.

KK seemed to be reading these pronouncements from a piece of paper. He wore a glazed expression, like that of a person under sedation. A cock could be heard crowing loudly in the background, suggesting both that the film had been recorded in the early morning and that the room in which he was sitting was of flimsy construction.

Farrukh knew KK to be a man of immensely strong character and nerve. He knew these nonsensical "confessions" could only have been extracted from KK under the most horrific forms of persuasion. His appearance suggested as much. He looked ghastly.

Although seeing KK in this state was upsetting for Farrukh, and harrowing for KK's son, Usama, they tried to take comfort from the fact these so-called confessions would be dismissed by everyone who knew KK. Even in his horribly frail state, KK had given the world a clear indication these were not his own words. At one point, he'd referred to his beloved wife, Shamama, by the wrong name—Farrukh knew that was to be read as a sign.

Farrukh remembered the events of the Lal Masjid massacre. He knew that, on the very first day of the operation, KK had been abducted by the security agencies— they wanted to prevent him from helping his friends on the inside—and that the *maulana* whose escape KK now stood accused of masterminding had, in fact, been coerced by the army into fleeing. Officers had threatened to rape his wife.

When Farrukh showed the video to Nudrat, her response was visceral. She clutched her stomach and sank into a chair, sweating. The vile images from her nightmare in Istanbul flashed into her mind. A bearded man, a razor, the beard shaved off first. Then the hair. Then the skin.

Usama called Farrukh. He'd been in touch with Shah Abdul Aziz, who had news. Mullah Omar had sent a delegation to Waziristan to speak at the *jirga*.* Mullah Omar's representatives had conveyed the message that it was wrong to take hostages for ransom. Usama also drew comfort from his continued conversations with Usman Punjabi, who was still assuring him all would be well.

But Farrukh remained unnerved by the video of KK and the coverage his "confessions" had received in the Pakistani press. He had a feeling that something terrible was about to happen.

Farrukh called our sister, Rakhshindah, in the UK and asked her to keep Mum and Dad away from the television news, in case KK's video was shown.

He couldn't shake off the strong sense of imminent threat. Driving to his office with Asghar, he asked his friend whether God was punishing him or testing him.

"I don't know. But a person who is punished is abandoned by God. God stays with a person who is tested and opens doors to help."

Farrukh's phone rang. He pulled it from his pocket and fumbled with the recording device. Asghar grabbed it and connected it to Farrukh's phone.

"A North Waziristan number."

Farrukh nodded.

"Hello?"

"Hello. Farrukh Karim?"

"Who is this?"

"This is Ali Raza."

"Yes. How are you?"

"I am fine. Tell me, have you thought of something or not?"

"Mr. Ali, I will do as you say. As you know, the British government will not do anything. We are at your mercy. We, the family, are the only ones who can do something. After God, it is up to you to end this problem. A Pakistani man like me could not begin to raise even one million dollars. How can I come up with ten million?"

"You tell me your limit. Then we will think about it."

"We are simple people who are victims of circumstances. Give us a reasonable figure and I will talk to my family and see what we can arrange."

Farrukh was implementing the A Team's plan—shatter the notion of a major ransom payment, by keeping the government and the TV channel out of it, and stressing to the kidnappers that no one but the family could be expected to raise money, then modify expectations further with a picture of the family as simple people with limited means.

---

* The assembly of tribal elders which takes decisions by consensus.

It was a risky strategy. Farrukh wasn't at all convinced it was the right one. Ali Raza's voice registered impatience.

"Talk to the government. See what is their demand. Otherwise talking to you is a waste of time."

"As I have already told you, the government will not get involved. They are not even responding to me."

Farrukh was pushing it and he knew it. He couldn't tell Ali Raza that he had absolutely nothing to offer. At the same time, he couldn't give the impression that he had something to give. A rock and a hard place.

"Fine." Click.

"Hello? HELLO?"

Silence. Then his heart in his mouth. What had he done? He'd followed the A Team's instructions but he'd only made the situation worse. And he'd embarrassed himself by telling the kidnapper that, after God, he was the only one the family were looking up to.

Asghar assured him he'd handled it as well as anyone could have, and better than most. But Farrukh was left with a deep sense of unease.

Later that day, a long conversation with Nudrat did nothing to dispel this feeling.

"I don't want to raise their hopes too high. But I must not make them think Asad is not worth their time. That he's dispensable."

"What is your limit?"

"Not that much. I am spending a lot on keeping my family in England. Remember, I am earning in rupees and spending in pounds. And the way business is now, I will be broke soon."

Again Nudrat's nightmare flashed through her mind. The bearded man, the razor … She turned her head so Farrukh wouldn't see her discomfort. Farrukh decided to go to the A Team and tell them about the call.

The team were pleased Farrukh had stressed that the British government wouldn't get involved and were delighted the kidnapper had not mentioned the channel. Simon, the channel's security adviser, was keen to build in more delays.

"Just keep emphasizing you're not a rich man and you won't be able to meet outrageous demands."

"I will try."

"The ransom deadline is just a few days away. We need to buy more time. We also need to establish if this man, Ali Raza, is who he says he is. We need to know if he's the one actually holding Asad and his colleagues. Or is it Usman Punjabi? Or are they both part of the same gang? Did Ali Raza send the videos? We need to know that."

"How do we go about that?"

"I suggest you set up a new email account. Send an email to the address the videos were sent from. Ask outright if it is Ali Raza. You have a right to know, and they will acknowledge that. It'll show you're taking the ransom seriously. And sending emails back and forth will buy us more time."

Farrukh resolved to go to England—he wanted to see our parents in person, to prepare them for the heat that would be turned up as the days passed and the deadline approached. Having made these decisions, Farrukh felt a little easier when he arrived home that night. After his routine 2:00 a.m. call to Mum and Dad in England, giving them the news of his impending visit, he settled down in the hope of catching a couple of hours of sleep.

The following day, he decided it was time to be proactive with the kidnappers. Nudrat had set up an email account a few days earlier, exclusively for use in contacting the kidnappers. Farrukh would follow the A Team's advice and use it. He was desperate to keep a channel of communication open. His email was deliberately brief and forthright:

Regarding the video, please call me, but not before Tuesday, April 27.

A few hours later, Farrukh received a call from Rodney Henson, the channel's senior news producer in London.

"I just wanted to inform you the British High Commission in Islamabad has received a call from the kidnappers."

"What did they say?"

"If the commission doesn't take them seriously, they will kill Asad."

"What was the commission's response?"

"The kidnapper hung up after delivering his message."

This was it. Farrukh had seen it coming. Had felt it. He'd tried to play it cool and be the hard man the team wanted him to be, but he'd only succeeded in baiting them, these animals who thought nothing of doing the most despicable things. Now they were angry. And now he was committed to a trip to London. He felt like he was fleeing the scene.

The following morning, he found himself in the departure lounge at Islamabad Airport, waiting for his early flight to Leeds, with a rock in his stomach.

He emailed Jacqueline:

Dear Jacqueline,

As you are aware, the deadline set by the kidnappers expires in four days' time, on April 24. I understand a phone call was made to the High Commission yesterday and they have threatened to kill Asad unless their demands are met within that time. You are also aware I've been told to convey the ransom demand to the British government. The kidnappers are asking the government for money. The family has not, to date, been directly asked to pay any ransom.

Mr Robert Muir, from the Foreign and Commonwealth Office, contacted my family in the UK earlier this month and informed them that Asad was fine and would be back in a few days. I've tried to contact him since but without success. When I call, he is not at his desk. When I leave a message, he does not get back to me.

As you can imagine, the whole family is extremely concerned about Asad's safety and health. It would be reassuring to know exactly what the government has done so far and what it proposes to do in trying to bring this ordeal to an end. I would also like to know whether the government intends to formally/publicly respond to the kidnappers' demands, as silence on the government's part could jeopardize Asad's life as well as those of his colleagues.

I am leaving for England in order to speak with my family in person, as this incident has now started to receive international media attention. I will be back in Islamabad after the weekend.

Nudrat was tasked with checking the dedicated email address for a response from the kidnappers. She checked every ten minutes. The first day of Farrukh's absence came and went. Around noon on the second day, she received a one-line response.

"who are u introduce ur self"

She contacted Farrukh in England. He responded to it right away, holding his breath while he typed, playing the long game the A Team wanted.

"I am Asad's brother, Farrukh. I am traveling. Call me on that number, but not before Tuesday."

The A Team told Farrukh that, once the first deadline had passed, things would become easier. For that reason, he'd planned his trip so he'd be unreachable on the day the deadline expired.

He prayed the A Team's tactic was the right one. He was gambling with my life.

Farrukh went to visit Mum and Dad. He could see Dad's natural optimism had begun to fray at the edges. Mum spent the entire visit in tears. Never had it been more important to wear his mask of confidence and emotional strength. He comforted them as best he could, hoping his assurances didn't sound as hollow to their ears as they did to his own.

Then he visited his wife and children. Although she hadn't seen her husband for quite some time now, Rhuksana knew her husband's mind would be a whirlpool of thoughts and emotions. She didn't ask questions; she listened when he volunteered snippets of information.

Spared from making his now-regular 2:00 a.m. phone call to Mum and Dad, Farrukh went to bed early. But sleep still eluded him. When he closed his eyes, all he could see was Dad's furrowed brow and Mum's tears.

The following morning, April 24, he read Pakistani newspapers online. More bad news:

Missing ex-ISI Men May Face Revenge

The captors of two former ISI officials and a British journalist, who went missing in the North Waziristan Agency nearly three weeks ago, are unlikely to spare two former ISI sleuths as they are sure that the two have been spying on them.

Qari Zia ur Reman, an Afghani leader of the Taliban, had revealed that all the efforts made by the Islamic Emirate of Afghanistan to secure release of the two former ISI officials and the British journalist have failed. They were not in the hands of the Tehrik-e-Taliban Pakistan but of scattered groups of Pakistani militants, whether they were Punjabi Taliban or some other organization. He said the captors seemed to be very close to former clerics of Lal Masjid, Maulana Abdul Aziz, and Maulana Abdul Rashid Ghazi. This is the reason they forced Khalid Khawaja into making the confessional statement that he worked for the CIA and the ISI. Thus it had been confirmed Khalid Khawaja had been helping the Musharraf regime when it launched the operation at Lal Masjid.

The captors believed that, by detaining the two former ISI officials and a British journalist, they had succeeded in smashing a network that had been spying on them. Different groups of the Afghan Taliban made strenuous efforts to secure the release of the kidnapped men but the captors did not oblige them.

The Punjabi Taliban group were extremely annoyed with the two former ISI officials, particularly Khalid, because they believed they played an important role in the arrest, by the Pakistani authorities, of their operatives and leaders.

So Farrukh knew the Afghani Taliban had become involved in attempts to release us, and also that the captors had refused. It seemed our guilt had been established before a *jirga*. And there was no one to speak on our behalf.

Farrukh spoke to officials at the Foreign and Commonwealth Office. Their response was the same as Jacqueline's at the British High Commission in Islamabad. They did not want to get involved in a hostage situation. He met Rodney from the channel and asked him again about the protection the channel could offer. What rights did our team have? None. Nothing.

That evening, at the dinner table, Farrukh's phone rang. The polite but emotionless voice of a British High Commission official gave him some chilling news. A report, as yet unconfirmed, had come in from the region. Three men had been beheaded by their captors. Farrukh's eyes filled with tears, but he could reveal nothing. *As yet unconfirmed.* Hold on to that.

He brushed aside Mum's question.

"Oh, just a client. Nudrat will deal with it."

His phone rang again. Usama told him that the same story had just been aired in Pakistan. KK's daughter had been standing next to the TV when the report came on. She fainted with shock. Farrukh redoubled his efforts to keep our parents away from television news.

Farrukh called Nudrat in Islamabad and told her about the reports. He argued that it seemed unlikely. Why send a list of prisoners to be released and demand millions of dollars in ransom money, and then just torpedo the entire plan? It didn't seem feasible. He clung to that thought and decided to return to Islamabad.

Usama had told him Shah Abdul Aziz was due back in Islamabad any day now. He'd have firsthand news from the *jirga*.

As soon as he landed in Islamabad, Farrukh switched his phone on. Now he was available for the kidnappers to call. Then he went to the office and sat with Asghar and Nudrat, in exhausted but composed silence.

He scoured the Islamabad papers. One newspaper carried a story in which Jawaid Ibrahim Peracha claimed he was being approached by the Asian Tigers to negotiate with the authorities on their behalf. This was a new and encouraging development.

Why would the kidnappers want Peracha to negotiate on their behalf if they'd already killed their hostages?

Cracks were starting to appear in the reports of beheadings. Then somebody spilled the beans. Rumors of three headless corpses thrown onto a street in Waziristan had been fabricated by a Pakistani TV channel eager to steal a march on its rivals. This ruthless ratings war in the Pakistani media trampled on all notions of ethics. It was disgusting.

When Farrukh met with Shah Abdul Aziz, he confirmed what the newspapers and TV channels were now saying, that the headless corpses story had been a fake.

But that was the only good news from Waziristan. The Taliban hierarchy was in favor of our release and had made a very strong case for it, but the Asian Tigers had clung to their demands. There is a pact among Taliban groups that they will not fight each other. So the only way forward was negotiation. The long game.

But how long? We'd been gone for thirty-four days.

16
Soon You Will Hear Good News

Returning from a dispiriting visit to Mr. Z, during which the cleric had emphasized how gloomy the situation was, Farrukh sat in his office with Nudrat. She seemed uneasy. The story about the man with the American business card was still haunting her, as well as Mr. Z's story about the kidnapped doctor. But, as things stood, Mr. Z seemed like their only hope.

An anxious evening dragged by, with no contact made by the kidnappers.

It was not until late the following day that an email pinged into the dedicated inbox. Nudrat called Farrukh over and showed him the text.

aoa

I hope u are fine what is ur last demand

take care

quick reply

ur date is over

What were they on about? What is your last demand?

Farrukh was demanding nothing. He was not in a position to make demands. They read it over and over, at least fifty times in the following couple of hours. Was this some kind of game? Were they baiting Farrukh to lose his temper and issue some sort of ultimatum?

Then Nudrat had a lightbulb flash of insight. It was Ali Raza. Ali Raza was the writer of the email. She thought back to the phone calls. She could hear his voice. Hear him instruct Farrukh to speak to the British government. To ask for their demand. Same mistake. By *demand*, he did, of course, mean *offer*. *What is your final offer?*

Well, at least here was a clear indication they were dealing with a single group, not a hotchpotch of disparate factions as they'd previously feared.

The kidnappers had asked a question. Farrukh needed to come up with an answer.

Meanwhile, a newspaper report had signaled another development. Jawaid Ibrahim Peracha was making comments in the press that suggested he knew something of the kidnappers. Peracha was the politician at whose house in Kohat we'd stayed as guests before heading into Waziristan. Two men, from the group Ulema-e-Islam Fazal, had visited him and given him names of people they wanted released, Peracha was saying. To his knowledge, the group calling themselves the Asian Tigers consisted of ten to twelve men, comprising Punjabi and Mehsud militants.

If the report was to be believed, the Asian Tigers were looking to negotiate our release through Peracha. Was it a coincidence that, apart from Abbasi, our driver, Peracha had been last man we'd spent time with before our abduction?

The fog had lifted briefly, revealing a path, then it had descended once more, leaving Farrukh groping around for the way ahead.

He discussed the matter with, in turn, Nudrat, Asghar, Dawood, Salim, and the A Team. Still, he had no answer to the kidnappers' question. He knew the ten million dollars was out of the question, even for someone with his wealthy connections. And he'd only be able to raise a fraction of that in the short time he had. For the moment, he'd have to gamble that the kidnappers were bluffing and would be prepared to settle for very much less.

But it would be good to get some reassurance that this was a sensible way to proceed. Perhaps Mr. Z could help with that.

"I have talked to all my friends and family. As you can imagine, at a time like this no one wants to know me. My friends are reluctant to get involved. My family is not well off. I have talked to everyone I know and, on the basis of the pledges made to me, I am fairly confident that I can come up with about four million rupees."[*]

"Well, if you have only four million rupees, and the kidnappers are asking for ten million dollars, it might take a very long time to negotiate your brother's release. The kidnappers will certainly settle for less than they are demanding, but I do not think they will want to settle for less than ten million rupees. Certainly not less than eight."

"What can I do?"

"I suggest that, if you have four, you tell the kidnappers that you have only two. Then perhaps the negotiations can end on the four you do have."

"I will find it very difficult to lie to them. As I can give them four, I think I should just tell them four."

"Well, I appreciate your truthfulness. But there are times when one has to lie for one's own sake and for the sake of others."

[*] Around $40,000.

Farrukh thanked Mr. Z for his advice and left, still in a quandary as to what exactly he would tell the men holding me.

Although it was well below the kidnappers' demands, four million rupees was still a substantial amount of money, and Farrukh needed to convince the kidnappers it was an offer worth accepting, and it was the only offer they were going to get.

But would they bite? Well, it was a good sign they were clearly prepared to negotiate with him directly. They seemed to have accepted that the channel was out of it, and the British government too.

Yet he was still nervous. For a man who had the confidence to win extremely complex legal cases, in which his clients were awarded millions of dollars, in this matter his self-assurance had deserted him.

That evening, he went to the Serena Hotel to meet the A Team. They sat in the hotel's sumptuous gardens, on a lush lawn, the air thick with the perfume of azaleas, a pink sun setting over the high, thick walls that protected the hotel's many foreign guests from the constant threat posed by vehicles carrying Taliban bombs.

Brian was the first to speak.

"It's time you gave a figure to the kidnappers."

"What figure should I say?"

"How much can you give?"

There it was again. The stonewall refusal to get the channel involved. *You're on your own.*

"I'm not sure. Maybe as much as four million rupees."

"Well, tell the kidnappers how much you can arrange to get. But tell them you need two or three days to get it. Buy more time."

"Okay."

"And you still need to convince the kidnappers that the channel and the British government will not become involved."

"Okay."

"Direct them to the High Commission's website. The categorical statement that it does not deal with terrorists or pay ransoms."

Brian handed Farrukh a script, reiterating the points he'd just made. No government involvement. No channel involvement. Look at the High Commission website. The same mantra.

Farrukh noted there was no mention at all of Rustam. He'd been completely overlooked in all this. The A Team clearly weren't bothered whether or not he got out alive.

Well, if Farrukh had, however reluctantly, accepted Mr. Z's advice to disregard Khalid Khawaja and Colonel Imam in negotiating for me, he was not prepared to abandon Rustam. At least Usama and Major Nauman were dealing with Mr. Z on their own behalf, pleading the case for the release of KK and the Colonel, but nobody was fighting in Rustam's corner.

Well, now Farrukh was. He penciled Rustam's name into the script.

Nudrat was waiting for him when he got back to the office. Ever the loyal assistant. Without her, he'd have gone mad by now.

Farrukh flopped into a chair and let the A Team's script fall to the floor. The moment it hit the marble tile, his phone started ringing.

The kidnappers. Were they watching him? How?

He snatched up the script and set it on the desk, then answered the call.

"Hello. This is Ali Raza."

"Hello."

"So what is your final demand?"

Demand. A faint smile played on Farrukh's lips for a fleeting second.

"I have spoken to family and friends and explored every possible avenue. But I am afraid I will not be able to come up with more than four million rupees."

"That's not even one tenth of what we are asking. It seems you don't want to see your brother again."

The buzz of a dial tone in Farrukh's ear. Panic in his brain. What had he done? He'd blown it! All the advice, the scripts, the coaching … and he'd jumped right in with both feet and offered the maximum.

The phone call, when it had come, had caught him completely off guard. He hadn't had time to think. To keep his calm and play the game. The fighter plane had burst out of the clouds, deployed its missile, then twisted up and away into the stratosphere. What devastation had it wrought on the ground?

Nudrat stared at him in horror.

"What will you do now? What will you say to Mr. Z?"

"I don't know. If I can't follow a simple piece of advice, he might not think it worth his while to help us."

Shaken by the gravity of the situation, and desperate for some kind of reassurance, he called Salim.

"Salim *sahib*, I need to tell you something. The kidnapper just called me. I offered four million rupees."

"You did what?"

"I panicked. I told them four instead of two. I was caught off guard. I told the truth. I gave the game away."

"Farrukh *sahib*, I understand your brother's life is on the line here. But we must follow Mr. Z's instructions."

"I know. I'm sorry."

"Let me talk to him tomorrow. I will try to convince him to stay onboard. But I am not sure how he will react. *Inshallah.*"

Salim made his way to Mr. Z's compound and was ushered in to see him. When he explained Farrukh's mistake, the cleric was visibly annoyed.

"Salim *sahib*, if Farrukh *sahib* negotiates directly with the kidnappers in this way, he is going to make things extremely difficult for me. I wonder if he realizes the embarrassing position he's put me in."

"He knows he has made a mistake. He is truly sorry."

"It is not easy to deal with these hostile people. Now it will be twice as difficult."

"I know."

"You see, I have sent a message to the kidnappers, telling them Farrukh *sahib* could pay two million, just like we agreed. Now he has offered four million, which puts me in a very bad position. I have not had the chance to build any trust with them. Now I have been exposed. Now the kidnappers will be thinking that I wanted to keep two million for myself."

"I understand."

"Why would they want to deal with a middleman who wants to keep half the money for himself? I'm not sure I can continue talking to them, given Farrukh *sahib*'s disregard for my instructions."

A long pause. The cleric seemed to be thinking. Salim kept quiet for perhaps two minutes. A long silence. Then a shadow on the cleric's brow. Salim became worried that this spelled the end of his association with the negotiations. The end of all hope. Time to speak up.

"Sir, he's under a lot of pressure. It's not just his brother he's worried about, but his elderly parents too. He has no one else but you to rely on. You are his only hope. He is not a wealthy man. They will surely kill his brother if you pull out. I beg of you to find a way forward. I can assure you he will do exactly as you tell him from now on."

Another long pause. Mr. Z was a man who thought long and hard before speaking. Salim looked on nervously. Just as before, he'd rattled off an imploring monologue.

"Okay. Tell him to stick to four million."

Salim was elated. He rushed back to tell Farrukh the good news. That there was still hope. That Mr. Z was still in their camp.

Farrukh was relieved that, from this corner at least, there was some hope. Because, in the Pakistani media, the vultures were circling again.

Asia Times Online has learned that Khalid Khawaja and Colonel Imam wanted to hammer out a formula of peaceful coexistence between militants and the military in North Waziristan, and in the broader context to seek a way for the US to withdraw from the region in such a manner that the Taliban would have a role to play in Afghanistan and Pakistan.

All of which painted KK in a good light vis-à-vis the kidnappers. But it was not all good. After his forced retirement, the article said, KK became active in politics. He'd formed an understanding with former US Central Intelligence Agency director James Woolsey in the wake of the 9/11 attacks. He'd been involved in the crackdown on the Taliban-sympathetic Lal Masjid.

The article was depicting KK as a straw blowing with the prevailing wind:

Depending on the issue, Khawaja is clearly not afraid to act in the establishment's interests, or against them, and he is comfortable speaking to Americans and to the ISI.

A Pakistani Taliban spokesman was quoted extensively in the article. He mentioned an earlier trip KK had made to North Waziristan. One sentence in particular made Farrukh sweat:

However, everybody noticed their suspicious activities.

Farrukh knew that the word "suspicious" was poison. The spokesman went on to say that, during this visit, KK had been given the use of Mufti Mehsud's four-wheel drive vehicle. Then, a few days after KK and the others returned to Islamabad, the vehicle was hit by a US drone, which killed six people. Although Waliur Rehman Mehsud had escaped with his life, he said. The clear implication was that KK had planted a microchip target for the drone. Then the language became chillingly direct:

If we get proof that a person has a connection with the ISI, he is an enemy. We have reports that, in addition to having ISI connections, Khawaja frequently meets with the CIA. Furthermore, he offers people access to the CIA in return for money.

The spokesman was effectively saying KK was in the pay of the Americans. No worse allegation could be made:

Mum and Dad. Still smiling after all I've put them through.

My brother, Farrukh, the real hero of this story

Farrukh's assistant, Nudrat. She could not have worked harder in support of Farrukh.

Ashgar, Farrukh's trusted friend. He helped keep my brother sane throughout this whole ordeal.

Khalid Khawaja.
An enigma.

Colonel Imam in a screen
grab from his appeal
video. He was a strong,
brave man.

Proof of life

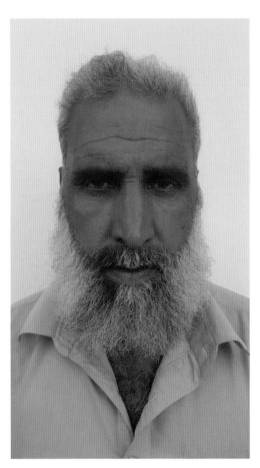

My assistant, Rustam. A fearless, hardworking
man. *Courtesy Mohammad Iftekhar Yazdani*

Qari Zarar, who risked his life for me on
several occasions

Dad. This is the photo Farrukh sent to me in captivity. I signed the back of it as further proof of life.

Fazlur Rehman Khalil, the "Mr. Z" who helped negotiate my release

Sherry

My Persian cat, Sunny. I still miss her.

Landing with a local cameramana in Buner in the Khyber Pakhtunkhwa province of Pakistan, during filming for the BBC's Panorama in 2009, a few months before our kidnapping

An abandoned Taliban brainwashing compound for suicide bombers in Waziristan, showing a depiction of heaven and a dedication to a Taliban "martyr" written in the blood of Pakistani soldiers

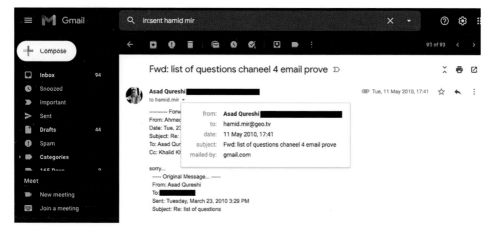

A screen grab of one of the emails forwarded by the kidnappers from my account during my captivity, shows the recipient of the email to be Hamid Mir, the prominent Pakistani broadcaster.

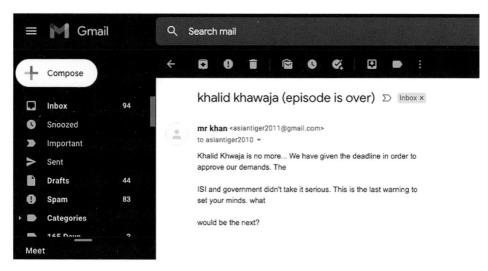

A screen grab of an email sent by one kidnapper to another, callously giving the tragic news of KK's murder

At KK's grave in Islamabad. I think of him every day.

A tribute to Colonel Imam, in the village of Chakwal, 80 miles outside Islamabad. *Courtesy Col Safir Tarar (brother of Col Imam)*

KK shopping for green tea at a market in Chaman, on the border between Pakistan and Afghanistan. This is the last photo I took of him before we were captured.

At the Friendship Gate in Chaman, during the first phase of filming

Happier times with Fazlur Rehman Khalil, on a return trip to Pakistan three years after my release

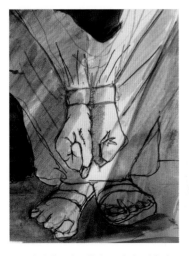
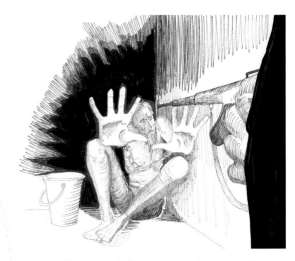

Hooded, handcuffed, and shackled
Courtesy Judy Mella

Handcuffed and naked, down the barrel of a gun *Courtesy Judy Mella*

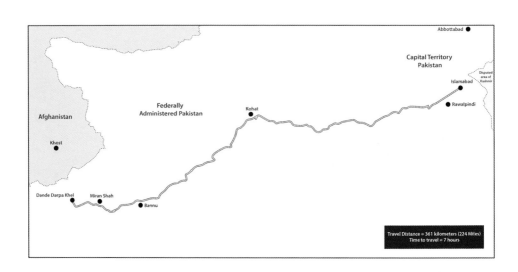

Khawaja and the others left North Waziristan. He said he would soon be back, with a British journalist. We concluded that he had come with an agenda. When he came back, we caught him immediately. The journalist he brought with him also worked for the ISPR, making documentaries. They are all Pakistani army assets and our enemies and they will be dealt with according to their crimes. It has been decided.

The article made terrifying reading. The Taliban spokesperson quoted so extensively was named as Usman Punjabi, the man making constant phone calls to KK's son, Usama. So he was not only in the eye of the storm but was prepared to state his hardline position to the press in the strongest of terms.

For Farrukh, this was the bleakest development yet. Our entire group had been declared to be spies. Our guilt had been established. Our fate sealed.

The *Asia Times* article had been explicit about my connection to the ISPR. In order to conceal from the kidnappers exactly how much work I'd done for them, Farrukh asked the A Team to arrange for my website to be taken down.

The deadline had passed. A new deadline had not been issued by the kidnappers. April was coming to an end. The kidnappers seemed increasingly unpredictable. Usman Punjabi was playing games and clothing himself in several disguises. Farrukh and Nudrat both wondered if Ali Raza and Usman Punjabi were, in fact, one and the same person.

Farrukh contacted Usama and was told Punjabi was still calling him, almost daily, with news of supposed progress in the negotiations for his father's release. Given the tone of the *Asia Times* article, this had to be a bluff. But Farrukh couldn't help hoping it might be a sign that behind-the-scenes negotiations with the families were under way.

Farrukh just wanted the whole group home now. He felt like he'd be willing to do anything, to pay anything, just to get everyone released.

He thought of KK, well aware of the dangers of Waziristan, and felt the familiar resentment. He should never have taken me into that danger zone. And yet he knew it would be a source of immense pain to KK that his rash decision was causing my family such terrible grief.

And he felt angry at me. To his mind, I ignored my parents' feelings. I didn't understand the pressure my job placed them under, the constant worry they felt about what might happen if things went wrong.

He started putting himself in my shoes. At lunch with Nudrat, he'd suddenly stop eating.

"I wonder if Asad and Khalid are getting any food."

In the office, he would sometimes stare out of the window at the hot, dusty city below.

"Asad and Khalid will be sitting in filth, with no fresh air."

Then he'd get up and switch off the air conditioning.

Asghar and Nudrat were hurting with him, but they kept quiet. The deadline had passed, apparently without incident, and he'd not heard anything. He remembered what Robin had told him—once the first deadline passes, deadlines stop being an issue.

A day or so later, Usama walked into Farrukh's office. There was a change in his demeanor. He no longer looked edgy, nervous, hunted. He looked at ease.

Farrukh asked him for an update. Usama told him that, in the past twenty-four hours, he'd had a great deal of contact with Usman Punjabi, and with another man by the name of Ilyas Kashmiri. Punjabi was confident Usama's father would soon be released. Usama was elated.

To Farrukh, with whom the kidnappers had been so demonstrably hostile, this news seemed almost too good to be true.

He asked Usama if he'd recorded his conversations with Punjabi, but he had not. Farrukh asked if he did indeed sound Punjabi or if he sounded Pushtun. Usama wasn't sure.

Serendipitously, Usama's phone rang and the call was from Usman Punjabi. Usama put his phone on speaker so both Farrukh and Nudrat could hear. The voice was certainly very different from the voice of the man who'd identified himself to Farrukh as Ali Raza. It was a calm voice that kept repeating that Usama would not have to wait long to see his father again. Usama was delighted. He replied with respect. With gratitude. With warmth.

But Farrukh was unnerved. He did not like the voice. Did not like its calmness. Its coolness.

Did not like the bald, emotionless statement that brought the call to a close.

"Soon you will hear good news."

17
The Move

Krishan Lal entered my room and asked me to stand up. He was carrying long strips of black cloth.

He proceeded to blindfold me, wrapping one strip of cloth on top of the other till I couldn't see at all. I was led out of the room, still in handcuffs and shackles. After I'd shuffled a few steps out of the room, I was told to stand still and not move.

Numerous voices swirled around me. The sounds of people moving, on either side of me. Was this it? The end?

I felt some sort of cloth garment being draped over me. The all-encompassing weight of it made me gasp for air. A burqa. I could feel it tight around my blindfolded head. A sickening stench of perspiration mingled with the sickly sweet smell of cheap perfume. It had been worn by a young woman.

I was left standing for several minutes while frantic activity went on around me. I played a scene in my head. A dusty yard, a wall, gunfire. Darkness.

I pictured myself in a burqa. Ridiculous. I remembered that the veteran BBC news reporter, John Simpson, had worn a burqa in Afghanistan. "It seemed like I was invisible," he said of the experience. And, of course, Maulana Abdul Aziz of the Red Mosque had tried the old burqa trick—nobody notices a woman in a burqa—in a failed attempt to escape from the besieged mosque.

Someone grabbed my right arm and pulled me toward them. I started walking, taking each shuffling step carefully so I wouldn't trip. I felt some steps. I was being led out of the house.

Then I was held and told to stand still. I heard Mukhtar's raised voice. Someone was being pushed, forcefully. Then the sound of punching. Heavy blows punctuated by exhausted grunts. Colonel Imam. Mukhtar seemed to have it in for him.

"Move," Mukhtar shouted. He pushed me forward.

"Take a step up."

I slowly raised my right foot and felt for the step and put my foot on it. Someone pushed my head down. I was in a vehicle. Quite a high step, so an SUV.

Another person climbed in next to me, then others. We were packed in tightly. Just like the first day. The day we'd been taken.

Krishan Lal barked a command.

"If we are stopped, not a sound."

The vehicle pulled away. I prayed to God that He would protect us from these terrible people.

The sound of water splashing as we drove. Puddles. A breeze on my face. The first time I'd had that refreshing sensation for a while. About a month.

The vehicle stopped. A whisper from Krishan Lal.

"They're watching us. What shall we do?"

Nauman's whispered answer.

"We should keep going."

So Nauman was driving.

We drove on for what felt like twenty minutes or so before coming to an abrupt halt. One by one we were led out of the vehicle. Krishan Lal held my arm and guided me.

"We have trip wires here that could electrocute you. Lift your feet high as you walk."

Life is precious. Maybe I was being led to my death anyway, but I didn't want death by electrocution. I lifted my feet high, knees almost up to chest level, as I stepped forward gingerly. A prancing man in a burqa. I must have looked absurd.

The air around me changed. I was now in a room. I was told to sit. I felt something soft, perhaps pillows or bedding rolled up on the floor.

A loud voice said, "Finger on the lips."

There was a slight echo to the voice. And no smell of earth. A different kind of place. A building of bricks and mortar.

A new voice. An odd accent. I couldn't place it. Russian? American? Either way, it didn't bode well. If this new man was Russian, he'd be well versed in exotic methods of torture. If he was American, we'd almost certainly be shipped off to Guantánamo Bay, where more-traditional methods of torture would await us.

I sat still. Finger on my lips.

The sound of someone else being brought into the room. A mumble. Then the sound of a heavy punch. A resonant sound, like contact made on someone's back.

"What was *that* for?" KK's voice.

"I told you to put your finger on your lips."

"I didn't understand you."

Although my treatment was bad enough, KK and the Colonel were clearly being much more roughly treated. I felt a very uncomfortable mixture of anxiety, sympathy, and shame.

My blindfold was untied. I saw Krishan Lal's face in front of me. Then I saw Khalid, for the first time in a month. He looked pale and gaunt. His chains were tighter than mine.

His blindfold was removed. He looked at me. I gave him an imploring look in the hope he wouldn't say anything to antagonize Krishan Lal.

"I don't want you two to talk to each other, or even look at each other. We have listening devices in this room and cameras right outside. If I hear you talking, I will take you downstairs to the cold room. You will have to run to keep warm. The only place to sit will be a big block of ice."

The thought of the cold room terrified me. Krishan Lal rolled a straw mat out on the floor and laid what looked like a sleeping bag on top of it. He told us to lie down, with our backs to one another.

Once Krishan Lal had left the room, I heard KK's chains jangle as he turned around to face me. I could see he was trussed up differently. Although we both had the same Hiatt-type handcuffs on, which were a design from the 1990s, KK had two extra rings inserted in each cuff, which led to his shackles, leaving less room for his wrists. I had only one ring which went round the chain connecting the two handcuff rings. My wrists had a good bit more freedom.

He looked tired and pale. His voice was weak.

"I am so glad they put you with me. Trust no one. And whatever you do, don't tell them you gave me any money."

His advice was fruitless. I had written everything down in the diary they had surely read, including notes about the money Asif had given him, and Asif's statement that "KK was spending money like a sailor on shore leave." Well, maybe they hadn't been able to decipher my terrible handwriting.

I looked away and faced the wall, hoping he'd understand my fear about us being monitored. Thankfully, he took the hint and rolled back onto his side. A new chapter in our captivity had begun.

A few hours passed. Krishan Lal came into the room with some food. I asked him if I could use the bathroom. He proceeded to unlock my handcuffs and shackles.

"When I go outside and knock on this door, then you can go through that door. Not before."

He pointed to a metal door on the side of the room.

When I heard the knock, I walked over and opened the door. It revealed an adjoining bathroom. Basic, but better than the one in the last place. At least there was running water here.

I closed the door behind me. Then I heard Krishan Lal bellow at KK.

"Why are you telling my people to leave us for something better? Why?"

The sound of blows.

But it had been me, not KK. I was the one who'd spoken to Mukhtar, not him. I couldn't just stand back and allow him to be punished for something I'd done. That would constitute the height of cowardice.

I dashed back into the room.

"It was me. I said those things to Mukhtar."

His turned his face toward me. He was full of hatred. He took a pistol out of his holster. He pointed it at my feet.

"Who are you to advise my people?"

"No one. I'm no one."

"I am going to shoot your toes off, one by one."

His mouth was twisted with rage and spittle was flying from it. The veins on his neck looked like they were struggling to contain his boiling blood.

He cocked the hammer with his thumb. I was never going to walk again.

I joined my hands like a beggar.

"Please forgive me. Please. It won't happen again. I promise."

KK spoke up.

"Please have mercy on him. He didn't mean it."

I kept my hands in their begging position and lowered my eyes. I didn't want to provoke him any more. And I didn't want to look at the gun. KK had clamped his mouth shut, too. In the silence, I could hear Krishan Lal's heavy breathing as he struggled to contain his outrage. At the last place, he'd killed someone outside my door. He'd offered to show me the dead man's blood. I knew he wouldn't lose any sleep over shooting my toes off. He was a trained killer.

There was a knock on the metal door.

"*Hoi! Kiya ho raha hey?*" Oi! What's going on?

A voice I'd not heard before. A voice with authority. Krishan Lal started.

"*Kuch nahin.*" Nothing.

I looked up at him. His face relaxed. Then he shook his head up and down. *This isn't over.* He turned around and left the room.

I stopped holding my breath. Relief. I looked at KK. His intervention had probably saved me the use of my feet. He looked so exhausted. He'd been beaten twice in as many hours.

Then the door burst open again, and Krishan Lal marched into the room with a second person, a young boy who looked no more than twelve years of age. He had his turban pulled down over his face but I could tell his age from his slight frame. He was carrying an AK47 assault rifle. It looked heavy.

"You see him? You think you can turn him against us?"

"No. No."

I looked at the boy. The boy pulled his turban up and stared back at me, like a boxer in the ring. Like he'd seen plenty of people like me. Men old enough to be his father or grandfather. He'd seen them beaten, tortured, even killed. Perhaps he'd even done the killing.

Even in my pathetic, shackled state I felt so sad for this boy. He was just a child, but one that had been robbed of his childhood. Oblivious to the difference between right and wrong and ignorant of the ethics of war and peace. Of human rights. Of the value of human life.

"He will shoot you without blinking an eye."

"I believe you."

He signaled to the boy to leave the room. He wagged his finger at me. *I'm warning you.* He followed the boy out.

Again I breathed. Hopefully that was the end of the matter.

I looked at KK. It was better not to engage him in conversation. I was done being shouted at and threatened. I didn't want to give Krishan Lal any excuse to mistreat me.

I looked at the food Krishan Lal had brought earlier. Lentils and chapattis. I took some. Too much oil in the lentils, and too much salt. So I just broke off little pieces of chapatti.

KK ate a little. We didn't look at one another.

I wondered where we were. This place was better but I still had no desire to be here. The windows had fine wire mesh on the inside to keep out mosquitoes. The troublesome little beasts would have had no chance of getting in anyway—in place of glass, sheets of metal had been set into the windows, which both prevented us from seeing outside and offered us no material we might break and use to do harm to ourselves. They were clearly experienced at holding prisoners.

As night began to fall, Krishan Lal came in and switched on all the lights—twin bulbs on three walls and two fluorescent tubes on one wall. (There was a fan on the ceiling, so all lights had been fitted to the walls, so as not to create a strobe effect).

The bright lights were another form of torture. Sleep deprivation. I was wide awake in a brightly lit room. On top of the light, the chirping of the crickets outside was loud and constant. It was going to be a long night.

I looked around at the place. It was not at all as Krishan Lal had described it, after my last interrogation. He'd told me we'd be going to stay in an American compound. We'd enjoy all their American luxuries. There'd be a big-screen television and good food, and our stay with the Americans would be short before we were released. In my desperate hope for the miserable ordeal to be over, I believed him. Now it was clear to me that he told lies for the sake of it. I resolved not to believe him in future. There was no point getting my hopes up only to have them dashed.

A cricket sat on the bare concrete floor in front of me, chirping steadily in the bright light.

I was restless. On my makeshift bed, I tossed and turned, my chains jangling with the movement. There were many questions I was dying to ask KK, but I didn't dare, for fear of being heard.

When the lights were finally turned off at dawn prayers, I had a terrible headache and felt very fragile. But I washed for prayers and tried to feel positive about my situation—at least this new place had a relatively clean bathroom with a proper sink. I looked around. As prison cells go, it was okay. There was a little hole high up in the wall, probably made for an extractor fan but very small. Too small to squeeze through. They'd thought of everything.

My second day with KK had started. I smiled at a little irony. I was no longer in solitary confinement. I had a companion. But one I wasn't allowed to talk to.

Occasionally, KK and I would look at one another, each wanting to talk but knowing we couldn't.

A long, silent, and uneventful day passed. As evening drew closer, I started to dread the bright lights and the thought of another interminable, sleepless night. Whoever said "Time flies" is an idiot.

To pass the time, and engage my brain in some activity, I began my old counting trick, hoping it would lull me into a restful sleep. American states again, in alphabetical order—Alabama, Alaska, Arizona, Arkansas ...

Early the next morning, Krishan Lal came in. He hurriedly blindfolded KK and led him out of the room. No explanation. Another interrogation, perhaps. Or maybe they'd put us together to listen in on our conversations but, as we hadn't said much, they'd given up. I was working hard not to think the worst. I said a prayer for his safety.

After a few hours, Krishan Lal led Rustam into the room. With his right hand he held Rustam's shoulder. In his left he was carrying a wooden box. Rustam was blindfolded and looked dreadful. Drained. His beard was very long and straggly.

Krishan Lal told Rustam to stand in the middle of the room. Then he gestured to me to walk over to him. He opened the wooden box. Tools. Tools for torture.

He pulled out a set of pliers and gripped Rustam's fingernail. I let out a yell. "NO!"

Krishan Lal looked at me and threw his head back and laughed like a torturer in a horror movie. He pulled away the pliers and untied Rustam's blindfold.

Rustam and I looked at each other and hugged, like long-lost brothers. I was relieved to see he was alive and, if not well, then at least not disabled or disfigured.

I had learnt a new lesson. Krishan Lal was not only a liar but also a sadist. He had reveled in my frantic outrage at the pliers. He was still laughing.

He told Rustam to take the bed KK had occupied. He left us, locking the door behind him.

I clung to Rustam, a deep sense of responsibility invading me. He was in this mess because of me.

I asked Rustam how he was, a ridiculous question under the circumstances. He was bearing up.

"I'm sorry for asking you to come on this shoot with me."

"It is not your fault. I was happy to come."

The response of a true friend.

I worried about his large family and how they were coping, since Rustam and his eldest son were the only breadwinners in the family, and they barely scraped by. His first wife didn't get along with him at all; she had borne him ten children and he went off and married someone else. After having a son with his new wife, he went back to his first wife, for whom the damage was done. I could never understand his follies; he had enough problems without creating more.

I asked him for news of Colonel Imam. In contrast to where Khalid and I were kept, Colonel Imam was not so lucky, it seemed. He was locked in the bathroom similar to the one KK and I used but at the other end of the building. The room measured no more than 5 feet by 8. The windows had metal sheeting on the outside and a small hole on the wall, like in our room, the only way for fresh air to enter the room. The small room was claustrophobic, smelly, and impossible to get comfortable in.

Colonel Imam was over 6 feet tall and in order to lie down he had to contort himself. When he stretched out his legs, his feet touched the pedestal of the sink and he had to put one foot either side of the pedestal. If he wanted to turn on his side, he had to put both feet on one side of the pedestal. The Eastern-style toilet was raised by about 6 inches from the ground, impeding his movement even more.

This was to be his home for the next twelve days, where he would eat, sleep, pray, and the rest. Strictly speaking, in the Muslim world a person is not allowed to pray in a graveyard or a bathroom. However, locked up in a bathroom through no fault of his own, it was acceptable for him to offer his prayers.

While Rustam and I were talking, Nauman came in. He took the magazine off his AK47 and took the bullets out and started throwing them at us. The bullets from these guns are about 3 inches long and very heavy. We held our arms up to protect our faces. A bullet hit me on the wrist and a sharp pain shot up my arm. This was Nauman's idea of fun.

Then he told us to collect them all up. Rustam and I were on our hands and knees picking up the bullets. He was reveling in making us crawl all over the floor. Krishan Lal entered the room and asked him to stop. Nauman insisted he was missing one bullet and said we were hiding it. He knew full well all the bullets had been returned to him—he just didn't like Krishan Lal stopping him.

I hated him. I wanted to jump on him and tear him to bits. But of course that would have been the end of me. In my state, I was no match for him, and he had a gun. At the same time I was grateful to Krishan Lal for asking him to quit. Krishan Lal was friendlier in this location than he was in the last place, at least toward me. But he seemed to have an aversion to KK, which puzzled me.

After he left, I updated my diary with the recent events as usual and put it under my mattress. I had crammed so much information into it and was desperately short of space. I hoped they'd soon give me another book to write in.

18
The Unthinkable Happens

The following morning, Krishan Lal came in. He blindfolded Rustam and led him into the bathroom and locked the door. Then he blindfolded me and told me to sit up straight.

What was going on?

I heard the door open and close. Footsteps approaching. My stomach tightened.

"*Asalaam alaikum.*"

"*Walaikum salaam.*"

A new voice. No Pushtun accent.

After the usual pleasantries, the man settled into a lecture. How they were protecting Islam from the infidel Americans. If they stayed in Afghanistan for another two years, it would be the end of the United States. It would break up, just like the Soviet Union had done.

His people were the guardians of the world, he said. But the world needed to change. A new world was needed, and the defeat of the allied forces in Afghanistan was the start, the man said. I'd later learn this man was Usman Punjabi.

I shuddered to think what kind of a world that would be. I thought back to a film I'd made for the BBC's *Panorama*, "The Battle of Swat Valley." In it, I'd included footage of Taliban fighters digging up corpses, decapitating them and hanging them by their feet in the town square, newly renamed *Khooni Chowk.** They'd killed people for not having their trousers above their ankles. Using a mobile phone, they'd filmed a girl being held down and beaten because she refused to marry a Taliban man.

This was the kind of world Punjabi wanted. A continuous holocaust.

I listened to his diatribe with all the apparent impassivity I could muster. Then he mentioned Farrukh.

"Your brother is coming to collect you."

If this was true, and my release was imminent, this was great news indeed.

But it might be a trap. They might seize Farrukh too.

---

* Bloody Square.

Why wasn't someone else coming? Someone from the channel? Or the government?

Then his tone changed. More serious. Inquisitory.

"Do you know General Shuja Pasha?"

General Pasha was the head of the ISI, someone these people would regard as the enemy.

"No, I don't know him."

"Did you give Khalid Khawaja any money?"

The rug had been pulled from under me. KK had known they'd ask this question. I thought again about my diary. I hoped again they hadn't read it.

I had to answer quickly. Hesitation would be interpreted with suspicion.

"I don't handle money. My job is to shoot the film. All financial matters are taken care of by the producer. I don't get involved in those decisions."

"I see."

He seemed convinced. Still, I prayed they hadn't looked at my diary.

And why did they need to know about KK and money? What was behind that question?

But Punjabi asked no more questions. In silence, he got up and left.

My blindfold was untied. Krishan Lal's face again. Then he ushered Rustam back into the room. He'd been standing in the bathroom during that brief interrogation.

I thought about KK and the irony of his situation. This man was always doing so much to support the families of missing people, himself now captive and—to the outside world—missing.

I remembered an interview I'd conducted in Karachi with KK. Two men had been released after being held by the security agencies for nine months. I'd listened to the painful experiences of the men, but I'd been marked more by the gut-wrenching stories of their mothers. The fear. The pain. Which only a mother knows.

I thought of my own mother and of the agony she must have been feeling at that very moment. And there was nothing I could do to bring her any comfort. I felt horribly powerless.

By now we'd been in captivity for thirty-six days. Each day had seemed like a month.

* * *

On Wednesday, April 28, 2010, Mohammad Raashid, an experienced journalist with good contacts in Waziristan, received a call from one of his sources in Mir Ali. He was told that a *jirga* had made a ruling on KK and he would be killed on April 30 after Friday prayers. Only a swift and impressively persuasive intervention could save KK's life. Raashid immediately went to see KK's family and told them they had only twenty-four hours to save KK. He implored them to hold a press conference and ask Maulana Abdul Aziz of the Red Mosque to appeal to the kidnappers to spare KK and the rest of us. Usama didn't take Raashid seriously—he suspected the kidnappers had sent him to put pressure on the family and he clung to the belief that his father's connections were a talisman. A cloak of invincibility. He was confident nothing would happen to him.

The unthinkable happened on Friday, April 30, 2010.

KK was transported to the town of Mir Ali. The Asian Tigers celebrated Friday prayers. After prayers, they led KK to an area by a stream. People gathered round him, just as in Nudrat's nightmare in an Istanbul hotel three months earlier.

One man stepped forward and at point blank range shot KK once in the forehead. As his body fell, the man shot him again in the chest. Death was instant.

As KK's blood seeped out of his body, the dry ground started to absorb it. The monsters pinned a note to his chest, accusing him of being a spy, in the pay of the Pakistani government and the CIA. Young children looked on, unmoved. Just another day in this lawless hell. Nothing new. To some it was entertainment. A spectacle.

KK had left home with just the clothes on his back. He'd told his wife that was all he'd need.

* * *

At Farrukh's office, Nudrat was taking advantage of a rare moment of focus to get Farrukh to deal with a few bits of urgent work that required his input.

Farrukh's phone rang. Brian from the channel had received an email. An Asian Tigers spokesman had released a statement to the media. Khalid Khawaja had been executed because the government had not met their demands.

Farrukh's receptionist came in to say the phone lines were jammed. They'd seen bad news on television.

Nudrat switched it on. The former ISI officer's corpse had been found near Mir Ali. Two gunshot wounds.

Farrukh's legs gave way. He collapsed onto the sofa and stared straight ahead.

Nudrat saw again her Turkish nightmare. The bearded man defamed, tortured, brutalized, and murdered. It was chilling.

And yet, in her dream, only one man had died. The other man had been there, in the dark, being fed slop and filthy water from a dog's bowl. She had not seen this second man die. *Asad will come out of this alive.*

Usama heard the news of his father's death on television.

He remembered the premonition as he'd waved goodbye to his father. Through his tears, he turned to his mother. She was incredibly strong. A gracious, God-fearing woman who accepted her fate. For her, everything had a reason. And she'd always supported Khalid in his various projects, never objecting when he'd brought refugees home, never complaining when they'd stayed for months on end.

She remembered Khalid's parting words. *If we succeed in this mission, we will save many lives.*

So typical of him to value other lives above his own. She'd loved him for that. Usama hugged her. They cried in each other's arms.

Farrukh gathered his staff. They all knew KK well and were all deeply saddened by the news of his death. They went en masse to KK's family to offer their condolences.

KK's family was in mourning. The house full of relatives and friends. Surrounded by reporters.

Like a family elder, Farrukh moved through the house, trying his best to console everyone. Usama, whom Farrukh had known as a young boy, now looked like a grief-stricken old man. He was on the phone, frantically trying to contact people to make arrangements to bring his father's body back to Islamabad.

He tried to persuade Farrukh to speak to the press. The journalist who'd contacted him had proved, fatefully, to have very accurate information. Perhaps speaking to him was the best way forward for Farrukh.

But Farrukh was in no mood to contact the media. Besides, the Pakistani press, notorious ambulance chasers, would be salivating over the prospect of footage of the return of KK's body. He couldn't trust himself to stay calm in the face of all that shameful baying. Best to sneak back to the office unnoticed.

He sat alone for hours, watching the seconds tick away on the white enamel wall clock. Nudrat stayed on long after the others had gone home, but Farrukh was in a place where she couldn't reach him.

When finally she left him to his own dark thoughts, he called Asghar and, despite the very late hour, together they went to see the A Team. Farrukh's mood was somber, but the team did what little they could to try to keep up his morale.

Back in London, Asif had not been contacted by anyone involved with the negotiations. Farrukh had wanted him to remain detached from the crisis, partly for his own safety but mostly in order to limit communication. The more people in the loop, the greater the risk information would be leaked. Information that might jeopardize my release.

But Asif didn't need direct contact. He'd been monitoring the Pakistani news channels online. He already knew about KK's death.

Asif had known me since 1984. We'd collaborated on many projects. He knew the risks I was prepared to take. As a result, he worried about me. And he felt guilty.

Before we'd set out for Waziristan, he'd suggested we employ a local cameraman to do the filming. It wasn't safe for me, he'd said.

I was against the idea. Such an opportunity couldn't be squandered by having some unknown cameraman handle the filming. We'd have no idea what kind of footage he'd bring back. And I couldn't countenance sending someone else in danger while I remained at a safe distance in Islamabad.

"If we were to hire a local cameraman, well, he'd have a mother too. She'd worry about her son just as much as my mother will worry about me."

Now Asif was wishing he'd insisted. Wishing he'd overruled me and, as producer, prevented me from going.

My younger sister, Farhat, telephoned our sister Rakhshindah at school. It was lunchtime and she was in the staff room.

"What is it?"

"They've killed Khalid."

Rakhshindah got up and walked to her classroom. She must try to keep calm. Farrukh had told her they must all do everything in their power to keep the news from getting out to the British media. If my kidnapping became an international news story, it would put me in even more danger.

A pupil walked past her in the corridor, staring.

"Are you all right, Miss?"

"I'm fine."

She was far from fine. The news of KK's death had suddenly made the prospect of my death very real. It was clear the kidnappers wouldn't think twice before taking my life.

Farrukh's immediate problem was what to tell Mum and Dad. He knew that, despite getting everyone in England to keep them away from TV news, word of KK's death might still get to them. How to proceed?

If he didn't tell them, and they found out from other sources, they'd instantly fear the worst for me. That would have a devastating impact on their already fragile health.

If he were to break the news to them, carefully explaining that KK's case was different to mine, and that mine was still under negotiation, that would produce two results. It would give them hope for me. And it would go some way to preparing them for a similar fate for me if things didn't work out.

He dialed the number. Mum answered the phone. She sounded drained.

"Hello."

"*Asalaam alaikum.*"

"*Walaikum salaam.*"

"Mum, I need to talk about Asad and his colleagues."

"What has happened?"

"I need to explain to you that each case is different."

"What do you mean? What has happened?"

"Asad's captivity has money attached to it. Khalid and the Colonel are being held so that a demand can be made for prisoners to be released in exchange for them."

"I understand that."

"But the government does not deal with terrorists. The terrorists have killed my friend, Khalid."

Mum let out a scream.

"Where's my son? What have they done to him?"

"Mum, don't worry. It's very sad. But Khalid's case was very difficult. There was nothing we could do. Asad's case is entirely different. He's just a filmmaker. They won't harm him. They just want money."

"Can you get the money?"

"Rest assured I will bring him back, safe. I promise you."

The sound of Mum sobbing.

"Please don't cry."

Ten minutes later, Farrukh had succeeded in calming Mum down. Then he talked to Dad and repeated the same story. Dad barely said a word. Since the kidnapping, he'd gone into a silent stupor. He was grieving quietly.

In the hours that followed, my whole family called each other. Tears. Long periods of silence.

On hearing this news, the mother-in-law of my younger sister, Farhat, suggested my parents stay with them in Oxford for a while. A change of scenery and company might do them good. Farrukh thought this was a good idea.

Out of the blue, Farrukh received a call from a former client, Mrs Shakir, resident in Germany. Three years previously, her husband had abducted their son and taken him to Pakistan, where he'd enrolled him in a *madrassah*, telling the boy they were just visiting for the day.

Mrs Shakir had been horrified and frightened. She'd asked Farrukh to find the boy and bring him back.

It had taken Farrukh three long years to track the boy to a secluded *madrassah* in Lahore, from where he'd personally escorted him to Germany, to be reunited with his mother.

Every year since, on the anniversary of their reunion, Mrs. Shakir phoned Farrukh to thank him. Today was that day.

Farrukh listened politely and patiently as Mrs. Shakir gave him the highlights of their last twelve months together. Once again, he accepted her effusive thanks and her good wishes for the future, never once letting the mask slip.

When he put down the phone, he was exhausted. Nudrat managed to convince him to get some sleep, while she kept her eyes on the dedicated email for a message from the kidnappers.

At just after two in the morning, it came. Nudrat roused Farrukh and they read it.

Aoa
only give me final demand
we have no time
may be this is last email
u can ask uk press
and international media
quick reply

Another push to hold a press conference and make the kidnapping more public. He'd resisted so far, on the advice of the A Team and also because he himself believed it was wisest to contain the situation.

But, with Khalid's death, everything had changed. And what about the Colonel? He was also linked to the ISI. Was it safe to keep insisting on his release with mine? Should he now come clean and tell the kidnappers how much he could pay? Wasn't that playing into their hands? Should he move fast? Should he move slowly? So many questions. But no easy answers and no clear guidance.

He went to meet the A Team.

They assured him all would be well but suggested he reply immediately, repeating the line that the government doesn't pay ransoms, and he was talking to the family and trying to come up with the money. They should give him a reasonable ransom figure and call back in forty-eight hours.

In spite of the A Team's insistence on an immediate but repetitive reply, Farrukh had a strong feeling that now was not a good time to get in touch. Nudrat and Asghar agreed. He was, in some way, grieving, they said. He needed some time to formulate a proper reply. And the last thing he wanted to do was appear weak and vulnerable.

He thought about the money again.

Although his own personal savings constituted a substantial figure, it was still short of what he wanted to offer. He'd already called in some favors and chased some clients who owed money, and now he was also looking at his investments. Some friends were offering to remortgage their houses. This man who had never had to bother about money could now think about little else.

But still Khalid remained on Farrukh's mind. Sadness. Disbelief. One of his closest friends dead. And Farrukh powerless to help. A miserable, violent death. A death alone.

Which was how Farrukh felt now. No one to turn to. No one to lean on. No one to bear the burden. As much a prisoner of the kidnappers as I was, his whole life revolving around their emails and calls and how to respond. Noise in his head. Incessant. Denying sleep.

The following morning, he read a newspaper report:

PESHAWAR: On Friday, militants in North Waziristan killed Khalid Khawaja, a former officer of the Inter-Services Intelligence, who was kidnapped on March 26, along with another ISI officer and Taliban sympathizer Colonel (retired) Amir Sultan Tarar and British journalist Asad Qureshi. Khalid Khawaja was shot in the head and chest. A little-known Asian Tigers group has claimed responsibility for the kidnapping.

The newspapers contained more confusing statements from Jawaid Ibrahim Peracha, the local politician who'd played host to my team in Kohat.

In the report, Peracha said KK was a friend of the Americans and had helped to get a Taliban leader killed in a drone attack. Yet, on the other hand, he claimed KK had told him the recent trip to North Waziristan had been made to work on a pro-Taliban documentary highlighting collateral damage caused by US drone attacks.

It was obvious to Farrukh that the latter statement had been prompted by a visit to Peracha from KK's son, Usama, desperate to paint his father in whatever light would be most favorable for his release.

Confusingly, Usama's own statements to various private television channels claimed his father had gone into Waziristan on a peace mission. He'd set out with the aim of persuading the Taliban to end suicide bombings and attacks inside Pakistan and, instead, focus their attention on combating the United States and NATO forces in Afghanistan.

The media message was very mixed, with many reports claiming KK was pro-Taliban and some claiming he was pro-American.

Precisely what motives had driven KK to make the trip into Waziristan Farrukh could not be sure. KK had taken the answer with him. But Farrukh resolved to believe he had gone there to make arrangements for the documentary to be shot by me.

He knew KK had been pro-Taliban—no secret had ever been made of that—and, following the Lal Masjid siege in 2007, KK's tireless work in tracking down "missing people" had earned him a widespread reputation as a humanitarian.

The ambulance carrying KK's body stopped many times en route to Islamabad and crowds of people gathered round it to offer prayers. At the Kohat/Islamabad fork, the driver took the right fork for Islamabad.

If only we had done the same on that fateful day in March.

The ambulance arrived in Islamabad much later than anticipated, on account of the frequent stops. By this time, a considerable media camp had been established outside KK's house, ready to pounce as soon the ambulance showed up.

A tearful Usama and his younger brother, Huzaifa, received their father's body. The pain of seeing the body was evident, not just the reality of his death but the terrible appearance of the body itself. Point-blank gunshots make for very grisly wounds indeed. In addition, KK's body was peppered with cigarette burns, marks of the torture used to extract the false confessions that had been broadcast.

According to Islamic law, a deceased person has to be buried on the day of death. By this point, KK had been dead for three days, a further ignominy.

His body was placed in the garden and people paid their respects, many sitting and reading the Qur'an.

As KK had been murdered while trying to do good work, he was deemed to be a martyr. The ritual bathing that precedes an Islamic burial is, in these circumstances, dispensed with.

Journalists were surrounding Usama, clamoring for an interview. KK's son was in no state to talk at all, let alone coherently to camera, but Pakistani journalists are the most persistent and heartless in the world.

As Usama stood in front of the cameras, he could barely utter the few words he chose to speak.

"My father was a very truthful person. He was a harmless man. He was always trying to help other people."

That was all he could say.

Usama had approached Maulana Abdul Aziz, imam of the Lal Masjid, to lead the funeral prayers for his father, but he'd been initially reluctant. Any association with KK would stir up memories of the Lal Masjid massacre, an issue still very fresh in the public mind. The Taliban were still blaming KK for, as they painted it, leading Abdul Aziz into a trap that ended with his arrest, which Farrukh knew was a complete fabrication.

Farrukh also knew the Pakistani government was pressurizing Abdul Aziz *not* to lead the funeral prayers, so his refusal would make it seem KK had in fact been responsible for Abdul Aziz's arrest and the government could distance itself from KK's death.

But Usama, together with numerous friends, had continued to implore Maulana Abdul Aziz to lead the funeral prayers and, finally, he'd agreed.

Although many people stayed away from the funeral, for fear of a terrorist attack, nevertheless, on May 4, 2010, four days after his brutal execution, KK's funeral service was attended by loyal friends and a huge media contingent, to whom Generals Hamid Gul and Mirza Aslam Beg gave interviews.

After prayers had been said, the body of this brave, selfless, enigmatic man was gently lowered into a grave. His sons, Usama and Huzaifa, sprinkled earth on their beloved father, then left the gravediggers to their grim work.

Farrukh had kept a low profile throughout and managed to leave the funeral unnoticed by the press.

It was the end of the journey for his trusted friend. But Farrukh was acutely aware that, for Colonel Imam, Rustam, and me, the journey's end was still some way off.

For now, the state of limbo continued.

19
The Humiliation

It was now early May.

Rustam and I had settled into our room. Not exactly comfortable but more bearable than the last place.

KK and I had been forbidden from talking to each other. They relaxed this rule for Rustam and me. I spent my day writing in my diary, reading the Qur'an, praying, and talking to Rustam. For his part, Rustam just lay on his bed stroking his beard and staring at the ceiling. I often wondered what he was thinking, but to ask seemed like an intrusion so I never did.

I went to get a glass of water from the water cooler at the other end of the room. My shackles jangled as I shuffled. No handcuffs now, though, which was something of a blessing.

A shiny object on the floor caught my eye. I bent down to pick it up and saw it was a paper clip bent into the form of a key. A key that might unlock shackles.

I was gripped by fear. If they found the key on me or Rustam, we'd get a beating. No doubt about it.

The most sensible thing to do was to hand it over to Krishan Lal.

After a couple of hours he came in, with food. I held out the paper clip.

"I found this. I want to give it to you."

He took the piece of bent metal and looked at it. Then he lifted his eyes toward me, slowly.

"It was on the floor. I saw it when I went over to get some water. I don't know where it came from."

I was babbling.

He laid the food down on the floor. He looked at me again. Then he left. Relief.

I looked at the food but didn't take any.

The food we were given had not been agreeing with me at all. I'd begun to feel unwell. I was having serious stomach problems and couldn't digest anything. Lack of exercise was also doubtless playing a part.

The kidnappers could see I was genuinely unwell. After consulting their so-called doctor, they gave me some medicine, the laxative Ispaghula. It didn't work. A couple of hours later, I was in absolute agony.

Nauman went out to a shop in the nearby village. He came back with a small brown paper packet. Inside the packet was another smaller packet, tightly wrapped in dusty white cotton cloth. He opened it carefully. Inside were a few round black seeds known locally as *jamalgota* and to the medical community as *croton tiglium*.

I'd heard of the seeds. They contained what is possibly the strongest purgative known to man. I'd heard of people who, wanting to get revenge for something, would use the seeds to spike food at some formal occasion—a wedding or other celebration—and the result would be widespread instant diarrhea. The ultimate embarrassment for the hosts.

I knew *jamalgota* could kill a person if it were not administered properly, and I could tell from the care Nauman was taking with it that he appreciated its potency too.

But, such was my agony, I thought it was worth the risk. Things couldn't get any worse.

He handed me the open packet.

"Take half of one of these seeds."

The seeds smelt distressingly pungent. What havoc was it going to wreak on my insides? Half a seed seemed too much for me to take in my weakened state.

"Half?"

Nauman stared at me threateningly. He'd made the effort to go out and get the stuff and here I was arguing with him.

I broke one of the seeds in half and swallowed it with some water.

Almost instantly, I felt queasy. Psychosomatic perhaps, but I really felt very nauseous.

"It will start to work soon," Nauman said. Then he left.

The unease mounted. I started to feel dizzy. Then a wave of nausea broke in my abdomen and I sprang up, only just making it in time to the bathroom to vomit. I coughed and groaned noisily, a terrific pain in my chest and stomach. I staggered back to my bed. Rustam tried to comfort me but nothing would.

The door burst open and Nauman and Krishan Lal strode in, furious with me for throwing up the medicine they'd made the effort to get for me.

Nauman pulled a pistol from his waistcoat and pressed it hard against my temple.

"So you think you are so delicate and special, do you?"

Krishan Lal pushed me toward the bathroom. I stumbled but managed to hold the door frame. Krishan Lal gave me another push and forced me inside the bathroom. Nauman's gun was still pointed at me.

"Take your clothes off!" Krishan Lal barked.

This wasn't good. I tried to pretend it wasn't real. I wanted to believe he wasn't serious and I held my ground.

Nauman pulled back the hammer on his pistol. My heart was racing. I was cornered. A trapped animal. I looked down at the floor, hoping they'd have pity on me and walk away.

"Did you hear what I said?"

I began to tremble. I was afraid of the gun and of a potential beating, but I was more afraid of the humiliation they were about to inflict on me. So far, through all the threats, the starvation, the sleep deprivation, the vile beatings, I'd held on to my dignity. Now that was about to be stripped away as well.

Never in my life before had I succumbed to an instruction to strip. Once, in the UK, I'd been involved in a car accident and had been taken to hospital. The doctor wanted to examine me all over, to make sure there were no injuries. I wouldn't allow it. I drew the line at his examining me below the waist. He was very angry but I was adamant.

I have always been a very private person where nudity is concerned. After PE lessons at school, I'd always wear my swimming shorts in the shower. I was the only one with anything on. The others would stare at me.

It's connected to my fastidiousness, I think. In the school showers, I'd fold my toes inward and upward, so only my heels were touching the shower floor.

I know that, to some people, my attitude might seem a little squeamish, if not downright precious. For me, it's about basic decency and dignity.

"Take your clothes OFF!"

I could see Rustam from the corner of my eye. He looked at me helplessly—there was nothing he could do. In situations like this, your instinct tells you not to get involved. It's better for one person to get hurt than both. Intervention would be pointless.

Krishan Lal lunged toward me. He grabbed hold of my shoulders and shook me violently. He pushed me backward and I fell. The hammer was still raised on Nauman's pistol.

I began the mortifying task of removing my clothes.

Rustam was still looking at me. I wished he'd look away and allow me to suffer this abuse on my own. But I dared not say that, for fear of further antagonizing my tormentors. I made the slightest of motions with my head, sending a sharp pain through my whole body in the process, but hoping to get through to Rustam. He saw the gesture and looked away.

I was now totally naked in front of these monsters. Through access to my email account, they had knowledge of my life. Now they had knowledge of my body too. It felt like I had nothing left that was mine.

"On the toilet!" Krishan Lal yelled.

Nauman stepped closer and pressed his pistol against my forehead.

"Please stop. Please."

But these barbarians were not going to back down. I crouched down on the toilet. No humanity left.

"Okay, okay," I sobbed. "Please leave me now. Please close the door."

They stared at me. I prayed they'd go. The standoff continued for perhaps a minute. An eternity. The two raging figures towered over me while, utterly degraded, I squatted helplessly on the toilet. Surely they'd realize they'd gone far enough.

Nauman pulled his pistol away. They both took a step back. Then they backed off completely. They left the door ajar, but it was still some comfort to be left alone.

But I was not alone for long. Minutes later, they came back into the bathroom, Nauman still with the pistol in his hand.

To avoid further humiliation, I stood up. Krishan Lal turned the tap on and started to fill a bucket of water. He signaled me over to the bucket. Nauman still had his gun trained on me.

"Here. Wash."

I took the bar of soap from the sink and crouched down by the bucket, next to it a big plastic mug, its maroon color blackened by the build-up of soap scum. I picked up the mug, scooped up water, and poured it over my head. I lathered my hands and rubbed them through my hair, which was thick with dirt and only became more matted as the fat in the cheap soap mixed with the dirt.

Through my overgrown beard, I could feel how thin my face had become. My arms and legs looked about half their usual thickness. I'd clearly lost a huge amount of weight.

Krishan Lal threw a towel at me, which I just managed to catch before it touched the floor. I felt like an animal in the zoo, being gawped at by strangers.

I wrapped the towel around my body and went back into the room. I sifted through my bag to find clean clothes and took them back into the bathroom to get dressed.

When I came back into the room, Nauman was rifling through my bag. I grabbed the bag but he pulled it away violently.

"Give it to me!" He growled at me like a mad dog.

He turned the bag upside down and let everything spill out onto the floor—two pairs of *shalwar kamiz* that had belonged to my father, a pair of pajamas, underwear, several handkerchiefs, and my shaving kit. He rummaged through the contents like a shopper at a bargain bin. He selected a few pairs of socks. Then he lifted the *shalwar kamiz*. My father's clothes. He tucked them under his arm with the socks and left.

Feeling bereft of all humanity, and robbed of my connection to my dad, I lay on my bed. I faced the wall and slowly curled up into the fetal position. I felt degraded, as if I existed just for their entertainment. Tears rolled down my cheeks. If ever there was a time I needed my mother, it was now. I longed for her to hug and comfort me. Then everything would be all right. I cried myself to sleep.

Some hours later, Rustam nudged me awake. It was time for evening prayers.

I knew my religious duty and took it very seriously, but part of me wished he'd left me alone in my slumber, far away from this place.

I was still traumatized by my earlier humiliation. And I was angry. If the roles were to be reversed right now, I felt sure I wouldn't show my tormentors any mercy at all. They were ignorant cowards. Robbers masquerading as religious zealots. The injustice of the situation was eating away at me.

The following morning, Nauman walked into our room wearing the clothes he'd taken from me. My father's clothes. The *shalwar* didn't fit him at all—he was a much-broader man than me or Dad.

He noticed me staring at him.

"These are not your clothes. They're mine. I bought them."

I was disgusted at this unscrupulous behavior. To compound theft with a bare-faced lie made him inhuman in my eyes. I decided not to engage in conversation with him. He wasn't worth it.

Besides, when my father wore these clothes, he looked resplendent. Nauman looked like what he was—an impostor.

No doubt he'd derived a great deal of pleasure in taking the clothes from me. I was satisfied that, in these fine clothes, he looked ridiculous. I was having the last laugh.

He strolled round the room, showing off the clothes. His posing was interrupted when Krishan Lal came into the room, carrying a large brown paper bag. He pulled out a board for the game Ludo (known in the US as Parcheesi), some counters, and a dice.

"Here, this will keep you busy."

After the previous day's odiousness, this was indeed a turn-up. Perhaps he was feeling guilty.

Rustam thanked him. He led Nauman out of the room, and Rustam and I were left alone.

"Do you want to play?"

Rustam was clearly keen, so I decided to oblige him.

He arranged the counters on the board and rolled the dice, making rules up as he went along, insisting you had to roll a six to start.

It had been a long time since I'd played, so I accepted what he said. Besides, we were just passing time. Who cared about rules?

In no time at all, Rustam was storming round the board while I hadn't even got off the mark. It wasn't long before he'd won. We played another game. I was surprised at how good he was. It was a game of chance, but Rustam won every time.

When I asked him why he was so good at the game, he told me he was good at all games of chance. He was naturally lucky. He often gambled with his friends, and he'd won and lost thousands of rupees.

I was disappointed and wished I hadn't asked him. I'd never thought of this hardworking family man as a gambler.

For hours, time had passed quickly and we had fun. But the fun was short lived.

Krishan Lal came into the room and told us to stop playing games. It was un-Islamic. The devil's work. Before we could protest, he took the board and tore it up.

It made no sense. But that was the point. A kind of mental, emotional upset was the point. It was almost laughable. If playing a board game was the devil's work, what about stealing, threatening, brandishing a gun?

But, with the board game gone, time slowed down again. The hours stretched ahead.

The days were long but, with the lights left on, the nights seemed longer still.

I'd recite prayer after prayer, hoping to calm myself into a state ready for sleep, but sleep was always hard to come by.

Often I'd reflect on how I'd come to be in this situation. The world had become a very different place since 9/11. But invading Afghanistan and Iraq and declaring war on terror wasn't going to solve the problem. In fact, it was having the opposite effect. And the phrase "war on terror" itself was nonsensical and impotent. It was like saying that all the bacteria in the world must be eradicated.

My present predicament seemed a direct result of the "war on terror," particularly of Pakistan's alliance with the USA. Opposition to President Musharraf's policy of alliance had effectively created a civil war.

I'd lie awake at night thinking of world events, of the Pakistani nation as a victim of terrorism, and of its international status as the most dangerous country in the world.

It was all a far cry from the time I'd traveled the length and breadth of the country, making a film for the tourism corporation. I used to be proud to tell people how beautiful Pakistan was. It was embarrassing now to think anyone visiting Pakistan would be putting their life in danger.

Every night, I would imagine a courtroom and hold an imaginary trial of Presidents Musharraf and Bush, Prime Minister Tony Blair, and US secretary of state Condoleezza Rice. They were world leaders, but this was my court and my word was final.

Condoleezza Rice had made a speech that incensed me at the time.

What we're seeing here is, in a sense, the birth pangs of a new Middle East, and whatever we do, we have to be certain we're pushing forward to the new Middle East, not going back to the old Middle East.

Now, in my imaginary court, I told her how angry I was about that speech. I told her it wasn't right to go around interfering in the internal issues of other countries, irrespective of the consequences.

She gave me a stern look, as if asking who the hell I was to put her on trial. I reminded her this was my court.

And then there was Musharraf. I hadn't liked him since I'd worked for the Ministry of Information. In a room one floor below my office, the National Security Council used to meet once or twice a year. For Musharraf's safety, they always blocked off a staircase at my end of the building. This had also blocked off a fire escape, leaving only one exit point on the far side of the building. Their side.

If he'd been a true leader, he'd have had regard for other people's lives too.

So, in my court, there was nothing he could say in his defense. He was found guilty of causing many deaths. Bush and Blair were judged in the same way. But I couldn't think of a strong enough punishment for them.

The following night I'd do it all over again, till I fell asleep.

I was still very busy with my diary. I wrote up every incident with as much description as possible, taking pride in crafting the words. It kept me busy and, to an extent, kept me sane. It allowed me to think that making it out of here was a possibility. If I did make it out, the diary would be a good record to share with the outside world.

Krishan Lal walked in with cold juice and sweets. He saw me making notes in my diary. I looked up at him. I told him I'd mentioned him in my diary. I thought he'd be pleased.

He grabbed me by my collar and hauled me up from my sitting position. He snatched the diary from me, then punched me in the face. He grabbed me again and slapped me, catching my right ear several times, very painfully.

Self-defense or retaliation would have been dangerous. Rustam and I both knew that. I had to just grin and bear it.

My right ear was throbbing and felt very hot, but he continued to punch me in the face. One of his punches made contact with my nose. It made my eyes water but, strangely, my nose didn't bleed. But I began to feel some swelling in my face. Then, satisfied he'd roughed me up pretty badly, he stopped the barrage of punches and slaps, picked up my diary, and left.

Rustam tried to comfort me, but I waved him away. I lay on my bed facing the wall. I was full of anger at myself for having mentioned the diary. Now I'd lost it.

When Krishan Lal came in later that day, I asked him if I could have my diary back.

"No. I have torn it up."

"Doesn't matter. I would still like it back, please."

I thought of the US hostages in Iran who had shredded all documents before the Iranians could get their hands on them. But the Iranians had painstakingly stuck all the documents back together again. I was willing to go to the same trouble. I had committed my innermost feelings to paper, with vivid descriptions of the horrors I'd suffered, and these were things I would not be able to recall again with the same clarity and fervor.

"I have burnt it."

This broke my heart. The diary was my friend. Someone I could talk to and share my feelings with. Someone who helped me pass the time and gave me hope and comfort. But the friend had been taken away by a madman.

When he came in the following day, Krishan Lal told Rustam and me we'd be learning the Qur'an in Arabic. One of them would teach us, daily.

Mukhtar turned out to be our teacher. Rustam had never attended school, so he had to start by learning the Arabic alphabet. I knew some basic Arabic already, so I started from the first chapter, progressing by memorizing two lines a day. Rustam was stuck on two letters a day and found it difficult enough to remember even that little.

Mukhtar was patient with us but tried to indoctrinate us at the same time. He'd talk about Raiwind, the large *madrassah* in Lahore that had become the site of an annual Muslim convention but also a place where terrorists were now being radicalized en masse. He'd encourage us to settle there and make a life.

If I was ever to get out of here, there was no way I'd be going to Raiwind. I'd had enough of these crazy people.

In this new location, we saw more of the kidnappers, and new members of their group, than we'd seen at the last place. Sometimes we'd get a visit from a man called Mohammed. He always had his head covered. He took an instant dislike to me and was openly hostile.

He talked a lot about an Indian actress he liked—Preity Zinta. I'd never heard of her. I wasn't a fan of Indian films. He'd obviously seen all her films and was taken with the glamor of them. Such a hypocrite. On the one hand, reveling in Bollywood magic. On the other, stopping drivers at gunpoint and ripping out their CD players because listening to music was un-Islamic.

Hypocrites, murderers, and liars. I hated them more each day.

One day, we heard a violent commotion in the next room. When Krishan Lal came into our room, I asked him what was going on.

"Haji *sahib* is being punished."

We'd never heard of this man.

"It is all very well going to Mecca for pilgrimage. But dealing in drugs is wrong. So we are punishing him."

We could hear the sound of a brutal flogging. I imagined an overweight man dressed in white, hung upside down. I could hear the heavy breathing of the man doing the flogging. He was working hard. The flogging continued throughout the call for afternoon prayers. Another contradiction. Another religious rule broken.

After about an hour, there was complete silence. I feared the worst for Haji *sahib*. Krishan Lal had killed a man right outside my door in the last place, so I knew he would have no compunction about killing this man.

When Krishan Lal came in later, I asked about Haji *sahib*.

"He was so clever, he had false caps on his teeth. He hid drugs inside his hollow teeth. When we beat him, he bit his tongue. His own drugs killed him."

I didn't believe a word of it. It was like something out of a James Bond film. I was convinced they'd flogged him to death.

When Krishan Lal left our room, he left the door ajar. I peeked outside and saw Mohammed walking past. I recognized him from his clothes. He had his head uncovered and it was the first time I'd seen his face. It was so badly pockmarked, he looked disfigured. I wondered what his beloved Preity Zinta would have to say about that.

I remembered what an acquaintance of mine, a Harley Street dermatologist, had said when he'd seen excerpts from my film *Defusing Human Bombs*.

"People who are terrorists normally have very low self-esteem. Their faces are often covered in scars or acne. They're usually not what most people would call good-looking."

Looking at the people holding us, his assessment seemed a fair one.

At that moment, Mohammed came into our room. His face was hidden under a hood as usual. He had a book in his hand.

"I want to read you my favorite story."

"Okay."

As if we had a choice. He sat down and opened the book at a marked page. He read.

"There was a battle going on and seven men were killed. As they lay there on the ground, all of a sudden fairies dressed in red and green floated down from the sky and sat on a wall nearby the *shaheed*.[*] One by one, the fairies floated over to the dead men and kissed them. Then, each of them taking a man, they flew straight up into the sky. All except one. As the fairy kissed the man, he was still conscious. Realizing he was still alive, the fairy left without him. He regretted not dying, for, if he had, he too would have been in heaven with his colleagues."

[*] Martyrs.

He looked at me. This was clearly a message aimed at me.

"*Isi leiay hum fadaeen hamla karnay say dar thein nahien.*" It is for this reason that we are not afraid to be suicide bombers.

The brainwashed trying to brainwash others. As for his favorite story, well, it wasn't that impressive.

The call to prayer came and Mohammed left the room. Krishan Lal shouted in to us from outside the room.

"You can pray with your shackles on. God will give you a greater reward."

Who was he to comment on the reward God might or might not give us? He was just too lazy to unlock our shackles. By his twisted logic, what reward would they receive from God for all the harm they'd caused?

It gave me comfort to think God would one day pass judgment on them and it wouldn't be in their favor.

I remembered my friend Susan quoting the Chinese military strategist and philosopher Sun Tzu: *If you wait by the river long enough, the bodies of your enemies will float by.* My contempt for these people was immeasurable.

My mind was strong but my body had suffered a lot of punishment. Add to that weeks of near-total inactivity and my muscles had begun to waste away. I felt incredibly weak. Standing required seven or eight seconds of sustained effort.

Krishan Lal could see something needed to be done. He said I could exercise outside on the veranda. A door on the side of our room opened onto it.

He hung sheets from the veranda canopy so I wouldn't be able to see into the courtyard.

At the far end of the veranda was a *charpoy.** Behind it stood a young boy with a Kalashnikov rifle, the same boy Krishan Lal had brought into our room some time back. I was told I could walk back and forth on the veranda, stopping short of the *charpoy.*

This was the first time I'd properly stretched my legs for several months. My muscle weakness made me very unsteady on my feet and, initially, I stumbled several times. But the boy didn't flinch. He just left me to gather myself each time.

Three rooms led onto the veranda. Perhaps there were other rooms on the other side of the hanging sheets, but I couldn't see them. The first room was ours, and the one next to it was where Haji *sahib* had been flogged. I wondered who was in the last room, beyond the *charpoy.*

As I approached it, the boy pointed his gun at me and told me to keep my distance. I could see in his eyes that, despite his young age, he meant it.

The sheets not only blocked my vision but blocked out fresh air too. They radiated a concentrated odor of sweat and mustiness that made me feel sick.

---

* A traditional bed with a base made of woven rope.

I walked back and forth a few times but, although I could already feel the benefit of the exercise, I needed to get away from that awful smell, so I retreated to my room.

I still hadn't properly recovered from my stomach problems, and now I began to feel not at all well.

Krishan Lal came in and felt my pulse, then put his hand on my forehead. I wondered whether he'd had medical training or whether he was just trying to impress me.

He left the room and returned with an intravenous drip bag and started to set it up. I was concerned he might not have much of a clue what he was doing, but I was too weak to argue with him.

He looked for a suitable vein to insert the cannula, but there were none. He dug in his pocket and pulled out a piece of cloth that had been used as a blindfold. He wrapped it round my upper arm as a tourniquet.

I gave myself up to Krishan Lal's treatment. If he killed me, well, it didn't look like I was getting out of this place anyway.

With the tourniquet on, he found a vein. He inserted the cannula, not as smoothly as a nurse or doctor would have done but not bad. After adjusting the drip flow, he injected a red liquid into the intravenous bag.

"This will give you strength."

It was one thing surrendering to a doctor's experience in London but quite another giving myself up to a quack like him in this God-forsaken wilderness. But I had no energy left to fight. I just nodded. Then I fell asleep.

The next thing I knew, I was being shaken awake by Rustam and cajoled into eating some food. Krishan Lal stepped over and removed the cannula so I could move freely.

"Do you think you could leave the lights off tonight? So we can sleep."

"Okay."

Indulgence. Kindness. The fact of it almost made me weep.

But it didn't last. Of course it didn't.

The following morning, Krishan Lal strode into the room. He was holding a long stick with a truck's transmission belt nailed to one end. He swung it violently, slamming the belt into the floor. The swishing noise recalled Haji *sahib*'s flogging. My God. No wonder he'd died.

"Everybody has to be punished."

He beat the floor repeatedly, while Rustam and I cowered on our beds. He turned to me, eyes full of venom. I was terrified.

One minute, he was a good guy. The next he was a sadistic monster.

"Draw me a map of the Miranshah army air base."

He shouted for someone to get him a sheet of paper and a pencil. Now I was in trouble. My brain wouldn't work, and, although I knew the base well, I was hopeless at drawing. In any case, part of me was reluctant to provide any information that might jeaopardize the safety of friends and colleagues.

He continued to whip the floor with the belt. I imagined, in my weakened state, it would only take two, perhaps three, blows from the belt, and that would be the end of me.

A piece of paper and a pencil were thrust into my hands. I looked at the blank sheet, my mind devoid of any idea how to begin, with the belt swishing through the air and smashing into the floor. I needed to come up with something.

Trembling with weakness and fear, I drew a large rectangle. Inside this I drew a runway and a helicopter landing pad. I added a hangar. It could have been anywhere. All the ancillary buildings would rightly come outside the rectangle, but I'd left no room for them.

Krishan Lal walked over to look at my drawing. It looked like something a four-year-old child would draw at nursery school. He grabbed it from me. I trembled. Then he threw his head back and laughed.

"I know the place backward anyway."

He walked out of the room, clutching the drawing and laughing heartily. He'd just wanted to see me squirm. He enjoyed it.

When I'd recovered my composure, I took up an English translation of the Qur'an, which I'd started reading weeks ago in the previous place. I only had a few pages to go.

When I finished the reading, I said a short prayer, naming my parents as the beneficiaries of this reading. As I said their names, my eyes filled with tears.

I had no idea what state my parents were in, or even if they were still alive. I longed to be with them.

20
The Tape

Farrukh still hadn't replied to the kidnappers' email. After Khalid's death, he needed to think clearly before taking any action. He didn't want blood on his hands. Certainly not mine.

My sister, Rakhshindah, wound up her Religious Studies class in Bradford and, on her way to the staff room, took out her phone to take it off silent. There were thirty-four missed calls from her daughter. In a blind panic, she called her back.

"Mama. I wanted to be the first one to tell you the news. Asad uncle has been released."

"*Alhamdulillah.*"*

For the rest of the day, she repeated the phrase over and over. She couldn't concentrate on her teaching.

"Miss, why are you saying Alhamdulillah?"

"I got some really good news. Something fantastic has happened."

There'd been a report of my release on the lunchtime news. When she got home from work, Rakhshindah called Farrukh and told him the British media was saying I'd been set free. The mood in her house was jubilant. Her doorbell rang and a friend who'd seen the news brought flowers.

In his office in Islamabad, Farrukh couldn't believe what his sister had told him. After the horror of KK's death, it was difficult to accept this apparent U-turn in the kidnappers' behavior. He was mystified. Was KK's death all they'd wanted? Had he been the target? And now they'd settled that score, the rest of us were of no interest? If so, why all the shenanigans with phone calls and threats and ransom demands? Was this really all over? Was I really coming back?

Minutes after the call from Rakhshindah, the office came to life. One after another, there were congratulatory phone calls from friends and colleagues. Someone switched on the TV and all the channels were broadcasting the breaking news. A dazed Farrukh had a broad smile fixed on his face.

* Thanks be to God.

Farrukh asked the reception staff to go out and buy sweets to celebrate. They returned with bagfuls of multicolored sweetmeats of various shapes and sizes, and everyone sat around smiling and laughing and dipping their hands in the bowls. Everyone except Atique.

"I will not eat any sweets until I see Asad with my own eyes. Only then will I celebrate."

Usama called Farrukh. He'd received a call from Mohammed Raashid, the journalist in North Waziristan with whom he'd been in touch about his father. Raashid had told Usama we were now in the hands of the Haqqani group. The group were supporters of KK and Colonel Imam, so we were among friends. Farrukh asked how reliable Raashid's information was likely to be.

"He phoned me the day before my father's death. He told me that was the last night for my father, but I should do whatever was in my power. Another day and it would be too late. He was right."

The Pakistani news channels were giving minute-by-minute updates on our release, increasing Farrukh's excitement. The office was filled with happiness. Although it wasn't clear to Farrukh who we were with, the channels were naming Taliban groups that Farrukh knew to be pro-KK.

Then one of the channels announced we'd been handed over to the army and would be flown home by them early the following morning.

Farrukh called Mum and Dad. They'd been following the coverage on the UK channels, and they were overjoyed at this latest news.

For Farrukh, it was a bittersweet moment. Although delighted and hugely relieved at the news of our release, he couldn't help feeling desperately sad we'd be coming home without his friend, Khalid. KK had trusted the wrong man. Farrukh knew that, if KK had gone with his original contact, who'd first taken him to see the Taliban leadership, he'd have still been alive.

Nevertheless, that night Farrukh enjoyed the best sleep he'd had for months.

The next day dawned bright and Farrukh tried to hold on to the positive mood of the previous day, still not quite believing it was true.

He walked through his empty house to the dining room, where servants were serving breakfast. His usual sheaf of newspapers was laid out on the table. He picked one up.

ISLAMABAD: Former ISI official, Colonel Imam, and a British journalist of Pakistani origin, Asad Qureshi, were released on Thursday in North Waziristan by a militant group calling itself the Asian Tigers.

The group is believed to be operating in North Waziristan and kidnapped the two on March 26, 2010, together with former ISI official, Khalid Khawaja, recently killed by the group. Khawaja's body was found near a stream in Karam Kot, seven kilometres south of North Waziristan's main town of Mir Ali. Locals said they had seen Khawaja's body but did not recover it for fear of attacks from the militants.

A senior official said a jirga of residents and clerics deputed by the local administration finally retrieved Khawaja's body.

Officials said Khawaja's body was taken to Islamabad and handed over to his family. A note was found with his body which said he was working for the Americans and anybody else working for them would meet the same fate.

Many of the papers carried sickening details of KK's murder, along with reports of my release. Others concentrated on the details of our abduction and captivity.

It should be mentioned that the kidnappers released a video of former ISI man Sultan Amir, alias Colonel Imam, Squadron Leader (Retired) Muhammad Khalid Khawaja and a British journalist Asad Qureshi on April 19. Khalid was killed on April 30 and his body was thrown onto a street in the suburbs of Mir Ali. According to local sources, the remaining abductees were released via a Haqqani Group during a jirga in Miranshah. The abductees were lifted from Wana while on their way to Waziristan from Kohat on March 25, on charges of spying. Khalid Khawaja and Colonel Imam were in Waziristan in connection with peace negotiations.

Our expected imminent arrival created a buzz of excitement in the office. People stood at windows, sat by phones, fidgeted in chairs. Nobody did any work.

Then morning passed into afternoon and still there was no word of our return. Farrukh thought there would probably be an army debriefing session to go through first, and this was the reason for the delay. But surely the army would let us call home first?

He spoke to the A Team. Their local sources were saying we'd be back today. But when night fell and there was still no news, Farrukh grew very tense. Was news of our release too good to be true? On the one hand, there was seemingly reliable information from Raashid; on the other, why would the kidnappers release me after demanding a ransom of ten million dollars? Even if it was clear they weren't going to get anywhere near that sum, to release me and having nothing to show for it seemed odd.

In the silence of the night, the truth of our release began to seem shaky.

The following day, the mood in the office had gone from jubilant bustle to morbid silence. There was a sense of guilt over the previous day's celebrations. Atique's cautious response to the news looked sensible.

Rakhshindah called Farrukh for an update. He told her he was hearing the same news as she was. There was nothing new.

Usama called Farrukh. He'd heard that no less a person than Mullah Omar, the supreme commander and spiritual leader of the Taliban, had become involved in our situation and had issued a *fatwa* declaring it not permissible to kidnap and demand a ransom for any person, whether Muslim or not. The Taliban in Afghanistan had condemned the murder of Usama's father and had demanded the immediate release of the hostages.

Everyone was telling him of our release, but we still hadn't arrived. The only way to find out what was really going on was to see Mr. Z, so he found Salim and, once again, the two of them paid the cleric a visit.

Mr. Z was sitting on the floor of his drawing room when Farrukh arrived. He assured him we were safe and he shouldn't worry. The intervention of the Afghani Taliban would ensure none of the remaining hostages would be hurt. The kidnappers had entered a binding pact.

But he also said we wouldn't be coming home anytime soon.

Farrukh returned with mixed feelings. I was out of danger and my life was no longer under threat, it seemed. But there was no clear timetable for our release.

He called Mum and Dad. He told them we were safe and there was no need to worry any longer. Mum asked when we'd be home—people on the news were saying we'd be home the following day. Farrukh told them it might take a week or so.

He was angry at the heartlessness of a media that ran stories based on speculation or hearsay without bothering to establish the facts. They had scant concern for people's feelings.

Mum's mind continued to work overtime, churning out worries and what-ifs. To her mind, I'd always been a liability in Pakistan. She often cited my outspoken intolerance with beggars in the street. The people you see are often professional beggars working for organized groups. I usually send them away with a flea in their ear. I find my own ways of giving money to people who are genuinely poor. But my mum is superstitious. She thinks the professional beggars will put a curse on me if I don't give them money.

And now this superstition was at work again. She'd convinced herself that the fact I kept birds as pets was responsible for my captivity. And for my delayed release. She asked Farrukh to set the birds free.

So Farrukh spoke to Jawaid and asked him to release the birds. The cage door was duly opened and Jawaid stood back to watch the birds take flight. Nothing happened. The birds stayed put. Jawaid left the door open all day, and still the birds didn't budge. He phoned Farrukh to let him know. When Farrukh told Mum, she became upset and saw it as a bad omen.

Farrukh wondered if there was a less paranormal explanation for the birds' behavior. They'd simply become institutionalized. The cage was where they were fed so the cage was where they were staying.

He mentioned his theory to Dawood, who agreed. Dawood's advice was to leave the cage doors open at night. This was done and, the following night, the birds flew away, allowing Mum to pack her superstition away and liberating her from the referred guilt of having a son who kept birds captive.

Usama came to see Farrukh, accompanied by Raashid, the journalist from North Waziristan. After KK's murder, Raashid had been contacted by one of his sources in Mir Ali. The source had a *patta* (a Pushto word for a CD or an audio tape). Raashid had initially thought it might be a video of KK's murder. The source wanted 100,000 rupees. Raashid was to go to the bus station in Rawalpindi, where a man would make the exchange.

But it wasn't a video. It was an audio tape of a conversation between two men, a conversation about KK, a recording, made at a public call office, possibly in North Waziristan.

Raashid took the tape to Usama, and they listened to it together. Raashid seemed to recognize one of the voices as belonging to Hamid Mir, one of Pakistan's most prominent broadcasters and the presenter of *Capital Talk*, a current affairs programme on Geo TV. The other voice he didn't know at all. But Usama did. It was the voice of Usman Punjabi, the kidnapper who was in constant touch with him. If this was true, that a prominent broadcaster was communicating with the kidnappers, it was an explosive revelation.

Usama and Raashid went to see Farrukh.

"You should listen to this tape."

"I don't have a cassette player in the office. We'll have to listen to it in my car."

Farrukh and Nudrat recognized the voice of the kidnapper they'd spoken to on the phone. And the other voice they took to belong to the well-known broadcaster.

Some details of the conversation suggested it took place before KK's execution. At one point, the voice they believed to be Hamid Mir's alluded to his sacking from the *Daily Ausaf*, one of Pakistan's Urdu newspapers.

Early on in the conversation, Usman Punjabi claimed to have abducted Khalid Khawaja and asked the other man for information on KK. The other man went into considerable detail about KK's background, claiming he had links to the CIA, to an international network of Qadianis, and to a pro-Israeli American named Mansur Ejaz, who offered to solve the Kashmir issue.

This other man went on further to link KK to the Red Mosque operation, claiming KK and his wife were directly responsible for the death of Ghazi Abdul Rashid and for the humiliating capture of Maulana Abdul Aziz and his family. The other man urged Punjabi to cross-examine KK about his relationship with Mansur Ejaz, with the Qadianis, and with CIA chief William Casey. He also mentioned Jawaid Peracha, the Kohat-based lawmaker who offered to mediate KK's release.

Toward the end of the tape, Punjabi said he'd relay the information this man had given him to the senior Taliban commander, Hakimullah Mehsud.

Farrukh and Nudrat were shocked. The tape seemed to suggest a member of the media was spreading lies about KK, lies that had clearly prompted his murder, although, in the absence of incontrovertible evidence, it could not be said that the other man in the recording was indeed Hamid Mir.

I should say that I know for a fact that these claims are ridiculous and untrue: KK was *not* a CIA agent, KK was *not* involved with a pro-Israeli US businessman, and, during the Red Mosque crisis, KK had been picked up early one morning on his way to the mosque and jailed, to keep him quiet. I'm sure the order to take him off the streets had come from high up. So, KK had emphatically not been involved in Ghazi Abdul Rashid's death *nor* in the Maulana's capture.

Usama asked Farrukh if he should go public with the tape. Farrukh suggested that he should do what he thought best. Usama asked who should keep the tape in the meantime, as merely possessing the tape was dangerous. Farrukh held out his hand.

* * *

By a strange turn of events, this wasn't the only copy of the recording in circulation. News of its contents soon spread online, firstly on the *Let Us Build Pakistan* blog, then on YouTube, then widely on social media networks.

Within a couple of days, the tape was headline news.

Now that the revelations were public, Usama took the opportunity to appear on television and publicly accuse Hamid Mir of his father's murder. He further stated his belief that, given Mir's involvement, the Asian Tigers were actually a group working for India's primary foreign intelligence agency, the Research and Analysis Wing (RAW).

As he stood at the microphone, he held a printed phone log.

These calls were made on the nineteenth of April and my father's confessions came on the twenty-third. All the things Hamid Mir said about my father are the same as in the confessions. Those confessions were made on the basis of this audio tape. I can prove it, here on this programme, that Hamid Mir knew these were all lies about my father because Hamid Mir himself is an agent for CIA and RAW and he has links with the Asian Tigers. I am sure he has taken money to have my father killed. I want to ask him how much money he has taken to make me an orphan and destroy my family.

The audiotape had now become powerful evidence in the charge that Hamid Mir had played a signifcant role in KK's murder. Usama went ahead and filed an FIR, so that the police would investigate the charges against Mir.

It also became known the ISI were investigating what role Mir had played in the assassination. As soon as there was a whiff of ISI involvement, Hamid Mir issued a rebuttal:

Lahore, May 19: Noted Pakistan television journalist Hamid Mir has sent legal notices to the *Daily Times* and the Business Plus television channel for running a report claiming he had a telephonic interaction with a Taliban spokesman which actually led to the killing of kidnapped former Inter Services Intelligence (ISI) official Khalid Khawaja.

Mir, executive editor of *Geo News*, has termed the story being published and aired on the newspaper and the television channel respectively, as defamatory, which was based on mala fide intentions. In his notice, Mir has demanded an official apology from both media houses within 14 days and also payment of 250 million rupees as compensation for damages done to his reputation, failing which legal action would be initiated. The points of interest mentioned at the end of column were also aimed to cause hatred and dislike for Mr. Mir in specific sections of society. Further, the publication of an editorial titled "Shocking Revelations" in the *Daily Times* on May 17, 2010, wrongly propagated Mr. Mir's involvement in Khalid Khawaja's murder, Mir's notice states.

The said column and transcript was published in the *Daily Times* in breach of professional conduct and without verifying the accuracy and authenticity of the source of information, it added. Both Mir and the Taliban have denied having any conversation with each other concerning kidnapped ISI officials. Earlier, Mir had said the leaked audiotape was an attempt to malign his image by his enemies in the government.

"I never said these things to these people. This is a concocted tape. They took my voice, sampled it, and manufactured this conspiracy against me," Mir had said. On the other hand, Khawaja's son Usama Khalid has claimed one of the voices on the tape was certainly that of Usman, a Taliban militant with whom his family had several negotiations for his father's release.

Days passed. Still there was no concrete news of our release.

Farrukh was becoming increasingly anxious. The deafening silence from the kidnappers was weighing heavily on him. They'd asked him for his final ransom offer and, against the A Team's advice, he'd chosen to remain silent. He felt he'd been right, although he struggled to find a logical explanation for his actions.

He had thought the kidnappers might kill Rustam first, just to flex their muscles. Instead they'd murdered KK. It was impossible to guess their next move. He still focused on Rustam. He still thought they'd be likely to consider Rustam less valuable. With Khalid dealt with—a separate score—they might now kill Rustam to put more pressure on Farrukh to pay up. Farrukh thought about Rustam's family. All those children, all dependent on their father.

Farrukh kept preparing himself for the kidnappers' call. He rehearsed the things he wanted to tell them: that the UK government and the channel had refused to get involved because I was a Pakistani national and came under the jurisdiction of Pakistan; that I was not an employee of the channel but a self-employed freelance cameraman for whom the TV company felt under no obligation to provide help; that he insisted on speaking to me so he could be sure they hadn't already killed me.

He knew he was the only one in a position to negotiate with the kidnappers. With these bullet points fixed in his head, Farrukh waited for the kidnappers to call. No call came.

He sat at the dining table in his house, an empty house no longer filled with the sounds and sights of family. The housekeeper brought him his lunch—chicken curry, two chapattis, and a glass of water at room temperature. Farrukh couldn't bring himself to eat. To placate the housekeeper, he played with the food for a while, took one bite, and left the rest. He felt exhausted.

He got up and walked through the big empty house. He felt an overwhelming desire to sleep, so headed for the stairs. He got to the top landing before the realization hit him. He'd left his mobile phone on the dining table.

Frantic with worry, he raced down the stairs and through to the dining room. He lifted the phone. The display showed a missed call. From the kidnappers. They'd called him from a public call office, so he had no way of calling them back.

How could he have been so careless?

They'd think he was ignoring them. Trying to play the big man. Their macho pride would be wounded. They'd be incensed. My God, what would they do now?

Once again he visited Mr. Z for advice and reassurance. He and Asghar paced up and down the compound, waiting for the cleric to receive them.

The compound was a huge complex with a mosque at its center and countless ancillary buildings, including a *madrassah*, where numerous children studied, and, in the distance, rows of residential buildings.

Asghar looked around.

"For all we know, Asad is being held right here. Mr. Z could be colluding with the kidnappers. Acting as their front man."

Farrukh shook his head.

"You know, just like in the movies. Asad might be locked in a basement. He might be looking at us right now. Shouting to get our attention. Only we can't hear him."

Farrukh smiled. It was kind of Asghar to try to lighten the mood.

Once again, Farrukh talked to Mr. Z about our parents. The impact the false reports of my release had had on them.

"Don't worry. Everything will be all right. This is a waiting game. We have to be patient. Tell your parents to have faith. You must have faith. Faith in me. Your brother is safe. We are working to get him out of there."

"It's just that the process is so slow. Each day Asad is with them… each extra day is hell for my parents."

"If we rush things, their demands will be high."

On the way home, Asghar broke the silence.

"Do you think he is playing with us?"

Farrukh thought for several seconds before speaking.

"To tell you the truth, I don't trust anyone. But he's our only hope."

After the usual circuitous route back to Islamabad, to ensure no one was following them, they pulled up at the A Team's hotel. As usual, Asghar waited in the lobby while Farrukh took the lift to the sixth floor.

Brian told him to send an email to the kidnappers, asking about my welfare. It was a fair question to ask, as they'd know news from the television and the newspapers couldn't be verified.

"What makes you think they will tell me the truth?"

"They have a vested interest. They want the ransom. They have to assure you Asad is all right."

Farrukh was frustrated and couldn't help but show it.

"Well, they could always cut his ear off. Send it to me as proof of life."

Brian was taken aback and braced himself for a verbal onslaught. But Farrukh was too much of a gentleman to fly off the handle. He composed himself.

"Mr. Z is saying we have to be patient. If we push the kidnappers, they may stick to their original demand of ten million dollars. Do you have ten million dollars?"

"No."

"Then we do as Mr. Z says."

Silence from the A Team, which Farrukh took as agreement.

Farrukh's law business had been suffering for a while. Nudrat was holding the fort admirably in Islamabad but operating his Turkey office had become unsustainable, and he made the decision to close it down. One less headache.

And, in focusing on Rustam and me, Farrukh was aware he'd rather neglected the fate of Colonel Imam, although he'd spoken periodically to the Colonel's sons. He phoned them again now, to offer reassurance and also to ask what news they might have. But they didn't say anything he hadn't already heard from Mr. Z. We need to play the waiting game.

The army and the ISI were making vague promises about the safe return of their father. But nothing concrete seemed to be happening.

21
Betrayal Revealed

These were very dark days for Farrukh.

There was no news. Not from the kidnappers, not from the channel, not from Mr. Z. The atmosphere at the office was still very somber. KK's death had left everyone reeling. The prospect of further terrible news hung in the air like the smell of fear.

Farrukh needed to do something. He wasn't sure he'd made a strong enough case with Mr. Z so, with Salim and Asghar in tow, he went to see the cleric again.

Patiently, respectfully, my brother again explained the situation from his and the family's point of view. Our parents were old and would not survive the stress much longer. I was a freelance cameraman, not any kind of employee, and the English TV channel would do nothing for me. My life did not matter to any of the agencies or the governments or the channels. The kidnappers and Mr. Z had to understand this. Farrukh felt there was no more he could say. Mr. Z sat in silence for a whole minute before speaking.

"I understand your situation. But you must appreciate that these are criminals we are dealing with. Their only language is violence. They have proved that, by killing Khalid Khawaja. So there is no room for mistakes, delaying tactics, or dishonesty. We have to build a strong case if your brother is to get out of there alive. Which will be a miracle."

Mr. Z went back to counting his rosary beads. Nobody spoke. These were things Farrukh didn't want to hear. He was painting such a bleak picture that Farrukh was beginning to lose faith in Mr. Z's influence. This nightmare wasn't going to end any time soon.

"I think you should persuade the British government to get involved. Just in case."

Farrukh was confused. It sounded rather like Mr. Z was taking the kidnappers' side, suggesting something they wanted. Or was he genuinely thinking of a strategy for my release?

"Don't worry, Farrukh *sahib*. I will do everything in my power. *Inshallah*."

Farrukh left and went again to meet with the A Team. On the way, he spoke to Asghar about his concerns regarding Mr. Z. But Asghar couldn't see any other way forward.

"We have to trust him."

Brian told Farrukh to email the kidnappers and ask to be allowed to speak to me, as proof of life. This was imperative, and a reasonable request in circumstances in which news about me couldn't be verified.

"It's not unknown for hostage takers to kill their victims and still demand money."

Farrukh was becoming impatient both with the A Team's negativity and with their tendency to state the obvious.

"What you're telling me is not rocket science. Do you think I haven't already thought of that? And if I can think of it, so can they. It is easy for you to give me advice. All day long you sit in the luxury of this air-conditioned hotel. But I am the one who has to run around in the heat, begging people. Begging! Something I have never done in my life. Look!"

He pointed to his feet.

"Look at my heels. Look at how they're all cracked. Because now I have to wear sandals. I have to dress down to meet these people. I can't wear a suit and shoes. Because they would disapprove. They wouldn't help me. But they are the only ones I can turn to."

He stared at Brian. Brian looked away. An embarrassed silence. This lack of response made Farrukh angrier still.

"You are so scared you don't want anyone to know you are here. You ask me not to come and see you on the same day as I'm meeting Mr. Z. In case I am being followed. Well, today I came directly after seeing him. Why? Because I don't have time to waste while the noose around my brother's neck is tightening. You call yourselves experts. Well, come up with some proper advice. I am leaving for England while you lot sit here and twiddle your thumbs."

Farrukh slammed the door behind him.

Farrukh sent an email to the kidnappers. It was May 10:

Raza sahib AoA,

My family and I want this matter resolved and we want my brother and Rustam returned to their families safely. This is why we have worked so hard to collect more money than I thought was possible.

You have my offer and I do not know where to turn to next. I cannot give you what I do not have.

There are other groups making claims they have my brother. The TV, newspapers, and radio stations are all saying different things. The situation is confused. I need to know I am talking to the right person. I take you very seriously. I know this is no game. I know what happened to the other man.

I need you to allow me to speak to my brother and to Rustam, so I know you are in control of the situation and are the right man to do business with. I can be contacted on the cell number that you already have.

I will be unavailable on Monday afternoon from 1:00 p.m. as I am traveling to speak to the man my brother mentioned in his video.

To make sure I don't miss any more calls, from Tuesday I will be available daily exclusively to you at 2:30 p.m. Pakistan time. Please call at this time so we can work to solve this problem for both of us.

Farrukh hoped the kidnappers would respond soon, and he prepared himself for their call. He would insist neither the UK government nor the channel would get involved. He would insist on talking to me.

He thought of Mr. Z's words. *Getting him out will be a miracle.*

Well, the first step was to establish I was still alive. And he needed to hear my voice to be sure of that.

He also needed to clarify the position on the ransom amount, to repair the earlier damage he'd caused to Mr. Z's credibility.

His phone would never leave his pocket.

Farrukh took the next available flight to England, to visit the family. Mum greeted him with tears. Dad was locked in silent thought. The sharpest contrast to the jubilation of only a few days ago. They both looked exhausted. Broken.

Farrukh tried to reassure them everything would be fine but patience was the key. If he tried to push the kidnappers into acting quickly, he'd never be able to negotiate the ransom down to a realistic figure.

My father understood Farrukh's reasoning. My mother just wanted me home.

Farrukh's phone rang. Atique told him KK's wife had given a press conference, in which she talked about her husband's accomplishments and achievements. But that wasn't all she'd said. She'd mentioned that Farrukh's family had left Pakistan for the UK. And she'd mentioned Sherry. Had revealed her nationality.

Farrukh was livid at Shamama's indiscretion. All of Farrukh's secrets were coming out, one by one. First the secret of my being a British national, then the revelation I'd been working for a UK news channel. And now the long-held secret of my American wife.

He'd been avoiding press conferences for this very reason. It was simply too easy to say the wrong thing, off the cuff and in the glare of the spotlights and flashbulbs, in response to some pointed question from a journalist.

But all his caution had been for nothing.

Farrukh went outside into the garden and called Usama. He lost his temper and shouted at him. What was his mother thinking? Didn't she understand how dangerous this information was?

He spent a long and wakeful night imagining how the kidnappers had reacted to these revelations. *They'd now be labeling me a spy. Just like KK.*

In the early hours of the morning, Farrukh received an email.

Asalaam Alaikum,

Thank you for your kind words. We don't have enough time to give explanations or proves. You have our email address on which you can contact us any time. Tomorrow from 2:00 to 2:30 p.m. most possibly we call you. Our contact person's name is Ali Raza. As a pass code remember these phrases: when receiving the call, you need to ask whose friend you are. In reply, Ali Raza will give you the answer: I am a friend of Rustam.

You are running out of time, my friend. There is no question for the custody of hostages since media is just creating a scene. If you like we can send you same videos when we release them to other media. You have to contact the channel and other media bodies. As an advice we can give you a hint; if you do some press conferences revealing all these matters in public, citing the role of UK and Pakistan governments. Also his wife who is a US citizen. Do the press conference. Just a single press conference will solve all your problems may be.

There is no possibility to talk to your brother since government banned the cell phone services.

As he'd feared, the kidnappers were using the revelation about Sherry to press for a high ransom demand. To leave Farrukh little room to maneuver.

He also feared these latest revelations would compromise Mr. Z's credibility with the kidnappers to such an extent he might even pull out of the situation altogether, to save his own reputation.

Farrukh called the A Team and told them what KK's wife had said. Brian told him that if the kidnappers mentioned Sherry, he should just laugh and tell them they were wrong if they thought the American government would get involved in this.

That was easier said than done. Farrukh was all too aware of the Taliban's sensitivity where America was concerned. And, although the kidnappers seemed to be ruling it out, he was determined to insist on some sort of proof of life.

On the morning of May 11, Farrukh left Bradford and pointed the car toward London. It was promising to be a warm, sunny day.

As the clock in the car was nudging 10:00 a.m.—2:00 p.m. Pakistan time—he pulled in at Woodall services near Sheffield, on the southbound M1, and prepared himself for the kidnappers to call.

He sat in the car, too nervous to go inside and get a coffee. Too nervous to be around other people. He didn't want to end up making a scene.

He became aware of his heart beating faster, and of a slight tremble in his hands. He'd been thinking the worst since Shamama's press conference. The kidnappers definitely had the upper hand now. They would not show any mercy. This was it.

Farrukh watched other people pull into the car park, get out, and walk toward the cafes and the shops, talking about what they'd eat, what they'd buy, what time they'd get to their destination and see their friends. Relaxed. Happy. Living a normal life.

He could almost not remember what that felt like. He didn't dare allow himself to try.

The phone broke his reverie. The kidnappers. With a trembling hand, he turned on his recording apparatus. This would be the first contact since KK's death. He'd need to put that horror out of his mind and stay calm. *For my sake.*

"Hello."

"Hello, Farrukh." Ali Raza's voice.

"Yes, whose friend are you?"

"I am Ali Raza. Rustam's friend."

"Okay."

"Where have your negotiations reached?"

"Well, Mr. Ali Raza, we are trying our best. Please tell me what I am to do."

"You are to get in touch with the British government and demand ten million US dollars. If you cannot do this, in a few days you will get second news. Khalid Khawaja's news you have heard, right? We did not tell anyone beforehand that we will kill him. But we are in contact with you now, and if you do not give the right response then anything can happen in a few days."

"The British government will not help us. So my repeated request to you is please tell us what to do now. We will do what we can. He is my brother. My mother is very concerned. My father too. My father is ninety years old and my mother is seventy-eight years old. We are all very worried. My brother has nothing to do with this. He is a worker. He had his equipment. He went like a driver goes on a job."

"How much can you arrange? You tell us. If it is in accordance with our estimation, then we will settle. Otherwise …"

"I have been running around. Speaking to everyone I know. From family and friends, I have 4,280,000 rupees at the moment. Which I can give you today, tomorrow, whenever, wherever you say."

"Okay. I will inquire from my elders."

"Mr. Ali Raza, you have said you are not able to arrange for them to speak to us. In that case, please get me an answer to a question, so we can be satisfied that they are alive and still with you. Because of the confusion created by other people calling me, I need an answer to a question."

"Okay."

"I need an answer to a question. From Asad. Please ask him, 'Who got married in April?'"

"Okay. Who was married in April?"

"Yes. And please ask Rustam, 'What was the business carried out by Ghaffar?'"

"Okay."

"Once you give me the answers to these two questions, we can talk further."

"Okay."

Ali Raza hung up.

Farrukh's hands were still trembling. He lay back in his seat and tried to relax and gather his thoughts before getting back on the motorway.

There'd been so much more he'd wanted to say but he'd found it difficult to think on the hoof. He'd wanted to make it clear about the two million rupees—that he'd been genuine in giving that figure to Mr. Z, that he'd only later been able to arrange more, and Mr. Z wasn't playing some double game and keeping money for himself.

Late in the afternoon, Farrukh checked into the Marriott Hotel in Grosvenor Square. He'd stayed there often. He liked its central location and its proximity to Bond Street station. He liked that he could leave the hotel and, within seconds, be lost in the hustle and bustle of Oxford Street.

In the evening, he met Asif for dinner. The conversation was to take a turn that Farrukh had not expected.

"I don't understand why the channel hasn't used their insurance."

"What do you mean?"

"To pay the ransom. They have insurance. For ransoms."

"They have told me explicitly that is not the case."

Asif looked Farrukh in the eye. "Then they've lied to you."

Farrukh felt sick to his stomach. For some time, he'd suspected the channel had not been entirely honest. Jacqueline at the High Commission had told him the channel had paid ransoms before. Now Asif was assuring him that, not only were they in the habit of paying ransoms, but insurance was in place for that very purpose.

Asif continued. "You have to assert Asad's rights. Make a claim. Quickly."

"Are you sure? They would have told me. Surely."

"Asad signed papers before he left. I saw them. Stating there is insurance in place, for just this situation, where someone is killed and the others are threatened. Well, now, with what's happened to Khalid Khawaja ..."

Papers. Documentary proof of an agreement.

"You need to make a move now and tell the channel that Asad has rights."

Farrukh couldn't believe it. He was paying a subsistence allowance to KK's family. They were almost destitute. Their landlord didn't want publicity. Didn't want images of his house on TV. He was about to kick them out.

If what Asif said was true, the channel could have paid the ransom right away. All this might have been over. KK might still have been alive.

Clearly, they were only looking after their own interests. They didn't care about him or about us. The A Team had simply seen Farrukh's name on the form, as my next of kin, and they'd put pressure on him to sort things out and raise the money. They'd left him alone in the wilderness.

He felt used.

"I had to tell you. Because Asad is not here to speak for himself. I've known him for a long time."

"Thank you. You were right to tell me."

"Thank you for saying that."

"What about Colonel Imam?"

"Unfortunately, there's no protection for him. It was KK's decision to involve him. It's only because of KK that he's in this mess. The channel has no duty toward him."

After they'd eaten, Farrukh sat alone at the table and thought about what Asif had told him. He'd never be able to trust the A Team again.

He left the restaurant in Edgware Road and made his way back to the hotel on foot with, once more, normal life swirling around him—a boy of four with his nose pressed against a shop window, three men with loosened ties doing their best not to look drunk, a couple holding hands.

Of course, everyone has a story. But he wondered how many stories were as bad as his.

Why had the A Team kept this information from him? Were the lives of their colleagues worthless to them? The more he thought about it, the more agitated he became.

* * *

Nauman came into my cell and blindfolded me.

"What now?"

"Another visit. Sit up."

A familiar crackle of menace announced Sabir Mehsud had entered the room. I felt him crouch down close to me, press his face close to mine.

"Tell me, who got married in April?"

"It was my niece, Aisha."

Silence. His feet moving slowly away. Why had he asked me *that*?

* * *

The following morning, Farrukh received an email from Nudrat. It contained the names of Taliban prisoners the kidnappers wanted released. He recognized a few names on the list. While he was scanning through it, Dawood called from Islamabad to ask if he'd seen the list.

"Yes. I'm looking at it now. But it's changed."

"Yes. It's different from the one they gave earlier."

"Some of the men on *this* list are hardened criminals. The government will never release them. This list is like a death warrant for the hostages."

"You have to stress that Asad is separate from the rest of the group. That's what you have to do."

A huge dilemma. Negotiating for the release of the group as a whole would be to link my fate with that of Colonel Imam, someone Farrukh knew the channel had even less commitment to saving than they appeared to have to saving me.

Dawood was stressing my case be negotiated separately, and that was also Mr. Z's view and therefore one to be taken seriously.

But Farrukh was an honorable man. He knew Colonel Imam would never have gone to Waziristan had it not been for KK.

Yet, taking responsibility for Colonel Imam was a huge burden. Besides, Colonel Imam's sons were keeping themselves distinctly separate from Farrukh and pursuing their own negotiations. With their army connections, perhaps they were confident they could secure their father's release. Perhaps Farrukh shouldn't concern himself.

Perhaps, as it had seemed from the beginning, it was every man for himself.

An image came into Farrukh's head. Me, his fastidious brother, sitting on a grubby concrete floor crawling with the insects that repulsed me, at my feet a discarded bowl of foul gruel thrown together by a filthy cook in an unsanitary kitchen. Weakness. Malnutrition.

He didn't get much sleep.

The following day, he met with Rodney Henson from the TV channel. The conversation started pleasantly enough. Farrukh was marshaling all his reserves of self-control to keep a lid on his anger and his deep sense of betrayal.

Then, using his tactical skill as an attorney, he got to the point. He asked Rodney for a letter, to send to the kidnappers, stating the channel would not become involved in the matter and could not be expected to contribute to a ransom payment. He knew the letter would make little difference to the kidnappers but at least he would have the letter and could, if matters came to a head, use it as evidence the channel had broken the agreement, which he now knew I'd signed, to support me and pay a ransom in the event of a kidnap.

Rodney promised to have a letter to that effect delivered to the hotel by the afternoon.

The conversation was interrupted when Farrukh's phone rang. He looked at the screen. Ali Raza.

"Hello."

"Hello. This is Ali Raza."

"Yes, Mr. Ali Raza."

"Here are the answers to your questions. The wedding was of the youngest daughter, Aisha, of the eldest sister."

"Yes. Right."

"Okay. And second answer is, Mr. Ghaffar has died."

"But didn't he say what Mr. Ghaffar's business is? That's what I asked."

"His son, Waqar, has a shop on Murree Road."

Farrukh was satisfied. Now a white lie to stall for time.

"Okay. Thank you. I am trying my best to get in touch with the man Asad mentioned in his video. He's not been answering his phone. So I have come to London to meet him. To find out how he can help us. I am trying my best. Whatever I can do. Our wish is to bring Rustam and my brother back. Your desire we will fulfil to whatever extent we can. I have told you how much we have arranged. I am trying to arrange some more as well. Next Sunday or Monday I will be in a position to tell you how much more I can get."

"You should talk to the people at the TV channel."

"I have still not been able to meet that person. He will be able to tell me what the channel's role was in all of this."

"Asif Jameel?"

"Yes. He is not answering his phone. I have met him only once or twice. He is a very old friend of Asad's but I don't know where he lives. So I have come myself to find him and meet him. Please be content that I will fulfil your demand to whatever extent I can."

"Okay, okay."

"How are Rustam and Asad?"

"They are fine."

With that, Ali Raza brought the conversation to an end.

Rodney commended Farrukh on how calmly he'd dealt with the situation. Farrukh joked they might offer him a position on their team when all of this was over.

A couple of hours later, the promised letter from the channel arrived by courier.

When Farrukh arrived back in Bradford, he noticed a change in Mum. She'd stopped taking care of her appearance.

"What does it matter? That can wait until Asad his home."

Farrukh coaxed her into going to the hairdresser's. He dropped her off and went to run some errands. Later, when he came to collect her, the hairdresser said, "Your wife is ready." He smiled. "My *mother*, actually." The hairdresser flushed and apologized.

Farrukh translated the hairdresser's remark to Mum and noticed the ghost of a smile on her lips.

My parents had been grateful for Farrukh's presence and his reassurance, but they were keen for him to return to Pakistan. Mum, in particular, could not shake off the feeling that, with Farrukh in the UK, I was alone and abandoned.

At the airport, Farrukh received a call from KK's son, Usama, asking him to check a link he'd just emailed. Farrukh asked him what it was about.

"I don't want to talk about it on the phone."

"Is everything all right?"

"No."

Farrukh checked his email. The link was to a blog. The blogger had heard a recording of a conversation between the Pakistani broadcaster Hamid Mir and Usman Punjabi, the same recording Farrukh had listened to in his car with Nudrat, Usama, and Raashid. The blogger did not mince words. Hamid Mir had instigated the murder of Khalid Khawaja.

Now that this development had been broadcast on the internet, Farrukh knew the Pakistani media would be all over him. He couldn't risk going home or going to the office. He called Nudrat and asked her to book him at the Marriott Hotel in Islamabad.

Farrukh checked into the hotel on the morning of May 14, carrying with him two letters—one from Jacqueline at the British High Commission and the other from the channel, each one formally refusing help, each one serving no real purpose in the negotiations.

In the afternoon, he picked up Salim, and they went to see Mr. Z. Following Shamama's very public indiscretions, the situation would need to be reassessed.

Farrukh was incredibly nervous. He feared there'd be questions about the channel, and about Sherry in particular. He feared Mr. Z would feel betrayed and, to preserve his credibility, he would simply cut them loose.

In the end, Mr. Z was very gracious. There was no mention of Shamama's revelations. But Mr. Z did suggest the best way forward was for Farrukh to hold a press conference of his own. For my sake.

Farrukh was hesitant.

"I'm camera-shy. Besides, the media will twist my words. They have no respect for the truth. Only for sensation."

"This is my advice."

Nudrat didn't like it. She was concerned Mr. Z always seemed to be saying what the kidnappers were saying. As if he were their agent in Islamabad. Farrukh was clinging to Mr. Z as their only hope.

He didn't know what else to do.

22
Reunited with Colonel Imam

The weather was warming up, and the days were getting longer. Insect activity had increased. I would often hear crickets and there was a train of ants walking up the wall. I hoped they'd keep away from me. We'd been here for several weeks. The worst thing was boredom and inactivity, and of course the fact of not knowing what might happen next. I thought if I survived this ordeal, I'd be dining out on the story for a long time. If I didn't survive, which seemed likely, the only dinner I'd be attending, in spirit only, would be the dinner served by my family after my funeral.

I worried about the terrible time I was putting my parents through. I felt immensely guilty for causing them so much pain.

I turned the possibilities over and over in my head. I'd ask Rustam what he thought might happen. He'd assure me we'd be going home. This would contain my worries for a while. Then I'd ask him again. A merry-go-round of anxiety.

The temperature was becoming unbearable in the room. The metal sheeting on the windows absorbed the heat, like an oven. The place seemed specifically designed for the mistreatment of hostages. Krishan Lal brought us a cold drink, which was enormously welcome. I decided to push my luck and ask if it was possible to open one of the windows. He laughed.

"You know our Amir al Momineen, Mullah Omar, lives in a place where there are no electrical appliances—no fans, air conditioners, or refrigerators. The electrics in them might attract the attention of the drones. How do you think he manages?"

So that meant no.

I thought about the mango season, which I reckoned would soon be upon us. I asked Krishan Lal if I would be released by then. The thought of a fresh, cold mango was tantalizing.

"Maybe. There's a chance."

I noticed a change in Nauman's behavior. He became arrogant. The others, with the exception of Krishan Lal, were now addressing him as *sahib*, which he clearly enjoyed. I wondered why the sudden attitude. Rustam noticed it too.

"Who fathered this son of a bitch?"

"I don't know. But whoever he was must be regretting it now."

I was surprised Krishan Lal was giving him the freedom to throw his weight around. From the outset, Krishan Lal had made it clear he was in charge, and Nauman was his subordinate. But Nauman was now insufferable. He strutted round our room with his face hidden in his turban, wearing my dad's clothes, and brandishing his Kalashnikov. *Oh yes. Very brave. We're handcuffed and shackled and defenseless. If only the roles were reversed, my friend, I'd show you no mercy.* I had visions of gouging his eyes out with my bare hands and throwing them on the floor and stamping on them, squashing them like overripe tomatoes.

Nauman was in midstrut when the door opened and a broad-shouldered, hooded man came in. I'd seen his fancy watch before, and his knuckleduster-type ring. Sabir Mehsud, the leader. Nauman composed himself and stood behind Mehsud, who stared at me intensely, his menacing eyes piercing the gauze of his hood.

"How are you?"

"Okay."

"Do you want to film one of our operations?"

I didn't like the sound of that. They'd always hidden their faces from us, but surely they'd take off the hoods during an operation. I'd see their faces. Then they'd never let me go.

"I'm too weak. I wouldn't be able to keep up with you."

He nodded. He seemed to accept my reasoning.

"Your wife has gone to America. On vacation."

Was this true? Would Sherry leave at a time like this? Was he just messing with my head?

"Do you think the Americans will pay for you?"

"No, they won't. I have nothing to do with them. Besides, they never pay money for hostages. Take the American hostages in Iran. They were held for 444 days and their government didn't pay. I'm no one to them."

He stared at me for several seconds in silence. I think he realized I had a point. Then he signaled to Nauman and the two of them left the room.

I was glad he hadn't pushed me on the filming. I didn't want to get involved in anything that might bring accusations of Stockholm syndrome.

If Nauman had become more belligerent, Krishan Lal seemed to have softened toward us. He continued to bring us sweets and cold drinks and sometimes stayed to talk to us. As a joke, he'd keep changing his name. One day he said his name was Talib Hussain, coincidentally the name of a boy I was at school with. I wondered where *he* was now.

I told Krishan Lal I'd finished reading the Qur'an and wanted to dedicate the reading to my parents. As I said this, my eyes filled with tears. This was all I could do for them.

A couple of days later, Krishan Lal asked Rustam a question out of the blue.

"Can you use a gun? If I gave you a gun, do you think you could find your way out of here?"

Rustam nodded his head enthusiastically.

I wasn't sure where Krishan Lal was going with this. Leaving this place on our own would be suicide. We were in Afghanistan and had no papers for traveling and no money. We probably wouldn't make it farther than 10 feet from this compound. Even if we did, we'd probably be picked up by another group.

Maybe it was a trap. KK's words came into my mind—*Don't trust anyone.* I didn't want Rustam getting us involved in some doomed escape attempt. I decided to pipe up.

"No, no. We'll take our chances here."

Rustam looked disappointed. Had he seriously thought we could make a break for it? I wasn't going to take a chance with his life or with mine. We were too weak to survive on our own on the outside. Let them kill us if they wanted, but I wasn't going to give them an excuse by being tricked into an escape. After all, why would they go to all the trouble of kidnapping us and interrogating us and asking for a ransom of ten million dollars, only to let us go scot-free? It didn't make sense.

I wondered if Nauman's change of attitude meant Krishan Lal was losing his authority. If we escaped, with his help, he could blame Nauman and regain control of the situation.

Then, a couple of days later, Krishan Lal came into our room. He told us he was leaving. He'd already said goodbye to Colonel Imam, he said. After spending several days in the bathroom, Colonel Imam had been moved to the room adjoining ours, a storage room with several of the fold-up beds we were sleeping in, as well as a pile of other stuff covered in sheets.

We'd later learn from the Colonel it had been an emotional farewell. The kidnapper had stared at the Colonel, but this time without the usual anger.

"I am sorry I beat you. Please forgive me."

Colonel Imam had been dumbfounded by this abrupt reversal in behavior.

Krishan Lal had dropped to the floor and kissed the Colonel's feet. He'd begun to cry. Colonel Imam had stroked Krishan Lal's hair.

"I forgive you."

"If I don't leave this place soon, they will kill me."

"Then you must go. And I will pray for you."

They'd both stood up. Colonel Imam had hugged Krishan Lal, and the inexplicably contrite kidnapper had turned and walked out.

And now he was bidding us farewell. Out of habitual politeness, Rustam and I stood and shook his hand. He said he hoped we might meet up some day, in Islamabad. Then he left.

This explained Nauman's behavior. A new regime was in the offing. This wouldn't be good for us. Of the two men, Krishan Lal had been the lesser of two evils. Though why on earth he'd think I'd want to meet up with him in Islamabad was bewildering. Here was a man who'd torn up my diary, beaten me, and lied to me. If I ever got out of this place, which was now unimaginable, he'd be the last man I'd want to see. Did he know something I didn't?

The following morning, Mohammed came in and told us to sit facing the wall. Any such orders unsettled me greatly. You never knew what was going to happen.

I heard them fold our beds and carry them out of the room. Our time had come. I should have taken Krishan Lal's offer and made a run for it. He knew something was up and he'd offered us a way out. Now it was too late.

Mohammed returned. He blindfolded and handcuffed us and led us out of the room, me carrying the chain of my shackles so it didn't drag on the floor. I could tell we were walking down the veranda where I'd been exercising. After about twenty paces, we stopped. I heard a metal door being unlocked. I figured we were at the other end of the veranda, where the young boy had stood guard. We were led into the room and told to sit down.

My heart was racing. Suddenly the whole thing seemed unreal. Events I'd only ever imagined or seen in films. Dirty places. Violent thugs. Guns held to the head. How had I got here?

I was scared, but I was also angry. These monsters had shaken the very core of my outlook on the world. I hated them and hoped the worst possible fate awaited them, a fate I'd be happy to administer if the roles could be reversed.

I had an image of myself as a superhero, ripping off my shackles and handcuffs, seizing my captors by the throat and, one by one, squeezing the life out of them. They fire shot after shot at me, but I'm impregnable and I defeat them all.

Then Mukhtar's shrill voice. "Turn around."

My blindfold was removed. I saw a whitewashed wall with bedding rolled up against it, the same kind as in the other room. To my surprise, Colonel Imam was sitting at the opposite end of the room, with Rustam between him and me. I felt a wave of relief wash over me. But where was KK?

I greeted the Colonel.

"*Asalaam alaikum.*"

Colonel Imam looked at us perplexed.

"*Walaikum asalaam.* Are you the film team?"

"Yes, we are."

"I didn't recognize you. You look so different."

His observation was correct. We were beyond recognition. Bearded, disheveled, gaunt. We hadn't seen each other for a few months.

The Colonel's *shalwar kamiz*, once brilliant white, was now a dirty cream. The back of it was a network of dark red stripes where he'd been flogged, hard.

Mukhtar burst into the room. He barked at us.

"No talking. And no looking at one another."

He pointed at the wall and we took our cue, each sitting on the floor and turning away from each other. He brought in two plates of lentil curry and some chapattis, one plate for Rustam and me and the other for Colonel Imam. He distributed a few chapattis between us, then told us to eat separately, me at one end, Rustam in the middle, and the Colonel at the other end, not looking at each other.

Then Nauman came in carrying an assortment of things—a new Ludo board, a ceiling fan, and a stepladder. He surveyed the ceiling and selected a beam, just past the middle on the Colonel's side. What was the fan all about? Was it just about making us comfortable? Or did it signal that we'd be here, or be alive, for some time to come? We had no way of knowing.

Above where Colonel Imam lay, there was the familiar hole in the wall for an extractor fan that had never been fitted. The hole was open to the elements. I was furthest away from the new fan but, as a consolation, I was best positioned to get a view through the hole.

Blue sky. The sight brought me some comfort. I thought about KK again. Why wasn't he with us?

"Where is Khalid Khawaja?"

"He has gone to Islamabad to negotiate your release."

Before I could ask more, Nauman left the room and locked the door behind him. We all looked at each other. What was going on? Rustam was the first to break the silence.

"I *told you* he was responsible for all this. I saw him on the roof of the *madras-sah*, in Karak. He was making phone calls."

"That doesn't mean anything."

"Okay, so why has he been allowed to go? Why not you?"

"He has more connections than any of us. If anyone can get us out, it's him."

Rustam shook his head.

"I don't like it."

Rustam didn't know KK like I did. This was good news. I imagined KK in Islamabad, speaking to officials, using his contacts, pulling strings.

Rustam set out the Ludo and, like little boys with a new toy, straight away we started to play. I didn't care about winning the game. Time was the adversary—simply by playing, I was winning.

Colonel Imam went back to his books, occasionally looking at us over his glasses and smiling.

In the evening, Mukhtar came in and shackled and handcuffed us. In addition, he tied a long chain to a rickety old table and chair and ran the chain through the shackles of my right leg and then Rustam's right leg, and lastly Colonel Imam's left leg. A new security measure. There was no escape from this place, but they weren't taking any chances. If there was a drone strike, we'd have no chance of survival.

And it wouldn't be great for our sleep. If one person turned over, he'd pull on the chain. Then we'd all feel the chain pull. As a light sleeper anyway, I braced myself for a long night.

I heard the buzz of a mosquito. I hated them but they loved me. Sweet blood. I swatted at it, pulling at the chain and waking up Rustam and the Colonel. They both sighed at the ridiculous futility of my action and turned over.

I looked at all the junk in the room. A wealth of hiding places for insects of all sorts. My flesh started to crawl.

I can date my insect phobia to an incident at school. We'd gone camping. A friend asked me to close my eyes and hold out my hand. When I opened them, he'd placed a dead beetle in the palm of my hand. It had made me panic. The story got round. In a biology class, a girl had taken my pen and poked it among a pile of worms. I'd never used the pen again. To people in Pakistan, my phobia about insects is laughable. Insects are everywhere.

In the daylight hours, to distract myself from the thought of insects, I'd often lie down and look up at the ceiling. I'd count the metal joists running from one end of the room to the other. Then count all the concrete slabs that made up the ceiling. I often lost count and had to start all over again.

Rustam would lie on his back and gently stroke his long beard, seemingly deep in thought. Colonel Imam spent most of his time reading. Our captors had given him numerous books, and he'd sit in the middle of his bed with books scattered around him. He wore very old, red-framed spectacles that had seen better days, the lenses badly scratched, the frames stretched so much with wear the arms could almost open to 180 degrees. They must have been next to useless. Nevertheless, he was happily absorbed in his literary world, briefly removed from the reality of being a hostage.

On one such day, our escapist peace was broken by Nauman. Rustam and I sat up. It was always politic to show a little respect. He looked at us, then turned his attention toward Colonel Imam. He walked over and sat down opposite him.

"Have you learnt the statement?"

"I have been reading it but haven't learnt it all yet."

"So why are you reading *these* books?"

Nauman lifted his hand and slapped the Colonel hard across the face, catching the arm of his spectacles and dislodging them. It was upsetting to see the Colonel, such a strong and dignified man, brutalized in this way. I decided to intervene.

"Please don't hit him. Please understand we are all under stress here. It's difficult to concentrate. He will learn the statement."

Nauman turned to look at me. Even though he was hooded, I could feel the rage on his face. I froze, expecting him to see me as a suitable vent for his anger. That's how it is with these people. Anger needs an outward expression. They're so brain-washed and desensitized they don't have feelings like normal human beings. You can't even say they're animals. Animals are better than them. No animal tortures another animal or harms it simply for its pleasure. Calling these thugs animals would be an insult to animals.

Rustam also appealed to Nauman in their native Pushto language, which seemed to calm him. He finally took his gaze off me and left the room.

I'd been spared a beating. And a severe one. I'd suffered, but I knew the Colonel had suffered more. His beatings had been particularly brutal and sadistic. But, old and frail though he seemed, he had reserves of strength I didn't possess. I wouldn't have survived the treatment he'd withstood.

I felt such a deep sense of responsibility toward him. He wouldn't have been here if it hadn't been for me. Now this great man was subjected to humiliating treatment. When we'd left Islamabad, all those weeks ago, he'd told me his wife was recovering from surgery. He'd told her he'd only be away for a few days.

His ancient spectacles were now damaged beyond repair. I had two pairs in my bag—a photosensitive pair for use in sunlight and a standard pair. I used the standard ones for filming, as they were better for judging exposure. I wondered if Colonel Imam might benefit from the other pair.

He put them on and looked at his book. He smiled.

"That is much better. Things look brighter."

"Good. Now, if they've given you a statement to learn, please learn it."

He picked up a piece of paper.

"When we get out of here, I'll buy you a new pair."

Late in the afternoon, we were all lying on our mattresses when Nauman entered the room, carrying a chair. He placed it by the bathroom door, nearest to Colonel Imam.

"Sit up. *Sahib* is coming to see you."

I wondered what Sabir Mehsud wanted this time. We all sat up and moved to the edge of our mattresses. Nauman withdrew and another, very tall man replaced him, his head covered in a black hood (we'd later learn his name was Shaukat). He was carrying what looked like a Thompson automatic rifle—a Tommy gun. He towered over us, holding his gun at the ready. He must have stood there, statue still, for a good fifteen minutes before Sabir Mehsud walked in.

Mehsud was a man who inspired fear. We stood and walked over to shake his hand as a gesture of fearful respect. I saw again the expensive watch and the silver ring studded with zircon stones. I imagined myself on the outside recognizing this hand, knowing it was him, driving a knife into his chest.

Sabir Mehsud surveyed us attentively.

"You know, if I wanted to, I could have had you all killed. But instead I asked them to bring you in alive. I wanted to see what you looked like."

He paused and looked at us, as if waiting for a response. Did he expect thanks? We stared at him in silence. I imagined an ugly, misshapen face behind the hood. The face of a monster. I didn't know whether to feel sorry for his parents for what he had turned into, or to feel angry with them for creating such a demon.

He turned his attention to Colonel Imam and picked up one of his books.

"How are you finding this book?"

"Very informative."

The book Colonel Imam was reading was compiled by a member of the Sipah-e-Sahaba group.* The book consisted of photocopies of writings by Shia scholars, with a dismissive Sipah-e-Sahaba commentary.

"The author of this book had put up a reward of ten thousand rupees for anyone who could answer his questions on Shias. Shias killed him with a remote-controlled bomb."

The Shias were monsters. He was a saint.

"But we've killed enough of them too."

"You yourself have killed people?"

"Yes. Many."

"Shot?"

"Yes. And beheaded." He laughed.

I had shaken a hand that had beheaded people. I felt sick. I started to shake.

"When my time comes, please shoot me. I don't want my mother to see ..."

He found my distress amusing.

"Don't worry. We still shoot. In the head. Sometimes also the chest."

---

* Sipah-e-Sahaba Pakistan is a Sunni sectarian group alleged to be involved in terrorist violence, primarily targeted against the minority Shia community in Pakistan. Its stated goal is to deter major Shiite influence in Pakistan in the wake of the Iranian Revolution. The organization was banned by the Pakistan government in 2002.

23
Mr. Z Sends an Envoy

Mr. Z could see that the false reports of our release had hit Farrukh hard. His mood was dark.

The cleric decided to take direct action. He arranged for his close associate, Zarar, to travel to North Waziristan to negotiate a settlement with the kidnappers. Farrukh was hugely encouraged by this move, and when Mr. Z told him he could send some things with Zarar to pass on to me, Farrukh immediately assembled a comprehensive package—a notebook and a pen (he knew I'd be keeping a diary), two pairs of *shalwar kamiz*, some undergarments, some socks, toothpaste, and a toothbrush. He typed out a letter telling me everyone was fine and Mum and Dad were out of harm's way in England. He added a small photograph of Dad.

Comforted by the knowledge that, for the first time, proper contact would be made, he put the lot in a small holdall and placed the bag on the edge of his desk, awaiting further instructions from Mr. Z.

Salim called him to say Zarar had to delay his trip to Waziristan for a few days. Farrukh tried to busy himself with work, glancing all the while at the bag and wondering when it would be leaving his office.

Usama sent Farrukh a copy of an email exchange between his younger brother, Huzaifa, and the kidnappers. Huzaifa had been confrontational. When the kidnappers had addressed him as their "brother," Huzaifa had responded furiously: "I would prefer to die a dog's death than be your brother." Huzaifa went on to threaten them with a fatwa. The kidnappers' response was chilling. "A fatwa is already issued for Colonel Amir Sultan and Asad Qureshi."

Farrukh was desperate. The delay in sending a negotiator was now intolerable. He went to see Mr. Z, to persuade him to send his man right away.

Mr. Z explained he'd been contacted by Badar Mansoor, an Al Qaeda member. While conducting negotiations on our behalf, Mansoor had told him a few members of Al Qaeda had suggested kidnapping one of Sabir Mehsud's men in turn, and forcing him to lead them to where we were being held. Their intention was to storm the place and get us out. But others feared we'd be spread out around the compound and we'd either be killed in crossfire or be killed by Mehsud's men; they'd shoot us rather than let us go free without a ransom, it was argued.

They'd toyed with this dilemma for several days. This was the reason Zarar's trip to Waziristan had been delayed.

Mr. Z had finally told them to stand down. The plan was too risky. They'd stick to the original plan and send Zarar to negotiate.

Salim collected the bag from Farrukh's office the following day, June 11. Things were moving. Farrukh felt easier.

Arriving in Miranshah, Zarar met up with Badar Mansoor. He knew all about the various militant groups scattered around North Waziristan. He told Zarar the Asian Tigers consisted of two splinter groups—one headed by Usman Punjabi, a slightly built, dark-complexioned man in his thirties, formerly of Lashkar-e-Jhangvi,* and the other led by Sabir Mehsud, a stocky man with a long beard also in his thirties and formerly of Tehrik-e-Taliban Pakistan. Mehsud was the leader and Punjabi was his deputy. The plan to kidnap us was hatched by Punjabi.

The two men met with Usman Punjabi. He outlined the Asian Tigers' twin demands: the release of 159 prisoners, and a ransom of ten million dollars for my release. I had come from England, and I was associated with a television channel there. The figure was appropriate to those circumstances.

Zarar told him it was not. It was true I was making a film, but filmmaking was just a hobby of mine. I wasn't associated with any channel. It was down to my family to raise any money for a ransom. The sum of money the kidnappers wanted was impossible. If they pursued that sum, they'd be holding me for a very long time.

Then Zarar met with Sabir Mehsud. He suggested Mehsud convene a *jirga* and reach a solution to release us. Mehsud was incensed. How dare Zarar presume to tell him how to handle the situation? He threatened Zarar with dire consequences if he didn't leave Miranshah right away. Zarar ignored the threat and walked away.

Zarar found a shop with a telephone and called Farrukh to give him an update. In the middle of the conversation, Mehsud's men grabbed Zarar and whisked him away.

They took him to a compound. They put him in a room like an office cum armory—a table and a few chairs and, on the walls, Kalashnikovs, loaded magazines and bandoleers, rocket-propelled grenades, and IEDs. A well-armed group. Was this meant to impress and intimidate?

From there, Zarar was driven to a house built of mud. He was led into in a small room where animals were kept. It was baking hot inside. He was told to sit on the floor and was given a different set of clothes to wear, heavy clothes of coarse cloth that made him feel hotter still. They left a bucket of water next to him.

The following day, Sabir Mehsud returned with two men. Without a word, the three men set about flogging Zarar. Then they punched him repeatedly in the face and stomach. When he crumpled to the ground, they kicked him. They accused him of working for the ISI. They wanted to know why he was still in Waziristan. Zarar said nothing.

---

* A Sunni jihadist organization.

For the following three days and nights, he was allowed no sleep. Then they used the bucket to enrich the torture. They tied his hands behind his back, blindfolded him, and pushed his head into the bucket. Zarar struggled and fought for breath, but Mehsud's henchmen kept a firm hold of his head. After a minute or so, they yanked his head out of the water, giving Zarar ten seconds to gasp for breath before pushing his head down again. They continued this routine for thirty minutes. When they finally threw him to the floor, Zarar was close to death.

* * *

Asghar had been Farrukh's shadow ever since the hostage crisis began. He was determined to keep his old friend's mind busy and try to take the pressure off him. On this hot summer evening, Asghar persuaded Farrukh to go for a walk in the commercial area of Islamabad. Seeing the hustle and bustle of people shopping and enjoying the evening would help them relax, he thought. Smoke billowed out from the many alfresco eating places as the cooks fanned the kebabs and chicken tikkas on the charcoal. Tantalizing aromas wafted through the air, and many people responded by sitting down and ordering food.

Asghar suggested a place and the two of them sat down. A waiter appeared with a menu and handed one to each of them. Asghar had had a busy day trying to keep his friend's mind occupied and now he was ravenous. He ordered himself kebabs and chicken. The waiter turned to Farrukh, who shook his head. The waiter disappeared and Asghar leaned in toward his friend.

"What's wrong?"

"I can't. I just can't."

"Can't what?"

"Sit here and eat. Here, in the open air, relaxing, having a nice time. Knowing Asad is locked up in some far-off place eating God knows what."

"I understand. But you must eat. You can't allow yourself to become ill. You have to stay strong enough to fight for him."

"*Inshallah* I will fight for him. If it is the last thing I do."

Asghar was worried about his friend. He was becoming more and more impatient. He was often short with his staff and people were avoiding him, staying out of his way.

Farrukh's phone bleeped. It was an email, forwarded by Sherry:

Hi. Regard salaam and good morning.

You peoples are informed by Asian tigers nickname Islamic tigers that me Abdullah the new man that to contact you from now. Before this I want to clear this point that before my friends contact you peoples at yet now they are busy in another duty and I am pointed out for this duty.

Some days later we send some of the videos and also letters of both Colonel Imam and Asad Qureshi separately, I hope you people will receive it, before this you peoples contact my friends but now contact me and abort all the contacts with them. After now you contact me on same E-mail address or through the man which bring the video cassette. I say all this because that 3rd person will not use our name to black mail you peoples. If anyone does then say to him that give us the new evidences. If you peoples having any doubt about me then ask the questions and we will give the answers, Inshallah.

The actual point is that we demand some of Rupees. As 10 million dollars but you peoples will not give this and you peoples demand is just 10% as we demand. 3 or 4 corer rupees are nothing as compare to the health of the man … You peoples try to complete our demands as soon as because the Qureshi is so much medically tense here as you will be see in the video also. We have not more time for you people so if you peoples will not then be remember the results of Khalid Khawaja we will do the same work to kill the Qureshi also.

Thanks and wasalam.

The kidnappers emailing Sherry was a major blow. They saw her as the weakest link in the chain. And how had they got her email address? It had been extracted by means of torture, perhaps. The situation was becoming impossibly complicated. Yet another player in the drama. Abdullah. Who on earth was he?

Sherry went on to ask Farrukh if she should get the FBI involved. He thought not. Doing that would be giving the kidnappers exactly what they wanted—global recognition. He wrote back. *Do not respond to the email. Talk to no one.*

He knew that turning the situation into a global media event would make the ten-million-dollar ransom harder to resist. Either that or they'd just kill me for the publicity.

Sitting out in the warm summer evening was now the last thing Farrukh and Asghar wanted to do. They rushed back to the office, only to receive another blow.

Mr. Z called and told Farrukh Zarar had been captured by the Asian Tigers. Negotiations were on hold for now. Mr. Z was planning to go to Mecca for *Umra** for two weeks.

---

* A lesser pilgrimage that can be undertaken at any time of the year.

Farrukh was speechless. Why couldn't Mr. Z's plans for *Umra* be postponed? He seemed egregiously casual. Away for two weeks! His envoy now a prisoner! What on earth was going on? Why had Farrukh trusted this man? What was he going to tell Mum and Dad?

With no other options, Farrukh went to see the A Team. They'd been against Mr. Z's involvement from the start and they suggested Farrukh pursue negotiations on his own, although, with no contact from the kidnappers for several days now, this wouldn't be easy.

Nancy thought they'd hold on to me for as long as possible but ramp up the pressure on Farrukh by killing Rustam, the member of the group of least value to them. Farrukh didn't want to imagine that scenario. He insisted on Mr. Z's continued involvement.

"I don't want to deal with the kidnappers alone. He speaks their language. It's frustrating, but it's better to wait till he returns from *Umra*."

Another email arrived from the kidnappers:

Greetings,

We have received the things that you sent for your brother which included clothes, toothpaste, brush, letter, photo, and a note book etc.

The person named Zarar who was talking to you on the phone who was telling you not to talk to us or make contact on the phone or reply to our email we arrested him when he was talking to you on the phone. He has tried to sabotage the negotiations between us. He will be punished for this.

What you have told Zarar about the demand i.e. 4,000,000 rupees; this amount has no meaning for us because we demanded 10 million dollars. This offer is an insult.

Greetings

Abdullah Ghori

Well, one good thing was that the clothes and other things had been delivered. But what of Zarar? *Punished*? Farrukh felt desperately uneasy about that.

With Mr. Z away, the A Team giving advice he didn't want to follow, and now another name—Abdullah—to deal with, Farrukh's head was spinning. He felt helpless. The only thing to do was wait for another contact from the kidnappers. But days went by and he heard nothing.

Eventually the radio silence was broken by a phone call from a man who identified himself as Usman Punjabi.

"Can you tell me where you are with the situation? Because they have to give a final deadline now."

Farrukh recognized the voice from the tape but wanted to know Punjabi was a legitimate representative of the kidnappers. He invoked the code from his exchange with Ali Raza.

"Whose friend are you?"

"I am a friend to you. I can help you solve this matter."

Wrong answer.

"I'm afraid you have no authorization to talk to me."

Punjabi was not deterred.

"How is your mother?"

Farrukh was incensed at such a personal question but he held his temper.

"She is not well, of course. This worry is too much for her to bear. You have parents too. How would they be feeling?"

"Yes. I know it must be pretty bad."

"What group are you with? If you don't give me the code word, I can't talk to you."

"Come on, you can talk to me. You've asked questions, about the wedding of someone. And you got the answer you wanted. I know that. I have been asked to facilitate your deal."

Farrukh didn't like Punjabi. He was wheedling and overfamiliar, but Farrukh knew he was part of the group, although he didn't understand why it was Punjabi who was phoning, not Ali Raza. But some contact was better than none, so Farrukh decided to continue the conversation.

"How is my brother?"

"He is well. But you must try hard to raise the money. You must stay involved. And you must stay in touch with me."

"And how is Colonel Imam?"

"He is fine. Negotiations are good. His case carries more weight than your brother's because of his history with the Taliban. Many people on the outside want to save him. As for your brother, the only people interested in him are you and your family. To the rest of the world, he is a nobody. He needs your help. How much can you pay?"

Farrukh said he was trying to raise as much as possible, but reiterated the full amount was completely out of the question. The maximum would be a much smaller sum. Punjabi urged him to keep trying and to stay in touch.

Farrukh wanted to clear up the lines of communication. He wanted to know why Usman Punjabi was getting involved. What was his role? Were the kidnappers playing games or was the chain of command in the group now a little uncertain? He sent an email to Ali Raza:

Ali Raza sahib, AoA.

I have been called twice in the last few days by a man called Usman Punjabi. He claims to be your spokesperson and uses the telephone number that only you should have. He knows some details of our discussions so far.

I need to know who has your authority to talk to me and I will only talk to one person to resolve this situation. This is too important for our talks to be confused by outsiders using their own ideas.

Please call me tomorrow (Thursday) at 2:00 p.m. so that I can be clear as to who is the right person to speak to. After our last conversation, you said you would speak with your elders and call me back the same day. I am still waiting for your call.

Ali Raza responded the same day:

ASALAAM ALAIKUM
I hope u are fine
mr punjabi is spokesman taliban media center
we discuess about this meter
no tension
may be me punjabi role is middle man
u can talk with mr punjabi
no our represent
mr punjabi high value in media and taliban
many time talking about on this topic with mr punjabi
take care
ALLAHA HAFIZ

Another email followed shortly:

aoa
i hope u are fine
code
Waziristan
When he calls ask the code
Second code
Pakistan

Take care

ALLAHA HAFIZ

Tell me your last demand

Well, at least Farrukh had been told Usman Punjabi was authorized to talk to him and now a code word (however unimaginative) was in place. It brought a degree of clarity, but it was not the answer Farrukh was looking for.

He was not comfortable talking to Usman Punjabi. The emails suggested Punjabi was involved in some capacity but was not a representative of the Asian Tigers. It was unsettling.

In the days that followed, Punjabi called Farrukh on several occasions, always pushing him to hold a press conference and raise the ransom money. Farrukh wondered if he was negotiating part of the ransom money for himself.

* * *

The kidnappers had relaxed the regime a little. We were now allowed to talk to each other.

My conversations with Colonel Imam were a revelation. It turned out he hadn't known KK very well at all. He'd been fiercely opposed to making the trip and being part of our group, but KK had been very persuasive, and the Colonel had agreed at the last minute.

"I don't know what made me drop everything and come."

"Well, it was a surprise to me too. KK never told me you were joining us."

"He didn't know I'd be coming until the day we left."

"And I don't know why he didn't want Rustam to come along. We argued about it. I persuaded him."

Despite my opposition to KK at the Kohat junction, I felt that, between us, he and I were responsible for the terrible predicament these two men were in now.

In the days that followed, we got to know each other pretty well. We slept and washed and undressed in front of each other. The Colonel was very proud of a shirt his daughter had made for him, out of a silky brown fabric with a gold panel across the chest.

But it wasn't long before we started to get on each other's nerves. Meal times were the hardest for me. Colonel Imam had some disgusting habits. There was always too much oil in the curries the kidnappers gave us. When the Colonel got oil on his fingers, he'd flick it back onto the plate. And whenever he took a drink of water, he'd swill it around his mouth noisily before swallowing it. One day, this swilling noise was too much to take and I exploded.

"PLEASE! SOME DECORUM! Is it TOO MUCH to ask!"

The Colonel swallowed his water and set down the cup.

After five minutes of stony silence, I apologized.

The days were longer and warmer now, which placed a strain on the water supply. We were asked to use less water during ablutions for prayers. Nauman wanted us to wash just once, in the morning, and make that do for all the five prayers of the day. I protested. That was impossible. If we were to doze off, even for a second, or if we had to use the bathroom, it was required we wash again before praying. Nauman said there wasn't enough water. The usual religious practices could not be observed. He could see this placed him in an awkward position and, in the end, he agreed to three ablutions a day.

Sometimes Colonel Imam would fall asleep. He snored terribly. Whenever it was time for prayers, Rustam and I would wake him, so he could lead. I'd often remind him to make his ablutions before praying, as he'd fallen asleep. He'd always deny he'd slept and, in the end, I stopped making a point of it.

Rustam and I passed most of the time playing Ludo, a ridiculously boring game but good enough when it was all we had. Rustam always beat me but I didn't care—I just wanted time to pass.

Colonel Imam spent most of his time reading but, whenever Nauman came in, the Colonel would ask him the time, a habit I found increasingly frustrating. What was so important about the time of day? Knowing the hour just made the day longer. What was wrong with the Colonel? Did he have a train to catch?

On one occasion, I became very agitated at the Colonel's question. I shouted to Nauman.

"Please! Please don't tell him!"

Nauman looked at the Colonel. He said nothing and locked the door behind him. I turned to the Colonel.

"Why do you want to know the time?"

"It is my habit. I like to know the time so I can prepare for prayers."

"But when you hear the *azan*,[*] you can prepare then. Please spare us this incessant clock-watching. It just lengthens our days even more. You are a soldier, Colonel *sahib*. You know about psychological operations. You should be helping us to survive."

"I don't have an escape plan."

"I'm not talking about an escape plan. I'm talking about a survival plan. How we should behave with one another. How to avoid cracking up. As a soldier, you must know all about that."

[*] The call to prayer.

Colonel Imam looked at me and smiled.

"You know, you would have made a good commanding officer. A lieutenant colonel. The most exciting rank in the army. You would have been good at it."

I was flattered. But I also wondered if this was his way of absolving himself of the role of leader. We'd regarded him as the elder statesman. Perhaps he'd had enough. We all had.

We were now very jumpy indeed. Always fastidious about cleanliness, I now became obsessive. When a mouse darted across the room, I panicked and froze. Rustam crawled around our cell on his hands and knees, hunting for it. He cornered it and killed it with his sandal. He wrapped some toilet paper round his fingers and picked the mouse up by its tail. Seeing the squashed mouse in his hand made me sick, and I shouted at him to get rid of it.

Nauman came in to see what the commotion was about. Rustam held up the mouse and Nauman took it off him and left.

Rustam sat down and picked up the dice, ready to continue our game.

"Aren't you going to wash your hands?"

"What for? I was holding it with a tissue."

"I know, but I have this feeling in my stomach. Please wash your hands."

"No. I won't."

I was incensed. He was my assistant. He should do as I say.

"If you don't wash your hands, you'll never work with me again!"

"I'll never work with you anyway because we'll never get out of here! And, by the way, I don't use soap after I've used the bathroom!"

"What? You've been touching my cameras with dirty hands? All this time?"

He nodded, a smirk on his face.

"Wash your hands!"

Rustam continued to smile. He wasn't going to back down.

Rustam was a Pushtun, just like our captors. Pushtuns have a reputation for being short tempered and stubborn. Once they've said no, they'll never say yes.

Nauman shouted in to us to keep the noise down. We sat in silence.

When lunch was brought in, I thought Rustam would do the decent thing and wash his hands. There was no way I was going to eat from the same plate as him if he didn't. But he'd really dug his heels in. He showed no sign of going to bathroom to wash. I stared at him, as if looks could kill, but he was shameless. Colonel Imam looked away, preferring to stay out of it.

Rustam leaned toward the plate.

"Don't touch the food!"

I lifted my cup, scooped some water into it, rinsed it, and threw the water under the door. I heard Mukhtar's voice outside.

"They are still arguing."

I poured some of the curry from the plate into my cup and took a piece of chapatti and sat down, well away from Rustam, and began to eat.

The door burst open. Nauman strode in, a black hood over his head, in his hand the stick with the transmission belt nailed to it. He stood over me.

"We don't tolerate people like you. Who do you think you are?"

He slammed the belt into my back. A bolt of lightning shot through my body, as if I'd been branded with a red-hot iron. A wave of nausea rose in my stomach. Instinctively, I looked away, not wanting to invite a second blow.

Rustam and Colonel Imam stayed still and silent. They didn't want Nauman turning his attention on them.

I glanced back at Nauman. His cold, sadistic eyes stared at me through the eyelets of his hood. I looked away again.

After perhaps a minute, he left the room.

I rubbed my back, working hard to suppress the sobs that filled my chest. I was angry with Rustam. It seemed to me he had absolutely no sense of loyalty or camaraderie.

He and the Colonel began to eat, but I had no appetite at all now. I turned toward the wall and closed my eyes.

24
Proof of Life

As if to placate me after the flogging, Nauman asked me to teach him English. Although I hated him, and was not at all minded to help, I knew a refusal would likely bring more mistreatment, so I agreed.

I wrote a simple sentence at the top of a sheet of paper and asked him to copy it all the way to the bottom of the page. He picked it up quite quickly. Once he'd finished, I wrote out another line for him to copy. He was excited.

"You know English well, and you have a British passport. When you go back to England, you will be sleeping with English girls."

A stupid man full of contradictions. People like him style themselves as religious zealots but, if you spend enough time with them, the mask slips.

"What makes you say that? Muslims in the West don't behave like that."

"It's what people tell us."

"They're lying to you."

If he wanted to get personal with me, I wasn't going to let him in. I wanted to keep him at a distance.

"Here. Let me write another line for you. I have traveled to … You need to fill in which countries you have been to."

"I have been to Afghanistan, Pakistan, and America. Can you write the words here for me to copy?"

I wrote out the names of the countries at the top of the page. I was curious as to why he'd gone to the United States.

"Why did you go to America?"

"I was in Guantánamo Bay."

That was certainly an answer I hadn't expected. Colonel Imam looked up in surprise.

"You know Guantánamo Bay is *not* in America. It's in Cuba."

Nauman seemed disappointed to learn he hadn't been to America after all. Another contradiction.

"How were you treated there?"

"It was a difficult time. We were kept in cages. It was very hot. To give us shade, they put us in a hole in the ground with a huge cover over it. They would throw food in to us as if we were animals. We'd have to fight over it. Whoever got hold of it would eat it. There was never enough to go round."

"So they eventually let you go. Why?"

"I was innocent."

I thought of Abdullah Mehsud, the one-legged, publicity-hungry Taliban fighter who'd been released from Guantánamo only to go right back into the fighting. And here was Nauman. Another blunder by the US authorities. And I was paying for their mistake.

I wondered if Nauman had picked up training tips in Guantánamo. He behaved like a trained hostage-taker, as Krishan Lal had. I wondered what he was doing now.

Then I thought of KK and of where he might be. I wondered who he was speaking to and how the discussions were going for our release.

"Have you heard from Khalid Khawaja? Do you know where he is now?"

Nauman smiled. "He's probably eating mangoes with his wife."

That wasn't funny. He was amused by the disapproving look on my face and decided to play me some more.

"Actually, he was in Miranshah and wanted to come back and see you. I told him that was not possible because we'd moved you and you were now far away. We didn't want him here. He might leave a microchip for a drone strike."

"Sure. Let's just carry on with the exercise."

After that, we didn't see Nauman for a few days.

Mukhtar came and went, and there was the big guy, Shaukat. He chatted quite openly, claiming to be working here as an unpaid volunteer ready to die for the group's cause. He was much nicer to us than the others. Sometimes he even came in without a hood, not caring that we saw his face.

Then, a few days later, Mukhtar asked me to teach him English as well. But secretly. I was not to tell the others.

What was it with these guys? They professed hatred for the West on the one hand, while on the other they wanted to learn English.

I wasn't keen on teaching Mukhtar, nor on keeping his secret. He'd grassed on me before, and I'd nearly had my toes blown off. But I needed to humor him.

Nauman returned a few days later, bringing the voices of children with him. We'd hear them moving around in the areas outside. Nauman started coming into our room with items he wanted to store there—mostly ancient pots and pans that didn't look worth holding on to—and we reckoned he was emptying out another room to move his family into.

Once all the removal activity had finished, Nauman came in and told us Sabir Mehsud was coming to see us. As usual, we were to sit up straight. Show the murderer some respect.

The two of them came into the room. Mehsud handed me an old plastic bag. It contained some clothes, a toothbrush, toothpaste, and an envelope with a letter in it.

I took out the letter. It was from Farrukh, assuring me he was doing his best to get me out. I'd always known he'd be working hard for our release, but it was nevertheless good to hear it from him.

There was also a message from Mum, telling me to keep praying, telling me how much she loved me. A photograph of Dad was also enclosed. Precious contact with my family.

Farrukh's letter talked about an enclosed notebook, which wasn't there.

"My brother mentions a notebook. Where is it?"

"The notebook contained a secret message. We can't give it to you."

An outright lie. Any notebook from Farrukh would be a smart piece of stationery. They'd obviously fancied it for themselves.

Mehsud looked at me.

"Your friends sent someone. They want a *jirga* to talk about your release. They think we are weak. But we are not. We are warriors of God."

He didn't like his authority being challenged and he saw me as directly responsible for that challenge. His eyes were full of rage.

I looked away. He said nothing, but I felt him staring at me. I picked up the things he'd given me and went to put them into my bag. Rustam jumped up and grabbed the bag from me and hit it with his hand. A scorpion had been sitting on the side of the bag. It scurried away. I shrieked with horror, and Nauman and Mehsud laughed at my discomfort. A city slicker with no stomach for the real world. They left the room, still laughing.

I emptied my bag, to make sure nothing else was hiding inside, then put everything back. I took the letter and read it again, several times, thinking of Farrukh and Mum and Dad. It was tremendously comforting just to read Farrukh's words. To know Mum and Dad were okay. To know Farrukh was doing his best to help us.

Colonel Imam asked me to show him the letter. He read it out loud. When he got to the part where Mum said she loved me, his voice broke and tears ran down the old man's face. No matter what our age, a mother evokes powerful emotions.

* * *

Farrukh felt he was losing his grip on the situation. Things seemed worse now than when they'd first started. Too many people were involved. He was inundated with phone calls and emails. He had no idea what was going on. He felt as if all his decisions were made on an emotional level at a time when he needed more than ever to be clear-headed, rational, pragmatic. The email Sherry had received from the kidnappers had put more pressure on him, and he felt weakened and exposed by all the information that was coming out, information he'd wanted to keep hidden.

And with Mr. Z out of the picture for the moment, everything was left to him. Above all, he wanted to be sure of my welfare and my whereabouts.

He decided to send another email to the kidnappers:

Raza sahib AoA,

My family and I want this matter resolved. We want my brother and Rustam returned safely. There are others making claims that they have my brother. The TV, newspapers, and radio stations are all saying different things.

Because of this confusion, I need to know that I am talking to the right person. I take you very seriously. I know this is no game. I know what happened to the other man.

I need you to allow me to speak to my brother and Rustam, so that I know you are in control of the situation and are the right man to do business with.

The kidnappers responded immediately:

Asalaam alaikum

We don't have enough time to give explanations or proves. You are running out of time my friend. There is no question for the custody of hostages since media is just creating a scene. There is no possibility to talk to your brother since government banned the cell phone services. New contact is Abdullah Shah. Email address below.

The response was frustrating in the extreme.

With Zarar arrested and with no proof of life, how could Farrukh continue with the negotiations? For all he knew, they might have already killed us and were just stringing him along to get money.

After consulting with the A Team, he sent a short email to the new man, Abdullah Shah, asking for questions to be passed on to me, hoping for answers that would prove I was alive:

Please ask my brother for the answers to these two questions:

    1. Who is Guddu?

    2. What does Sajid say after lunch?

Rustam and I were playing Ludo when Nauman came in. He was singing.

"Papa doesn't need to pay any more."

He looked at me meaningfully as he sang the words.

"What are you saying?"

He repeated the line. "Papa doesn't need to pay any more."

"Do you mean the ransom? The ten million dollars? You don't want the ten million?"

"That's right."

I turned to Rustam. He was smiling. I felt like crying with relief. I felt I could taste freedom. See freedom ahead of me, somewhere. Perhaps we wouldn't die in this place after all.

Nauman told me to get up and follow him into the bathroom. I didn't like the idea of being separated from the others. I felt very uneasy.

"I have some questions for you. Two questions. If you can answer them, you will be able to go home in a week."

One week. Seven days. Then I'd be out of here.

But what about Colonel Imam and Rustam? I couldn't leave them here.

"Who is Guddu? Question One. And, second, what does Sajid say after lunch?"

I was perplexed. "Guddu is the nickname of my cousin, Saqib. But … the second question? I don't know. I don't know the answer to the second question."

Nauman nodded toward the room. "Go back in and think about it."

Rustam and the Colonel stared at me as I crossed the room and sat down on my bed. I could think of nothing to say. I just lay on my mattress and looked up at the ceiling, thinking about the second question.

Who on earth was Sajid? And what would he say after lunch? Why would Farrukh ask such a question when I had no chance of answering it? Had the question really come from Farrukh or was Nauman toying with me? Again.

When Nauman came in later, I gave him other information to pass to Farrukh, information about where I take my mother shopping for clothes and the name of her tailor, information Farrukh would know could only have come from me.

Could it really be true I was going home soon? I thought about my family. I imagined our reunion.

I thought about Sherry and how she'd be coping without me. I thought about how good it would be just to be with her. To be in her company. To sit with her, maybe watch a film together. To feel her squeeze my hand at a tense point in the film. To see her tears at a sad ending.

She was so delicate. She had the softest heart I'd ever known in a person. Things had been pretty strained between us—we hadn't been getting on well at all. Perhaps this experience would make us close again. Change things for the better.

I certainly hoped as much.

And I thought about work. I wondered if the ISPR were going ahead with *Defusing Human Bombs*, the film I'd started shooting. I hoped they were waiting for me and not finishing it with another director.

* * *

The following day, Farrukh received an email:

Salaam and regards to you.

This is what your brother says. Guddu is the nickname of Saqib, my aunt's son and my cousin. Regards the second question, I don't know a Sajid or what he said after lunch. Instead I can tell you that I take my mother shopping for cloth at Sheba Silk and Waheed is her tailor.

At this point we release the video of Colonel Imam and Asad Qureshi and we give you 10 days only. After this it's your wish that you complete our demand or wait for the same results as Khalid Khawaja.

The other important thing is that you people do not trust the third man. If the third man say anything more and disturb my demand or he take the money then the result will be very bad as then we will kill Asad Qureshi.

Walaikum asalaam.

Farrukh was deeply confused. He couldn't believe I'd failed to answer the second question. How could I not remember Sajid, the kitchen boy who served lunch in Farrukh's office? He was learning English and making good progress, but he'd often get words mixed up. If there was a sweet dish to follow, he'd always warn Farrukh to leave room for it. But, instead of "sweet," he always said "sleep."

This had become a standard joke for Farrukh and me, and years later, we were still asking Mum to make us some "sleep."

Why hadn't I answered the question? How could I not remember this? Had I been brainwashed? Was I losing my mind?

And this *third* person? They must be referring to Mr. Z. The visit from Zarar had made them suspect Mr. Z wanted to cheat them out of their money.

And now a ten-day deadline.

Farrukh showed the email to the A Team. Brian tried to convince him that, like the earlier deadlines, this one would also pass without incident. They were just using scare tactics. But, at this stage, Farrukh was not minded to take anything lightly.

And the picture was still hazy. He was now dealing by email with Abdullah Shah. But what about phone calls. Whose calls was he to accept?

* * *

For Zarar, the torture continued.

They withheld food and deprived him of sleep. They pressed a pistol into his temple and shouted in his face.

But Zarar was stoic in his faith. He accepted the inevitability of death. If it was his fate to die in this place, so be it. They could do what they liked to him. But he insisted they allow him to write his will and, as was their responsibility under Islamic law, they should make sure that his will reached his family.

So he wrote to his wife:

Asalaam alaikum

By the time you receive this letter, I will no longer be alive. I have been accused of being a spy and you should know that I am not and that they killed me for no reason. My instructions for you are to educate our children to the highest level and I want you to build a house near to where my parents live. When the girls grow up, one should be married into your family and one into mine. Our son Abu Bakr is to be given religious education and taught to memorize the Qur'an, and be a scholar in other fields.

Goodbye and be strong for the sake of the children.

Allah hafiz.*

Nauman warned us that another man would be using our bathroom, and we were to remain silent when he was in there. But he didn't trust us, so every time this other man was in the bathroom, Nauman came to sit with us, to make sure we didn't talk. This aroused our curiosity enormously. After Nauman was gone, we'd speculate about who it could be.

---

* God be with you.

Nauman started spending a lot of time with us, not just for his English lessons but also to play Ludo. Rustam and Colonel Imam would team up against Nauman and me. I was the worst player by far, and we'd always lose, which often put Nauman in a mood. It was like playing with a seven-year-old.

Sometimes, he'd serve mango with our lunch—a real treat—but, as a punishment for repeatedly putting him on the losing side, I was forbidden from eating it. When he'd gone, Rustam and Colonel Imam tried to coax me into eating some, but I refused. He'd be able to smell the mango on my hands, and that would only lead to more beatings for all of us. So I sat back and watched them eat my favorite fruit.

But it never did any good to start taking kindness for granted. After a few days of mangoes, one day Nauman brought in a plate of mango stones, with a few shreds of flesh hanging off them. Rustam was incensed.

"These are just like bones with no meat on them. I have a good mind to send them back." Like we were in a restaurant.

It was a move calculated to wind us up. On Rustam, it was working. He wouldn't let it go.

"But there is nothing on them!"

"I know. But just show that you at least touched them." The only way to avoid a beating, and to hold on to your sanity, was to play along.

But Rustam pushed the plate away.

When Nauman came in an hour later and saw the plate untouched, he left the room. Then he came back with a long hard stick and spent ten minutes softening it up on my back and my legs.

Then we were hauled onto the merry-go-round again and good food started to appear. It was clear Nauman's wife was now doing the cooking. And, in our water, the novel and welcome addition of ice. Well, welcome if you didn't think too much about the conditions in which it had likely been produced. I tried not to imagine Mukhtar chipping pieces off a big block of ice resting on the tiled floor of a grimy bathroom used by all and sundry. I tried to concentrate on the delicious coolness of the water as it washed down my throat.

But having Nauman's family around also brought challenges. One day, for a period of several hours, we were prevented from using the bathroom. Instead, it was given over to Nauman's children to use as their playground. We spent the day listening to them splash about while we lay on our beds in silence, our bladders bursting.

The weather warmed up and our kidnappers issued us with sachets of mosquito repellent cream, which brought some relief. But there were now also bees in our room, flying in through the hole meant for the extractor fan at Colonel Imam's end of the room. Because I'm pretty nervous around insects of any kind, the presence of the bees unsettled me.

Then I got stung. A sharp pain on the back of my left hand. I let out a little yelp. Rustam took the pin of my shackle and rubbed it on the sting. Remarkably, it immediately felt better.

"Iron. If you get a bee sting, just rub iron on it."

A useful tip, and one I was grateful for. Then I looked at Rustam's grimy hands. I got up and went to the bathroom and scrubbed mine as best I could.

I was aware of how weak my body had now become, through lack of exercise. And my stomach, never very settled, began to complain.

I asked Nauman for some medication for my stomach. He brought the medication, and he also brought us a cream cake each. The aroma of vanilla from the cake immediately made me nauseous, and I politely declined it.

This infuriated Nauman and he stood over me, ordering me to eat—for him, I had insulted him by rejecting an act of kindness. I thanked him and asked him to leave the cake for me to eat later, when the medication had made my stomach feel better. But he picked up the cake and flung it at the wall and stormed out, slamming the door behind him.

Some of the cake had stuck to the wall and the rest had dropped onto the floor. If the mess wasn't cleaned up quickly, the room would soon be invaded by ants. Rustam and I picked up as much as we could, and I went over the area with wet toilet paper.

A while later, Nauman came back, apparently a little calmer. I told him I'd taken the medicine. I asked him to leave me unchained overnight, and leave the bathroom door unlocked, in case I needed to use it in an emergency (leaving the bathroom unlocked didn't mean we could escape—there was another locked door leading to the outside).

He refused. Rustam pleaded with him, but Nauman was adamant. With my stomach in knots, at that moment I'd probably never hated him as much. I thought of the indignity I'd suffer if I couldn't control my bowels.

I lay on my mattress, willing my body to control itself. Then I noticed the pots and pans Nauman had stored by the wall and wondered if I'd have the courage to use one of them as a makeshift toilet.

Thankfully, it didn't come to that. I lasted until morning. God had watched over me.

A few more days passed. I woke one morning—my diary tells me it was June 21—with my head full of what Nauman had said, about my going home soon. For some reason, on that morning, I was convinced I was going to be released.

This feeling was sharpened when Nauman came in with a newspaper and handed it to me. It was *Dawn*, the most widely read English newspaper in Pakistan. A rare treat to have news from the outside world.

I gave some pages to Colonel Imam. Most of my section was devoted to Benazir Bhutto—it was her birthday. There was a long article waxing lyrical about her party and its achievements, written by judge Ali Nawaz Chowhan, a friend of my family. I chuckled at the sycophantic tone of the piece, written from a perspective of pure self-interest.

Colonel Imam and I exchanged sheets and continued reading. Time passed, and I was eager for news of my imminent release. Nothing. I read all the articles again, then began to read the classified ads. Anything, just to make the time pass.

Evening came. I convinced myself they'd be releasing me at night, once the heat of the day had fully subsided. Nightfall came, and I eventually gave in to sleep.

I woke at first light. Still in my room. Rustam and the Colonel were fast asleep. An overwhelming sense of disappointment gripped me.

Nauman came in. I turned on him.

"You said I was going to be released soon."

"What?"

"You said you didn't need the money."

He laughed. "I was joking."

"What?"

"Do you think we are just going to let you go? We have spent at least 800,000 rupees just in feeding you."

He was still laughing as he locked the door behind him.

I lay back on my mattress, my head once again heavy with the death sentence that still hung over it. I thought of Sherry and I thought of my mother and father and of the hell they'd be going through.

I thought of Nauman's wife and mother. How would they feel if they knew the torment this monster was inflicting on another man's wife and mother? I couldn't imagine that his wife didn't know exactly what was going on. If that was the case, as far as I was concerned she was an accessory and she deserved to be punished just like him.

In the days that followed, I was emotionally very unsettled. Everything irritated me. The days were unbearably hot and, at night, I felt like the room was alive with insects. I often had the sensation of little hairy legs on my face, and I was forever jumping up in the middle of the night to shine my flashlight around, only to see nothing. Rustam and the Colonel would stare at me, a mad pathetic person. Then they'd be unable to get back to sleep and we'd all lie awake, in mutually hostile silence.

One evening Nauman came in. He sat down and looked at us and put his finger on his lips. Keep quiet. We heard someone go into the bathroom and take a shower. Ten minutes later, another person knocked on the bathroom door and shouted in to the stranger.

"Finished?"

"Yes." An unfamiliar voice.

We heard the door open and close. Then we heard the stranger being led away.

That evening, they served us a meal of chicken biryani. Rustam and Colonel Imam devoured the meat. I took some rice. It was probably the best meal they'd ever given us.

I wondered what the special occasion was.

25
The Cat Out of the Bag

Farrukh learnt from Salim that Mr. Z had returned from *Umra* and, much to his surprise, Zarar had been released. He was anxious to speak to Zarar, to get a sense of what was going on with the kidnappers, and to ask if he'd seen me. They went to see Mr. Z straight away.

Mr. Z told them there were the beginnings of a split among the kidnappers. It seemed some of the kidnappers wanted a separate ransom for Rustam, while others said he was a poor man who should be spared. There'd apparently been a very angry exchange between Sabir Mehsud and Badar Mansoor. Mehsud had grabbed Mansoor by the collar and threatened him. Afterward, Mansoor was very angry and said he wanted to kill Mehsud.

Mr. Z asked one of his aides to bring Zarar in. Farrukh was shocked at the sight of him. There were visible signs of torture on his body. The skin on his hands had been burnt by acid.

"I was talking to my emir, telling him you shouldn't be sending lots of emails, when they apprehended me. Usman Punjabi told the rest of the group you'd offered fifty million rupees, while we were telling them four million. That's why they arrested me and beat me."

He took a breath. Then he continued the tale of his ordeal.

"I was blindfolded all the time. They only took it off to let me read the Qur'an. They beat me daily."

He looked at Farrukh.

"They asked me about your finances. I told them you were not a very rich man, and you were offering all you could afford after selling your valuables. They pushed my head in a bucket of water every day, asking for more details about you. Then they put acid in the water and pushed my hands into it."

Farrukh looked away. How would he ever be able to repay this man for what he'd done? Zarar continued.

"Abdullah Ghori and Sabir Mehsud are the same person. The film of Asad in front of the green painting was made in Mehsud's house—I was there during the initial negotiations. It was Mehsud's faction who kidnapped me, and Mansoor's group who got me released."

Stories of the tension between the kidnappers unsettled Farrukh. He knew KK had been tortured to get the confessions used in the video, and he was concerned they'd be doing the same to me. They certainly hadn't held back in their treatment of Zarar. And given that Zarar hadn't told them much about Farrukh, Farrukh thought it was conceivable they'd tortured me for more information about his finances.

He thought of me being tortured by these animals, and a wave of anger flooded over him.

"They should all be bombed! The whole lot of them!"

When he saw Mr. Z's face, he immediately realized the awkwardness of what he'd said. The cleric looked calm, but there was steel in his eyes.

"I can understand your feelings. But we have to proceed with a cool head. The kidnappers want you to get desperate, so you'll pay the full amount. The more relaxed you remain, the better chance we have of paying less and getting your brother out of there. We have to make them desperate so they take as little as possible."

Farrukh nodded. He was being reprimanded. Mr. Z knew the building that the kidnappers used as their headquarters, and he knew which mosque they attended.

"Next time they call you, tell them you know their location. Mention it. Let's see how they react."

Farrukh was amazed Mr. Z had been able to uncover this information. But he was still no closer to getting me out. And he knew how ruthless the Taliban were. And yet, Mr. Z had been able to get Zarar out. After Zarar's intervention had caused such discord, this was no mean feat. Farrukh felt encouraged. But he was concerned this loss of face might be pushing them into mistreating me, in some sort of twisted *quid pro quo*.

It had emerged Punjabi had been making mischief in suggesting Mr. Z was trying to deceive the kidnappers. Given Punjabi had been unmasked as a troublemaker, working to his own agenda, Farrukh wondered what would happen to him now.

He spoke to Nudrat and wondered aloud if he should offer himself in my place, but Nudrat argued no one else had the strength to face this battle on the outside. He seemed to accept this, but Nudrat feared he might do something like that anyway, without telling anyone. She knew he was feeling desperate.

Then Farrukh's anxiety was ratcheted up further. Usman Punjabi called him. There was disagreement in the group (confirming what Mr. Z had said). Sabir Mehsud was threatening to kill Rustam, in order to put pressure on Farrukh and extract more money.

But the *ulema** were conducting their investigations into how guilty each of us was and who could be condemned by fatwa. They said my crime was making films for the army, which marked me out as a spy, but Rustam was not guilty of any misdemeanor. Sabir Mehsud wouldn't accept their decision, and now the kidnappers had split into two factions. This meant, in order to secure my release, Farrukh would now have to pay a ransom to *both* groups.

* Scholars.

Punjabi said unless his group was paid soon, they'd take possession of me from Mehsud, and the ransom would go up. Or they'd simply kill me.

The conversation with Punjabi left Farrukh feeling wretched.

On top of all this, frequent power cuts brought everything to a standstill and made daily life very uncomfortable, with everyone baking in the stifling summer temperatures without the relief of fans and air conditioning.

Being outdoors was almost unbearable, but Farrukh and Asghar bore the heat bravely, running around between Mr. Z's compound and the A Team's hotel on a daily basis. Farrukh was exhausted all the time, and his feet were in ruins from the open sandals.

But he was still putting on a brave face for Mum and Dad, making his nightly phone call, reassuring them the kidnappers couldn't hurt me because they needed the money, making out he was in control of the situation and was intentionally delaying things to make the kidnappers settle on a lower figure.

In truth, Usman Punjabi was now pestering Farrukh with calls, sometimes several a day, demanding money for his group. Farrukh lost his temper and told him to stop calling, saying he'd only deal with Ali Raza from the other group. Punjabi told him his own group were looking into the involvement of the British government and the British TV channel. Farrukh should take him seriously and pay him, he said, or there'd be dire consequences.

Farrukh was at his wits' end. There was no news from Ali Raza and the ransom deadline was just around the corner. But Mr. Z had told him to wait. But after what Punjabi had said, Farrukh wondered if the A Team's presence in Islamabad had been exposed. Should he be insisting they leave?

He felt like the man in the circus who spins plates on sticks. He had to keep all the plates spinning. If one plate were to fall, the lot would come crashing to the floor.

Farrukh shared the Punjabi conversation with the A Team. They were stunned. They understood the consequences if their presence was detected. Everything he'd told the kidnappers would be treated as lies. Everything would end. Including my life.

He suggested they leave the country. They were reluctant to do this, even given what Punjabi had said. A compromise was reached, and they agreed they'd now meet much less often.

They assured Farrukh this latest deadline would pass without incident, just like the previous ones.

Farrukh wasn't so sure.

Usman Punjabi became relentless, making constant demands for money. A payment of two million rupees would guarantee my safe passage to Islamabad. No payment and they'd pick me up, and I'd be in their possession.

Farrukh went on the offensive.

"Sabir Mehsud told me he will kill you if you continue to interfere."

Punjabi sounded shaken. "I will kill him first. I am not afraid of him."

"If Sabir Mehsud is holding my brother, then he is more powerful than you. I will deal with him only."

"Okay. Now I will kill him. Then the price goes up, and if you don't pay I will kill your brother."

Punjabi hung up.

Farrukh had recorded the conversation. He copied it to a CD and took it to Mr. Z. Mr. Z said he could use it to bring things to a head.

Mr. Z could see Farrukh was becoming desperate, but he urged him not to show any desperation. Farrukh was running out of energy.

"It's not just my brother. My parents can't take this much longer. And they shouldn't have to, at their age."

"I understand. But this is a war of nerves. If your nerves are strong enough, this will end. But if they see the slightest hope of getting more money, they will keep on turning the screw. They have nothing to lose and have all the time in the world."

Several days passed, with no news from the kidnappers. Even Punjabi stopped calling. Farrukh met with his friend, Dawood. He suggested sending the kidnappers an email in Urdu—they were clearly struggling with English—and this might get the ball rolling. Farrukh thought it was worth a try, so he drafted an email for Dawood to translate:

Abdullah Ghori Sahib,

I am sending this email in Urdu so there can be no confusion.

On behalf of my father and mother, I appeal for mercy. Please take the money we have collected and set my brother free. If we could mortgage ourselves to get some more money we would gladly do that too. My work has been halted since this nightmare began and debts are mounting. The more you delay, the more our condition will deteriorate. What we have collected might also start to decrease. May Allah have mercy and resolve this matter.

Respected Sabir and Muhammad Ghori Sahib it is our appeal to you that you consider my request with compassion and take what we have collected and set my brother free. Your demands are too high. We cannot get ten million dollars and we cannot arrange for 159 prisoners to be set free.

Have mercy on my old mother and father.

I urge you to take what I have to offer and end this nightmare.

Farrukh

Within hours, he received a reply:

Mr. Farrukh Qureshi we are not dacoits* or criminals. Alhamdulillah,** we are Muslims and Mujahedeen.*** We are not Asian Tigers, we are Islamic Tigers. As regards the demand, that too is permitted in Islam because what your brother and his people were doing is not in accordance with Islamic teachings. It is synonymous with harming Islam.

Our group contains many scholars and their declarations, which are in accordance with Islam, are complied with by us. It is permissible in Islam to take money for captured prisoners, as the Prophet (Peace be upon Him) did in the war of Badar. It is also permissible to kill and it is also permissible to try to free the Mujahedeen companions who have been captured. It is up to you now. Thanks to God, we do not sell our faith for money. If our demands are not fulfilled, then it will be permissible by the teachings of Islam to kill the prisoners. We were getting millions of rupees for Khalid Khawaja, but his crime was unforgivable. That is why we killed him in broad daylight.

Sir, also remember this. Neither Badar Mansoor nor any other group can persuade us otherwise. Alhamdulillah we ourselves are a strong network. We do not care whether people approve of us or not. We only want the will of Allah.

Our first and last wish is that you fulfil our demand if you want to save your brother's life. And if you are relying upon any other personality to save your brother, then this is your biggest mistake.

Several days ago, we gave you a deadline of ten days. If our demand is not met by that deadline, we will take the next step. Do not think that we are greedy or in need of money.

The demand for Colonel Imam is also the same. If our companions are not released, we will also kill him. You and your old mother should be worried about your brother only. You can save the life of your brother. You have until June 30, 2010. Your brother has already told us that he would like to be shot, not beheaded. We will carry out his wish.

Greetings

Abdullah Ghori messenger of Sabir Mehsud.

Farrukh was devastated. So my method of execution had been discussed, and I had chosen. It sounded like I'd given up on being released and accepted my fate. Like I felt defeated.

He felt helpless. He wrote back immediately with another appeal for mercy:

* Bandits.
** Praise be to Allah.
*** Warriors of Allah.

In the name of Allah who is the most merciful

Respected Mr. Sabir and Mr. Abdullah Ghori,

Asalaam alaikum

I got your email. I read your stance. It informed me of the situation. You talked about the deadline of ten days and required that your demand be fulfilled. I have listened to that and this is what I've done. I have talked to friends and to all my brothers and sisters. I have been abroad and talked to my brother's friends there and appealed to them for help. I have sold whatever I could sell. You have my final figure. Everyone has given what they can. No organization will help me.

Farrukh.

No response.

The deadline approached. There was nothing Farrukh could do. He didn't sleep. He worried about Mum and Dad. What if the A Team was wrong? What if the kidnappers actually killed me on June 30?!

He thought about the date. It was a Wednesday. They'd executed KK on Friday, the religious day. Perhaps Wednesday would pass without incident. Perhaps. But you couldn't predict the kidnappers' moves. They were *Khawarijis.** As we are told by the Prophet Muhammad, peace be upon him, "*There shall come a people who will recite the Qur'an but it won't pass beyond their throats. They will slay the followers of Islam and spare the people of idolatry. They will pierce through the religion just like an arrow which goes clean through a prey.*"

With three days to go, Farrukh didn't know what to do. If the kidnappers killed me, where would he want to be when that happened? In Islamabad, or with Mum and Dad in England? He decided to travel to England.

He arrived in London on June 28. The clock was ticking. Two days to go.

So far, he'd played it cool about the deadline. Pulling that off in front of Mum and Dad would be a big test of his character. It had been more than three months since he'd had a proper night's sleep. As he drove to the family home in Bradford, he felt every day of that.

It was good to be part of the family again, and to sit around a table with everyone. But he'd only been in bed for twenty minutes when he started to feel a pain in his chest, like heartburn but stronger. He got up and took some indigestion tablets and went back to bed.

* People who had become separate from Islam.

He didn't sleep a wink. Around three in the morning, the pain had become unbearable. He couldn't keep still. He woke his son, Umer, and told him to start the car. They were going to Bradford Royal Infirmary.

In Casualty, Farrukh threw up. He was acutely embarrassed. He'd never vomited in public before. He asked Umer to clean up the mess—he didn't want a nurse to have to clean up after him.

Nurse after nurse filed in, taking blood, checking his blood pressure, hooking him up to an EKG. The heart trace showed nothing, but Farrukh was still in tremendous pain. A doctor asked him if there was anything unusual going on in his life and he mentioned the kidnapping. The doctor told him this was doubtless the body's reaction to traumatic stress, a physical demonstration of the mental pressure he'd been under for the past three months.

The nurses gave him a strong morphine injection, which eased the pain and sent him into a deep sleep.

The following morning, Farrukh discharged himself from the hospital and went home to worried parents. He made light of the situation. It was June 29, the day before the deadline.

No news from Mr. Z or the kidnappers. He called Salim and learned that, ever loyal to Mr. Z, Zarar had returned to Waziristan and would meet the relevant people in the evening. Farrukh was overwhelmed by Zarar's willingness to return after all he'd been through. Salim had also been told by Mr. Z that there'd been positive developments, both in relation to Colonel Imam and to me. He hoped to have more news later when he got an update from Zarar, but he expected an early settlement. The message from Mr. Z was to "be ready."

Time passed at a snail's pace, and Farrukh was still incredibly weak from the night's exertions.

In the evening, Salim called. Zarar had sent word the kidnappers had opened negotiations with a demand for fifty million rupees but had finally settled on the figure of thirty million. No less.

Farrukh told Salim even this was a figure he couldn't raise. Salim said it sounded like there was no room for maneuver.

Farrukh decided to take a gamble. He told Salim Mr. Z should convey the message that the kidnappers might as well kill both Rustam and me if they weren't willing to negotiate below thirty million, as no more money could be found.

Salim told him the kidnappers had said, once agreement had been reached, Rustam and I would be home within three days.

Farrukh was on tenterhooks. Pakistan is four hours ahead of BST, which meant the deadline was only hours away. Terrified they might kill me, and horrified at the thought of being asleep when that happened, he tried to stay awake but was overcome with fatigue and drifted off.

Mum and Dad were already having breakfast when Farrukh was woken by Umer. He quickly looked at his watch. Eight o'clock. Twelve o'clock in Pakistan. He checked his phone for messages. Nothing. Frantically, he dialed Salim's number.

"Have you heard from Mr. Z?"

"His phone is constantly busy. He must be negotiating with them. Don't worry. I'll keep you informed."

At breakfast, he assured Mum and Dad negotiations were under way, and there was nothing to worry about. Mum read her Qur'an and Dad fingered his rosary. Both prayed for a miracle.

Finally, Farrukh got a call from Salim with the news the negotiations had broken down. The kidnappers had somehow discovered I had cats—fancy animals valued at fifty thousand rupees each, who ate fancy food imported at great expense. Any man who had money to waste in this way clearly belonged to a rich family. Farrukh's line all along, about us being a family of limited means, was clearly nonsense. They were angry at having being lied to. Taken for fools. Now they were looking for more money.

Farrukh pointed out to Salim that the kidnappers were wrong. The ginger cat, Sheroo, had died of kidney failure. And the white cat, Sunny, had disappeared one day and never returned. And they'd been bought for five thousand rupees (around thirty pounds), not fifty thousand. But I didn't have them anymore.

Farrukh wondered if the kidnappers had somehow managed to contact the domestic help at Mum and Dad's house—that was the only way they could know anything about the pets.

And he shook his head at the absurdity of a situation in which my path to freedom was being blocked by a nonexistent cat.

His worries about Rustam and Colonel Imam returned. He felt he was the only one looking out for poor Rustam, and there was no way the government would release 159 terrorists in exchange for the Colonel. But the Colonel's sons were negotiating on his behalf, so Farrukh tried to persuade himself to focus on my case only. It still didn't feel right. It felt like he was abandoning the old man.

On July 2, before returning to Islamabad, Farrukh went to London to meet another representative from the channel, who agreed that the best course of action would be to show resistance and stick to the offer previously made—four million rupees.

And in any case, there was no guarantee that payment now would bring me and Rustam back. An offer might prompt the kidnappers to double or quadruple the price.

And there was a genuine risk to Rustam's life no matter which course of action was taken.

There was also the important matter of having the funds in place. It was not wise to offer any amount unless Farrukh could lay his hands on it quickly.

After this meeting, Farrukh took a flight back to Islamabad. Asghar, ever faithful, was waiting to take him home. Instead, Farrukh asked him to drive to the A Team's hotel.

Once again, Brian tried to convince Farrukh to drop Mr. Z and deal directly with the kidnappers. Having Mr. Z involved was just complicating the issue. Witness the breaking down of talks.

"You have to listen to me. I know what I'm talking about. We told you the deadline would come and go. We told you it was just a mind game."

"You did. But I know these people. In this region. We're playing with lives here. My brother's life. So we have to think like they do. And the best man for that task is Mr. Z. Your brother's life is not at risk. So now you have to listen to me."

Brian's jaw dropped. Farrukh was in charge.

"This last deadline passed without incident because of a cat. A cat that Asad doesn't even have any more. The kidnappers took their eye off the ball. We won't be that lucky again. If I negotiate directly with them, the price will just go up and up."

"Okay."

"I don't play with people's lives. We have a death penalty in this country. That's why I don't practice criminal law."

"Okay, okay. We'll do it your way."

Farrukh went home to rest for a few hours. The electricity was back on. He lay on his bed and watched the ceiling fan go round and round. And he thought about money. If the kidnappers called him now with a new, inflated price, he couldn't appear to even consider it. To do so would mean Mr. Z's credibility with the kidnappers would be completely destroyed. They'd have to stick to the four million figure already on the table.

What Farrukh didn't know was that Salim and Dawood had been to see Mr. Z without him. They'd told the cleric they could raise an additional four million rupees. They'd asked Mr. Z to keep this from Farrukh—they didn't want to embarrass him. So a total ransom payment of around eight million rupees was credible.

But what to do about this new demand?

Thirty million rupees.

26
Congratulations

Colonel Imam tried to relieve the tensions in the room by regaling us with tales of his wartime experiences. He talked about his time among the Mujahedeen in Afghanistan, fighting the Soviets. The Soviets were so scared of the Mujahedeen they would not leave the security of their tanks and would have to urinate in their helmets. The Mujahedeen, dressed only in *shalwar kamiz*—no helmets or boots— were superior modern fighters, he said. He talked about their success with Stinger missiles and quoted an 87 percent success rate.

And the Mujahedeen were merciless when they captured enemy troops—an enemy soldier might find himself tied by the neck to the turret of his captured tank, then the turret would be slowly raised. Death would be agonizing. Flies would gather and settle and an infestation of maggots would follow.

During the war, the Colonel had been friends with the US senator Charlie Wilson, played on screen by Tom Hanks in the film *Charlie Wilson's War*. The senator had been instrumental in securing funds for the Afghans. After the war, the Colonel proposed a plan to rebuild Afghanistan but the Americans just packed up and left. From that point, relations between the Colonel and the senator soured.

The Colonel was a deeply devout man. He'd made a commitment to himself, during a trip to Turkey, always to pray as part of a congregation whenever he had the chance. For him, prayer was more powerful that way. And, for him, prayer was paramount.

But not for everyone, it seemed. The Colonel had been Consul General at the Pakistan embassy in Herat, Afghanistan. Whenever he came to Pakistan, his first port of call was President Musharraf, for a briefing. The two men worked closely together.

On one visit, the Colonel arrived at President Musharraf's residence just before prayer time. The Colonel asked the president's aide de camp to let him know when prayers were starting in the local mosque—he wanted to be part of the congregation. Later, during the meeting, the aide came up to the Colonel and whispered it was time for prayers. The Colonel rose to excuse himself, but Musharraf told the Colonel to pray later. The Colonel refused—he wasn't going to have the president come between him and God.

After that incident, Musharraf refused to meet with him.

His stories were fascinating. And he taught us to recite the prayer the prophet Jonah recited while in the stomach of the whale—*La ilaha illa anta subhanaka inni kuntu minaz zalimeen.** This is one of the most powerful prayers there is. I learned it by heart.

I thought to myself, if ever I'm invited onto *Desert Island Discs*, the BBC radio program in which people imagine they're stranded on an island and have to choose what music and what luxury item to take, my luxury would be Colonel Imam. In spite of his snoring.

Every time Nauman came into our room, he had some sort of object with him. It was always different. A rucksack, which he claimed the group had made in their own factory. A string of grenades round his waist. A pistol, which he'd use to demonstrate how to disarm a man by putting the palm of your hand on the barrel. On one occasion, as a show of strength, he cajoled Colonel Imam into a grappling contest. The Colonel, forty years his elder and weakened by months of captivity, gave him a run for his money. After all, he'd been a commando in the army.

Nauman had mentioned a few times that, one day, he'd get Colonel Imam to show him how to make a Molotov cocktail. Today was the day.

The Colonel told him to get hold of a few bars of soap, a bottle, a rag, a bowl, and some petrol. He was to make shavings of the soap and mix them with the petrol. The soap would soften and become like putty. This he was to put into the bottle, then add more petrol, then stuff the rag in as a fuse. When the fuse was lit and the bottle thrown at a tank, the ignited soap would stick to the tank and burn fiercely.

Nauman seemed pleased with this tutorial. After he'd left, the Colonel turned to me and smiled.

"But it's not as easy as that. He might get hurt."

Nauman became more and more friendly. But we'd been stung before. And I remembered KK's words—"Don't trust any of them." I pretended I was in awe of his bravery, while inside I despised him, knowing he was neither a true Muslim nor brave.

And Nauman was an inveterate show-off. He tried to impress us with stories of his power over others—he'd been up all night interrogating a Chinese woman accused of spying, he'd say, or they'd captured an American soldier and Nauman had persuaded him to convert to Islam and join them. I didn't believe a word of any of it. He was just trying to make himself look big.

He talked to Rustam more than he did to me or Colonel Imam, because Rustam spoke Pushto, and one day he offered to give Rustam a haircut. He took him into the bathroom and, while in there, removed his black hood, revealing himself for the first time. Rustam told me after that Nauman's beard had never been touched by a razor. I visualized a sparse and unkempt growth.

---

* "There is no God except You. Blessed are You but I am among the sinners."

July brought with it more heat and a water shortage. Bathing became increasingly rare. And we hardly ever washed our clothes. I craved cleanliness.

Occasionally, I'd be allowed a small bucket of water to wash my clothes. When I put the dirty clothes in the soapy water, the water turned black. And there was only enough water for one rinse. Add to this the fact I was too weak to wring the clothes out properly and the result was clothes far from clean and with a residue of soap clinging to them.

Almost as much as the beatings and the sleep deprivation, I found that this lack of hygiene was pushing me to the brink of despair. I wondered if I'd ever get to wear a clean garment again. The others didn't seem bothered. I was the weakest of the three of us. I didn't feel I could survive much longer.

Then, one day, Shaukat came into our room. He moved us into the bathroom—he had something to do in our room, he said. While we were locked in the bathroom, we heard things being moved around. I thought maybe he was looking to plant listening devices in order to spy on us.

When he opened the bathroom door to let us back into the room, he'd forgotten to pull his hood back over his face. I pointed that out, but he wasn't bothered. I wondered why.

There'd been a chance of me going home, he said, but things hadn't worked out. Good news and bad news. On the one hand, Farrukh was clearly doing all he could do to secure my release. But things had gone wrong, and now our kidnappers were lax about hiding their identity. I was going to die in this place.

I hoped I'd have the courage to accept my fate.

Then we were made to sit up, once again, for the imminent arrival of Sabir Mehsud. He came in and glared at us with his customary menace. Then he launched into a rant, banging on about how he and his colleagues were *mujaheds** and about how this world was no place for non-Muslims. He challenged me with not being a Muslim. My command of Urdu was poor, he said, and I'd lived in the West, which had corrupted me. And, worst of all, I had an American wife.

He talked of dead Taliban soldiers. They were martyrs, he said, and their graves smelt of perfume. By contrast, dead soldiers of the Pakistani army were infidels and their graves had a putrid smell.

I felt anger surging within me. These people had no proper knowledge of Islam. Because of them, the world thought all Muslims were terrorists. For people outside the faith, Islam was a religion of violence. Yet these murderers thought they were the chosen ones, when in fact they were the ones bringing about the apocalypse.

But there was nothing we could do except listen to the ravings of this mad megalomaniac.

* People engaged in jihad.

For some time, the Colonel had been trying to learn the very long text the kidnappers had prepared for his video appeal. Now the time had come to film it.

Mukhtar brought some hair color. He told the Colonel to dye his beard and wash his turban. Once he'd completed these operations, he looked in the mirror.

"They've made me look like a cartoon character."

I thought he looked fine, but he wasn't convinced. "You know, when I was young, my mother made chapattis for dinner. She'd always make an extra one, for the *Talib ul-'Ilm*,* who'd come around each evening from their *madrassahs* and collect food from the neighborhood. Look at these men. They are also taught in *madrassahs*. Look at how they treat us by comparison."

"I know. We have to believe no bad deed goes unpunished. They claim to be Muslims. But they have no knowledge of Islam."

Mukhtar called Colonel Imam to the bathroom doorway and showed him a newspaper but told him not to disclose the contents of the newspaper to me. I wondered what was in it that they didn't want me to know. And why was it okay for the Colonel to know?

The Colonel was told once again to go over the statement the kidnappers had given him. Half an hour later, Nauman came in, blindfolded me, and took me into another room. My camera equipment was lying on the floor. Nauman told me to set it up—they wanted to film the Colonel's video appeal.

I smiled at the irony of this situation. I'd brought this equipment to film interviews with Taliban commanders—now the Taliban were using it to film us.

I explained to Nauman he should hold the statement up next to the camera so Colonel Imam could read it—he'd never be able to remember his lines. Then I was blindfolded again and taken back to our room, by which time the Colonel had already been taken away.

An hour or so later, the Colonel returned. He seemed remarkably composed. I asked him how it had gone.

"Fine. I stumbled a few times, but it was fine."

I was just relieved they hadn't beaten him again.

* * *

Nudrat and Farrukh stayed in the office till late into the night. To pass the time, they took a test on the internet. Are You Depressed? Farrukh scored 10 out of 10, with Nudrat trailing behind with 7 out of 10.

---

* "Students of sacred knowledge," religious scholars who have taken a vow of poverty.

Nine days had now passed since the last call from the kidnappers. Farrukh had hardly slept and was extremely jittery. When he thought of the kidnappers, and of how submissive he'd had to behave toward them, it made him furious.

"Me calling them Mr.! SIR! These are people I wouldn't even hire to WASH MY CAR!"

The monsoon came with a vengeance, causing widespread flooding. Soldiers had been drafted in to help with the relief effort, taking them away from the fight against Taliban insurgents. Farrukh wondered if we'd been affected by the flooding. He hoped at least the cooler weather was bringing us some relief.

More days passed. Then more. July was almost over. Still nothing from the kidnappers. In the news was a story about a plane crash near the Margalla hills. No survivors. This grim news deepened Farrukh's despair. But he reflected that the passengers' families *knew* their loved ones were never coming back. What did *he* know?

The monsoon season would soon be over, and then it would be Ramadan. Fasting would begin, in temperatures in excess of a hundred degrees. No food or water for eighteen hours a day. Farrukh wondered how I'd cope.

Mr. Z's instructions were *not* to contact the kidnappers—to do so would be interpreted as desperation and weakness. But Farrukh was beside himself with impatience and anxiety.

Another week passed. Then on August 9, Farrukh's phone started to ring. News channels were showing a video of me. Farrukh sprang up and switched on his television. Rustam and me, sitting in white clothes. Two hooded men at our sides, holding AK47 assault rifles. A black backcloth with the monogram *Ya Allah Madad.*[*] In Farrukh's mind, God had very little to do with all this. He closed his eyes as he listened to my words:

This is the last message of my life. We were abducted on March 26, 2010, Khalid Khawaja, Colonel Imam, Rustam Khan, and I, Asad Qureshi.

We are in the custody of Lashkar-e-Jhangvi al-Alami of Abidullah Mansoor group. And the man sitting beside me is Rustam Khan. He has been working with me for the last several years in Islamabad.

God is great.

I respectfully reappeal to please accept the demand of Lashkar-e-Jhangvi al-Alami of Abidullah Mansoor group. Otherwise this group is going to kill us, one by one.

This is the last message of my life. These people may not give us any more time. You have seen this before and you will see it again.

---

[*] May God help us.

I ask my dear father and mother to please pray for me and also my dear brother Farrukh Karim Qureshi and all my family members to pray for my release.

Asalaam alaikum

Farrukh's nerve deserted him when he replayed those words in his head. The last message of my life. His eyes filled with tears. He saw me as a little boy, riding my tricycle. He saw me as a grown man, filthy, disheveled, scrawny, pleading for my life.

His email pinged and the video clip landed in his inbox.

He and Asghar and Nudrat watched the whole video again. Nudrat seemed shaken. Asghar had tears running down his cheeks. Nudrat saw him reach for a tissue.

The following day was the beginning of Ramadan. Daily timetables were turned upside down.

Farrukh would lie down to sleep at 1:00 a.m., then wake at 3:30, then try to sleep again at 5:00, then be up again at 6:00, awake then for the whole day.

Having neglected his work commitments for weeks and weeks, he now found himself with three major arbitration cases imminent. Each one would normally take a month to prepare.

But he had no space in his head for work. He had to leave Nudrat to deal with the work alone. Three times the normal workload. Half the professional support. During Ramadan. She was swamped.

Mr. Z called to say he was sending Zarar again, as a show of strength. Farrukh felt terrible that Zarar's safety was being put at risk yet again, knowing what he'd gone through the first time. But Mr. Z was convinced that, as a tactic, it would demoralize the kidnappers.

* * *

Nauman told us, as it was Ramadan, naturally no one would get anything to eat or drink during the day. The hunger was hard, but the thirst was worse. I decided to sleep as much as I could, to keep both at bay.

It was an exhausting month. I'd never felt weaker. The day began at 3:30 a.m., when Nauman came in to unlock our handcuffs and shackles. Our fast would continue until about 7:45 p.m., when there would be food and water.

Colonel Imam noticed, in the mornings, I always rushed into the bathroom first. One morning, he commented on it.

"Why are you always first to get to the bathroom?"

"Well, sir, I really don't want to be going in there after someone else has emptied his bowels."

He seemed bemused by my fastidiousness. For me, it was a tiny shred of dignity and self-respect I was managing to cling to.

Mealtimes were difficult. During Ramadan, breakfast was parathas and tea, shared with our captors. I dreaded this communality. Mukhtar brought in the breakfast. He laid a teapot and the woven basket containing the parathas on the floor, then he handed us each a cup. The cup's handle and brim were greasy where the hands and lips of the previous drinker had touched them.

Mukhtar could see the look of distaste on my face.

"Drink. We are Muslims too."

He glared at me. I felt sick to my stomach and utterly dehumanized.

"Hurry. Eat. It will soon be time for prayers."

His eyes were fixed on me. Rustam and Colonel Imam had poured some tea for themselves. I was still debating whether to drink or not. Mukhtar poured some tea into my cup.

"Drink."

I froze. I looked at the cup. Rustam and Colonel Imam carried on eating and drinking—they'd accepted the situation. But my hygiene hang-up was a major obstacle. As was Mukhtar—he wasn't going anywhere.

I took a deep breath. The only way out of this was to create a mental block. This isn't real. I'm not really doing this. I deliberately blurred my focus, trying not to see the residual tea on the cup's brim, and I tightened my grip so the greasy handle wouldn't slip. As I lifted the cup, I spotted a section of the brim that looked clean, so I tilted the cup, imperceptibly I hoped, so it was that section that made contact with my lips. A small compensation. A small triumph as I stared at my nemesis.

While I ate and drank, I silently recited the prayer the Colonel had taught us—"*None has the right to be worshipped but You, O Allah. Glorified and exalted are You, above all evil. But I am among the sinners.*" The Holy Qur' an, Surah Al-Anbya 21:87.

The days were now unbearably hot. And the metal sheets that covered our windows absorbed and radiated the sun's heat. They were like storage heaters, amplifying the temperature to an intolerable degree.

A thin film of perspiration covered my whole body, and my clothes were perennially damp. On a typical Pakistani summer's day, I'd normally bathe four or five times, each time putting several kilos of ice in the bath. Here, in this grimy hellhole, I was as far from my true self as I could possibly be.

I tried to get into a routine. Asleep by 6:00 a.m., awake again around 1:00 p.m. for afternoon prayers. With this schedule, I could make it through the day without any food or water.

But sleep was elusive. Power cuts had stopped the ceiling fan. Flies buzzed around us in the thick air. When I couldn't sleep, I wrote in my diary.

Lack of sleep and lack of food didn't seem to bother Colonel Imam. He just sat working his way slowly and quietly through the huge pile of anti-Shia books our captors had given him. Having no skills in the areas of reading and writing, Rustam just sat there, apparently deep in thought. Here we were, three very different people from very different worlds, all stuck in the same room, trying to get along, trying not to get on each other's nerves.

It reminded me of some of the film crews I'd worked with. Different people thrown together in quite claustrophobic conditions, trying not to let each other's quirks drive them mad.

We'd occasionally hear Nauman's children playing directly outside our room. A couple of times, when the door was opened, a little boy of four or five put his head in and peeked at us. I wondered what the children had been told about our presence there. Had the brainwashing started? I imagined the sweet young boy as a teenager—a hardened, ruthless killer. The image was heartbreaking.

I thought again of the US senator Charlie Wilson, who'd asked the Senate for one million dollars to fund a school-building program in this area. The Senate had refused. But they're happy to fund billion-dollar military campaigns. Thousands of lives are lost. Nothing is learned. No end is in sight.

In addition to the sounds of children playing, we'd sometimes hear a sound like someone banging loudly on a metal gate, giving us the impression we were in some sort of compound. A fortified place.

And often, in my sleep, I heard a distant call to prayer. Half awake, I'd imagine people going over to a mosque, getting on with their daily routine, oblivious to us and our torment.

The daily routine continued. The afternoons were longest. After prayers, we had nearly six hours to kill before we could eat or drink. Reading for Colonel Imam, and more Ludo for Rustam and me. Then, bored with mindless games, I'd flop back onto my bed and stare into space, trying to keep my thoughts off my family. Sometimes, in a state of near-hypnosis, my mind would take absurd flights of fancy. I imagined myself as the captor, a gun in my hand. What would I do next? I'd use it.

That's how dehumanized I'd become. I, who hated guns and had never held one, I who abhorred violence, now feeling the impulses of a killer. I thought again of the children playing outside our room.

My reverie was broken by Mukhtar. Food.

I was chewing on a date when Nauman came into the room.

"Stand up."

We all looked up at him, but it was me he was looking at. He signaled to me with his finger, reaffirming his order. I felt my heartbeat increase. Rustam and Colonel Imam looked away, feigning inattention, continuing to eat—intervention on their part would have been foolish in the extreme.

"Let me get my glasses."

"You won't need them."

My heartbeat stepped up a gear. Not needing my glasses could mean only one thing—I was going to get another beating. Or worse.

Nauman took a rag from his pocket and put it over my eyes and tied it at the back of my head. He adjusted it, making sure I couldn't see. A click announced he'd turned on his flashlight, checking if I could see the light. I couldn't. He held my left arm and led me out of the room.

We walked through the bathroom (I could smell it) and into another space. Then he made me do a 360-degree turn, in an attempt to disorient me. It didn't work. Then we walked four paces and entered another room, stepping over some shoes as I crossed the threshold. It was the room next door, where we'd been taken to record our video messages. Nauman pulled at my arm, and I walked on a few more paces. Then he stopped me.

There was a terrifying stillness around me. I stood, still blindfolded, for perhaps a whole minute. Helpless.

I felt a hand at the back of my head untying the blindfold. As the cloth came away from my eyes, I saw several people standing in a circle around me, seven or eight of them, all wearing hoods, all staring at me. Directly in front of me, I recognized Sabir Mehsud, their leader. Through the gauze on his hood, I could see his eyes fixed on me. I could feel his anger.

He took a step toward me and the others did the same. They were all big guys. I imagined each of them laying into me in turn, passing me on to the next guy, just like in gangster films. The silence was deafening. I couldn't bear it any longer.

"What is it?"

Sabir Mehsud said nothing but he pointed at the floor with his right index finger. I knelt down. The posture of a man about to be beheaded. Images from execution videos flashed through my mind. I dared to glance up. He towered over me.

"The British government has sent a lot of money. Your brother is sitting on it. Like a snake."

"The British government?"

"Yes. We want that money."

He slipped his right hand under his shirt and pulled out a revolver. With his right thumb, he pulled back the hammer. I heard the snap of metal on metal as the bullet slipped into the chamber.

He raised the gun to the level of my eyes and stepped toward me, so close I could see down its barrel. I rushed through prayers in my head, asking God to forgive me and to help my parents and brothers and sisters to accept my death with patience and not to grieve. My stomach heaved, and I trembled uncontrollably. I couldn't breathe. He pressed the gun to my left temple so hard it hurt. I winced.

"Don't be so dramatic."

I shouted back. "This is not a drama for me! This is real!" Since I'm on the verge of death, I thought, I might as well answer back.

He pressed the barrel even harder into my temple, pushing my head to one side.

"Your brother has five days. If not, you will die. Just like Khalid Khawaja."

What had he said? KK was dead?

He pointed to one of the others.

"Fetch the newspaper with Khawaja's picture."

"No! I believe you. I don't want to see it."

The man shuffled through a pile of newspapers.

"You will look at the picture."

Mehsud signaled for the man to show it to me. Two photographs on the front page—one of KK alive and the other of him lying on the ground, a gunshot wound in his head, blood on the ground around him.

"Okay, okay! I've seen it."

I turned my head away. I had to work hard to suppress the sobbing that rose up in my chest.

"Your brother is ignoring our demands. He has been sent the money to meet our demands. But he's keeping it. He wants to pay us less and keep the rest for himself. We don't like to be messed around."

I didn't know what to believe. They'd lied about KK, telling us he was on the outside, negotiating our release. And now this story about Farrukh. I couldn't believe he would hesitate for a second to pay them if he had the money.

Sabir Mehsud grabbed my collar and pulled me onto my feet.

"Your brother doesn't care about you. I should hang you by the feet from this ceiling and let these men beat you."

I glanced up at the ceiling and remembered Haji *sahib*, the Pushtun whom Krishan Lal had beaten as a punishment for drug dealing. They'd hung him from a metal hook and flogged him brutally. I thought I'd rather be shot.

"But I'm stuck here. There is nothing I can do. Let me talk to him. Let me call him on the telephone and persuade him."

Sabir Mehsud turned to Nauman.

"Bring a satellite telephone tomorrow. Let him talk to his brother."

Nauman nodded.

I was blindfolded and led back to my room. Colonel Imam and Rustam had finished eating, and there were remnants of food in the dish. I was still trembling from my ordeal and fell onto my bed. I lay there facing the wall.

KK was dead.

I thought about his family. Then I thought about how the news of his death would have affected my family. Then, stripped of all physical and mental feeling, I fell asleep.

"Get up."

Nauman kicked my leg. I woke with a start.

"We have to move."

"What?"

"Drone strike. Get up."

I started to gather my things. How did they know of a drone strike in advance? Was he telling the truth?

"Leave your things. We're only away for one night."

He lined the three of us up at the bathroom door. Mukhtar and another man came in. The three men led us out of our room by the arm. No handcuffs or blindfolds. Into a moonlit night.

"Keep your heads down," Nauman ordered.

But I'd already surveyed the area. A much smaller compound than I'd imagined. The small yard was very rocky, as if only recently cleared. We reached a gate (the banging we'd heard) and were made to stop while one of the men went outside.

A moment later, he came back, and they led the three of us to a car parked outside the gate, pushing the three of us onto the back seat and putting a sheet over our heads.

"Keep your heads down." Nauman again.

I wasn't going to give anyone a reason to point a gun at me again, so this time I looked at the ground.

We drove for about twenty minutes over some rough ground and then came to a halt. Nauman opened the door and led us out of the car one by one. In the moonlight before us was a derelict-looking mud hut.

I stopped. I took a breath of refreshing night air. I could smell the earth and hear the crickets chirping. The pure pleasure of simply being outdoors was overwhelming.

"Walk this way. And keep your heads down."

Nauman shone his flashlight on the ground like a cinema usher, making sure we didn't trip over rocks. We walked round the side of the mud hut and were led across a courtyard to a room at the far end.

Inside the room, the only light was from Nauman's flashlight. The place was dank and, in the dim light, looked grim indeed. A small platform at the far end, 3 feet by 3 and a foot high, was the toilet. Three mattresses were laid side by side across the floor. I dreaded the thought of sleeping on the mattress at the toilet end, but I didn't want to make an unseemly rush to take the one by the door. Thankfully for me, Nauman assigned us our beds, giving me the mattress by the door, Rustam the one in the middle, and Colonel Imam the one at the far end. The toilet end.

I looked around. This place was the worst we'd been in so far, worse than the first mud hut and infinitely inferior to the brick-built place we'd just come from. The ceiling was thatched and seemed to be crawling with insects. Every now and then, in the darkness, I felt something land on me.

I wondered why they'd really brought us here. The story about the drone strike just didn't ring true.

Early the following morning, before sunrise, Sabir Mehsud invited Usman Punjabi and a few of his men for talks. Two disagreements had caused a rift between them, both prompted by Punjabi's desire to be top dog—the killing of KK, and the future of the widow of a wealthy Arab Taliban member killed in a drone strike.

Mehsud wanted to settle the disagreement between them, he said. He invited Punjabi for *sehri** and the two groups gathered in the room we'd vacated a few hours earlier. Punjabi sat down. Without warning, Mehsud pulled out the revolver he'd held to my head hours earlier and shot Punjabi in the face. Within seconds, Mehsud's men had killed all five of Punjabi's men. Mehsud then killed one of his own men—that way, if the incident were to be investigated by a *jirga*, Mehsud would claim Punjabi had killed the man and Mehsud had killed Punjabi in revenge. The others had been killed in the ensuing gun battle, a battle that had left our belongings spattered with blood.

On August 29, Sabir Mehsud, using his alias Abdullah Ghori, placed a phone call to Farrukh.

"I am calling to congratulate you on the death of Usman Punjabi and his followers. He won't trouble you again."

Farrukh went to see Mr. Z. The cleric already knew of Punjabi's death and confirmed it was true. Perhaps they were now one step closer to my release.

Farrukh reflected on the old adage—"If you live by the sword, you will die by the sword."

* Breakfast before fasting, during Ramadan.

27
The Final Countdown

This place was the worst we'd been in.

There was a pungent stench of stale urine. Mixed with the damp smell of the mud from the hut, it was stomach churning. And the place was crawling with insects. In the night, they dropped onto my face from the thatched roof above. And the room was tiny. The three of us were wedged into it. With an open toilet in the corner, there was no privacy and no preservation of dignity.

Compared to this, the last place had been luxury.

Nauman came in to tell us that, from now on, a no-nonsense guy by the name of Jaffar would be in charge of us. There'd be no messing about with him, Nauman said.

Jaffar's first order was we were only to use the toilet in the room for urinating. If we needed to empty our bowels, we'd have to wait until midnight, when we'd be taken individually to a toilet on the outside.

We were still in Ramadan and so fasting continued as usual. But Mukhtar came into the room one morning and told us we were not allowed to fast that day. Colonel Imam asked him why. Mukhtar shrugged and retorted, "Order from above." He poured water from a jug and ordered us to drink. We looked at each other. Rustam and I picked up a cup each and took a drink, breaking our fast. Colonel Imam began to cough.

"I don't want water. My throat is troubling me."

Mukhtar stared at him for a few seconds, then left.

After he'd gone, I felt angry at the kidnappers for forcing us to break our religious rule and at myself for giving in. It just confirmed what I already thought about them— they were hypocrites, portraying themselves as deeply religious on the one hand, and riding roughshod over religious principle on the other. They didn't have an ounce of Islam in them. I commended the Colonel for sticking to his principles.

Even though the month of Ramadan is the month of fasting, actually more food is eaten during this month than in any other. Once evening comes, people sit down to enjoy an abundance of delicious dishes prepared with special care. Here, we were served yesterday's leftovers on plates our captors had eaten off. I closed my mind and my eyes as I ate, trying not to contemplate the possibility that the disgusting swill on the plates had insects from the roof mixed in with it.

The midnight toilet routine was dispiriting. Jaffar was a short man with a big ego. In the darkness, he'd pull each of us outside by the neck then push us into the tiny, pitch-black hovel that had a hole in the ground. No electricity. Just a flashlight with a weak battery casting a circle of watery light.

One evening, Nauman and Jaffar came in and told me to stand up.

"You're coming with us."

"Where are we going?"

"Phone call."

They led me out of the hut without a blindfold. Outside, I walked through thick, long grass to a waiting car. Then Nauman blindfolded me and pushed me into the back.

We must have driven for about ten minutes. When we stopped, I heard the sound of shutters. Some sort of shop, presumably.

Nauman untied my blindfold. We were in the main street of a village. All the shops were closed up for Ramadan, apart from the one we'd stopped in front of. Nauman led me into the shop. Inside, it was littered with gas cylinders. I was led to the back of the shop, where there was a row of telephone booths. Jaffar asked me for Farrukh's number. I gave him a mobile number.

"And you'll need the 92 prefix for Pakistan."

"No need."

I'd thought we'd been held in Afghanistan. We'd been in Pakistan all along.

Jaffar handed me the phone. It was ringing. I suddenly became incredibly excited at the thought of speaking to my brother after all this time. I was aware my hand was shaking. The phone rang and rang. No answer. I looked at Jaffar and shook my head.

"Perhaps he's at my parents' house."

I gave Jaffar the number and he dialed. After a few seconds, he handed me the phone. No answer.

"We could try my sister's house in England."

The same routine. After several rings, a woman's voice answered.

"Rakhshindah?"

"Who's this?" I recognized the voice of my niece, Asma.

I'd been instructed to speak only in Urdu—no English. Asma had never heard me speak Urdu before. What she heard now was an alien whisper crackling down the line from 4,000 miles away.

"It's me. Asad."

"Who?"

"Asad."

"I don't understand."

She passed the telephone to her mother. I heard my sister's voice.

"Hello? Asad? Is it really you?"

"Yes. It's really me."

"How can I believe you?"

I was so frustrated I burst into tears. I shouted in English, "I have a white cat."

Nauman grabbed the phone off me and cut the call. He slapped me hard across the face.

"I told you, NO ENGLISH!"

I was blindfolded and shoved back in the car. Then taunted all the way back about my brother caring so little about me, he couldn't even be bothered to pick up the phone.

* * *

Farrukh and Asghar were in Dawood's office, with Salim. They sat round a glass coffee table, and Farrukh put his phone in the middle of it. They all stared at it. Nobody dared move or speak. Farrukh had missed a call before. He didn't want to miss this one.

Two hours later, they were still staring. Asghar wondered what had gone wrong. The arrangement had been made and the kidnappers had sounded serious. Were they just messing about?

Then Farrukh picked up his phone and saw there was no signal.

When he got home, Rakhshindah called him and told him about the brief conversation she'd had with me before they'd been cut off. Farrukh was furious with himself for going out to Dawood's place. He should have stayed at home, where there was always a good signal.

He stayed up all night, hoping the kidnappers would call again, but his phone never rang.

For the first time, he began to feel afraid to talk to them. Missing the last call had knocked him off his stride and his confidence had left him.

The following day, he asked Nudrat to take the call, if it came. She should pretend to be one of the women of the household and tell them Farrukh had had an accident when coming home after *maghrib* prayers and was still unconscious, and they should call back in a few days.

They waited the whole day but no call came. In the evening, Nudrat told Farrukh she thought the made-up story was a bad idea. If they called, he should talk to them. He should tell the truth and explain he'd been in a place with no signal. God would help him.

* * *

Two days later, Nauman and Jaffar took me out to the village again, to make a call to Farrukh. In the car, Nauman threatened me.

"Listen to me very carefully. If you cry today, I will personally beat you. If your brother does not answer our call, we will hand you over to people who will show you no mercy. I will no longer be responsible for you."

"I understand."

"But if you do as I say, I will buy you a cold drink."

He placed the call. He didn't pass me the receiver but I could hear it ring and hear Farrukh's voice answer.

"Hello?"

"Hello. How are you?"

"Fine, thank you."

"Did Mr. Ghori call you yesterday?"

I wondered who Mr. Ghori was.

"Yes."

Nauman looked at me. "Talk to Asad." He passed me the phone.

I heard my brother's voice. "Hello, Asad. How are you?"

"Better for hearing your voice. How are you? How are Mum and Dad and the rest of the family?"

"We're all fine. We just want you home."

"These people are saying you should meet their demand quickly or this is my last phone call."

"We are doing all we can to bring you home."

"Can you do it this week?"

"We are doing our best."

"The 22nd of Ramadan* is the last deadline. If they don't have the money by then, they'll kill me." My voice started to wobble.

"Okay. Just stay calm. We're doing all we can."

"Tomorrow would be good. It would be really good if you could arrange the money tomorrow. Do you think you can do it for tomorrow?"

"Well, if they talk to us. We're trying to contact them. If they talk to us, we have a good chance."

"Please talk to them. What day is tomorrow? It's Tuesday, right? By Wednesday evening I could be home."

* In 2010, this was September 1.

Nauman grabbed the phone from me and spoke to Farrukh.

"Did you hear him?"

"Yes."

"Then do it quickly. The 22nd of Ramadan. Bear that in mind."

"Where is Mr. Abdullah Ghori?"

"Mr. Ghori has sent us. If things are not done by the 22nd of Ramadan, then know this was your brother's last call."

With these words, Nauman hung up.

We drove round for a while until we saw a shop that was open. As promised, Nauman bought me a cold drink. Two, in fact. One bottle of Fanta and one of Mountain Dew. The bottles were beautifully chilled. I gulped the Fanta down in a flash and decided to hold on to the other one to share with Rustam and Colonel Imam.

When we got back to the hut, I got out of the car. Nauman removed my blindfold. I stood for a few seconds and looked at the moon. A beautiful sight. A glimpse of freedom. I wanted to stand there all night.

* * *

Farrukh was elated. It was the first time Nudrat had seen him smile in months.

"It was Asad! It was Asad!"

"What did he say?"

"If we can pay now, he'll be home by Wednesday!"

"That's wonderful news! Thank goodness the call came through this time! How did he sound?"

"Weak. But he's alive. I can tell my parents in all honesty I've spoken to him and he's alive."

Farrukh switched quickly into pragmatic mode. Arrangements would now have to be made to gather the ransom money together. Various withdrawals would have to be made from various banks. A range of different currencies would then have to be converted into rupees, counted, and put into a locker at a designated bank. Farrukh would split the money into batches, so that only he would know the final figure—the fewer people who knew, the better. The safety of others, present and future, might depend on discretion.

Then Farrukh went to see Mr. Z. He was told Badar Mansoor would travel to Waziristan first thing the following morning to survey the situation and make contact with the kidnappers, in advance of the money being taken.

Nudrat was thrilled to see everything was coming together. She'd been concerned that recent flooding in the area might hamper arrangements for a handover, but, despite new floods being reported in Sindh and other areas, the water had receded in most parts. Displaced people were returning home. A good omen.

But there were further frustrations ahead.

Salim called Farrukh and told him Badar Mansoor had waited several hours in the appointed meeting place, Sabir Mehsud's office, but no one came. Farrukh was concerned Badar Mansoor would feel he was being given the runaround by Mehsud. If tempers frayed, some sort of shootout might easily ensue and we'd be back to square one.

After much agonizing, Farrukh asked Mr. Z to recall Badar Mansoor. On the one hand, he felt like he was letting his brother down, but the risk that some messy situation would develop was too great.

* * *

I told Rustam and Colonel Imam there was a chance we'd be going home on Wednesday.

As I lay down on my filthy bed, I told myself I only had a few more days in this bug-infested hole. I closed my eyes and thought of the ice-cold shower I'd have. I'd run the water for an hour, just to feel it on my skin. Then afterward, clean clothes. A clean bed to sleep in. I couldn't wait.

Wednesday came and went, and there was no sign of us going anywhere.

Rustam became angry. He said Farrukh wasn't even trying to get us released. Restless, he got up and peeped through a hole in the door. He saw Mukhtar and Jaffar sitting without their hoods on. I signaled to him to come back, in case one of them barged in and caught him watching them. But he ignored me. I didn't want a confrontation with him, so I turned my attention to Colonel Imam.

"You seem very quiet today, sir."

"I've been thinking about Afghans. About how Afghan women are subservient to Afghan men. Except in one village. There, women take the lead and men are regarded as inferior. These women compete with the neighboring village over who can send more boys to their death as suicide bombers."

"What kind of mother does that?"

"Well, they take pride in making their sons into martyrs."

"I'm not sure I believe they're martyrs."

"If one village finds out their tally is lower, they simply prepare another boy. So they can catch up."

"That's horrible. While they are playing their macabre game of one-upmanship, hundreds of people are dying."

"They think they are sending the boys to heaven."

"I don't believe they are."

I found this story more disturbing because it was women who were breeding these suicide bombers, literally. I've seen such cruelty in men, but I wouldn't have believed it of women. Perhaps that's naïve.

I heard a scuffling noise and quickly shone my flashlight around the room. A scorpion was rushing toward me. Quick as a flash, Rustam slammed his foot down on it then kicked it toward the wall at the foot of my bed. It was dead, but I still wasn't keen on it being so close to me. I wondered what other things were lurking in this filthy hole. I started to feel itchy all over. I felt like running away. I felt like I was going crazy.

* * *

Abdullah Ghori called Farrukh.

"Have you arranged for the fifty million rupees to be handed over?"

Farrukh was incensed. "What fifty million rupees? I do not have that amount of money! I have told you what I have!"

"That is disappointing. It is not what we asked for."

"It's what I have."

"It is not enough."

"Then kill Asad. Kill him if you want. But I cannot give more than I have offered. Take it or leave it. I'm not interested in talking any more or playing games."

"I will call again soon." And, with that, Abdullah Ghori hung up.

Nudrat was shocked at how Farrukh had talked to the kidnapper. Farrukh could see the shock in her face.

"Don't worry. We are close now. I think we have the upper hand. Mr. Z has assured us of that. Zarar went there, as a show of strength. It seems to have worked. He came back alive."

The following day, Abdullah Ghori called again. Again, he mentioned the figure of fifty million rupees. Again, Farrukh spoke in anger.

"I don't know why you call yourself Abdullah Ghori. You and Sabir Mehsud are the same person. So who are you, really?"

"I use both names."

"Well, Mr. Both Names, what I said to you yesterday still stands. So much time has passed now. If we're not reaching a conclusion here, then whatever is acceptable to God will happen. If a person has time remaining in his life, no one can shorten it. If it has ended, then no one can extend it. Before all this, I had never asked anyone for money. Now I've had to ask friends for loans. It's humiliating. But that money is depleting with time. Our position is becoming worse, not better. There is no advantage to anyone in delaying any further. I have given you my figure. We have nothing more. And we have no energy left now. Do whatever you choose. What happens must be God's will."

"Everyone understands this. Even if he is not a Muslim. Everyone knows we have to die sometime. In an accident, or through illness, or by someone's hand. What your brother was doing—did you know about it? Did you know about the people he was with?"

"They had gone to make a documentary about the peace process, and about innocent people suffering as a result of drone attacks. They wanted people to know the harm being caused by these attacks."

"They wanted to make a film, but they wanted to sell it for money. But who were they doing it for? Was it for the ISPR? Was it for non-Muslims? Your brother's association with Khalid Khawaja and Colonel Imam is a very serious problem. And they have to account for their actions too. We know Asad has worked before with the ISPR, in Swat."

"Rustam is innocent of all of this. He's just an assistant. But you have held him in captivity for five months. Why?"

"They are all together. They are a team. No one person can be released, just like that. Do you understand? According to Islam, he is as guilty as the others. America is bombing for money. And what spies do, they do for money too. Everyone works for money."

"My brother is not a spy."

"Let us talk about Khalid Khawaja. He offered us 130 million rupees for his release. If we had named a price of 200 or even 250 million, he would have found it. But our emir didn't want his money. We are not greedy for money. Khawaja's sin was so great that it was better to kill him. Your brother asks us why we don't show mercy. We tell him we have shown mercy. That is the reason he is still alive. Our group has a principle—when we decide something is to be done, then it is done. I will make every effort to talk to our emir and persuade him that he should do something for you. Decrease the demand. Show some mercy. Then it is his will. We cannot interfere in his decisions."

"May God give you the strength to do the right thing."

"Whatever I can do, I will do. I will try to end this matter soon."

"Thank you."

Farrukh was happy he'd been able to get across the message that their funds were depleting and there was a degree of urgency in the matter.

But he was concerned about the things Abdullah Ghori had said about KK. He knew KK didn't personally have 130 million rupees or anything close to that sum. How could he have made such a commitment? Well, KK had had contacts in the strangest of places.

The following day, Badar Mansoor again waited in the office of Sabir Mehsud, but again Mehsud didn't show up. Then Mehsud called Farrukh and told him he was too busy to see Badar Mansoor.

Farrukh was irritated by this constant game-playing. The kidnappers, always unhappy about Mr. Z's intervention, seemed determined to mess his envoy around as much as possible. Mr. Z called Farrukh and said he was concerned that, if this matter was not settled before Eid, it might drag on for several more months.

Farrukh hoped Badar Mansoor would keep his cool.

* * *

There was still no news about our going home. The prospect of imminent release had made this filthy hole even harder to bear.

My grimy body was repellent to me. I asked Jaffar if I could take a bath, but he wouldn't allow it. For some reason, he'd taken a particular dislike to me. I looked at my hands. In all my life, I'd never been so filthy. It was now weeks since I'd washed my body. I looked like a coal miner. A shirt that had started out white was now gray.

I looked at Rustam. He looked defeated. Again I was overcome with guilt for having asked him to come along and for getting him stuck here. One of his daughters had told him not to go with me, because she foresaw some calamity. And now, with Eid approaching fast, he'd be missing his children.

I thought of them. Remembering the names of his many children had been in my repertoire of sleep-inducing exercises. At least Rustam himself could remember their names. He'd told me a story of a man who, like him, had a dozen or more children. After child number five, he'd struggled to remember all their names. When he'd taken them to the tailor, to be measured for new clothes for Eid, the tailor had asked him for their names.

"Tell the man your names," he'd said to the little ones. He'd presented it as an exercise in self-confidence for the children, when it had simply been a smokescreen for his ignorance.

Eager to be ready when the time came, Farrukh picked up Asghar, and the two of them went to the various banks and withdrew all the sums that Farrukh had been able to collect. They then converted the money into rupees. Farrukh placed the money in a bag and put the bag in a locker in one of the banks.

He called Mr. Z and told him that everything was ready.

A few hours later, Mr. Z called back and told Farrukh that Zarar was making his way to Waziristan, to rendezvous with Badar Mansoor. Together, they would hand over the money when it was time and together they would take delivery of "the package."

Frustrated by what looked like delaying tactics on the part of the kidnappers, Farrukh was also upset that they were trying to coordinate action during the month of Ramadan, a time of year marked by inaction. Life in Waziristan would be especially slow. He imagined village shops with the shutters down and the streets deserted. People sleeping after *sehri* until it was time for afternoon prayers. Nothing happening.

More waiting. More uncertainty.

It was now Tuesday. Wednesday was the 22nd of Ramadan. The deadline.

Abdullah Ghori called Farrukh.

"We are releasing your brother."

"That is good news. What about his colleagues?"

"We are releasing your brother because he has told us the truth about everything. Call this number again in two hours, and we will give you instructions."

Badar Mansoor called Mr. Z to say he had finally made contact with Sabir Mehsud. Mr. Z told him and Zarar to return to Islamabad to collect the money.

The two hours passed. Farrukh placed the call. No answer. He called again. No answer. A third time. Nothing.

Hours passed and, scores of attempts later, contact had still not been made. Farrukh went to bed.

He got a call just after midnight.

"The phones here are not working. The cable is broken."

"I have called numerous times."

"Tell your man to come to my office at ten o'clock tomorrow morning. If my people are not there, tell him to wait ten or fifteen minutes. Someone will come."

Farrukh contacted Mr. Z. They arranged to meet early the following morning.

Farrukh went to the bank to retrieve the bag with the money. Nudrat wasn't happy about a third party handing it over. She felt uneasy about the possibility of it going "missing" on the way. But she knew this was the only option—it would be beyond stupid for Farrukh to set foot in Waziristan himself. When he handed the bag to Mr. Z, the cleric could see the worry in his eyes.

"The money will be safe. You have given it to me. It is now my *amanat*."*

The following day, Farrukh received a call from Mr. Z. The money had reached its destination. Badar Mansoor had counted it out in front of the kidnappers, at gunpoint. Satisfied that the promised amount was available, the kidnappers had said the release would take place later that day. Both parties would meet at an agreed location, and the exchange of money and prisoners would be made there.

"With luck, you will see your brother tomorrow."

"I don't want to wait another day. I've waited long enough. Please bring him home today."

"Your brother is being brought from a place some distance away. It will take several hours. It is not safe for them to travel at night. You will see your brother tomorrow. Be patient."

Patience. Farrukh had used it all up. A lifetime of patience deployed over the last five months. Now, *impatience* was eating him up inside.

* Something entrusted to someone who has the solemn duty of delivering it.

28
The Handover

It was the night of September 6. Our room was lit with our three flashlights. We'd finished offering prayers and were preparing to go to sleep.

Sabir Mehsud came to see us, with Nauman. An unexpected visit. He'd never come so late at night before.

I never liked visits from Sabir Mehsud. I hated him. He was arrogant and ruthless. I wondered what cruel threats he had for us this time.

He stood in the doorway. We all looked up at him.

"Although I am very busy, I have come from a long way away because I wanted to say goodbye to you personally."

We looked at him blankly.

"You are going home tomorrow."

At the sound of these words, my eyes instantly filled with tears of joy. Through the tears, I looked at Rustam and Colonel Imam. They were both smiling.

At last. At last our suffering had finally come to an end. At last we would be going home to our families. I couldn't believe it.

Sabir Mehsud sat down. Nauman stood guard in the corner with his gun. I remembered that Sabir Mehsud had once told me he would never release Colonel Imam. I was relieved he'd changed his mind and the Colonel would be going home with us. While Colonel Imam and Sabir Mehsud exchanged pleasantries, I plucked up the courage to ask Sabir Mehsud a question.

"Why did you kill Khalid Khawaja?"

Nauman quickly responded.

"Because he was a Qadiani. He worked for QTV and was a CIA agent."

This was not true. I knew for a fact that KK was not a Qadiani. Nor did he work for QTV, which, in any case, stood for Qur'an TV and not Qadiani TV, as our kidnappers thought. Qadianism is an Islamic movement based on the belief that the nineteenth-century religious figure, Mirza Ghulam Ahmad, was a reincarnation of the prophet Muhammad.

I was deeply saddened to hear that they'd killed KK on these completely false charges. The realization that we'd be going home without him suddenly hit me and took the edge off my jubilation. But KK had been a tremendously brave man with extremely strong convictions, and he'd died for what he believed. I knew this would mean a lot to his family. I tried to console myself with this fact. There was nothing to be gained from arguing his case with our captors now.

"I am going to give you some money in case you need it on your way home."

Sabir Mehsud signaled to Nauman, who distributed two thousand rupees to each of us. He then got up and walked to the door.

Colonel Imam escorted him. The two men stopped by the door and exchanged some words. Sabir Mehsud held the Colonel's hand for a long time and said, "This is the last time we will see each other."

With that, the two captors left. Then Colonel Imam led us in prayers of thanks for our release.

After prayers, we talked about our release. We were all excited at the prospect of being home for Eid. I lay back on my bed and thought about my family and how good it would be to see them again. I imagined the scene of our reunion. More tears, but this time tears of happiness and relief.

This elated daydream was interrupted. Mukhtar entered the room and addressed Colonel Imam.

"You need to come and make your statement."

I was puzzled. What statement? There was nothing else to say. We were being released.

"What statement?" I asked.

"Statement of release."

Colonel Imam stood up with a smile, and Mukhtar led him out of the room.

I didn't like it one bit. Something was wrong. There were no more statements to make now. Except, perhaps, "Goodbye—we never want to see you again." I was very uncomfortable about being separated from Colonel Imam when we all seemed finally to be so close to freedom.

Rustam and I stayed awake all night. We just couldn't sleep. Thoughts of our imminent freedom were running through my head, but also worrying scenarios involving the Colonel.

When it was time for *sehri*, Mukhtar brought food for us. It was the usual insult—cold lentils on a plate they'd already eaten from and last night's leftover chapattis. And only just enough for the two of us.

"What about Colonel Imam?" I asked.

"He has already eaten."

Now I was really concerned. It doesn't take several hours to make a video statement, even accepting that such a statement was necessary, which I didn't.

After morning prayers, Rustam and I still didn't sleep. Then something very significant happened.

Mukhtar came into the room and took Colonel Imam's pocket Qur'an. This could mean only one thing—the Colonel had accepted that he was not going with us.

I felt a surge of anger at Sabir Mehsud's wickedness. Still the mental torture continued, right up to the wire.

And I was livid at this upstart, Mukhtar, just following orders and unaware of the pain they were causing us.

"Colonel Imam is not going, is he?"

"If you ask too many questions, you won't be going either."

This was a gut-wrenching confirmation. Four of us had embarked on this doomed mission. Only two of us were returning. And Colonel Imam hadn't wanted to come in the first place. His wife had just been through surgery. He must have been over-joyed at the thought of being reunited with her.

I was so angry and upset and full of contempt and hatred. But these pieces of scum had killed so many people that they'd reached the stage where they enjoyed it.

I couldn't get Colonel Imam's image out of my mind. That last image of his smile as he left the room. I saw it now as a smile of resignation, of understanding, of acceptance. He'd known he wasn't getting out, even though we hadn't.

I missed him. I wanted him back in this room with us.

It seemed I had spent my last night in this awful place. I wondered how much longer Colonel Imam would have to endure it. He was a strong and brave man, but this cruel charade would have been a bitter blow. And now he was all alone. I was grateful we'd had the chance to talk and pray together.

There had, inevitably in a situation like ours, been times when we'd had our dif-ferences and got on each other's nerves, but I'd enjoyed hearing the tales of his adven-tures. This dreadful shared experience had built a camaraderie between us that I valued greatly. He had often said we should keep in touch once we were released.

Now that we'd been separated, I felt as if I'd lost a friend.

I pictured him alone in his room and wondered what he was doing. What was he thinking? What was to become of him?

Although I had, to an extent, come to accept the death of KK, walking out of here without Colonel Imam seemed like a defeat.

I thought back to the time I'd filmed the Mount Everest expedition led by my friend, the Pakistani mountaineer Nazir Sabir. He and his fellow climbers had been vilified for failing to reach the summit. The president of the Pakistan Alpine Club had even gone as far as saying they shouldn't have returned without the summit—in his view, they should have given their lives to reach the top.

This comment struck me, both at the time and again when I thought of it now, as scandalously misguided. The fact that Nazir had brought all his men back in one piece was a major achievement and cause for celebration when nine men from other expedities had died on the mountain that same year. In my eyes, there was absolutely no shame in not summiting—they could always go again, as long as they were alive to do so.

I had lost KK, and I was unsure of Colonel Imam's fate. In effect I was returning home from my expedition without two members of my team. It would be Eid in a few days. For KK's family, it would be their first Eid without him—a somber occasion indeed, as it would be for Colonel Imam's family.

I wondered what questions their families would have for me. I wondered what their reaction would be to my return. Would they share my happiness and that of my family, or would they be indifferent, perhaps even resentful?

Jaffar, our jailer, came into the room, acting tough, as usual.

"Get your things and go take a bath."

I quickly gathered a change of clothes. Jaffar led me out of the room toward the bathroom, with his hand clamped on the back of my neck, as usual. Thankfully, this was to be the last time I'd suffer this particular indignity.

This trip to the bathroom was the first I'd ever made in daylight, and it gave me my first real glimpse of the immediate surroundings.

The yard was dirty and strewn with litter. From the corner of my eye I caught sight of grubby cooking utensils strewn around a makeshift stove consisting of a few bricks. A cloud of flies swarmed around a heap of dirty metal plates. The place was a complete mess—they lived like savages.

We had to step in between the roots of a large tree to reach the bathroom, the unpleasant odor of which greeted me from afar. Again, so I thought, for the last time.

At the bathroom door, Jaffar pushed me in and locked the door from the outside. I quickly undressed and poured the cold water over myself (no luxury of warm water here) and rubbed soap all over my body. I'd not used shampoo throughout my captivity and my hair was matted with the grime of five months in this filthy netherworld. But I only had a single bucket of water, so my bath was soon over. This would have to do till I got home.

I knocked on the door and Jaffar led me back to the room. Then it was Rustam's turn.

So we were as clean and as ready as we were going to be. Time on the clock had ceased to be a reality for me, but I guessed it was around mid-morning. If we left right away, I thought there was a chance we could be home by nightfall.

But there was no sign of anyone coming to collect us. Time dragged. I was finding the wait agonizing.

Outside, the morning air was still, with a chill of autumn. I remembered the fresh spring breeze that had blown in my face when I'd stuck my head out of the car window as we'd first set out for North Waziristan. That felt like a different life in the distant past.

I wondered what kind of world awaited us now. The only news that had reached us was of floods in Pakistan, an air crash in Islamabad, and the match-fixing scandal involving Pakistani cricketers.

Sabir Mehsud had spoken about the disgraced cricketers with such disgust. I couldn't believe his outrageous double standards. A murderer accusing a fraudster of bringing dishonor on Pakistan and Islam!

Such people are always looking for ways to justify their view that they are the only proper Muslims and everyone else is a failed Muslim or a non-Muslim. These *Khawarijis* are fond of branding others as unbelievers and worthy of death.

But there is nothing Islamic about people who kill. In the Qur'an, it says, "If a man kills another it is as if he has killed the whole of mankind. If he saves a life then it is as if he has saved the whole of mankind."

My captors' view of Islam was totally distorted. They, and the dozens of extremist groups like them, have brought nothing but shame and disrepute on our religion. But, of course, an interview with these people is a Western journalist's dream come true, and the ranting and raving into the microphone makes for an entertaining article or broadcast.

And so now the entire world thinks of Islam as a violent faith.

It struck me I'd been in the company of these twisted and violent people for months. I was suddenly frightened by the thought my release, which might be greeted with unease or even suspicion. Would people think I'd been brainwashed by my captors? Would they suspect I'd fallen victim to Stockholm syndrome?

It struck me as ironic that I was known for making a film about the rehabilitation of young boys indoctrinated by the Taliban. People might think I'd suffered the same fate.

I looked at Rustam. I was relieved he was going home to his family. His status as a Pathan, and a poor man, had made our captivity less hellish than it might have been. And, although we'd lost KK, and we didn't know what was going to happen to the Colonel, I shuddered to think how the situation would have played out if the trip had gone ahead with the original lineup of relatively rich and influential friends—Major Mumtaz from the ISPR, the filmmaker Haroon Toor, and my friend in advertising, Fawad Naeem.

I heard someone talking outside. It was Nauman. He came into our room.

"Stand up."

He stared at me intently.

"Even though you are going home, we will be watching you. So you'd better not shave off your beard."

For many Muslim men, a beard is a sign of devotion to Islam. During the first few days of my confinement, my clean-shaven face was something with which my captors had taunted me. In their eyes, it marked me as a Western infidel.

I said nothing. Rustam and I stood up. Nauman blindfolded each of us in turn, for what I hoped was the last time, and led us out of the room. We were on our way home. I was elated.

Then I thought again of Colonel Imam. When we'd arrived, he'd been the first to be shackled and led away. Now he'd be the last one to leave. The only thing I could do was pray for his safe return.

We managed to negotiate the uneven yard and, once in the street, we were guided into a waiting car, me behind the front passenger seat and Rustam behind the driver's seat, with Nauman and Jaffar between us.

We drove on. After a while, the car stopped and two more people got into the back. There were now eight people in the car. Six of them guarding the two of us.

Nauman spoke to me.

"The people that we are going to hand you over to are boys in a man's game. When you meet them, you must tell them we spent the night in Kohat and have driven from there. If you don't tell them this, we will find out. And we will not be as kind to you as we have been in the past."

"I won't be able remember anything," I said. "Tell Rustam to speak to them."

I was still thinking about Colonel Imam, and I was in no mood to make up a story for whoever we were going to meet. Nauman repeated the information to Rustam, who readily agreed to tell the story.

For my part, I'd now reached the point where I disliked these men intensely, and I simply couldn't wait to be away from them. They had such contempt for human life and such ignorance of the destruction they were causing that I could no longer bring myself to cooperate with them.

As we drove, they chatted casually about how they were ready to take on the role of suicide bombers. Jaffar, in particular, became very talkative, a completely different person to the one back in the compound. He said both he and his wife were fully trained to operate a suicide jacket and were ready to detonate a bomb at any time and die in the process. He went on to say that God would look after his two-year-old son if both he and his wife were to die in such a way.

In the beginning, he told us, he'd been nervous about killing people, but once he'd got used to it, he began to enjoy it. He would disembowel the people he killed and make necklaces out of their intestines.

He and Nauman were reveling in telling us about their escapades. They were trying to scare us and prove to us what strong and brave individuals they were. But, to me, they were contemptibly ignorant people. Nothing more. I hoped they'd get their comeuppance soon.

Jaffar suddenly shouted.

"Look! Goat!"

The car stopped. Nauman prodded me on the shoulder.

"Give me one thousand rupees."

"Why?"

"Because we want to buy that goat for Eid."

"It's my money, and I need it."

"Do you want to go home or not? You have two thousand rupees each. I want one thousand from both of you."

Rustam was in no mood to argue, or perhaps he thought he was saving me from a beating, and he urged me to give them the money. I decided to go along with him. I didn't want to waste any more time. I just wanted us to get a move on. But I couldn't believe these people—they were always looking for opportunities to bully or terrorize us.

Nauman squeezed over my lap to get out of the car. I could hear him talking to someone in the distance. The others in the car seemed excited at the prospect of having a feast on Eid. As far as I was concerned, this goat was *haram*,* as they'd extorted the money to pay for it. I hoped they choked on the meat.

Nauman returned to the car.

"I have tied the goat at that shop, and we can collect it on our way back."

They seemed to have everything worked out. We accelerated away. I heard a crackly voice on their walkie-talkie.

"Are you on the bypass road yet?"

"No, not yet," Nauman responded. "I will let you know when we get closer. What is your registration number?"

There was a garbled response in Pushto that I couldn't make out, but it sounded like things were going according to plan.

I sensed we were just minutes away from freedom. Nauman reminded us of the story we had to tell the people we were being handed over to, and once again repeated his threat.

After a few minutes, we stopped. Nauman squeezed past me and got out of the car.

"Don't move. Not a sound."

There was no way I was going to disobey his instructions now. I heard the crunch of their AK47s being positioned, trained on whoever was here to collect us. No doubt the other men's guns were pointing at us too.

We waited in the car. No one spoke. The silence was overwhelmingly eerie, all the more so because I was still blindfolded and had no idea what was going on.

* Something forbidden under Islamic law.

This felt like a scene from the movies—an exchange is about to take place and, in the tension, the slightest hint of betrayal provokes a shootout. If that happened now, Rustam and I were right in the middle, blindfolded and unarmed. We'd have no hope of survival.

So near.

Jaffar sounded agitated.

"Come on. Hurry up."

My eyes were closed behind the blindfold. I was trying hard to take a pragmatic view. *Que sera sera*. Because, although Jaffar and his men must have gone through situations like this many times, the outcome was clearly never predictable. I knew our captors were desperate and trigger-happy. One slip of the finger could suddenly change the game plan.

I became aware of an oppressive stuffiness inside the car, blended with a stomach-churning stench of body odor.

I heard footsteps on gravel. My heart began to beat faster. The car door opened and I felt a waft of fresh air on my face. Then a voice.

"Are you Asad Qureshi?"

"Yes, I am."

I felt a hand untie my blindfold. I squinted up and saw a bearded man smiling at me. He offered his hand.

"My name is Eesa."

I reached out and took his hand, and he helped me out of the car. Another man was helping Rustam out of the other side. He introduced himself as Farhman.

I looked around and saw that what they called the "bypass" was in fact a dried-up riverbed—the Tochi River in the dry season.

Nauman stood about 20 feet away from the car, a bag over his left shoulder and a rifle in his right hand. He was watching the whole thing from a distance, but he looked ill at ease.

His unease emboldened me. I felt a strong desire to show him that all his bravado, his bullying, and his torture hadn't defeated me. To show him I still had my dignity and could rise above the horror he and his cohorts had subjected me to. To bid him goodbye as a gentleman.

I walked over to him and extended my hand. He just barked at me.

"Go now."

For the first time in many months, I felt strong. I could see this delay was making Nauman extremely nervous. I was no longer under his jurisdiction, and it was a great feeling. I had people with guns behind me. He couldn't scare me anymore.

I looked him in the eye. There was no hood covering his face this time.

Eesa beckoned me. I looked at Nauman and shook my head. I turned around and walked toward my new friends, knowing in my heart that Nauman wasn't brave. It's so easy to point guns at defenseless people. Even killing is easy. It doesn't take courage. It takes weakness, stupidity.

I was invited to sit in the front seat of an SUV. Everyone else huddled together in the back, at least ten of us packed into the car. The same smell of stale sweat.

We sped away in the opposite direction to that of Nauman and his men.

I was now anxious to get home.

"How long will it take us to reach Islamabad?"

"We will take you to Islamabad tomorrow."

"No. No. I want to go home today. Now."

"There is an army checkpoint, and it will close in half an hour. We won't be able to make it in time."

Tears rolled down my face. I felt I just couldn't wait another second to get home. After perhaps half an hour, we reached a town. I recognized it as Miranshah, the familiar capital of North Waziristan. We drove through a narrow street and stopped outside a house.

Everyone spilled out of the vehicle. A curtain made out of sackcloth hung in the doorway. One of the men held the curtain back, and we were ushered into a courtyard. There were a couple of beds of woven rope in the yard, which had rooms on three sides. Eesa pointed toward the bathroom.

"Go and wash. It is nearly time for prayers."

I made a beeline for the bathroom, ahead of Rustam. I was desperate to be properly clean.

Eesa led the prayers. It was the first time since March 26 that we'd prayed outside, in freedom. I thanked God for freeing us. I prayed for Colonel Imam's safe return.

When prayers were over, Eesa suggested I take a nap. I appreciated his kindness but I was far too excited about my newfound freedom to sleep. I wanted to absorb everything around me.

I walked round the courtyard. One of Eesa's men was pacing around. I spoke to him.

"Who are you people?"

"We fight for God."

"Taliban?"

"No. We are Al Qaeda."

From the hands of the Taliban into the hands of Al Qaeda in one day. I smiled at the irony of a situation in which Al Qaeda were the good guys. How would anyone ever believe me?

Now I understood what had prompted Nauman's comment that these were "boys in a man's game." He was jealous.

I walked back to the group. Eesa said something in Pushto to one of his men, who quickly disappeared, returning with some powerful-looking guns. He laid them on one of the beds. Eesa proudly picked up a large green machine gun.

"This is jewelry for real men. This gun can fire accurately for 2 kilometers."

Out of kindness, I pretended to be impressed, but the truth is guns have never held any fascination for me. Rustam showed genuine interest, which made the men happy. Then he picked up another one.

"See this? We took it from an American soldier."

I wondered what had become of the soldier.

It was getting close to the time for breaking our fast. Eesa and his men placed a big cloth on the floor. The younger men brought food and laid it on the cloth. Compared to what we had been fed in the last place, this was a banquet. There was rice, fish, chicken, and lamb curry, lots of chapattis, heaps of fruit, and Coke to drink.

After we'd heard the *azan*, we began to eat. Eesa sat opposite me and kept putting more food on my plate. It was a most enjoyable meal. We were being royally looked after. By Al Qaeda.

Eesa poured me some Coke.

"We are not as bad as people think, you know."

I smiled and nodded my head. Now was not the time to engage in a political discussion. I just wanted to go home.

After food, we hurriedly formed a line for prayers, which, as before, Eesa led. Afterward, he suggested taking Rustam and me to a public telephone office so we could call home. I was overwhelmed. The chance to speak to my family!

I thought Eesa would walk us to the office alone, but, in fact, the whole group came with us, for protection. They all slung their rifles over their shoulders, including Eesa's seventeen-year-old son, who was also wearing four hand grenades on his body. He wore these weapons even when offering prayers, so that if he was killed by a drone attack at the time of praying, he'd be considered a martyr.

It was getting dark. As we were about to leave, I said to Eesa, "Do you mind if I carry your gun?" Like a good host, he offered me the weapon. It was very heavy, and I put it over my shoulder. Although he didn't ask for one, I felt obliged to provide an explanation for this strange request.

"People have been pointing guns at me for a long time. I just want to carry one for a little while."

Eesa smiled.

The streets were dark. As we walked, the men lit the way with their flashlights. I could smell woodsmoke in the air. There was no gas in this region, so people burnt wood for cooking. I could smell the drains too. This was a pretty underdeveloped area.

The gun was feeling heavy, and, as it had quickly served its purpose, I returned it to Eesa.

We came to a small, dimly lit shop. Eesa told the man we wanted to make a phone call. I wrote down Farrukh's mobile number and the man dialed it. After a couple of seconds, he gave me the handset. I was excited and nervous at the same time. I badly wanted to keep my composure and not break down, but my heart was racing and a film of cold sweat had covered my body.

I had waited a very long time for this moment. The wait had made me ridiculously nervous. On top of it all, I had quite an audience. This was a very emotional moment for me and, ideally, I would have made the call in private. But Eesa had a smile on his face—he was obviously pleased for me—and I could not be rude and ask him and his men to go away.

"Hello."

"Hi Farrukh. It's me."

Tears leapt into my eyes, and I struggled to contain them. A lump had developed in my throat. Farrukh's question gave me the respite I needed to recover.

"How are you?"

"Okay. How are Mum and Dad and everybody?"

"Everyone's fine and looking forward to seeing you."

"Where are they?"

"In England. Can you be in Islamabad first thing tomorrow morning? There's a flight to England at midday."

"We're still a long way from Islamabad. I don't think we can."

"In that case, there's a flight at midnight."

"I think that's pushing it too. I need to clean up and get a haircut. I think it's best to wait and book the flight once I'm in Islamabad."

"Okay. I'll wait till you get here."

Considering I'd waited so long to speak to him, and had been through such a difficult time, I didn't have much to say to my brother. It just wasn't the right time for intimacy. We wrapped up this very prosaic conversation.

Rustam was asked if he wanted to make a call but he declined—he couldn't remember his son's mobile number.

We turned back toward the house. The dark streets were crowded with children lighting fireworks. They were already excited about Eid.

"So what time do we leave for Islamabad tomorrow?" I asked Eesa.

"Be ready to leave at eight o'clock."

By my reckoning, if we left at eight in the morning, there was a chance we'd be home by around three in the afternoon. I couldn't wait.

Not having walked for months, I felt exhausted after this short stroll. We were led to a different house, farther down the street, where we were to stay for the night. This house was newer and bigger than the initial one. It had a veranda and several rooms.

The others made their beds and prepared to sleep. I asked if we could sleep outdoors, in the courtyard. Eesa readily agreed and had two beds made up for Rustam and me.

But, with all the excitement, I wasn't ready for bed just yet. I walked round the courtyard, looking at the plants. There was a calendar on the wall, which attracted my attention. I walked over and studied the calendar. I found the month of March and began to count the number of days I'd been in captivity. I kept losing count and having to go back to the beginning. From March 26 to today, September 7, was a total of 166 days.

But we'd been taken at around three o'clock in the afternoon, and freed around midday, so not quite 166 days. More accurate to say 165.

165 days.

I was very possessive about time. The way I saw it, as soon as we were born we began our journey toward death. Every second that passed was one second closer to death.

Those people had stolen nearly six months of my life.

I walked over to my bed and inspected it. It was much cleaner than the bed I'd had in the last place. I lay on it and looked up at the sky. I took a deep breath. What a wonderful feeling! I was free. I was actually free. I couldn't believe it. No more shackles, chains, or handcuffs. I could move my arms and legs, breathe, think, feel.

I was free.

I'd missed the sky. Tonight it looked wonderfully black and full of stars. For months I'd shared a tiny cell with two other people. Now, here, before my eyes, lay an expanse of millions and millions and millions of miles. Lying on my back, I felt like I could lift my foot and strike out into this vast expanse of space.

A feeling of utter peace engulfed me. Mosquitoes were biting me everywhere, but that didn't bother me. I was determined to stay outside and enjoy my first night of freedom under the sky. It was late, but I didn't feel sleepy at all. I was too excited to sleep. Excited and nervous about tomorrow.

29
The Journey Back

September 8, 2010, was the first day of my new life. I felt invigorated and reborn. A new chapter had begun. Freedom.

It was still dark. I heard someone pottering about. It was almost time for *sehri*. I was fully awake. Another night during which sleep had passed me by. But it didn't bother me—this time I'd chosen to stay awake. And no handcuffs or shackles. Such a good feeling! I couldn't believe I was here.

I relished the prospect of being properly clean, so before the bathroom was invaded by all and sundry, I got up and washed myself at length. A very good feeling. Afterward, I sat outside and waited for the others to join me.

We were served tea, parathas, and curry. I delighted in eating and drinking from clean cups and plates. After months of eating leftover slops, this breakfast was delicious beyond words, almost as if I were discovering a sense of taste for the first time.

The call for morning prayers echoed around the town. A new day had begun, and I had a lot to look forward to. I was so excited at the thought of being reunited with my family and with Sherry. I just couldn't wait to get home.

Then, once again, my thoughts turned to Colonel Imam, and my spirits crashed. We would be driving to Islamabad in bright sunshine, while the Colonel was shackled in darkness and squalor, perhaps worse.

Our captors would, I was sure, pay for their deeds not only in this world but in the next.

By 7:50 a.m., Rustam and I were outside the house, waiting. We'd been told we'd be collected at 8:00 a.m. A smiling Farhman came out and waited with us.

I looked at him and once again reflected on the irony of a situation in which a Westerner should feel so happy in the company of such men. I had spent the night with Al Qaeda and would live to tell the tale.

I thought about the evening my captors had taken me into the street to call my brother, and I asked Farhman if he knew of a shop that sold gas cylinders and also had a public phone call office at the back. He said he did, and it was in the village of Dandey Darpakhel, a couple of miles from where we were standing.

I smiled to myself. Nauman and his men had driven for hours to get us from our prison to the exchange point—they'd clearly driven round and round in circles to make us believe we'd come a long way from some much more remote spot. They were certainly clever, but I still didn't believe the Asian Tigers had been acting alone—there had to have been some other, larger, outside influence at work in our kidnapping.

It made sense that we'd been held not too far from here. The helicopter activity I'd frequently heard would have come from the Pakistani army's base in Miranshah. The base was in a pretty dodgy area. I'd been there a few times and had seen that even the army personnel never ventured out of the base alone. They always traveled with a Quick Response Force of heavily armored trucks with jammers that would prevent IEDs from exploding in their path.

Oncoming traffic was routinely ordered to stop. The driver was asked to step out of the car. He would be asked only once. If a driver stayed in the car, he was shot where he sat. No second warning.

This was a volatile area. Danger on all sides—mines underfoot, drones in the sky, and terrorists all around. No wonder it's referred to as the most dangerous place on earth. It is. We'd witnessed it.

As a filmmaker, I'm always after the next big story. Many of the stories I've told have just fallen into my lap. Here I was standing next to an Al Qaeda operative. Perhaps here was another wonderful bit of serendipity. This man was certainly not hostile toward me. In fact, in my story, he was a good guy. Nothing ventured.

I asked Farhman if it was possible to make a film about their group. He gave me a wry smile.

"We have to ask for permission from our superiors."

A tactful refusal.

It would have been one hell of a scoop. But let's not be too disappointed, I told myself. Nearly six months ago, I'd set off to make a news report. Now I was lucky to have escaped with my life. One of my colleagues had not been so lucky, and the other was still their captive.

We'd now been waiting at the roadside for over an hour, and there was no sign of anyone coming to collect us. I was getting more and more on edge. I didn't want to spend another night here—I just had to get home.

I kept asking Farhman how much longer we'd have to wait. In typical local fashion, he pointed up at the sky—"only God knows."

I wanted a more precise answer, so I went back to the house to ask Eesa about the delay. He made a gesture that signaled I should be patient. I took the hint. After all, I shouldn't forget I was in a much better position than I had been just twenty-four hours earlier.

All the same, I was fasting and I didn't want a long and strenuous day. I just wanted them to hurry up and get here.

Feeling very restless, I went back outside. Although it was better than being indoors, the stench of the open drains was almost unbearable. I swore to myself that I'd never venture into this area again.

I heard footsteps and turned to see Eesa walking toward us. He was talking on the radio and a voice was squawking back to him. With a smile on his face, Eesa pointed to a car in the distance. Our transport to Islamabad had arrived.

An old brown Toyota Corolla came to a halt near us and two bearded men in their thirties got out. They came straight toward me and shook hands.

"Asad *sahib*? *Asalaam alaikum*. I am Badar Mansoor and this is Zarar. Sorry we are late. We had a puncture. Finding someone to fix it early morning in Ramadan is not easy."

"I'm just glad you're here."

"We have a long journey ahead, so let's go."

I shook hands with Eesa and thanked him for his hospitality. Farhman, it seemed, was coming with us.

Badar Mansoor invited me to sit in the front of the car while he, Zarar, Rustam, and Farhman got into the back seat. With the driver, that made six of us in the car. Farhman would escort us to the army checkpoint, after which we'd be back in Pakistani jurisdiction. I looked forward to that protection.

I waved to Eesa as we pulled away. Next stop Islamabad and civilization.

As the six of us started to engage in conversation, it seemed to me Zarar's voice was familiar. It had a distinctive, high-pitched tone. Where had I heard this voice before?

I asked him if he'd ever had dealings with Sabir Mehsud. He replied that he had. He'd been the envoy sent to negotiate our release. It seemed he'd not been well received. He touched his cheek, where there were several deep burn marks.

"Tell me, the last night you were there, did they feed you chicken biryani? You had a bath and then knocked on the door when you'd finished?"

"Yes, that was me."

He was the man I'd heard from our room. The man Nauman had told us would break the door down and kill us if we made a sound. Another one of Nauman's lies.

"How did you find us?"

"I had read about your kidnapping in the newspaper. Then Qari Abdul Salim came to see our emir. He told him you were his close friend's brother. Then we got involved in negotiations for your release."

I was intrigued. Here, in the car with me, was a man who had, it seemed, been directly involved in securing my release. Zarar went on.

"When I went to Miranshah for the first time, I met with Badar Mansoor here and asked him for help. He told me he had just met Sirajuddin Haqqani, the son of Jalaluddin Haqqani."

This was ironic indeed, as Jalaluddin Haqqani was the leader of the Afghan Taliban whom we'd originally intended to interview.

"Sirajuddin Haqqani had given him medicines for Colonel Imam, which he was going to give to Usman Punjabi. Usman Punjabi's group was called the Asian Tigers, he said. Well, as it turned out, the Asian Tigers are really two groups, one headed by Usman Punjabi …"

"Yes, a slightly built man in his thirties, with a dark complexion?"

"That's right. And the other is Sabir Mehsud, a stocky man with a long beard, about the same age."

"And both are leaders?"

"Well, Sabir Mehsud is the real leader. Usman Punjabi is his deputy. But the whole plan to kidnap you was hatched by Usman Punjabi. It was him we met with first."

"What did he say?"

"He told us they had two demands—the release of 159 prisoners and a ransom of ten million US dollars for you."

"That amount was never realistic."

"That's what I said. But he argued that you had come from England. That you worked for a television channel there. That they were rich and would pay the money. I told him this was not the case. I tried to persuade him filmmaking was just a hobby for you. That you were not associated with any channel. I explained to him that your family could not afford such a large sum of money. If they kept insisting on such a figure, they would be left with you for a long time."

"How did he react?"

"Well, I'm sorry to say that was when Usman Punjabi killed your colleague, Khalid Khawaja."

My heart sank. Poor Khalid. Once more, I shuddered at the thought of meeting his family again. Although it was KK who had driven the whole enterprise forward when the rest of us had wanted to turn back, I knew there'd be a part of them at least that would hold me responsible for his death.

"What happened then?"

"Well, this made Sabir Mehsud very angry. It was then he decided to take you into his own custody. Punjabi was not happy about this. The group began to fall apart. Then there were two groups."

"But which one was holding us?"

"Well, they argued. Since Punjabi had masterminded the kidnapping, he felt he was owed part of the ransom. He kept calling your brother and claiming he still had you in his custody. Farrukh was confused."

I could imagine how difficult this must have been for Farrukh. On top of all the worry and the stress, not knowing whom to negotiate with. He must have been going out of his head.

"Sometime later, I met Sabir Mehsud. He agreed on an amount to release you."

"So everything was settled then?"

"No. Not really. The very next day, he changed his mind about the amount. We had an argument and he threatened me. I took no notice and walked away."

"What did he do?"

"Well, I decided to call your brother to tell him what had happened. While I was on the phone, Sabir Mehsud's people came and took me away. They took me to a room full of weapons. Then they handcuffed and blindfolded me and put me into a car. We drove for about half an hour, sometimes on the road and sometimes off the road. Then we stopped. They pulled me inside some building and took my blindfold off. I was in a house made out of mud."

This must have been the place where I was held, I thought. This man who had risked his life to free me had himself become a prisoner, got himself tangled up in the hellish web that had been my life for the past six months.

"They put me in a small room. A room where they kept their animals. I was told to sit on the floor. It was very hot. They made me put on different clothes, made of thick material that made me feel even hotter. They left a bucket of water for me to drink from. But they didn't untie me so I couldn't drink."

"How long did they leave you there?"

"The next day, Sabir Mehsud and his men came into my room. They treated me badly. They accused me of working for the ISI. They wanted to know who I was meeting in Waziristan and why."

"What did you tell them?"

"I told them I wasn't ISI. They didn't believe me. So they didn't let me sleep. Then they put my head in a bucket of water, like they were drowning me. They beat me up and pointed a gun at me. I accepted I was about to die. Death is inevitable. If it was written for me, I wasn't going to change it. I told them they could do whatever they liked to me, but they should give me time to write my will."

"And they accepted that?"

"Yes. I wrote to my wife."

"Did they see the will? How did they react?"

"Yes. And, from what I'd written, they must have realized I was not a spy. I think they were under pressure from outside to do something with me, so after about eleven or twelve days, they took me to a new place. They gave me water."

I could imagine his relief. Memories of heat, dust, filth, confinement were still very fresh.

"Then they took my blindfold off. I saw black bags. Camera bags. I sensed you were nearby."

Tears came into my eyes. I suddenly felt incredibly close to this man. This stranger. Incredibly close and incredibly grateful. The feeling was almost overwhelming. Zarar went on.

"But I was very worried. If they were treating me so badly, I was worried about what they were doing to you. I was worried about how you were coping. When I asked about you, they assured me they were looking after you."

"Things had got better by then, yes."

"Then, after about a week, one night I was told to have a shower. They gave me clean clothes to wear. That night they made chicken biryani. As a send-off. Later, they put a burqa on my head and drove me back to the place they'd snatched me from. They handed me over to Badar Mansoor."

"You must have been relieved."

"Yes. It was good to be among friends again. But when I got back, everyone was shocked to see me. To see the state I was in. Especially your brother. I assured him I was all right."

"What did he say?"

"He looked worried. I understood why. Like me, he was concerned for your safety. Looking at me made him imagine the state you might be in. He was concerned that you wouldn't be coping well. He told me you were not used to rough living. That you were a fanatic about being clean. He was very anxious to get you home as soon as possible."

"So what happened then?"

"After about two weeks' rest, I was asked to return to Waziristan. To talk to Sabir Mehsud again about your release."

I was so touched and impressed by Zarar's story. By his bravery and by his devotion to what he'd seen as his mission. After suffering so much at the hands of these terrible people, he'd had the courage to go back and face them again. I owed him so much.

"Sabir Mehsud called Farrukh and asked him why I had returned to Waziristan. Hadn't I learnt my lesson the first time? I told him that the release of prisoners was not possible. Told him we should talk about you only. He agreed, reluctantly, and I left him and came back with his final demand. But Usman Punjabi was demanding a share of the money. Money which they had not yet received. They began to haggle as to who would get what, and it was finally decided that Punjabi would get a number of guns and vehicles as his share."

"And he was happy with that?"

"Well, Mehsud kept delaying the handover. Then he invited Usman Punjabi and his men over to his place, so that they could collect the guns and vehicles. But when they got there, Sabir Mehsud opened fire on Usman Punjabi and his men. He killed three of them instantly. Usman was badly injured. He died a very painful death the day after."

I remembered they'd moved us. That had been why. They'd used our room to lay a trap for Punjabi. Sabir Mehsud must have been very sure of his ground, of his status, to take such a step.

"That was risky."

"Yes, but Mehsud was clever. He killed one of his own men as well. A Punjabi living with him. So that if there was a *jirga* and questions were asked, he could say that Punjabi had killed his man first and he'd had to retaliate. After that, it was all over. We just had to hand over the money."

I was deeply moved by his bravery and his willingness to suffer on my behalf. This unassuming man with the piping voice was the epitome of honor, quiet strength, and religious conviction. I don't think I'll ever be so impressed by anyone again.

Badar Mansoor told us he'd been working with an NGO, helping with flood relief, at the time he was suddenly called upon to come for us. He'd not even had time to say goodbye to his wife or leave rations at home, and Eid was just a few days away.

"I had the *amanat* with me and had to be very cautious where I went. I didn't want to risk going to see my wife."

The *amanat* was the ransom money. I didn't dare ask how much it was. Right now, I just wanted to enjoy my newly found freedom.

The mention of his wife lightened the mood in the car. We knew his wife would be furious with him. So did he. In spite of the macho posturing that often goes on in our culture, we all know a wife is the real head of a family.

We all laughed at his predicament, and Badar Mansoor joined in the laughter. I was overwhelmed by affection and gratitude for both men.

Suddenly, Farhman's walkie-talkie crackled and we heard a Pushto voice. There was a gasp from Zarar and Badar Mansoor.

"What happened?" I asked.

"A drone strike," said Badar Mansoor. "It just killed two of Eesa's men. Right by the house, where you were standing. Fifteen minutes after we left."

I was stunned.

Farhman looked unmoved. For him, death was part of life. For me, well, I'd been close to death. For now, it seemed fate was giving me life.

Quite a coincidence that a drone strike should hit the very place where Rustam and I had stood for two hours, waiting for the car.

But was it a coincidence? About a year before, I'd been staying at the Tochi officers' mess in Miranshah and I'd heard a drone strike in the early hours. The target was about 5 kilometers away, but the deafening noise made it seem like it had struck right outside my room. That strike killed eight people. And, although it had taken place in a very remote area with poor communication, it had been no surprise to me that the incident had been reported in the news the very next morning.

The situation is so complex, it's extremely difficult to know who's who, or who's working for whom. Hence my first mistake in assuming I'd been held by the ISI.

I wondered now if the Asian Tigers had had something to do with this latest strike, on an Al Qaeda target. I would never know the truth.

After a few minutes, we stopped. Farhman, our Al Qaeda escort, stepped out of the car. His job was done. This was as far as he could come with us. The army checkpoint was quite close. Any farther, and there was every chance he'd be arrested. He smiled and said goodbye.

I thought nervously about the checkpoint. Rustam and I had no identity papers. I said this to Badar Mansoor. He told me not to worry—he had a letter of transit from a colonel based at the barracks in Bannu. The soldiers at the checkpoint wouldn't dare disregard it.

At the checkpoint, it was good to see the green uniforms. Our men. Now I was in Pakistan.

Badar Mansoor leapt out of the car and talked to the border guard. He produced the letter. After some discussion, the guard came over to have a closer look at me. I gave him a salute, and he waved us on. That was one hurdle crossed. Thank God.

Badar Mansoor climbed back into the car.

"We need to stop at the army headquarters in Bannu. I need to talk to a colonel about some friends they are holding as prisoners. We want them released before Eid."

I nodded but wondered what prisoners he was talking about. I'd assumed both Badar Mansoor and Zarar had been sent by Farrukh, who would never associate with people who had friends as prisoners. It just didn't make sense to me. I began to wonder who these people really were.

We arrived at the army barracks in Bannu. I remembered how it had been the last time. We'd been on a mission. We'd been raring to go, the fresh air of spring breathing excitement into me. I'd had the feeling I was on the brink of getting the scoop of my life.

And KK had still been alive.

I thought of something a friend of mine once told me—"If you want to make God laugh, tell him your plans."

We were led to an office inside the building and were invited to wait. The barracks were a remnant from the colonial era—high ceilings with fans suspended from long poles, good for keeping the room cool in the summer.

There was the standard-issue large desk, with a sheet of thick glass covering its entire surface and green felt underneath. There were four telephones and a pen set mounted in onyx—another standard issue. There was even a footrest under the desk. It seemed no expense had been spared to make the person behind the desk as comfortable as possible. The walls were covered with all kinds of army insignias.

On the wall behind the desk was a copy of a painting of Jinnah, the founder of Pakistan. Next to it was a wooden plaque with the names of the various colonels who'd previously held this post.

A smart uniformed man walked into the room. A lieutenant colonel—one pip and a star and crescent on his shoulder. We all stood up and Badar Mansoor introduced us.

"Colonel Imtiaz, this is Asad Qureshi, Rustam, and Zarar."

We shook hands and sat down.

"I am glad to see you, Qureshi *sahib*. We were all worried about you."

"Thank you. I'm glad to be out of there."

"I need some details from you. Exactly when were you released?"

"Tuesday, September 7th."

"Thank you." The colonel scribbled some notes.

"May I use your phone, sir?"

"Sure. Just dial straight out from this one. I will be back in a minute."

Colonel Imtiaz left the room. I dialed the number of my friend, Nazir Sabir. It was the only number I could remember—all the digits from the center keypad form his number.

"Hello, Nazir. *Asalaam alaikum*."

Nazir was surprised to hear from me.

"*Salaams*, Asad. How are you?"

"I'm fine, Nazir. I'm using someone else's telephone. I need you to pass on a message to Colonel Faisal—I can't remember his number."

"Yes. Go on."

"Please tell him that officers at the ISPR are to change their telephone numbers. My captors took my phone, with all the numbers of my ISPR contacts on it. And tell him they are to increase security at the compound—the captors asked me how many barriers there were on the outside. Please make sure he gets these messages. Their security's at stake."

"I will."

"I'm on my way home from Bannu. I'll see you soon."

It was good to hear Nazir's voice. I knew I could rely on him to pass on my message. All the personnel at the ISPR were known to me, and they'd been good to me. I felt it was my duty to let them know the enemy had some information that might be used against them.

After a short while, Colonel Imtiaz returned and took his seat.

"Did you get through?"

"Yes. Thank you."

It had been tempting to call Farrukh, too, but that would have been taking advantage of the colonel's hospitality.

Badar Mansoor jumped in with his request.

"Sir. About the prisoners. As you know, Eid is upon us, and we want them released before Eid."

"Ah, yes. The investigations are going on. It will take a few days."

I wondered what all this was about, but I was too full of excitement to enquire. And I didn't want to hold things up anymore. I was impatient for us to continue our journey. Thankfully, Badar Mansoor didn't press the matter further, and we were soon on our way.

On the road again, there were the usual crazy Pakistani driving conditions—weaving, horns blowing nonstop, drivers overtaking at dangerously high speed.

After a few miles, we reached the Kohat-Rawalpindi fork, and my eyes filled with tears as I remembered that fateful evening. I would have gladly gone through my months of captivity again to have KK and Colonel Imam in this car with me, the four of us all going home together. As we veered to the right, how I wished we'd taken this turn that evening! If only I'd stood up to KK and insisted on going home. But, as I have often reminded myself, one can never go back.

Badar Mansoor told us we were not going straight home. Farrukh would meet us at their compound, just outside Islamabad, where we were to eat.

We were approaching the highway. I suggested to the driver he take it. Rustam began to speak to the driver in Pushto, contradicting my instructions and causing us to miss the turnoff.

When I asked the driver why he hadn't taken the turning for the highway, he said Rustam had asked him to take him home first. Badar Mansoor and Zarar protested and asked the driver to turn back for the highway.

The driver hesitated and slowed. Rustam became furious, flung the door open, and jumped out of the moving car. Then he simply picked himself up and marched off without looking back.

I could understand his impatience. We were close to where he lived, and he obviously couldn't wait to see his family. But if we'd gone his way first, we'd have been late for *iftari*.*

Zarar and Badar Mansoor were disgusted at Rustam's abrupt departure, and Zarar said Rustam had been quite rude in general since we'd been picked up. He didn't seem to appreciate all the efforts that had been made to secure our release.

For my part, I thought it was a shame we weren't both finishing the journey together, after all we'd been through. But I knew Rustam was an impetuous man.

* The breaking of one's fast at sunset.

30
The Reception

There was a long line of traffic snaking up to the toll plaza. Everyone was in a rush to get home in order to break their fast. We inched forward at a snail's pace, watching the sun sink and our chances of eating sink with it. Any moment now, from some mosque we'd hear the call for prayers.

I thought about Farrukh. I felt nervous about seeing him again. It was going to be an emotional reunion, but I wanted to keep my composure and not break down.

After more agonizing minutes, we finally reached the toll gate. The driver tossed a five rupee note at the man behind the window and accelerated away, zigzagging between cars, wasting no time. We were on the home run now.

Soon we were leaving the main road and hitting a dusty track. The bumpy ride reminded me of the day of our captivity. I closed my eyes. I saw again the driver making a break for it, being gunned down.

We arrived at a huge metal gate, which was instantly opened by a long-haired man. We drove into a huge compound, similar to Shah Abdul Aziz's *madrassah* in Karak—it was like we'd gone full circle.

The call for prayers issued from a mosque in the foreground. We'd made it just in time. People were gathering for *iftari* and evening prayers. As we drove into the car park, I instantly saw Farrukh, standing with Asghar. I could see the anticipation on his face. The car stopped and, forgetting about my colleagues, I jumped out and walked toward my brother. I was suddenly aware of my appearance—long matted hair, straggly beard, clothes that, to put it mildly, had seen better days. I should have cleaned up at Eesa's house, but the excitement of coming home had got the better of me.

Farrukh stepped forward with a smile on his lips. I shook his hand and put my other hand round his shoulder and gave him a gentle hug. It seemed neither of us had words to express our joy.

Asghar took a couple of photographs of us. I walked over and shook his hand.

"*Asalaam alaikum.*"

"*Walaikum asalaam.* How are you?"

"Glad to be back."

"Where is Rustam?"

"He got out a few miles back, close to his house. He couldn't wait to see his family."

"That's a shame. I wanted him to stay here for a few days, to keep him away from the media until you're out of the country."

"I'm not planning on giving any interviews. And I don't think, where he lives, anyone will be able to find him anyway."

"To be honest, I'm more worried about the ISI. I don't want them picking you guys up for interrogation. That might be a worse experience than what you've just been through."

"I doubt it."

"No."

He looked away.

Then Farrukh put his hand on my shoulder.

"Come on. Let's break our fast."

We walked together into a large room. As we entered, Farrukh whispered to me, "I don't think Sabir Mehsud will see 2011."

People were seated around all the four walls. Plates and plates of food were laid out in the middle. Another banquet.

I was led to a distinguished-looking bearded man.

"Khalil *sahib*, this is my brother, Asad."

"*Asalaam alaikum.*"

"*Walaikum asalaam.* Asad *sahib*, you must have had a terrible time."

"Yes. It wasn't easy."

"Allah is great. Please sit."

More people were presented to me. Each time, I introduced myself as Asad Qureshi. Asghar nudged me and whispered, "Don't give your full name. Let's keep a low profile for now."

We sat down. Khalil *sahib* was at one end, the head of the table. Zarar and Badar Mansoor came in and sat by him. Khalil *sahib* put out his hands and said a prayer. Everyone in the room joined him in putting out their hands.

I said my private prayers. I thanked God for the simple fact of my being here. That fact was beginning to sink in.

Khalil *sahib* brushed his face with his hands, in the traditional way, and we followed his actions. It was time to break our long fast. I loaded my plate with food—I was ravenous. Farrukh looked over at me.

"Steady on. Leave some room. We're going to eat at Asghar's later."

I smiled. I knew his fear that I might overeat now wasn't his only concern. He'd also be suspecting this food might not have been prepared in conditions that were up to my fussy concerns about hygiene. He knew me well, knew I'd never normally eat out because I wasn't confident other kitchens lived up to the standards of our own home. Knew this water wasn't the mineral water I normally insisted on.

People started to filter out of the room and make their way to the mosque for evening prayers. Farrukh, Asghar, and I followed them and offered our prayers. Then we said our goodbyes to Khalil *sahib* and thanked him for his hospitality and climbed into Asghar's car to make the journey to his house in Islamabad.

It was now dark. I sat in the back and watched familiar landmarks whizz past, still trying to get used to the newness of being free. We were on the same road that had taken KK, the Colonel, Rustam, and me out of Islamabad, on that fateful day. A lifetime ago.

Within an hour or so, we hit the outskirts of Islamabad and we were soon pulling up outside Asghar's house. Asghar smiled at me as we walked inside.

"You know, this has been the toughest time of my life. I know it's been tough for the family, too—for Mum, Dad, and Farrukh."

"I think in some ways it's been tougher for them. For Farrukh particularly."

"You're right. It's like they've read the book, whereas I just watched the film. Things are always worse in your imagination. Not seeing. Not really knowing. But I was there."

We ate a fine meal, and afterward Asghar told me his mother wanted to meet me.

We walked over to the women's quarters, where his mother was waiting in the doorway. She put her hand on my shoulder and welcomed me back. I'd never met her before, and I was overcome by her concern for me—I had to work hard to stop myself from welling up. But, of course, she was a mother and knew what it was like to have children and worry about them. She could imagine the hell my parents had been going through. I pictured Mum and Dad. I wondered how this experience had changed them.

I thanked Asghar's mother for her concern, and we excused ourselves and left.

I wanted to feel like my normal self as soon as I could. I asked Farrukh to take me to get my hair cut.

We drove to his barber. The place was mobbed. Eid was just a few days away and people wanted to look good. Farrukh had a private word with the barber and he let me jump the queue.

My hair was all matted and coarse from the months of grime, and from using ordinary soap to wash it, and from never getting to rinse it properly. As he ran the scissors through my hair, it sounded like he was cutting cloth.

"Why is your hair stuck together like this?"

I was surprised he didn't know. My story was on the front pages of all the newspapers strewn around his shop.

"I'm an actor. I've been playing the role of a caveman. I like to be in character all the time."

"I see. You must be really committed to your craft."

I looked in the mirror at Farrukh and Asghar as they tried to contain their laughter.

"Yes, you could say that."

I felt enormously relaxed. It was good to know I hadn't lost my sense of humor. There might be difficult times ahead, and unpleasant memories to deal with, but humor would help. I'd been harmed but I hadn't been destroyed. And I hadn't succumbed to Stockholm syndrome. I was going to get my normal life back. Eventually.

My hair was beginning to look like an approximation of normal. The beard was next. I thought about Nauman's instructions, his threat. I didn't believe for a second they'd be watching me. They didn't have that much power. So the beard came off. A smooth chin. It had been a while.

I felt suddenly exhausted, so Farrukh drove me to his house. In the car, I thought about my wife.

"Where's Sherry?"

"It was best for her to leave. Get away from Pakistan for a while."

"Is she in America?"

"She's back with her parents. In Texas."

"I'll call her."

"Okay."

I must have stood in the shower for half an hour. My world was beginning to be clean again. I put on clean clothes, sat in a clean chair, breathed clean air.

Farrukh looked like he hadn't slept for months.

"Get to bed. You and I can talk in the morning."

Although I was shattered myself, I was eager to talk to Mum and Dad in Bradford, and to Sherry. I called my parents first. Mum answered.

"I'm relieved to hear your voice. I praise God for your safe return." Then she passed the phone to Dad.

"How are you?"

"Better. Getting better, now that I'm out of that hell."

The whole family was there. One by one, I talked to everyone. My niece, Aisha, was in tears.

"Uncle, if you'd come to my wedding, all of this wouldn't have happened."

"I know. I'm sorry. Work got in the way. I'm sorry I didn't make it. But I did think of you. On your wedding day."

She couldn't answer. She just cried.

After I hung up, I thought again about my cell. About the beam on the ceiling and my impulse to make use of it.

Then I called Sherry. In Texas, her day had just begun.

She saw the overseas number.

"Hello? Farrukh?"

"Sherry, it's me."

"Asad? Is it really you?"

"Yes."

"I can't believe I'm speaking to you. Are you okay? Where are you now? When can I see you?"

"I'm at Farrukh's."

"I missed you."

"I missed you too."

"You know I love you."

"Yes. I know."

"I want to see you."

"I've been making plans. Things I want to do with you. Places we should see together. And a car for you. A driver's license."

"Have you seen your parents?"

"They're in England. I'm going on Friday."

"I bet they can't wait to see you."

"I've just spoken to them on the phone."

"Good."

Then Sherry's mother called her away, and we said our goodbyes, with a promise to speak the following day.

I lay on the bed, staring at the ceiling fan. I thought of Colonel Imam. Here I was, showered with love and attention, enjoying good food and the comforts of civilization, while he was still in that awful place. It would be Eid in a few days. For his family, a huge dark cloud would hang over the festivities.

Then I fell asleep and, with no insects to bother me and no handcuffs cutting into my wrists, for the first time in many months, I slept like a baby.

I woke to the sound of the breakfast table being laid by the domestic help. I showered again (just bliss!) and walked through to the dining room—clean cups and utensils, tea with separate milk, toast, chocolate spread, peanut butter. My standard breakfast, no matter where I was in the world. Farrukh must have left a list.

After breakfast, I called my friend, Zaman, to ask if he'd drive me over to my parents' house—I didn't want to drive myself and risk being seen by the press. I was keen to see the old familiar place and to see my little Sunny, my beloved cat. Zaman came over, and I climbed in and lay down on the back seat.

I was greeted by our domestic help, Jawaid, and his wife, Shahgufta, and their two young daughters. Shahgufta did something that is not normally acceptable in our culture between men and women who are not related—she hugged me. Then she saw me look round the house. I asked her where Sunny was and her face grew solemn. She told me my little cat had disappeared months ago.

This news broke my self-control, and my eyes filled with tears. I sat on the arm of a chair and cried. They say it's the little things that get to you.

I gathered some clothes that I'd be needing for my trip to the UK and went over to Farrukh's office, where there was another reception committee. Smiles, handshakes, hugs.

Nudrat presented me with an Eid gift of a *shalwar kamiz*, a very thoughtful gift. Farrukh pulled me to one side.

"Call Asif."

"Sure."

On hearing my voice, he burst into tears. All I could hear was him weeping. Then there was a commotion in the background. Somebody rushed over to speak to him.

"What is it? Has somebody died?"

He struggled to get the words out through his tears.

"No. Somebody is alive."

When he'd stopped crying, Asif told me he was in hospital, recovering from surgery, so I kept my conversation brief and just told him I'd be back in the UK soon.

Then I called Sherry. The mood was very different from the day before.

"What is it?"

"My mother."

"What's wrong with her?"

"She's forbidden me from seeing you."

I was stunned. She'd never really liked me. But this seemed excessive even for her.

"She's torn up my passport."

"What!?"

"I've been making a new life. Here."

"A new life?"

"I've just started a job. I started yesterday."

"Oh."

"And I quit today."

"You've quit?"

"I love you."

"I love you too."

"But my mom …"

"I know. Don't worry. We'll sort it out."

It seemed like I had another battle on my hands.

That afternoon, Colonel Imam's sons came to see me. It was a meeting I hadn't been looking forward to. They'd want news of their father. I didn't know how much to tell them.

The eldest son was a major in the Pakistani army. He introduced himself as Nauman. The same name as the sadistic monster who'd tortured us. Tortured his father.

The two men sat pensively for perhaps a minute, looking at the floor, playing with their hands. They'd have preferred it to be their father sitting here, instead of me. I understood that. The silence was broken by Major Nauman.

"So, how is my father?"

The question was like a dagger through my heart.

"Well, he was in good spirits. He was sharing his many stories. About his army days. He helped us keep our morale up."

"Have they hurt him?"

The image of the Colonel's shirt striped with blood flashed into my head.

"Well, things were bad, but your father is very strong. And they gave him a lot of books to read. He was always busy reading."

"Was he okay? Is he healthy?"

I remembered what the Colonel had said about his wife, that she'd been recovering from surgery when we'd set off. The sons would want good news to take back to her.

"He's lost weight. We all have. But he was generally okay. Getting some food and water."

"Did he send any message for us?"

He looked me in the eye, imploring me to say "yes."

"I'm sorry. At the end, we were separated. I never had the chance to talk to him."

The brothers kept looking at the floor. They were reluctant to ask anything that would provoke a hurtful answer from me. I was reluctant too. For Colonel Imam, this was not the end.

After another uncomfortable minute or so, they stood up and took their leave. To be honest, I was glad. The brief meeting had been exhausting for me. Guilt was wearing me out. We'd gone out there as colleagues. A team. Now we were individuals. Every man for himself.

I thought again about KK. It was September 9, the night of *chand raat** and everyone would be out shopping for clothes, shoes, and gifts for their loved ones. For KK's family, there'd be no celebrations.

But, in the morning, Farrukh and I would be traveling to England, to celebrate with our wider family. A dual celebration, spent partly in Pakistan and partly in England.

The families were worlds apart.

Morning came. Farrukh got a call from the deputy British High Commissioner in Islamabad, offering us an escort to the airport. An offer of help at this stage from the British government was more than a little insulting. A case of much too little, much too late. But, gracious to a fault, Farrukh accepted on my behalf. He'd go on ahead to clear things at the airport, and the government car could drive me over later. I could see he was in a hurry to get me out of the country. He didn't want the ISI pulling me in for a debriefing session that could delay our reunion with the family.

A black Range Rover pulled up outside. I watched the driver step out and walk toward the house and ring the doorbell. As I walked toward the car, a man in a suit opened the back door and stepped out. He introduced himself as Nathan, the deputy High Commissioner who'd contacted Farrukh.

We pulled away. Nathan explained he'd arranged for the police to meet us at Manchester Airport. They'd escort me out of the terminal through a VIP exit, so I wouldn't be pestered by the press. Welcome news. I didn't have the stomach for a media interview.

At the airport, Asghar was waiting for me in the VIP car park. He walked with Nathan and me to the departure lounge, where Farrukh was waiting to hand me my boarding pass. We said goodbye to Asghar and Nathan, and we immediately boarded the plane. Meticulous timing by Farrukh.

Within minutes, the plane was climbing into the air. Members of the Business Class cabin crew fussed over me. Comfort. Luxury. I thought of Colonel Imam in that hellhole and prayed for his release.

Farrukh turned to me.

"So, the question about Sajid. Why didn't you answer it?"

* The new moon on the eve of Eid.

"I couldn't think who he was at first. Then I remembered him but still didn't understand the question."

"It was the thing about him always saying *sleep* instead of *sweet*."

"Oh. But that was what he said *before* lunch. Your question was 'What did Sajid say *after* lunch?'"

Farrukh looked at me and smiled. Even after months of torture and starvation, it seemed I still had the capacity to be irritatingly pedantic.

When we hit the cold air of a Manchester evening, two police officers were waiting for us at the gate, just as Nathan had promised. I wondered what the other passengers were thinking as the officers led me and Farrukh away. *Look, Bert. People being arrested. Drug smugglers, no doubt.*

The drive from Manchester to Bradford takes an hour. I've done it countless times. Now I was doing it for the first time as a free person who knows what it is to be free. Familiar sights flashed by—the woods by Newhey, the sign for Outlane Golf Club, the turnoff for Rastrick. I closed my eyes. Ten million dollars. The barrel of a pistol pressing into my forehead.

As we reached the end of our street, I took a deep breath. Be strong. *Hold it together. Don't break down.*

My mother was waiting. I hugged her. She kissed me, and then she cried a little.

I hugged Dad and shook his hand. He smiled warmly.

"I have done all my crying."

My sister, Rakhshindah, had cooked the Eid dinner. When we sat down together, Mum passed me a plate of chicken drumsticks. I was being asked to let my vegetarianism slip, if only for one night. To eat meat was to eat properly, eat well.

A mother wants to look after her son. After all I'd put her through, I wasn't going to refuse.

After dinner, one of my nephews opened his laptop and was flicking through news sites, looking for reports about me. I asked to borrow the laptop so I could check my email. The kidnappers had asked me for my address and password—the password would now need to be changed.

I looked in the Sent folder. Somebody had indeed been rooting around in my email account. They'd accessed a couple of emails in which I'd discussed with colleagues our plans for Waziristan and the film we hoped to make. These emails had been forwarded to the Geo TV presenter, Hamid Mir.

I can't prove it was the kidnappers who sent emails from my account. I can say that the emails were sent to Hamid Mir's email address from somebody using my account and at a time, May 10, 2010, when I was lying on the floor of a stinking room next to Rustam, my hands and feet shackled.

We all talked well into the night. My niece, Asma, was particularly attentive. She was still feeling a deep sense of guilt for not recognizing my voice on the phone, that day the kidnappers had let me make a call. To her, it seemed that, at the lowest point in my life, I'd reached out to her and she'd rejected me. In spite of my many reassurances since, it's something that still haunts her to this day.

Farrukh looked on. He'd promised to bring me home. He'd kept his promise. My brother. The real hero of my story.

I could not keep KK out of my mind. I talked of my regrets. Of that moment at the crossroads, when I'd given in to him. If only I'd stuck to my guns.

My dad told me that although death had beckoned KK, it had simply not been my time. He reminded me of a line from the ancient story about the angel of death and the prophet Solomon:

The purpose of death is to save you from dying, until your time is up. Then death will take you to the place where you are to die.

Epilogue

In the weeks and months that followed my release, something approaching normal life returned. But there were more challenges ahead, and more sadness.

Being apart from Sherry was devastating. I called her house all the time. Sometimes her mother would answer and simply hang up when she heard my voice. Other times, Sherry would answer but her mother would cut us off. But we did sometimes manage to have a conversation. Her guilt and shame at not being around at my release was what dominated our conversations. I tried to put myself in her place—alone for six months, culturally isolated, not knowing if she'd ever see me again. I tried to understand.

For her part, she'd tried to make a clean break, praying to God to make a decision for her. If I were not to come back maybe she could get on with her life without me being in the picture. But it was clear from our conversations that the break was anything but clean. She'd started to retrain as a financial planner, which involved a four-month course of study. After two months, she'd broken out in hives. The condition had been so bad, her whole arms had been bleeding. Then she'd gotten a job in telecoms, which she'd left after just one day, the day of my release.

Over the months that followed, there were terrible fights with her mother. She'd gone back to the US for good reasons, her mother said. She was settled there. A new life.

But Sherry couldn't settle, it seemed. And, without her, I couldn't settle either. Four months later, she came out to the UK and we were together again. This union lasted three months, and we divorced.

But we remain friends.

I was desperate to get back to work and finish my film *Defusing Human Bombs*. I needed to keep my mind busy.

The last footage I'd shot had been in January, a couple of months before our kidnapping. Under pressure from the film's financial backers, Asif had got a film-maker from Karachi to continue shooting. In London, he showed me the new footage. It was overexposed and not filmed in the style I'd established from the beginning. There was no alternative but for me to return to Islamabad and finish the film myself.

While I was in Islamabad, KK's wife Shamama and his son Huzaifa came to visit me. They asked me about his time in captivity.

I explained there wasn't much for me to tell—we'd only spent two days together, and most of that time in silence. She didn't press me. She just said she was pleased that he'd died a martyr.

She smiled when she told me a story about a dream she'd had. One evening, a few days after his death, she'd gone to take a bath but couldn't find the shampoo, so she'd gone to bed. In the night, he'd come to her in a dream and told her there was a sachet of shampoo in one of his bags. In the morning, she'd gone to the bag and there was the shampoo. Even in death, he was still helping her.

I was amazed at her strength and her sense of peace.

A day or so after this visit, I got a phone call from Farrukh. Mr. Z had been in touch with news that might interest me, he said.

Sabir Mehsud and Nauman had been captured by Hakimullah Mehsud, the supreme commander of the Pakistani Taliban. Hakimullah had been enraged at the killing of KK.

The two Asian Tigers had been brutally tortured for hours. Their legs had been broken with rifle butts. Then they'd been shot in the face, multiple times. Their bodies had been left beyond recognition.

I remembered Farrukh's words to me on my release—*Sabir Mehsud will not see 2011.*

Several months later, in January 2011, I héard the dreadful news that Colonel Imam had been executed by Hakimullah Mehsud and his men. A horrific video of the execution had been uploaded on YouTube, for everyone to see. A strong, incredibly resilient man, a loyal servant to his country, and a man of faith, treated like a piece of meat by a bunch of thugs.

The following year, in February 2012, Badar Mansoor was killed by a drone attack. He was revealed to be an Al Qaeda leader in Pakistan. That explained our stay at the house of Eesa, another Al Qaeda member.

In October 2013, of course, the whole world would hear of the death, in a drone strike, of Hakimullah Mehsud himself. So much violence.

In 2014, I would return to Pakistan again, arriving, as fate would have it, on March 26, exactly four years to the day since we'd been taken hostage.

One reason for my visit was to pay my respects to KK. I visited his grave in the company of Farrukh's close friend, Atique. KK's headstone reads:

Shaheed Khalid Khawaja.
Date of birth July 3rd 1951.
Martyrdom on the holy day of Friday, April 30th 2010.
Inna Lillahi wa inna ilaihi raji'un[*]

I stood there for a long time. I offered prayers for his forgiveness. I pictured him lying next to me on his mattress. He'd spent his last two days on earth with me. Now he lay in a grave. Alone. A generous soul and a true gentleman. I missed him.

The other reason for my visit was a meeting with Fazlur Rehman Khalil.

Mr. Z met me for dinner at Dawood's house. He arrived with a whole entourage of people, including a one-eyed bodyguard with a long beard, carrying a Kalashnikov.

The occasion was, for me, a very emotional one. Mr. Z talked me through the negotiations for my release, at every turn emphasizing how brave and gallant Farrukh had been throughout the crisis. My eyes filled with tears several times.

We talked about Zarar. I said again how grateful I was for his brave interventions, and how I had nothing but admiration for his fearless determination.

We didn't know it at the time, but there were further hardships ahead for Zarar. In April 2015, he was arrested by the Pakistan Crime Investigation Agency on charges of being a member of the Pakistan Taliban and of masterminding a number of kidnap-for-ransom operations, including, ridiculously, our kidnapping. Newspapers have carried reports of his apparent confession to having kidnapped us, and to having executed Colonel Imam and Khalid Khawaja. I will state here and now that these are lies, and he is being made a scapegoat because no one came to our assistance.

Mr. Z had uncovered some background to our trip into Waziristan. In 2009, KK had been imprisoned for speaking out against the government. While in prison, he'd used a smuggled phone to talk to someone by the name of Usman Kashmiri about a documentary project. This Usman could arrange access to Taliban leaders, KK had been told.

When KK had been released from prison the following January, he'd gone to Waziristan to meet this individual. The man KK knew as Usman Kashmiri had been none other than Usman Punjabi.

[*] Truly to Allah we belong and truly to Him we shall return.

According to Mr. Z, Punjabi had been planning to kidnap KK at this meeting but, when KK told him he'd later be bringing a British journalist to make the film, Punjabi had seen dollar signs and had decided to hold off with the kidnap and wait for a bigger prize. It had all been a trap. And we'd walked right into it.

I asked Mr. Z how much money had finally been paid for my life.

"You must ask your brother."

Since my release, to this day, and to his eternal credit, Farrukh has never mentioned the kidnapping. Only one man knows how much money was paid.

And he's saying nothing.

Afterword

I wrote this book not because I wanted some sort of catharsis—although the experience of writing was cathartic to an extent—but from an overwhelming belief that this story had to be told.

In the immediate aftermath of my release, I suffered from posttraumatic stress disorder (PTSD). I was having frequent nightmares, and my waking hours were intruded upon by intensely dark thoughts and governed by the pent-up anger I felt toward my captors. Physically, I was also very weak. My arms and legs were skinny, their muscles attenuated, and the slightest exertion made me breathless. The road to mental and physical recovery looked like a steep uphill climb.

At the insistence of the channel, I went for counseling to a psychologist in Harley Street, the area of London where the UK's foremost private medical practitioners have their clinics. Over a six-month period, I attended around twenty sessions. Members of my immediate family knew not to talk to me about my captivity—and they didn't want to relive the nightmare either—and I tended to shun conversations about my experience with friends and acquaintances, many of whom were looking for vicarious adventure from an ordeal that was, for me, unremittingly dark. But I have to admit I found it helpful to talk through my feelings with a trained professional. I offloaded some of the anger and some of the blame I laid at my own feet for not standing up to KK when he was persuading us to press on. By the end of the sessions, I was undoubtedly in a better place mentally. But I knew that memories of my ordeal wouldn't ever completely go away. My experience of captivity, torture, humiliation, and loss would be with me for the rest of my life. It was a case of accepting my reality and learning to live with it. I have done this, by and large, pretty successfully. The people who know me well often say they find it hard to believe how well I'm doing. People I meet briefly, whether socially or professionally, would never guess what I've been through.

My story is a very personal one, but behind it there are great forces at play, forces that deeply affect (and, in many cases, determine) the lives of millions of individuals just like me.

One of the forces I refer to is the human capacity for evil. Since I had the experiences you've read about in the book, I've often wondered how we, as humans, can do so much harm to our fellow human beings. We are supposed to be the most intelligent form of life, yet we are also the most barbaric and destructive.

I've asked myself many times how I would behave in the position of hostage-taker. How would I treat my captive? What would I be capable of doing to him or her? Each time, the answer is the same. Although at times I show the world a hard exterior (you have to be tough to run a film set), I'm at heart someone with a very soft interior. I know I'm not capable of inflicting serious physical or mental harm on anyone.

Our captors were very different animals. They were the most sadistic and ignorant people I've ever had the misfortune to come across. Not only did they ignore my pain and distress—they reveled in it.

But I don't believe these traits were innate. Neither do I believe our captors woke up one morning and decided to become terrorists. I think there is the *capacity* for evil in all of us, but I believe that monstrousness on this scale can only be the result of programmatic training.

Certain spheres of work require practitioners to maintain an emotional distance from the people their work brings them into contact with. A surgeon cannot effectively slice into a human brain without, to a large extent, mentally isolating the organ from the human being it is part of, and an attorney cannot effectively prosecute a case without, to a large extent, divorcing a set of legal circumstances from the human beings whose lives are affected by them.

So it is with terrorists. They are trained to develop an emotional and moral disengagement from the people whose lives they toy with. Such training requires logistical coordination, and serious financial backing. It's my view that the activities of the terrorists responsible for my ordeal were facilitated to some extent by the Indian government and, albeit indirectly, by the US administration's war on terror.

It's the view of many commentators that the India security service has had some success in fomenting terrorism inside Pakistan's borders, both for the purpose of destabilizing Pakistani society and with the aim of tarnishing Pakistan's reputation abroad. In the course of the numerous documentaries I've made in the region, I've seen evidence that strongly indicates the influence of the Indian state in terrorist activities in Pakistan. I've worked closely with the Pakistani army, and I've been near the front line on a number of antiterrorism missions. Many of the terrorists that Pakistani troops have killed, whom they assumed to be Pakistani Taliban, were revealed by medical examination to be uncircumcised males (and therefore not Muslim). And we have all witnessed the testimony of Kulbhushan Jadhav, an Indian spy captured by the Pakistani army in 2016, who has admitted to conducting terrorist activities inside Pakistan.

On the day we were seized by the Asian Tigers, Nauman repeatedly taunted us with the charge that we'd taken money from Manmohan Singh, the then prime minister of India. I think it's quite possible this was a case of transference, that Nauman was projecting onto us a transgression he knew his own group was guilty of committing. And I maintain that the presence of Krishan Lal, an Indian, in their group supports the view that India's Research and Analysis Wing (RAW) played a significant role in our abduction.

The human psyche feels most comfortable with a black-and-white worldview. Some philosophers and historians argue that this is particularly true of the *Western* psyche, and it is commonly held that the apotheosis of the Western psyche is to be found in the United States of America: the Hollywood good guy in the white hat, the bad guy in the black. Many would no doubt say the argument is debatable, the metaphor facile and outdated, and I'm not sure I'd disagree. But I would nevertheless make a very important point: I think Pakistan has suffered from, and has been bizarrely punished for, its role in helping to defeat the Soviet Union and making the United States the world's only surviving superpower.

A preeminent Western media seems to have identified Islam—incidentally the world's fastest-growing religion—as its new enemy, coining the words *Islamist* and *jihadist*, which in the minds of readers and viewers who lack discernment and cultural worldliness are mapped onto the word *Muslim*.

I've touched on the meaning of the word *jihad* elsewhere in this book, but it's a point worth repeating. The word appears frequently in the Qur'an, with and without military connotations. It means "striving in the path of God." Islamic jurists understood the obligation of *jihad* predominantly in a military sense, but they developed a set of rules pertaining to *jihad* that, importantly, prohibited acts that caused harm to anyone not engaged in combat.

In the modern era, jihad has lost its jurisprudential relevance and has instead been adopted into ideological and political discourse. Modernist Islamic scholars emphasize the defensive and nonmilitary aspects of jihad, while some radical paramilitary groups advance aggressive interpretations that go beyond the classical theory. These groups are naturally the most newsworthy and, before we know it, all brown-faced people who wear loose-fitting clothes and eat rice with their fingers instead of a fork are potential terrorists.

Pakistan allied itself to the war on terror instigated by former US president George W. Bush. The war was framed in clear terms: "Either you are with us or you are with them." Despite its cooperation, Pakistan itself was singled out for particularly harsh treatment, with President Bush's administration threatening to "bomb Pakistan back to the Stone Age."*

Since 2001, according to a study by Brown University's Costs of War project, more than 22,000 Pakistani civilians have lost their lives as a result of the campaign, with over 40,000 wounded. More than 8,000 Pakistani security forces personnel have lost their lives. The report makes the point that these figures "reflect just those killed directly. Many more have died as an indirect result of the wars and their destruction of infrastructure and community health."**

---

* This comment was reportedly made by US assistant secretary of state Richard Armitage to Pakistan's intelligence director, Mahmoud Ahmad, although it's important to point out that Armitage denies using those terms.

** The report's full findings are available online at www.costsofwar.org.

The seemingly endless war on terror, one might argue, has really been a war on Islam. And a war on Pakistan in particular.

Pakistan occupies an important strategic position bordering China, India, Afghanistan, and Iran. Of particularly recent significance, it lies at the Pakistani end of the China-Pakistan Economic Corridor (CPEC), the major highway funded largely by a Chinese investment of $62 billion. When completed, this road will stretch 1,865 miles from Xinjiang territory in northwestern China to Gwadar in Balochistan, where the seaport is being expanded and which opens into the Gulf of Oman and the Persian Gulf. This will make it quicker and cheaper for the Chinese to export their goods to the Middle East and Europe and, perhaps more importantly, make it immeasurably cheaper and easier for the Persian Gulf oil on which the Chinese economy depends to reach the emerging Asian superpower. CPEC will also, of course, be hugely beneficial to Pakistan. The mammoth construction project is already creating a huge surge in Pakistani employment.

In early 2018, I saw buses and taxis in London and New York carrying the slogan *Free Blauchistan*. Blauchistan, or Balochistan as Pakistanis call it, is the largest of the five provinces of Pakistan, and the separatist movement in the region has been active since the creation of Pakistan in 1947.

One can imagine that an economically strong and increasingly self-sufficient Pakistan—a nuclear state—with developing ties to an emerging superpower in the region, is not a progression that is wholeheartedly embraced in the West. If the development could be compromised by a rise in separatist fervor in the very region of Pakistan on which the enterprise depends, one can imagine the temptation to support such a rise would be difficult for some governments and politicians to resist.

Great forces at play. Dark forces, some might say.

But light shines out of the darkness.

After five and half years of imprisonment on ridiculous charges, in January 2020 the honorable Zarar was finally released, without warning and without explanation.

I spoke to him by phone a few months after his release, when the world was in the grip of the COVID-19 crisis. While in prison, he lost everything. And yet this destitute man was carrying out relief work, supplying food and medication to families deeply affected by the COVID-19 lockdown. Once again, he was risking his life for others. His selflessness is exemplary.

It's on these personal aspects of my story that my mind tends to focus. But the political aspects of life in that region are hard to ignore. And, as the world has recently seen, the regional sands of politics are shifting yet again.

In August 2021, when the United States Army pulled out of Afghanistan and Kabul fell to the Taliban once again, we'd gone full circle. It took the Afghans ten years to repulse the Soviets and twenty years to do the same to the United States of America. We live in a world where no nation can legitimately claim to be a super-power. No wonder Afghanistan is considered the graveyard of empires. As has been said many times, you can kill people but you can't kill the will of the people. So much time, money, and human life lost for no reason. Let's hope dialogue can provide a way forward in a region where military hardware has clearly offered no solution.

War is terrible. It creates suffering: families forced to struggle on without hus-bands, mothers, sons, and daughters; survivors, forgotten by their governments, forced to live out their lives with severe physical and mental trauma.

Meanwhile, more salt is rubbed into the considerable wounds of these victims as they see honors lavished on the very people who led them into these wars.

At the time of writing, the former British prime minister Tony Blair has been rewarded with a knighthood, in my view an appalling accolade for a man who has blood on his hands. Over one million people have signed a petition to have him stripped of the honor; I've added my own signature to the list. If the petition isn't successful, numerous families of dead soldiers say they'll return their loved ones' medals to Her Majesty the Queen.

But, always, my mind comes back to what is personal. And when I think of those dark times, I think mostly of my colleagues KK and Colonel Imam, who lost their lives in such a brutal manner.

KK's sons are still pursuing a case against the broadcaster Hamid Mir, but his influence is powerful and the case has been repeatedly thrown out of court.

Colonel Imam's family had to wait seven years from the dreadful events of this book for his body to be exhumed and finally given a proper burial.

May they both rest in peace.

We lost my dad in 2020, at the age of ninety-nine. Toward the end of his life, he said to my mum, "The one child we had no hope in has written a book." When she told me, I smiled, full of regret that my father, the great bibliophile, didn't live to see the publication of *165 Days*.

I hope he would have been proud.

Acknowledgments

I could not have written this book without the support of a large number of people.

First of all, I must pay tribute to my family. Not only did they suffer incredible emotional hardship during the months of my captivity, but they've spent the last five years reliving those horrors as I've quizzed them for material for this book. My brother, Farrukh, deserves a special mention in this regard. He suffered more on the outside than I did on the inside. And my parents, my sister, Rakhshindah, and my wife, Sherry, have all had to dust off the memory of a very unpleasant episode they hoped they'd put well behind them. I praise their courage, as I do the courage of my brother's friend, Asghar.

My brother's assistant, Nudrat, showed tremendous commitment and fortitude in her support for Farrukh during the terrible time of my captivity and I would like her to know how grateful I am for that, and for making her own invaluable notes available to me when I was writing this book.

I'm also very grateful to my friend Nigel Wooll for the kind things he says about me in the Foreword.

I should also like formally and publicly to express my gratitude to Fazlur Rehman Khalil, the cleric who helped negotiate my release, and to his envoy, Qari Zarar, who, in helping to secure my release, suffered extreme hardship with admirable fortitude. Their experiences have also informed this text.

I'm grateful to editors at *the Asia Times*, *The News*, and *Dawn* for their kind permission to reproduce news reports about me that appeared in 2010.

I'm also grateful to Lisa Leshne for her help and advice at several stages of this project.

I'd also like to thank Howard Sargeant, my freelance editor, who has worked tirelessly alongside me for the past seven years and whose skill and patience have played a significant part in helping to shape the text.

Finally, I'd like to thank all the people, known to me and unknown, who prayed for my safe return.